Seeing the Elephant

Seeing the Elephant

The Ties That Bind
Elephants and Humans

Eric Scigliano

BLOOMSBURY

First published in Great Britain as *Love, War and Circuses* 2004
This paperback edition published 2006
Copyright © 2002 by Eric Scigliano

Bloomsbury Publishing Plc,
36 Soho Square, London WID 3QY

A CIP catalogue record for this book
is available from the British Library

ISBN 0 7475 7471 5

9780747574712
10987654321

Book design by Robert Overholtzer
Printed in Great Britain by Clays Ltd, St. Ives plc

www.bloomsbury.com/ericscigliano

To Robert and June Scigliano,
who showed me elephants and so much more

L'éléphant est irréfutable.

— Alexandre Vialatte

Acknowledgments

A book is an iceberg, and the author's share the part that floats above the surface. Too many people have assisted this effort in too many ways to enumerate here; those not mentioned are not forgotten. Richard Lair was unstinting with his expertise and wisdom. Mick Elmore, Tuchpong Tulyayong, Dr. Suvit Yodmani, Daisy Tambi, P. S. Easa, Madhusudan Annadaana, Raman Sukumar, Dr. G. Paul Frederick, Lynette Hart, V. Krishnamurthy, and, especially, Jayantha Jayewardene opened windows onto the ways of elephants and other matters in Thailand, India, and Sri Lanka. Many along the elephant trail, from Tampa Bay to Taungoo, showed hospitality to a wayward writer. My thanks to Kathy and Robert Dodd, Alice Ray, Senerath Pahathkumbura, Mark Worth, Toby Old and Holly Gaskin, the Friends of the Asian Elephant, the Myanmar Beauty Guest House in Taungoo, Joshe George in the delightful village of Meloor, and the master animal healer Nigel Otter at the India Project for Animals and Nature, and to N. Baskaran, Rathinasamy Aruguman, Arun Ventakaram, and their comrades at the Indian Institute of Science's Mudumalai research station. The fearless elephant trackers of the Sri Lankan Department of Wildlife Conservation shared not only hospitality but adventure and songs.

Many archivists, librarians, and scholars opened their files and opened windows on rare lore and long-ago eras. Thanks especially to the keepers of the circus flame at the Somers Historical Society; to Professors Kumudu Kumara and I. V. Edirisinghe and the reference librarians at the University of Colombo; and to Erin Foley and Fred Dahlinger at the Circus World Museum, Pamela McClusky and Marta Pinto-Llorca at the Seattle Art Museum, Aaron Schmidt at the Boston Public Library, Judith Henchy at the University of Washington Libraries, and Pat Maluy and his colleagues at the Woodland Park Zoo. And to Brock Roberts for all his help digging out the nuggets from the stacks.

I am indebted to all those who read the manuscript in whole or in part and advised and dissented, including Anne Sheeran, Dan Zucker, Kate Pflaumer, Richard Lair, Mick Elmore, John Van Couvering, Diedtra Henderson, and Ken and Ivory Levine. Any errors are mine, not theirs, but are fewer thanks to them.

Thanks especially to Laura van Dam, a wise and patient editor, who nurtured this book from its conception and curbed its rogue tendencies each time it tried to stray. And to Lucia Hansen, who makes it all possible.

Contents

IV. The Circus Comes to Town

V. Endings

Introduction

> Of all the dumb beasts, this creature surely shares the most of
> Human Understanding: kind usage exercises their Ambition, con-
> tumely fires their Revenge.
>
> — The Learned Job Ludolphus, *A New History of Ethiopia* (1682)

> I've gotten to know elephants ... to appreciate the kind of people
> they are. If human beings were better than they are, they'd be like
> elephants.
>
> — Wayne Hepburn, Sarasota, Florida, January 2000

THIS BOOK is a love story, a murder mystery, a familial drama, and
a saga of biological and cultural evolution played out over the eons.
It is the story of the relationship between two types of animals, one
of them ourselves. Many books have recounted the baneful effects
of humans on elephants; this one will explore the ways humankind
has been affected, even shaped and defined, by its millennia-long
relationship with elephants — how we reveal ourselves through
that relationship, and how it has helped, in biological as well as cultural ways, to make us what we are. It is a relationship unique
among the planet's species, more influential, and in some ways
closer, than humankind's relationships to dogs, horses, and cats,
creatures that today seem much less strange to us than giant elephants. For humans, this relationship has alternated between worship, triumphant conquest, heedless exploitation, intimate coop-

eration, and sentimental delight. For the elephants and their vanished cousins, the tale has not been a happy one.

Perhaps it is elephants' mingled strangeness and familiarity — geologic in scale, extraterrestrial in appearance, but expressive in affect, with their melting, long-lashed, teary eyes — that draws children to them as to no other animal in the zoo or circus. I still remember when I first felt the allure, though I never saw circus elephants as a young child; we lived in Saigon, between Vietnam's French and American wars, where circuses followed European tradition and lacked grand animal spectacles. But Saigon's zoo had many beasts and few barriers separating them from visitors. Crocodiles lazed beneath a footbridge; monkeys would escape their cage; and a young elephant would reach her trunk across to visitors, nuzzling their faces and taking peanuts from their hands and whatever else seemed interesting from their pockets. I imagined that she recognized me out of all the kids who thronged around her. Elephants' noses and memories are so discerning — perhaps she did.

One day my father left on what was still a postcolonial rite in Vietnam, a tiger hunt. I remembered pictures I'd seen in some book or comic of pith-helmeted hunters sitting in baskets atop enormous elephants, their guns blazing at hideously contorted big cats. Yes, I thought, that's what I want to do — not kill tigers (I was relieved when his party failed to shoot any), but ride an elephant ship through a sea of vines.

As childhood fantasies go, this was ordinary stuff. What kid wouldn't dream of elephant-borne adventure? But I had unwittingly tapped into a fascination that goes back thousands of years, through paths as diverse as Hindu worship and Roman blood sport. For me, the fascination lingered into adulthood, and was rekindled by each unexpected elephant encounter. Near the vexing end of my first year at college, a small sawdust circus — something I hadn't seen in years — came to town, and I played hooky to go to it. I was so enthralled by the elephants (cheesy as their tricks doubtless were) that I announced I'd had enough of arid philosophies and dreary labs: I was heading over to the manager's trailer right now to see if I could get a job shoveling up after the elephants. My sensible companion persuaded me to finish the school year and catch up with the circus in the summer. By then no circus was in sight, and a proper summer job waited at the post office. Ah, misspent youth!

Ten years later, on a shutterbug safari in Kenya, I stood at a near distance but a safe height above a large water hole at day's end. One by one and ten by ten the local fauna trundled up to drink: warthogs, zebras, Cape buffalo, even a rhino or two. Suddenly lesser movement seemed to stop — or rather, the ground itself seemed to move — as a small herd of elephants, led by one impossibly large and heavy-tusked matriarch (those were more innocent days, just before the great slaughter of the '80s) strode to the water hole, while the others gave way. My sense of scale was toppled; a splendid rhino or buffalo now seemed puny and misplaced. The elephants did not just stop to drink: they stepped into the water, standing in apparent formation though they never turned to look at one another, and seemed to be conversing. (Thanks to subsequent research, we now know that they probably were, by infrasound — vocalizations pitched too low for the human ear to hear, and low enough to travel tremendous distances.)

The fascination was rekindled when, reporting on rebels and refugees along the border between Burma and Thailand, I came upon a couple of fellows nonchalantly leading an elephant as she dragged an immense teak log to a village sawmill. Later I puzzled over the seemingly impossible skulls and tusks and even hides of vanished proto-elephants in paleontological displays, and, as a journalist, interrogated elephant handlers about the tricks, and the danger and allure, of their trade. I realized that this fascination was hardly particular to me, nor to the people whose lives, in one way or another, revolve around elephants, from the circus workers who make them perform to the activists trying to make them stop. Everyone seemed to have a story to tell, to want to recount some point — at the zoo, overseas, even in the pages of *Babar* or *The Roots of Heaven* — when elephants had touched them.

When I told friends that I was contemplating a book about elephants in human life and culture, some launched into the subject as though they were proposing it themselves. "Elephants!?!?" one e-mailed back. "Omigod! Do we feel listened to and heard by 'such big ears'? Do we feel understood by such large hearts? . . . Oh yes, of course, how could we forget Horton?!!" Others would stare quizzically but then say weeks later, "You're right — I see elephants everywhere!" Not the proverbial pink ones, of course — though it's striking that the emblem of drunken delirium, the image we are supposed to see in our most uncontrolled moments, should be weirdly colored *elephants.*

I do not believe that the enduring, near-universal fascination with elephants merely reflects their size and appearance. Hippos, rhinos, and elephant seals are also big and bizarre-looking, and whales are much bigger, but they do not exert the same fascination. I suspect it lies in the paradoxes that elephants so poignantly embody. They are icons of reconciled opposition, at once wise and wild, enormous and delicate, monstrous and maternal — so unlike us in form but, we cannot help suspecting, so like us under their gnarled hides — with what Plutarch called "a refinement that seems not far from human." At times they seem the most disarmingly familiar of all animals, more "human" in their contemplative poise than our nearest cousins, the frantic chimps. We always imagine apes *as* apes, even when we make them giants (*King Kong*), surrogate family members (Burroughs's *Tarzan* books), or jackbooted thugs (*Planet of the Apes*). But we project ourselves into elephant protagonists — Babar, Dumbo, Horton, even elephant-headed Ganesha, the most humane and approachable of the Hindu gods.

It is both unsettling and deeply consoling to stand beside a five-ton creature, born in the wilds of Africa or Asia, that could snap your neck or crush your back in a hundred different ways — and to hear her purr, moan, snort, rumble, and sigh in a sonic syntax that seems nothing less than *conversational.* Her trunk, that great serpentine anomaly, greets you with a burst of warm wet air, then brushes, sniffs, and lightly prods you in a way that feels more like a human touch — uninhibited, like a young child's or a lover's — than the cool exploration of a snake. Here, you cannot help but feel, is a peer, an intelligence charged with discernment, curiosity, even empathy.

For all their immensity and exotic anatomy, elephants can even *look* disarmingly human. Asia's "true" elephants look like transitional creatures, changelings, with their smaller ears, rounder heads, curly fuzz of residual hair, and smoother skin, often mottled with pink. Their tuskless faces, with dewlap-like lips hanging in sweet goofy grins, seem far more expressive than the tusk-walled masks of their African cousins.

Until a few decades ago, the elephant images in our ads, art, and even dreams were largely images of *Elephas maximus,* the Asian or "Indian" elephant. Ever since the ivory- and circus-crazed Romans exterminated North Africa's herds, most of the elephants Europeans and Americans have known have been Asians. They filled the circus rings, picture books, and even early popular tales of fearless white hunters stalking rampaging pachyderms through trackless jungles, while Africa's elephants fed the market for ivory. It had been so long since Hannibal marched on Rome with African war elephants, the Africans were commonly considered too "primitive" to be trained, despite the Belgians' success at training forest elephants in the Congo. (This belief seems to have mirrored the differing degrees of condescension with which Europeans viewed Asia and Africa.)

By the late 1900s, however, the focus had switched. The defining image of "elephant" had become a big-eared, big-tusked, uniformly gray *Loxodonta africana.* Perhaps Babar had something to do with it, along with the emergence of once-remote African outposts as tourist destinations. But I suspect it reflected the ascendance first of movies, then television, as the dominant popular entertainment — and the way most people get to know elephants.

Recent years have brought a flood of television documentaries and big-screen films about the lives, loves, and ghastly deaths of Africa's elephants, punctuated by the occasional piece on Asia's. Accessibility is one factor: African savannas tend to afford much readier views and easier crossings than Asian forests. Their photogenic appeal is another; with their huge, sail-like ears, unisex tusks (only Asian males, and not all of them, grow tusks), long gait, and deeply furrowed skin, African elephants look more imposing and exotic. And so they have become the elephants we see, in everything from movies, to fundraising appeals from conservation groups, to ads for the latest four-wheel-drive gas-guzzler.

Wayne Hepburn, a passionate "elephile" in Sarasota, Florida, who doggedly tracks the use of elephants in advertising, says African elephants appear about ten times as often as Asian. This imbalance extends from advertising to other arts, and to places that should know better. "Save the Nature," a poster in Taungoo, Burma (Myanmar) urges — under a photo of an African elephant. A stirring painting in Malaysia's National Museum shows Malay patriots riding an African elephant into battle against European invaders. The silver elephants sold in the museum gift shop are all African. Several years ago, Ringling Brothers and Barnum & Bailey Circus outreach coordinator Peggy Williams told me, the cable TV channel Nickelodeon ran a feature on Ringling's Asian elephant breeding facility in Florida showing stock footage of — you guessed it — African elephants.

Such neglect has consequences. Though only about one-tenth as many Asian as African elephants now survive, the struggle to protect and conserve them is just starting to stir the same international enthusiasm as the campaign against African ivory poaching. This imbalance is one reason for this book's outsized attention to Asian and shameful neglect of African elephants; call it one small contribution toward balancing the record. The past three decades have brought shelves full of popular and insightful books on Africa's elephants by Cynthia Moss, Joyce Poole, Katy Payne, Ian Redmond, Ian and Oria Douglas-Hamilton, and others. The most nearly equivalent volumes on Asian elephants have been published in India, Thailand, and Sri Lanka, and are not readily available in this country.

There's another reason why a book like this, on humankind's relationship to elephantkind, focuses more on Asia than Africa: Asia is where that relationship has been most intimate and fraught, thanks to an unbroken, unfinished four-thousand-year history of capture and training. Africa's elephants remain wild animals, to be hunted and consumed, feared and avoided, or revered from afar.

They and their ivory have played rich and diverse roles in African art and religion, but these are deeply and widely explored in a single lavish volume, the Fowler Museum's *Elephant: The Animal and Its Ivory in African Culture*. The Asian animal has not received comparable treatment, and while it won't get all it deserves in this little volume, every bit helps.

And, finally, I write about Asian elephants because I remain helplessly fascinated by them — though I can sit and watch either kind until night falls, the chiggers bite, and the guards lock the gate.

It may be easy to dismiss the enchantment of elephants and identification with them as sentimental indulgence, but it would be a mistake. Understanding our species' elephilia, and all the other aspects of our enduring relationship with elephant species, may shed light on our current urgent and enormous predicament. As we enter an era of cascading extinctions and dramatic climate change, our greatest challenge is to decipher the effects of our heedless proliferation and development. We must understand *ourselves* in relation to the wider natural world, to appreciate how it has made us before we unmake it. If we are to rein ourselves in, to control our impacts upon this world that we may continue to survive and delight in it, then we must unravel our motives toward it — our impulses to exploit and dominate, and also to cherish and preserve. This special relationship is a good place to start.

A note on terms: I sometimes include mammoths, mastodons, and certain other now extinct proboscideans under the rubric "elephants" when discussing earlier humans' attitudes toward, use of, and effects on them. The more proper terms "elephantid" and "elephantoid" are cumbersome and smudge the many correspondences between these prehistoric interactions and interactions with the surviving elephant species. And "elephant" is already compromised: the true elephants (genus *Elephas*), including the sole surviving Asian species, appear more closely related to the mammoths (*Mammuthus*) than to Africa's forest and savanna elephants (both varieties, due to be recognized as separate species, of *Loxodonta*). But nearly no one calls the African animals "loxodonts."

I. Beginnings

1

Human Nature and Elephant Nature

The people of India assert that the tongue of the elephant is up-side down, and if it were not for that, it would have spoken.

— Muhammad Ibn Musa Kamal ad-Din ad-Damiri, *Hayat al-Hayawan* (ca. 1371)

By his intelligence, he makes as near an approach to man, as matter can approach spirit.

— Advertisement for "The Elephant," 1797

EVERY CREATURE, from a louse to a lyrebird, is a marvel of nature. But some marvels are just more marvelous than others — and none more so than an elephant. Look at one, a full-grown tusker, and see the image of the Other: huge and looming, weighing up to sixty times as much as a large man, by far the largest creature walking the earth today — "an animated mountain," as the promoter Edward Cross boasted in 1820, when he offered Londoners their first exotic menagerie show. Its legs are pillars, its inch-thick skin a fissured topography, its dark eyes unnervingly tiny and remote. Its front teeth are gleaming tusks growing nearly as long as goalposts — the mightiest of fangs, fearsome lances in battle and powerful chisels and levers in work, borne by a creature that eats only plants. Weirdest of all its wonders, the elephant defies the laws of quadrupedalism and bilateral symmetry. Its nose and upper lip have fused to form a fifth limb, a trunk (or *hasta*, "hand," in Sanskrit), the original multipurpose tool: a crane, forceps, whip, vise, noose, snorkel, shower, vacuum, jet blower, trumpet, bludgeon, and probe — a supple, writhing tentacle, moved by some sixty thousand muscles, which seems a thing of the sea, a precise but mighty instrument that can lift a log or a grain of rice and snap a man's back — as John Van Couvering of the American Museum of Natural History puts it, "the ultimate in giant mammal design."

Indeed, the elephant stands for the entire world in a Buddhist parable that has spread worldwide. The Buddha's disciples ask him to sort out the scholars' endless debates over whether the universe is infinite and eternal or finite and created, and whether the soul perishes with the body. He replies that a rajah once gathered the town's blind men and had each touch a different part of an elephant and say what he found. "A pot," said the man who touched the dome of the elephant's head. "A sail," said another who touched its ear (or a fan, in one retelling). Others mistook the trunk for a snake, a tusk for a plow (or sword), the back for a mortar, the belly for a sack (or wall), the leg for a tree, the tail for a rope, and the tail tuft for a paintbrush. They began quarreling. Just so, the Buddha explains, are the preachers and scholars who, knowing one side of a question, claim to know the truth of it.

If a camel is a creature designed by a committee, what army of artists and engineers could have conceived all the elephant's parts? Small wonder that when science-fiction pulp illustrators weary of bug-eyed insectoid monsters, they draw wrinkled, tentacled space elephants. Or that the fourteenth-century scholar ad-Damiri, in his treatise on the 931 creatures named in the Koran, noted that "if a woman dreams of an elephant, it is not a good thing, in whatever state she dreams of it." Or that John Merrick, the "Elephant Man" of late-nineteenth-century London and twentieth-century Broadway and Hollywood, should be called thus to evoke his extreme deformity and lure the gawking crowds. Merrick himself, in a brief promotional "autobiography," purportedly wrote, "The deformity which I am now exhibiting was caused by my [pregnant] mother being frightened by an elephant." This mumbo-jumbo was surely concocted by one of Merrick's exploiters, but "Elephant Man" is apt nonetheless. Like the actual animals, he was a gentle soul and a sensitive intelligence in an outlandish body. And he was dragged about and displayed, a virtual prisoner, in tawdry sideshows.

Consider this monster again and all it shares with us. Elephants live sixty to eighty years, the same span as humans, if they are not killed by humans first and don't wreck their health through bad habits; they also enjoy alcohol, and nineteenth-century captives were often given ale or whiskey to calm or reward them, and even as daily rations. The ploy sometimes backfired: some elephants were gushy, maudlin drunks and some turned mean — again, just like us. It's recorded that Jumbo, the most celebrated elephant of all time, would share a large bottle of stout each night with his keeper, Matthew Scott, who pitched his cot by Jumbo's pen. When Scott forgot himself and drank the whole bottle, Jumbo shook him awake and demanded his nightcap. Three of P. T. Barnum's elephants once took a chill after some winter labors and were given three bottles of whiskey each. The next day, now recovered, they put on the shivers to get more medicine.

A taste for intoxicants suggests intelligence, and anatomy affirms what mahouts and trainers have long attested: elephants are very smart animals. Their brains are by far the largest among land animals — about twice the size of humans', though much smaller as a share of body weight. Brain size alone is not a strict predictor of intelligence, but elephants' brains are richly folded and convoluted, indicating sophisticated development, with expansive cerebral lobes, the seats of memory (at least in humans). More telling is the degree to which their brains grow after birth, an indicator of learning ability. Most mammals already have about 90 percent of their ultimate brain mass at birth. Humans have just 26 percent, and chimpanzees about 50 percent. Elephants have 35 percent.

From Aristotle's day to the present, innumerable authorities have ascribed almost human "sagacity" and almost demonic ingenuity to elephants. When Seattle's zoo elephants were kept in a dank old barn, one named Bamboo would sneak in pebbles each night, then methodically toss them through the glass windows that stood out-side her bars. Keepers still puzzle over her motive: To get fresh air? To pass the time? (Elephants are famously restless at night, and sleep just two or three hours.) Or out of sheer mischief? A keeper at the Great Plains Zoo in Dubbo, Australia, once told me of the plea-sure, or at least distraction, her elephants seem to find in turning their home into a shooting gallery: "Every morning we have to wash the feces off the whole elephant barn, starting with the ceiling and working down the walls. They toss it at the possums that crawl on the rafters at night." A San Antonio keeper says his charges sling mud "whenever the gibbons next door make too much noise."

Lieutenant Colonel J. H. Williams, the legendary "Elephant Bill" who led elephant-borne refugees out of wartime Burma, spotted timber elephants plugging the wooden bells around their necks with mud, then sneaking silently into their masters' gardens to steal bananas. Another domestic elephant, chained in the path of a flood, piled up broken saplings to make a dry perch. A wild South African elephant was observed digging a drinking hole, then plug-ging it with a large ball of chewed-up bark, concealing it with sand, and returning later to drink again. This suggests several behaviors once considered uniquely human: invention, foresight, deception, and making and using tools; elephants have also fabricated fly swatters, back scratchers, water sops, and poultices.

Even when they sleep, elephants resemble us. They snore, take si-estas in the midday heat, and use hummocks and bushes as pillows. Most of all, they resemble (perhaps even surpass) us in the depth and durability of their familial attachments and affective commu-nications. Female elephants remain for life in the ultimate matriar-chies. Aunts and older sisters help care for the young, an important factor in the survival of a species with a long gestation (twenty-two months) and longer childhood. Elephants are among the few mammals, together with primates and sirenians, whose breasts hang between their forelimbs, allowing caressing while infants nurse and strengthening maternal bonds.

Like the love of humans and chimpanzees, elephants' affections endure after loved ones die. "Elephants' graveyards" may be fables, but elephants perform something like burial services: watching over and evidently mourning their dead, and even returning to the sites of death, fondling bones and tusks — and shattering them, as though to release their spirits.

They remember more than their dead; that old adage about elephants never forgetting bears some truth. Handler Jeff Pettigrew recalls returning to Ringling Brothers after five years away and being instantly recognized by the elephants he'd worked with. And, he adds, when the show played Wilkes-Barre, Pennsylvania, for the first time in forty-five years, the three old girls who'd been along the last time "knew exactly the route" from the train station to the arena.

At the Elephant Sanctuary in Hohenwald, Tennessee, a new arrival named Jenny met a lonely older cow, Shirley, whom she'd met briefly twenty years before. "Jenny became very agitated upon perceiving Shirley, and started calling," recounts sanctuary operator Carol Buckley. "After ten minutes there was an unbelievable exchange of vocalizations — the volume was so intense it was deafening. You could *see* the moment Shirley remembered Jenny. They climbed all over each other through the gate. When we let them through, we expected a huge dramatic scene. Not at all. They just melted into each other. Now, when Jenny naps, Shirley straddles her," sheltering her like a mother.

The singular nature of elephants has struck untold generations of observers dumb, or at least credulous, and magnified qualities that were already remarkable enough. Even before Barnum and other circus promoters, the original spinmasters, began inflating the measurements of their pachyderm stars, many who knew the animals firsthand saw them as even bigger — much bigger — than they really were. The colonial elephant catcher G. P. Sanderson noted that Madras elephants were variously accounted to be "seventeen to twenty feet high"; one mahout insisted his approached eighteen feet. Sanderson measured that giant and "it did not exceed ten feet." The tallest Asian elephants scarcely top eleven feet, and the tallest Africans twelve, perhaps thirteen. But stand beneath the stuffed thirteen-foot, seven-ton tusker in the lobby of the Smithsonian's Museum of Natural History and it's easy to see how imaginations ran wild.

Aristotle, Aelian, Bishop Ambrose, the Indian writer Nilakantha: from ancient authorities to nineteenth-century experts, writers on elephants routinely put their life span at one, two, three hundred, even *one thousand* years. Even the ordinarily reliable Sanderson opined that "the elephant attains at least 150 years" — twice the actual figure. Perhaps these authorities presumed that elephants needed so many years to acquire the wisdom they so evidently embodied. Wisdom and its companion, gentleness, are the elephant qualities most revered — or exaggerated — by ancients and moderns alike. Pliny saluted elephants for possessing "virtues rare even in man: honesty, wisdom, justice, also respect for the stars and reverence for sun and moon," and cited reports that "in the forests of Mauretania, when the new moon is shining, herds of elephants go down to a river named Amilo and there perform a ritual of purification, sprinkling themselves with water." Other Romans described elephants, which delight in bathing and water play, praying to the gods, purifying themselves in the sea, and raising their trunks to salute the rising sun. Even today some Indian temples handily exploit the animals' natural "prayer" gestures: at the Thepakkadu elephant camp, a young elephant performs a daily sunset *puja*, repeatedly circling a small shrine, then kneeling and saluting with its trunk.

The ancients saw elephants as not only reverent but romantic. Pliny, Aelian, and Plutarch all write of an elephant who "fell in love" with an Alexandrian flower girl. Pliny mentions another who fell for a young soldier. The ancients believed that elephants relished sweet scents and, by one account, preferred flowers even to food. In return, the giants afforded their own aromatherapy; their sweet breath was believed to be a "sovereign remedy for headache." Indeed, despite their reputation for flatulence, I've never detected a hint of halitosis in many close approaches.

Elephant flatulence is nothing next to elephant diarrhea, a desired sequel to constipation (which can otherwise be fatal). In 1998, according to the journal *Elephant*, a zookeeper in Paderborn, Germany, fed his constipated elephant Stefan twenty doses of animal laxative and a bushel of berries, figs, and prunes. He was trying to administer an olive oil enema when Stefan's dam broke. The torrent knocked over the keeper, who struck his head, passed out, and was suffocated under the dung. It was a death worthy of one of Peter de Vries's most absurdly unlucky heroes — and at the same time a monumental professional martyrdom.

And what should this selfless keeper's monument be made of? In 1999, elephant dung became the culture war's latest rallying cry, succeeding blood and urine as the most sensational and controversial art medium. That year the British-Nigerian painter Chris Ofili exhibited his *Holy Virgin Mary*, decorated with dried elephant dung, in the "Sensations" show at the Brooklyn Museum of Art. Mayor Rudolph Giuliani took the bait and tried to jerk the museum's city funding, declaring that "civilization has been about trying to find the right place to put excrement, not on the walls of museums." In the uproar over *The Holy Virgin Mary*, much cruder and crueler pieces in "Sensations" were overlooked, as was the longtime use of dung, especially elephant dung, in West African art and worship. Indeed, it could be seen as expressing the same great mystery as the Virgin herself: of spirit contained in corporeality, of supreme power — the elephant in African tradition — combined with fertility, fuel for fire, and fertilizer for crops.

In 1612 the greatest metaphysical poet, John Donne, pondered that mystery in a long verse meditation, "On the Progress of the Soul." It includes the most eloquent evocation of elephantine gentleness and dignity:

> Natures great master-peece, an Elephant,
> The onely harmlesse great thing; the giant
> Of beasts; who thought, no more had gone, to make one wise
> But to be just, and thankfull, loth to offend,
> (Yet nature hath given him no knees to bend)
> Himselfe he up-props, on himself relies,

And foe to none, suspects no enemies
Still sleeping stood; vex'd not his fantasie
Blacke dreames; like unbent bow, carelessly
His sinewy Proboscis did remisly lie. . . .

Reading such exaltations, one might think God created elephants in his own image and man just got in the way. Indeed, some elephant handlers seem to think that; at the least, they feel more comfortable around their giant charges than with other humans. But they harbor no delusions about elephant physiology and behavior, whereas Donne's knowledge of both was spotty. Contrary to widespread belief in his time, elephants *can* bend their knees, and would be in an awful fix if they couldn't. And far from being "harmless" and suspecting "no enemies," elephants can remember a wrong and nurse a grudge for years; they can kill suddenly out of long-brewed resentment or pique, or for reasons mysterious even to those who know them. Or some elephants can do so; most are loyal and — damn the anthropocentrism — loving, or at least submissive, passing softly through their long lives. Their temperaments and degrees of dangerousness vary as widely as humans'. Donne's fellow Englishmen would learn that, sometimes at the price of their lives, once they made the acquaintance of a few more elephants. Fourteen centuries earlier, Claudius Aelianus reported that "the elephant is even said [by the Moors] to possess two hearts and to think double: one heart is the source of anger, the other of gentleness" — the original Jekyll and Hyde.

This perceived dual nature reflects an essential difference between elephants and all the other creatures that humans have taken into their homes and stables. And it presents a paradox. Despite having one of the longest, richest, and most intimate associations with humankind of all animals (parasites excluded), the elephant has never been truly domesticated. It has never been bred for domesticity or, until very recently, captive-bred in significant numbers at all. Until the decline in wild elephants' numbers forced bans on their capture, nearly all captive elephants were caught wild or (in Asian logging camps) born from captive females allowed to mate with wild males. Thus, while a fat Hereford scarcely resembles its wild ancestors, and a dachshund looks not at all like a wolf, today's "domestic" elephants are still in form and genome full-fledged members of the wild stock, a fact some elephant breeders claim could save that stock if captive-bred animals can be used to replenish it.

This means that unlike beagles, bantams, and other animals bred to the bridle or feedlot, elephants are not wired for the tasks humans want them to do; they must be persuaded. Cooperation and coercion, partnership and intimidation, infuse their training and employment. Elephants are the only animals that can be tamed at any age — to the extent they are ever truly tamed. Indeed, elephant trainers have said that the largest, most defiant wild elephants make the most obliging captives once broken, while those raised in captivity are less trustworthy because they do not fear humans.

The elephant may also be the only animal that humans have both ardently hunted and used to hunt other animals. Elephant-back was long the preferred position for hunting tigers in India, and is still a favorite mode for capturing wild elephants. Trained monitor elephants, *koonkies* in India, exhibit an almost preternatural knack for both intimidating and mollifying their wild targets. And yet even the most outwardly docile sometimes turn on their trainers after years or decades of submission. The nearest equivalent to the taming of elephants is not the domestication of cats or cattle. It is the employment of humans by other humans — or their enslavement.

SEE THE ELEPHANT, GET A SIGHT OF THE ELEPHANT: To see the sights, to gain experience of life.

— Milford M. Mathews, *A Dictionary of Americanisms*

2

Mammoth Riches

The wisdom of the tuskéd domination
Holds up to shame the apery of mankind,
The malice and deceit and tribulation,
The tongue that wags and clacks, the vacant mind. . . .

Irremeable hour of mammoth tears
When elephants were turned out to browse
the prey to their inferiors' darts and spears!

— Henry Harmon Chamberlin, *The Age of Ivory*

AT THE HIGH POINT of the 1981 film of *Quest for Fire*, adapted
from J. H. Rosny's "Novel of Prehistoric Times," the questing Nean-
dertal heroes are about to be slaughtered by a larger rival band.
Desperately fleeing, they run into a herd of elephants wrapped in
shaggy body wigs, their size magnified through photographic fore-
shortening — a cinematic version of woolly mammoths. Caught
between the marauders and the mammoths, the Neandertals have
an inspiration: they pluck grass and offer it beseechingly to the giant beasts. Music swells; this is a Big Moment, a soulful meeting of
early man and primeval beast. The mammoths accept the offering
and stomp off to trample the heroes' enemies — just as Tarzan's elephant friends charge to the rescue whenever he summons them
with his trumpet-like call.

This scene is supremely silly, but it points up something plaintively real: humankind's abiding fascination with and affection for elephants, even elephants that vanished from the earth thousands of years ago. Of all the extinct prehistoric creatures save *Tyrannosaurus rex*, the woolly mammoth is probably the most pervasive in the current culture. But whereas *T. rex* emblemizes a nature that is brutal, ravening, and utterly foreign and inhospitable to us, the mammoths betoken a very different Lost World: an Eden that got away, or that we threw away, ruled by gentle behemoths resembling giant fuzzy stuffed toys.

I still remember when I first heard the call of this world, on a youthful visit to New York and the American Museum of Natural History. There, stretched out in a glass case, was . . . a mammoth! Not just bones wired together to approximate its former stance, nor a replica done in cement or rubber or pixels like the ersatz dinosaurs that sometimes seem as ubiquitous as real dinosaurs once were. This was the actual, though only partial, embalmed corpse of a baby mammoth — face, trunk, and foreleg — found frozen near Fairbanks, Alaska, where it lived and died some 21,300 years ago and was uncovered in 1948. It even had a name, "Effie," recalling the verse by e. e. cummings that begins, "here is little Effie's head / whose brains are made of gingerbread." That Effie's skull held only "six subjunctive crumbs" — the *would, should,* and so on of a life unlived and possibilities unfulfilled. Behold Effie the mammoth's head, and grieve for the lost evolutionary path she represented.

How much more piercing that feeling must be for those who view Dima, the best-preserved mammoth yet discovered, an infant male uncovered by Siberian gold miners in 1977 after an icy forty-thousand-year interment. Dima's corpse was withered but complete, down to internal organs and blood vessels. In a photo of workers lifting it out of the permafrost, it seems not a mummy but a living, if emaciated, baby elephant struggling shakily to his feet — a birth, not an exhumation.

The enchantment of bygone elephants has surfaced again and again with their buried bones, from ancient times until today and from the Mediterranean to the Arctic seas. Imagine a hunter, trap-

other; the survivors founded Thebes, the city of Oedipus and Dionysus. Even today, "sowing dragon's teeth" means to stir up strife. But in the fourth century B.C., the Greek skeptic Palaephatus — the original debunker — told the real story in his *On Fabulous Tales:* The dragon's teeth were actually elephants' teeth kept in a Theban temple; Cadmus was a Phoenician interloper who slew the Theban king Drago and claimed his throne. Drago's friends scattered to raise a force against Cadmus, bearing with them, evidently as tokens of sovereignty, the elephants' — "Drago's" — teeth.

Elephant fossils could become the relics of heroes as well as monsters. Mayor, in *The First Fossil Hunters,* suggests that the purported remains of the giant warrior Ajax, who fell outside Troy, were likely those of elephants. Likewise, a sixteen-foot skeleton uncovered by the Romans in Syria, which an oracle credited to an Indian giant named Orontes, was probably a mastodon or steppe mammoth. And gomphotheres and deinotheres were common in an area of Turkey where the Greek traveler Pausanias saw an immense skeleton that the locals identified as the giant Geryon, slain by Hercules.

The profusion of giant bones on the island of Samos presented an especially tantalizing riddle. The Roman historian Plutarch reported that at one site, Phloion, the earth was believed to have opened up and swallowed some shrieking giant creatures called the Neades, which handily explained both the buried fossils and powerful local earthquakes. Another site, Panaima ("Blood-Soaked Field"), was believed to hold the remains of a great battle between the Amazons and Dionysus, the god of fertility, wine, and ecstatic rites, who rode triumphantly from India into the West — atop an elephant.

Plutarch correctly credited some Samos bones to elephants — a true feat of observation 1,700 years before the French naturalist Georges Cuvier began classifying the vanished animals of the distant past. Other Greeks were all too ready to see oversized bones as proof that the heroes of the Golden Age walked taller than corrupt modern man. So were many of Cuvier's eighteenth- and nineteenth-century contemporaries. Yale College president Ezra Stiles ascribed American mastodon bones to human-like giants. Mammoth bones found near Gloucester, England, were hailed as relics of the giants mentioned in Genesis.

You might think tusks would be a dead giveaway. But most people could not imagine elephants inhabiting northern latitudes, and ascribed the tusks to all manner of zoological concoctions — "fanciful beasts resembling unicorns or oxen," as Lister and Bahn write, "or an enormous bird with the tusks for talons."

As the truth of the old bones emerged and intact Siberian carcasses were exhumed, the woolly mammoth became a sentimental cult figure, a prehistoric mascot for the Romantic age. With its tiny, humanoid ears (shrunken to reduce heat loss), beard-like mane, and fuzzy topknot, it looked like a benevolent fairy-tale giant or wise old forest god, a messenger from an earlier, purer age. Even its scientific name evokes a pristine past: *Mammuthus primigenius,* the "first-born" or "primitive" mammoth. But *M. primigenius* was anything but primitive. It was actually the last-born elephant, appearing only in the Ice Age cycles of the last few hundred thousand years — "the pinnacle of elephant evolution," in the words of the biologist S. K. Eltringham, and "more advanced than either of the living elephants." Like the surviving *Loxodonta* and *Elephas* genera, *Mammuthus* arose in Central Africa. But unlike *Loxodonta,* which stayed in Africa, and *Elephas,* which got only as far as China, the woolly mammoth was a truly global species, spanning the northern latitudes of Europe, Asia, and America in a blink of the geologic eye.

During its relatively short stay, the woolly mammoth played an outsized role in human life. It was essential sustenance for the Eurasian peoples living on the edge of glacial devastation, who relied on it much as America's Plains Indians did on bison. During the Ice Ages, mammoths may even have made human survival possible in the northern latitudes: a single kill could save a tribe from starvation. Paul Martin and David Burney, authors of a startling proposal for restoring elephant-based ecosystems, suggest that elephants, the most versatile foragers of all, would have led early human gatherers to many edible plants, such as agave and sweet mesquite beans in the American Southwest. They and the University of Nevada anthropologist Gary Haynes argue that the prevalence of mammoths may answer the long-standing mystery of how humans spread with such astonishing speed across the Americas. These immigrants would have followed the meat — along the "elephant roads" the mammoths had conveniently cut.

The Eurasian "mammoth cultures" didn't merely feed on killed and scavenged mammoths; they clothed themselves in mammoth hide and fur and made tools, weapons, even homes from mammoth bones. One representative bone hut at Mezen in the Ukraine rests on a foundation of twenty-five mammoth skulls; another hut held bones ranging up to eight thousand years in age. These bone houses resemble giant ribcages; the ancient steppe dwellers didn't just live off mammoths, they lived *in* them. Some authorities have suggested that the houses were designed for ritual use, to honor and invoke the animal that provided their materials.

From smaller bones the mammoth hunters made needles (probably for sewing mammoth wool) and what appear to have been musical instruments — which musicians of the Kiev State Orchestra used in 1976 to stage the ultimate revival concert, playing reimagined Ice Age music. Prehistoric artists painted mammoths, along with other valuable prey, on their cave walls and carved their sculptures — "Venus *impudique*" fertility figures, exquisite geometric forms, even other animal figures — from mammoth ivory.

The mammoths' largest leaps across the ages, enriching human life (and those lucky humans who find tusks) today as in prehistoric times. Mammoth ivory fueled a lucrative trade between Yakutsk and China two thousand years ago, and still supplies a flourishing carving industry. Conservationists hoped that it would divert demand for modern elephant ivory — and sure enough, when the elephant ivory trade was banned in the 1980s, prices for mammoth ivory climbed. But trade in prehistoric ivory also gives cover to smuggled modern ivory. And the pell-mell excavation of tusks is destroying valuable paleontological and perhaps genetic evidence.

*   *   *

But the treasures that Ice Age humans garnered from mammoths and mastodons may pale next to the contributions that the elephants of an even earlier era made to the emergence of humankind itself. To state the theory bluntly, elephants may have been evolutionary midwives, or at least nursemaids, to the human species itself. They helped provide not just food, clothing, shelter, and material for tools and art, but also the landscape conditions in which *Homo sapiens* could emerge, thrive, and embark on its global march of conquest.

This notion seemed far-fetched when it first occurred to me some years ago. But I took encouragement on finding it already proposed by the paleontologist John Van Couvering, who argued the "evolutionary nursemaid" case in a 1992 essay. This argument correlates observations, deductions, and speculations that aren't usually considered together, even though all derive from the same era in the same region: the vast swath of what is now savanna in eastern and southern Africa, where hominids first appeared and where most of the world's elephants now survive.

Until recently, one piece of the theory seemed a slam-dunk. For decades it was commonly thought that the qualities that distinguished first hominids, then humans, from other animals — walking upright on two feet, toolmaking and weapon wielding, cooperative hunting, food sharing, speech, couple bonding, cooperative parenting — developed in response to the exposed conditions of the open savanna, back when our apelike ancestors exited or were forced from the dense forests where they lived as chimpanzees live today. But the savanna hypothesis has taken some heavy hits recently, with the successive discovery of hominid fossils dating back 3.5, 4.4, 5.2, even (according to one controversial claim) 6 million years — much longer than the 3.2 million years of the previous earliest-known hominid. Unlike previous discoveries, these remains, with their indications of bipedality, turned up in places that had been forested. "The savanna is dead!" paleontology mavens proclaimed with the enthusiasm that typically accompanies new findings on human origins and often proves premature. "Long live the forest hominids!"

But in a thoughtful essay accompanying the announcement of the most dramatic new forest hominid discoveries, Henry Gee, writing in *Nature*, raised several cautions. The evidence that these were human rather than, say, chimpanzee ancestors seems inconclusive. "It is possible," he suggested, "that some of these fossils might not be hominids at all." And the question remains "whether bipedality is a diagnostic hominid trait." A now-extinct ape lineage might have started walking upright before humans did.

Even if hominids did start walking upright in the forest, the question remains *why,* when all the apes that have survived in the forest did not take that route. One possible answer: they would gain access to more resources, since they could travel between forests. (Fully bipedal humans can cover much more ground without tiring than occasionally bipedal chimpanzees, who sacrifice walking for climbing strength.) This would serve especially well in times of encroaching savanna and diminishing forest resources, when mobility would be at a premium. However and wherever bipedality developed, it would also confer other advantages in open country. Standing upright exposes less body surface to the scorching sun, helps the stander scan for prey and predators, and frees hands to wield tools and carry food from remote gathering sites or large kills.

Emerging from a forest where a monkey is a prize catch, the first hominids on the grasslands beheld a vast larder of meat on the hoof. But killing an eland, much less an elephant, was a bigger job than snagging a monkey. It required strategy, coordination, and communication and encouraged the refinement of toolmaking and throwing abilities that are rudimentary in apes. Monkeys and apes may fling sticks, stones, and feces to let off steam or intimidate interlopers. Elephants sometimes throw missiles and routinely toss dirt and leaves upon their backs to shield against sun and insects, and maybe just because it feels good. But only humans can throw hard, straight, and far — an ability that may be more "diagnostic of hominids" than bipedalism, and that seems to predate big brains, language, and fine thumb-forefinger coordination. The Peabody Museum's Barbara Isaac has assembled impressive archeological and circumstantial evidence for throwing as a primary skill, mastered by preliterate cultures worldwide. Ergo Van Couvering's exquisite definition of a human being: "An ape with a fastball."

This view gains support from a recent reexamination of Acheulian hand axes, ubiquitous tools of our *Homo erectus* ancestors. For more than 1 million years, these haftless stone blades were chipped out in the same almond shape, sharpened on all or most edges. Finally, someone — the University of Georgia's Eileen O'Brien — tested them in actual use. Their sharp edges couldn't be safely gripped for scraping or chopping. But O'Brien discovered with the help of trained discus throwers that they were splendidly balanced for throwing, always landing point first. And they are usually found in lakebeds and other watercourses, precisely where they would have been lost if they were thrown at prey.

And water holes, argues the University of Washington neurobiologist William Calvin, are where hominids would have stalked large prey, just as lions do today. Repeating O'Brien's trials, Calvin showed that a hunter needn't throw the sharpened "almond" precisely, or even target a specific animal. He could lob it into the teeming mass at a crowded water hole — a move a chimp could perform — with reasonable odds that it would land in some critter's back, making it buckle just long enough for hunters to dispatch it.

Hand axes, arrows, or guided missiles: at whatever level, throwing works better in open country than dense forest. And, as Isaac notes, it answers a question that had long stumped anthropologists: How could puny hominids survive in grasslands swarming with powerful predators? Consider how just pretending to reach for a rock makes the fiercest dog cringe; this response has been hardwired through thousands of years of confrontations between rockthrowing hominids and wary canids.

So even if the savanna environment did not make hominids diverge from other ape lines, it supported their development and success. But how did the savanna come to be on territory that had been forest? The most popular answer is global cooling, as deciphered by the South African–born paleontologist Elisabeth Vrba. She traced the appearance and disappearance of grassland antelopes in the fossil strata and concluded that around "2.5 million years ago a particularly marked and widespread environmental change occurred in Africa . . . an increase in open grasslands at the expense of wood and tree cover, probably resulting from a global reduction in temperature and associated changes in rainfall. The environmental changes caused the evolutionary changes in hominids that are observed in both eastern and southern Africa over the same time period." Other researchers have since affirmed that the world was cooling and Africa was getting drier around 2.3 to 2.8 million years ago, at the start of the Pleistocene epoch. But they debate whether a "faunal pulse" erupted then, or whether antelope numbers and diversity grew more gradually over a million-year period.

Either way, the climatic changes and the savanna growth credited to them both occurred well after the first hominids are now supposed to have appeared, which would seem to argue against the savanna hypothesis. But another factor lurks in the wings, which may be a link between the two phenomena. In the mostly warm, wet Pliocene epoch, 2.5 to 7 million years ago, Africa, especially East Africa, was a hotbed of elephant evolution, incubating three genera — *Loxodonta, Elephas,* and *Mammuthus* — that would dominate four continents right up to the modern epoch. The dominant African species, the now-extinct *Elephas recki,* spread across the continent in enormous numbers, outcompeting the loxodonts that still survived for millions of years. How would all these elephants have affected the African landscape? You can get a clue from the effects that African and, where they are numerous enough, Asian elephants have today.

The ability to transform the landscape is commonly considered distinctly human; in his noted *Conservation and Biodiversity,* Andrew Dobson calls it the "one ecological feature that distinguishes [humans] from all other species." But the difference is one of degree, not kind: beavers alter watercourses; termites, ants, and prairie dogs dig underground cities; strangler figs uproot human cities. And elephants most nearly approach the human ability to reshape the land itself, making them what Jeheskel Shoshani, founder of the Elephant Interest Group, calls "a super-keystone species." They dig wells, some as deep as they are tall, to find the channels flowing under parched riverbeds; they may gauge the depth of underground water by ground sonar, listening for echoes from their own footfalls.

Elephants also dig for dietary minerals. In Kenya they have tunneled out a whole network of salt mines — an entire new underground landscape. The biologist Ian Redmond spent stench-filled months observing these "underground elephants" and concluded that they alone had gouged out Mount Elgon's vast Kitum Caves, mouthful by mouthful. One elephant would crush and swallow about one gallon of tufa per visit; just twenty thousand visits would have excavated Kitum's main chamber. And the elephants came not singly but in large herds, until ivory poachers slaughtered many of them. For a while, mining protected them by wearing their tusks down; the poachers passed them by so long as they still had full-tusked elephants to kill.

If a gallon a day can carve out a cavern, imagine what six-ton gourmands can do to the countryside above. One study found that Tanzania's Serengeti elephants wrecked on average three trees every four days; those in one section of Uganda's Kidepo National Park were largely blamed for the loss of a third of its trees. Elephants extract less than half the nutrients in their food and compensate with enormous intake — three hundred to five hundred pounds of grass, leaves, fruit, twigs, and even sweet-sapped tree trunks each day. They distribute fertilizer and seeds — some of which sprout only after passing through an elephant's gut — each day.

Modern-day park managers, game officials, and even some ecologists tend to be less appreciative of the elephants' gardening role. They paint the endless stripping, chomping, yanking, smashing, and uprooting as devastation, pure and dreadful. In southern Africa, they insist that the only way to save the ecosystem is by slaughtering — or, in the operant euphemism, "culling" — elephants. Then they demand dispensation to export ivory so this killing can support the good work of conservation.

But eco-disaster usually entails a human factor. Elephants have overpopulated and defoliated parks such as South Africa's tightly fenced Kruger because they were stopped from migrating and browsing new territory while harvested-over areas recovered, and because they enjoyed year-round artificial water supplies, pumped for livestock or to lure wildlife within tourists' shutter range. Elephant breeding adjusts to water supply; guaranteeing water guarantees a population boom.

Even the alarming "desertification" of the once-lush Serengeti, which prompted some ecologists to call for culling in the 1970s, appears to have been a red herring — fire red. After monitoring the Serengeti for decades, the ecologist A. R. E. Sinclair concluded that it was fires set by herdsmen to improve the overgrown pasture, not elephants, that destroyed most of the acacia seedlings. Since then the Serengeti's famous million-strong wildebeest herd has recovered, cropping the grass and reducing the impetus to set fires. With ivory trading banned, elephants also bounced back; so did the acacias the elephants supposedly destroyed.

For most other large mammals — including *Homo sapiens* as hunter and herdsman — the elephants' partial destruction of woodlands is a boon. Dense forest may be heaven for bark burrowers and canopy dwellers, but it's notoriously poor habitat for most big critters. A mixed landscape is more congenial, especially when it grows lushly in a climate wet enough to support full forest. Elephants' foraging encourages plants — from grasses to acacias — that regenerate quickly, providing more fodder for gazelles, gnus, and, indirectly, lions. This foraging helps "maintain the present diversity of cover types and assure[s] a multispecific animal community," researchers in Uganda's Kigale Forest concluded. "The elephant population with its feeding behavior appears to be the key component in continued high total productivity of the entire reserve." Grass grew twice as high "in the area of greatest [elephant] droppings." Likewise, in an area of Rhodesia whose large mammals were destroyed, "land became parched, and the rich biotic community disappeared."

As today, so in the Pliocene. Elephants would have opened up a vast new country, loaded with game, for newly bipedal hominids to exploit. They even provided easy access, cutting pathways through the undergrowth and, being creatures of habit, maintaining these from generation to generation. Modern road builders sometimes follow these "elephant roads," whose routing human art cannot improve. Elisabeth Vrba, now at Yale, suggests that human ancestors learned to dig for roots and tubers by watching elephants do so. "I think the early hominids learned by imitating other animals — and there's a theory that tool use began with digging." Although she is an author of the climate-change explanation for the savanna's spread, Vrba readily concedes that "elephants are *major* factors in ordering the landscape" and could also play a role. "But it's all speculation. We can't verify this."

That speculation isn't confined to Africa. The ecosystem changes that overtook northern Siberia with the end of the Ice Ages are usually explained in terms strikingly similar to the climate-change explanations for Africa's savanna: Colder, drier Pleistocene weather favored grasses, which supported mammoths, horses, and bison, and the humans who preyed on them. Then wetter weather made this "mammoth steppe" revert to mossy tundra, starving the grazers. But researchers led by Sergei Zimov, director of Russia's North-East Scientific Station, found that precipitation remained constant throughout these changes. Instead, the "keystone" grazers — especially mammoths — had turned tundra into steppe by trampling delicate mosses and promoting grass growth through cropping. Because grass transpires more than moss, the soils dried out, further favoring grass — a feedback loop.

Then something else killed off the grazers, and mossy tundra returned. No longer would mammoths garden the tundra, reshaping it as the elephants do the African savanna, into rich habitat for humans and many other species — a contribution they would surely have regretted if they'd known how *Homo sapiens* would repay them.

SEE THE ELEPHANT: (American) To see the world; to "go out for wool and come home shorn"; by implication, to "go on the loose." Sometimes, TO SEE THE KING.

— J. S. Farmer & W. E. Henley, *Slang and its Analogues*

3

Overchill, Overkill, Over-ill, and Over the Hill

> Mindful of the elephants used by Hannibal and Alexander the Great in cold climes, Yasmilov plans to train the mammontelephases to earn their keep when they reach adulthood. They could pull immobilized convoy trucks out of the snowdrifts on the trans-Siberian highway. . . . The mammontelephases could also be used for logging, and there may even be a job on the trans-Siberian pipeline.
>
> — Diana Ben-Aaron, "Retrobreeding the Woolly Mammoth"

> As a result of the late Pleistocene extinctions we live in a continent of ghosts.
>
> — Paul S. Martin and David A. Burney, "Bring Back the Elephants"

THE DISAPPEARANCE of the mammoths and their Siberian steppe-mates is one chapter in the greatest murder mystery of all: the extinction of a bestiary full of giant creatures — twenty-foot monitor lizards, hairy northern rhinos, beavers big as pigs, sloths the size of hippos, and above all the ubiquitous and wildly varied elephants and their kin — which walked the earth just a few thousand years ago.

Imagine the vast plains and forests of America thirteen thousand years before they were planted with soybeans and shopping malls.

Imagine how all the world looked to the early humans fanning out from Africa. Everywhere, on every continent except Australia, they would have seen elephants. For over 20 million years, elephants and their cousins in the oddball order Proboscidea ruled the world, as much as any organisms larger than bacteria could be said to. They branched into some 162 species (352 by an earlier count), and into more weirdly varied physiognomies than any other mammal order save bats — from elongated shovel faces to bristling clusters of ivory. The proboscideans remind us that God has a sense of humor as well as a fondness for beetles.

These proto-elephants and quasi-elephants were, with the giant ground sloths, the biggest creatures to walk the earth after the dinosaurs departed, and probably the brainiest until the hominids arrived. They spread across every terrain, from tundra, desert, and mountains to tropical swamps and scattered islands, probably dominating them as today's elephants do the game parks of Africa. Vast size usually means smaller numbers, but the American mastodon is the most common fossil mammal in the northeastern United States. Remains of more than 167,000 mammoths have been uncovered in Siberia. Most of the large mammals found in Egypt's fossil-rich Fayyum basin are elephants and other proboscideans; most of the small ones are hyraxes, rodentlike creatures that are, with manatees and dugongs, the elephants' nearest surviving anatomical cousins. Gomphotheres, proboscideans with elephant-like upper and boar-like lower tusks, thrived in South America for 10 million years, until the human era.

And then the Age of Elephants ended everywhere except southern Asia and Africa — at different times in different places, but always with astonishing rapidity. Between ten and forty thousand years ago, as the Late Pleistocene Ice Ages neared their close, most of the giant land mammals disappeared — overnight, as things go on the evolutionary scale. For decades climate change was blamed for this as for earlier extinctions; absent a meteor strike or other planetary catastrophe, no other cause seemed sufficient to the effect.

But several questions still gnawed. Unlike the five much broader "great extinctions" that swept the planet, the Pleistocene die-offs seemed selective, affecting large land mammals greatly, smaller species much less, and marine species scarcely at all. They struck similarly at different latitudes — eliminating South America's tropical gomphotheres as well as North America's mammoths and mastodons — but very differently on different continents. The Americas lost three-quarters or more of their large mammal genera, Eurasia and Australia fewer than half, southern Asia fewer still, and Africa fewer than 15 percent. These extinctions struck Southeast Asia, Australia, and Africa forty thousand years ago, China twenty thousand years ago, and glaciated northern Europe, Siberia, and America ten to thirteen thousand years ago, just as the climate was warming and the glaciers retreating.

Paul Martin, a paleobiologist at the University of Arizona, considered these discrepancies and noted that the megafauna extinctions seemed to coincide with the perfection of Neolithic hunting techniques in Africa and Asia and the arrival of humans in America, Australia, and northern Eurasia. Martin noted that modern waves of extermination — of giant lemurs on Madagascar, big, flightless moas on New Zealand, and a host of smaller species in the Caribbean — occurred soon after humans arrived. And in 1966 he proposed a new culprit: as superefficient prehistoric hunters with fluted stone weapons spread across new continents, they slaughtered vast populations of naive animals that had no time to learn to fear them.

This "overkill" or, in its most extreme form, "blitzkrieg" hypothesis hit like a bombshell, and the debate between its advocates and defenders of the climatic explanation ("overchill") has raged, ebbed, and raged again ever since. Overkill seems to account for the discrepancies in climatic explanations. Because hominids evolved in Africa and inhabited tropical Asia for more than a million years, elephants and other large animals learned to avoid or repel them before they became master hunters. By the time humans reached the Americas, they were in their hunting prime. Big, trusting creatures — woolly dodos — wouldn't stand a chance.

Evidence for overkill was nearly nonexistent. But bit by bit, it has accrued: improved radiocarbon dating, the bones and ovens left by New Zealand's Maoris as they wiped out eleven moa species, a few mastodon-kill and meat-storage sites. Earlier findings had suggested that mammoths downsized quickly before they disappeared — a common evolutionary response to scarce resources, as when climate changes. Later findings suggest otherwise: if anything, mammoths' tusks — which, like trees, show annual growth rings — grew faster toward the end. That acceleration might reflect heavy predation, which favors the genes of individuals that mature quickly and mate before becoming prey. Likewise today, when poachers lop off the big males, fast-maturing upstarts get their chance at fertile females.

The climate case also rests on extremely narrow notions of what mastodons and mammoths ate. American mastodons' teeth were suited to browsing conifers; ergo they starved when warming weather made northern woods recede. Grazing mammoths starved when temperate forest replaced grassy steppe. But in 1989 a mastodon carcass was found in an Ohio bog with an intact gut full of moss, leaves, swamp grass, sedges — and no conifers. The next year, Kansas researchers found grass and aquatic plant residues on teeth from three mastodons.

It is presumptuous to think that mammoths couldn't adapt to their changing habitat as savanna elephants do, and that they ate only grass. Their nearest cousins, modern elephants, are supremely versatile herbivores, consuming everything from roots to bark to blossoms from up to two hundred plant species. Malaysian elephants prefer grass, as mammoths supposedly did, but feed more on palms, which are more plentiful. Elephants can also endure extreme changes and a wide range of environments, from Kilimanjaro's freezing slopes to Namibia's searing Skull Coast and all the swamps, forests, and grasslands between, and withstand extreme disruptions in them. They readily recover from catastrophic droughts and die-offs. "Proboscidean resilience," writes Gary Haynes, allows "recovery from nearly any environmental stress *except human overhunting.*"

But overkill still faces a basic hurdle of plausibility. As Haynes, who cautiously endorses it, concedes in conversation, "Most arche-ologists flat-out don't *believe* people with spears could have killed all the large animals."

That incredulity has prompted several variations on the overkill hypothesis. In 1987 the South African zoologist Norman Owen-Smith suggested that human hunters needn't have wiped out ev-ery species that vanished. They would have targeted the biggest and slowest-breeding "megaherbivores": elephants, rhinos, giant ground sloths. Without these keystone species to "maintain" them, grasslands reverted to tundra or forest, just as Zimov argues hap-pened in Siberia. Smaller grazers, plus the carnivores that ate them, followed the giants into oblivion.

In 1999, Ross MacPhee, curator of mammals at the American Museum of Natural History, proposed a more radical variation on overkill: the "hyperdisease hypothesis," according to which early humans spread some unknown pathogen — perhaps a rabies, flu, or morbili virus — devastating to scores of other species. It is a tan-talizing hypothesis without a shred of evidence.

Gary Haynes calls hyperdisease "a grassy-knoll kind of theory — people who just did not *believe* Lee Harvey Oswald could have fired all three shots said there must have been someone on the grassy knoll." MacPhee insists it deserves a chance, given the contradic-tions of the climate case and the sheer implausibility of a hunting blitzkrieg. "We'll never even approach proving the cause of death," he concedes. "All we can look for is patterns."

In North America two patterns converge: human expansion and climate change both coincide with the mammoths' and mastodons' disappearance. MacPhee has called the Pleistocene extinctions "a murder mystery with many victims, but no apparent means or mo-tive." Either that or too many means, motives, and suspects. Per-haps, as in Agatha Christie's *Murder on the Orient Express,* all the suspects had a hand in the killing. Hunters could have finished off populations already weakened by climate change and/or disease. Even Paul Martin, overkill's first and most persistent advocate, ad-mits he is now "inclining" toward accepting climate change as an underlying cause. "I guess at some point you need help" from ad-

ditional causes, he says. "I have to admit, the idea of stressed animals in their last throes succumbing to predators makes a lot of
sense."

Even if the great debate ends in a split explanation, the point will
hold. Early human hunters played a major role in exterminating
most of the largest land animals, including the ancient elephants
that helped make the world fit for humans. The debate over these extinctions does not happen in a vacuum; however much its protagonists aspire to scientific detachment, it remains politically charged
and freighted with troublesome moral and social implications.

Kill-off and die-off invoke divergent worldviews and opposite
notions of responsibility for ecological catastrophes past and,
maybe, future. Call it "nature versus murder": If impersonal nature
wiped out the mammoths and mastodons, humankind is off the
hook. But if early hunters swept through the Pleistocene fauna like
journalists at a buffet table, they may foretell the damage we ourselves will do in what the biologist Edward O. Wilson has called
"one of the great extinction spasms of ecological history." Ross
MacPhee complains that conservation biologists propound overkill
to bolster their dire and wrong-headed predictions of disaster —
and counters with his guilt-free hyperdisease hypothesis.

This is painful prehistory, with the power to offend. Overkill
challenges cherished notions of indigenous peoples, especially
Native Americans, living in exquisite harmony with nature. Debunkers are always waiting, sometimes with racist or expedient
motives, to claim a sort of earth-raping equivalence: See, the Indians then were just like leach miners and clearcutters today. At least
we're not butchering the last mammoth; we just want to keep our
big cars and houses and steaks. "I did not think scientific doctrines
were harmful," the Native American writer Vine Deloria, Jr., writes
in *Red Earth, White Lies.* "Then I began to hear how my ancestors
slaughtered the Pleistocene megafauna and I began to read about
this hypothesis. As I saw rednecks and conservative newspaper col-
umnists rant and rave over the supposed destruction of these large
animals, and saw a determined effort to smear American Indians as
even worse than our present industrialists, I decided to write this

book, offering an alternative explanation for the demise of the great animals."

Deloria's alternative is a nonbiblical creationism, although like other creationists he is glad to appropriate congenial scientific findings. His resentment at seeing what he calls "my ancestors" tarred as mass exterminators is understandable, but if they were, so were everyone's ancestors: overkill is a global hypothesis, varying only in degree from continent to continent. In surprising ways, guilt over it still haunts us today, inspiring plaintive longing and quixotic science. Frozen mammoths, flesh-and-fur messengers from another era, have become the stuff of not just bizarre banquets but a flamboyant quest, literally, to bring the Ice Age back to life — a quest that started as a hoax.

In the April 1984 issue of the MIT-published magazine *Technology Review,* an intern named Diana Ben-Aaron executed an April Fool's prank so ingenious I was briefly gulled when I happened across it on an electronic database. That database listed Ben-Aaron's article, "Retrobreeding the Woolly Mammoth," under such topics as "Genetic Engineering" and "Cell — Transplantation," not under "Hoaxes." The article reported that a Soviet veterinarian, "Dr. Svertbighooze Nhikiphorovich Yasmilov," and an MIT researcher had created hybrid "mammontelephases" by fertilizing long-frozen mammoth eggs with living elephant sperm and planting the resulting embryos in elephant surrogate mothers. Ben-Aaron recounted the steps to this breakthrough with a suspense worthy of the best science journalism, right down to a swaggering quote from the MIT hotshot: "Some scientists like to proceed in small, carefully thought-out steps. They are like accountants, and might as well be. I see science as high adventure, with enormous risks."

In one sense, this Tertiary Park gamble did come off: newspapers and other media reported the spoof as an actual event. But as every humbug and grifter since P. T. Barnum knows, gulling people means exploiting not only their ignorance but their desires and aspirations. In this case, people were so eager to see the mammoth return — to be reunited with this most endearing of vanished crea-

tures — that they were willing to believe a far-fetched gen
fantasy.

Or was it so far-fetched? If he were writing today, Marx
declare that all great events occur first as hoax, not tragedy. Fo
teen years after it appeared, *Technology Review*'s April foolery
started to come true, as not one but two international scientific
teams set out to do what Ben-Aaron had only spoofed. Not that
mammoth resurrection has become an entirely respectable en-
deavor. Although both teams were loaded with well-credentialed
brainpower, they were led by flamboyant, publicity-savvy business-
people. Neither was funded by the usual peer-reviewed agencies or
foundations. One was sponsored by a cable TV network that scored
a ratings bonanza for its contribution.

The first real-life scientist to try to make the mammoth dream a
reality was Kazufumi Goto of Kagushima University in southern
Japan. In 1986, Goto was toiling at the unglamorous task of gathering cattle sperm and eggs for artificial insemination to breed perfectly marbled Kobe beef when, as the journalist Richard Stone tells
it, he had an epiphany. He noticed that, contrary to the prevailing
macho image of furiously flagellating sperm cells thrusting themselves into receptive eggs, sperm actually died, lost their tails, and
were passively absorbed by the eggs. Goto wondered whether
sperm that were already dead might also fertilize eggs. He froze and
thawed bull sperm, injected it dead into live eggs, and — zygote! Viable embryos and, after implantation and gestation, live calves.

This breakthrough made it easier to store sperm and use it later,
and suggested other possibilities. In 1992, at a conference at Colorado State University, *Newsday* reporter Robert Cooke asked Goto
whether preserved sperm might be used to bring extinct species —
in particular that most charismatic of vanished megaspecies, the
woolly mammoth — back to life. (Cooke says he'd heard Colorado
State University's George Seidel toss out the notion.) Goto liked
the idea and pitched it to the advertising entrepreneur Katutoshi
Kobayashi, who had lately begun marketing inventions by Russian
scientists. Kobayashi was also excited by this novel form of entre-
preneurship: brokering mammoth DNA, and the mammoth itself,

from one epoch to another. "My friends always thought I was the most foolish person in the world," he told Stone, "but there before me was someone more foolish. I told Goto we would realize the dream together." Together they started the "Mammoth Creation Project."

For science director, Goto and Kobayashi recruited someone with grander credentials: Akira Iritani, head of the biotech department at prestigious Kinki University. In 1986, Iritani had pioneered the injection of sperm directly into egg cytoplasm, a technique now used for human fertilization and the basis for Goto's work with dead sperm. Then, Iritani had worked with rabbits; doing the same with mammoths would cap his career.

But breeding mammoths from ancient sperm presents at least two problems. First, feasibility: elephants' testes are buried in their abdomens, so just finding them in frozen carcasses would be difficult. And even if the animal died under cryogenically optimal circumstances — say, by falling into a crevasse — testicles insulated by so much body mass would not freeze quickly and cleanly. "Using frozen sperm to fertilize an elephant egg is not a likely event," says one microbiologist, Raul Cano of California Polytechnic State University, who, to his chagrin, found himself mistakenly associated with another mammoth-revival project. "Finding even a *single* cell with undamaged DNA is unlikely. We're always fighting entropy — cell death and decline." But Goto, with hands-on experience, counters that quick freezing, while desirable, is not necessary; because sperm DNA is so much hardier than that in somatic cells, it holds together in cattle sperm kept at room temperature for two days after death.

Another problem is *time*. If retrobreeding did work, it would yield a half-and-half hybrid — a "mammontelephas." If you got a female, and *if* it were fertile (unlike, say, horse-donkey hybrids), you could fertilize it with more mammoth sperm and get a three-quarters mammoth, and so on, the *Elephas* portion of the genotype shrinking by half with each generation. Elephants take so long to gestate and mature that it would require many decades to produce a near-complete (and very inbred) mammoth. "We cannot wait that long," Iritani told the newspaper *Yomiuri Shimbun*.

The faster way is one-generation genetic shopping: cloning. An intact mammoth nucleus would be swapped into an elephant cell, which would then be stimulated to divide, forming an embryo that would then be implanted. The result would be a mammoth borne by a modern elephant mother. But cloning depends on somatic DNA, which is much less durable than sperm DNA. And the Kobayashi team's first costly, ill-starred Siberian expedition did not even turn up a mammoth carcass, let alone the grail of intact DNA.

Cloning was also the goal of another, even more sensational mammoth-revival project, led by a passionate and charismatic French polar-tour leader named Bernard Buigues. In 1998, Buigues learned of a promising mammoth carcass on Siberia's far northern Taymyr Peninsula. He secured backing — $1 million, he has said — from cable TV's Discovery Channel and made television, if not scientific, history.

As "hyperdisease" proponent Ross MacPhee, a member of the project's science committee, notes, Buigues's enthusiasm was infectious: "There are very few people, certainly no scientists I know, who could ever have convinced anyone that there was a possible documentary in digging up mammoth bones." And Buigues's "Mammuthus" project proved a savvy investment. In March 2000 the first film about it, *Raising the Mammoth,* attracted not only the Discovery Channel's largest audience up till then but also, according to Discovery, the largest for any non-sports cable show that season — 26 million viewers on its first showing alone. The film itself was long on tease and short on actual revelations. It focused on sawing out the permafrost block containing whatever remained of "the Jarkov mammoth" and airlifting it to an ice cave for slow thawing. What was inside the block, much less what genetic magic might be worked with it, remained to be seen, in sequels. The press joined in the hype; Britain's tabloid *Sun* proclaimed the exhumation "one of the scientific finds of all time," right up there with oxygen, the double helix, and Archimedes' principle of displacement.

Six months later Discovery milked mammoth charisma with another heavy-breathing documentary, *The Last Mammoth,* about Raja Gaj, a huge, high-domed elephant in southwestern Nepal, whom the press had dubbed "the Beast of Bardia." After much drumbeating, *The Last Mammoth* concluded that the last mammoth was only an elephant — hardly surprising, since British researchers had already conclusively shown that Raja Gaj's double-domed skull was entirely unlike a mammoth's single dome and his size merely reflected his age and "the exceptionally large body size of the Nepalese [elephant] population."

That outcome didn't dissuade another drumbeat of media hype in December 2000, following reports of "large, hairy elephants" in the jungles of northern Thailand. Bangkok's *Nation* reported that "Princess Rangsrinopardon Yukol, the noted forest conservationist who coined the term 'Thai mammoth,'" was leading one of two expeditions endeavoring to find that fabulous creature. Sure enough, they failed.

In Nepal, and Thailand, the bait was the deceptive promise of a living mammoth. In Siberia, Buigues seemed sincere about cloning a living mammoth from long-dead DNA. But as MacPhee says, "Bernard's background is not in science." Those whose backgrounds were cast cold water from the start. Alex Greenwood, a genetics researcher at the American Museum of Natural History, was the most outspoken skeptic. After analyzing DNA from Alaskan and Siberian mammoth remains, Greenwood concluded that it was too fragmented and degraded for any hope of reproduction. Buigues's own science director, Dick Mol, called mammoth cloning "a crazy idea" in an interview on the Discovery Channel's "Raising the Mammoth" Web site.

Even if we could retrobreed long-lost species, and agreed that we should, one troublesome question would still loom: Why a mammoth? It would be more practical to revive a smaller Ice Age mammal — say, a dire wolf — that would need less space, food, and time to gestate and mature, and be more likely to breed in captivity (notoriously tricky with modern elephants). Also, ancient and modern wolves would make a better genetic match than mammoths and elephants, says John Critser, the director of the University of Missouri's Cryobiology Institute. Critser's team assisted the Indianapolis Zoo in the first successful artificial insemination of an African elephant and, by transplanting ovarian tissue, got mice to produce elephant eggs. He also hopes to undertake cloning from frozen prehistoric remnants. The problem, Critser told me, is funding: "Wealthy individuals who support zoos, and might support this, almost immediately and uniformly lose interest if [the conversation] moves away from the woolly mammoth."

Ancient rats and cats just don't shake the money tree the way mammoths, the definitive charismatic megarelics, do. "So many have a fascination with the concept of the mammoth and the fact of its relationship with early humans," says Critser. "They feel it would be wonderful if man could bring back this species which man helped drive to extinction. And in coffee-pot discussions here at the university, we say, 'Wouldn't it be great if we could undo that wrong?'"

After all the holocausts perpetrated by humans in the millennia since the mammoths vanished, against everything from dodos and sea cows to Bosnians and Tutsis, the faint prospect of undoing this one extermination still beckons powerfully. "Maybe there's a guilt complex involved," says Ross MacPhee. "We dream of saving not just the mammoth but ourselves," wrote the journalist Adam Goodheart, pondering "the strange potency of the story from Siberia."

Indeed, the dream extends to resurrecting the entire ecosystem that once centered on the mammoth. As a first step toward restoring the mammoth steppes, Sergei Zimov has proposed a demonstration "Pleistocene Park" stocked with wysent and wild horses and ready for the mammoths to come — tourist-economy counterparts to "Dr. Yasmilov's" heavy-hauling mammontelephases.

Soon enough, however, these dreams crashed against cold scientific reality. As the skeptics had predicted, the Jarkov block did not yield good DNA, or even intact organs or tissues, just the bones and scraps commonly found in the Siberian sod. And that was where the real science came in. As even Greenwood conceded from the start, "there's a lot you can learn" about mammoths past and elephants present from such relics. With the cloning hype dashed,

Buigues and the Discovery Channel turned to more grounded matters: the mammoths' ecology, lifestyle, and habitat, and, especially, the mystery of their extinction. "We're interested in many things other than DNA," says the paleontologist Larry Agenbroad, who joined the Jarkov team. "This is the first time anyone's had this chance to study a mammoth's chemistry, parasites, hematology, organs, to conduct hair analysis and tusk analysis, to analyze whatever is in its stomach and intestines, what it tells us about its environment." Agenbroad concedes that "the Russians have done some of that. . . . But most of their material is only accessible to Russian aficionados, in small publications that are hard to find even in Russia."

By raising an unheard-of budget, removing the block whole, and thawing it slowly (with hair dryers, a millimeter at a time), Buigues opened new doors for research. Scientists in a wide range of disciplines lined up to get aboard, and about thirty joined the project. After the first Discovery installment aired, Ross MacPhee dismissed it for what it was: entertainment that "promises everything and delivers nothing," with "almost no real science." Worse yet, he feared that the cloning hype would hinder serious research: "It's made it harder to get cooperation in Russia. The hunters and so on now want exorbitant prices for any samples. They think any mammoth is a potential gold mine."

A year later, in mid-2001, MacPhee's views had changed considerably, and not just because the second Discovery show afforded a pulpit for his hyperdisease hypothesis. Yes, he conceded, the "gold rush mentality" was disruptive in cash-starved outer Siberia: "It was not a great move on anybody's part to show that we had a great deal of money to burn, in effect, just for bones. It's always a hard thing, in field circumstances." But once the project's "adventure value was depleted after the first documentary," it became "much more like a regular scientific enterprise, and we're getting some very interesting results."

Svertbighooze Yasmilov might be disappointed, but the quest to clone a mammoth has undergone its own evolution, from hoax to hype to the hard scientific work of understanding the mammoth.

4

Elephants in America

He entered the room, wherein was working a taxidermist from Poplova who'd arrived that afternoon. The massive head rested on a table, tusks curling in the lamplight, and the old man was painting the skin of its head with translucent fluid. He saluted Bulnovka, and lifting the lip of the mastodon, pointed inside.

"Buttercups," he said, and extracted a small yellow flower from the great row of teeth.

— William Kotzwinkle, "A Most Incredible Meal"

Though we may as philosophers regret it, as men we cannot but thank heaven that its whole generation is probably extinct.

— William Hunter

THE RECENT SCHEMES to restore mammoths to the steppes are just the latest and most ambitious expressions of a recurrent and enduring impulse reaching far beyond Siberia, to the jungles of Central America and the drawing rooms of patrician Virginia. For more than two centuries, ever since the realization dawned that elephants might once have walked the hills and dales of the New World, otherwise sober people have craved to see elephants here again — or believed they had discovered them, or dreamed of restoring them.

America's first great mammophile was that powder keg of scientific curiosity, Thomas Jefferson. In the early 1780s, when word trickled in from the frontier of giant bones found along the Ohio River, Jefferson was avid both to possess and to explain them. He asked General George Rogers Clark, who led the conquest of what was then called "the Northwest," to buy him all the giant bones he could find. "You are also so kind as to keep alive the hope of getting for me as many of the different species of bones, teeth and tusks of the *Mammoth* as can now be found," Jefferson wrote in 1783. And he asked whether Clark would lead an expedition he hoped to help sponsor "exploring the country from the Mississippi to California."

America's premier statesman-naturalist had already written extensively on the mammoth discoveries in his *Notes on the State of Virginia.* He vehemently rebutted the renowned naturalist Georges-Louis Buffon's contention that these were the same elephants that inhabited Asia and Africa. Those elephants, Jefferson contended, could never withstand the northern climate: "Nature seems to have drawn a zone of separation between these tremendous animals."

Jefferson likewise rejected Ezra Stiles's "Doctrine of Monsters," which ascribed the bones "*not to Quadrupeds, not to Sea-Animals, but to Bipeds* of huge and immense Stature." He noted that the tusks found with the bones instead suggested a creature "of the same kind" as the mammoths lately uncovered in Siberia, only larger. This was a point of national, or hemispheric, pride. Determined to rebut Buffon's "very degrading" contention that "nature was less active" in the New World and its "degenerate" creatures smaller and weaker than their Old World counterparts, Jefferson declared it "certain" that the American mammoth was "the largest of all terrestrial beings." Just a few years later, dinosaur bone discoveries would prove otherwise.

Jefferson even suggested (and evidently hoped) that these "largest beings" still dwelt in the deep woods. Like many of his pre-Darwinian compatriots, he believed that "such is the economy of nature, that no instance can be produced of her having permitted any one race of her animals to become extinct; of her having formed any link in her great work so weak as to be broken." After also citing weasels, badgers, lynx, foxes, and moose as creatures that grew at least as large in the New World as in the Old, he conceded, "It may be asked, why I insert the Mammoth, as if it still existed? I ask in return, why I should omit it, as if it did not?"

In his *Notes,* he wrote that the Indians believed the mammoth was carnivorous and still lived "in the northern and western parts of America." He speculated that it might have vanished from familiar territory because fur-trading Indians had killed all the animals on which it preyed. And he recounted a Delaware chief's explanation of the giant bones found at the Ohio River "Saltlicks": "That in ancient times a herd of these tremendous animals came to the big-bone licks, and began an universal destruction of the bear, deer, elks, buffaloes, and other animals which had been created for the use of the Indians." Enraged, the "Great Man" (that is, the Great Spirit) blasted all the giants with lightning bolts, save the big bull, who deflected them with his forehead and, leaping over the Great Lakes, fled north, "where he is living to this day." He also described "a Mr. Stanley" who was captured by Indians in Tennessee, shown giant bones, and told that "the animal to which they belonged [lived] in the northern parts of their country; from which description he judged it to be an elephant."

Jefferson was not the only founding father with a special interest in mammoths. Robert Annan, a bone collector in upstate New York, recorded that "his Excellency, General Washington, came to my house to see these relics," and said that he had a similar "grinder" at his own house. But Jefferson's passion was in a class by itself. It endured as he rose to the presidency, becoming a distinguishing idiosyncrasy and a fat target for his Federalist critics. They parodied it so relentlessly that his defenders gave him a 1,235-pound "mammoth cheese" as consolation. Hearing of a new discovery of mammoth bones in the Hudson Valley in 1800, Jefferson implored New York's Robert Livingston to purchase them, especially "the head & feet. . . . I will gladly pay for them whatever you shall agree to as reasonable." Only after making that plea did Jefferson proceed to other business — the pending vote count in his election as president.

Eighty years before P. T. Barnum discovered the elephant superstar Jumbo, President Jefferson envisioned the money to be made amazing the public with elephantine marvels. In 1802 he wrote the painter and naturalist Charles Wilson Peale, who was about to send his son to Europe with a mastodon skeleton he had exhumed: "I hope and believe you will make a fortune by the exhibit of that one, and that when tired of showing it you may sell it there for another fortune."

The next year Jefferson fulfilled the dream he'd cherished for twenty years: he sent forth an expedition to explore "the country from the Mississippi to California," commanded by Meriwether Lewis and George Rogers Clark's brother William. Doubtless he wondered whether such an expedition might, among other things, find any mammoths still lurking in the western wilderness.

Lewis and Clark did not find any mammoths, but they may have heard stories about them. Tales of giant creatures endowed with extraordinary fangs and appendages were rife among the northern tribes of America and Asia. In 1744 the French Jesuit missionary Pierre F. X. de Charlevoix wrote that some Algonkians in the Northeast spoke of *"un grand Orignal,"* a moose so big that "others were like ants beside it" and "eight feet of snow bothered it not a bit." Weapons could not break this beast's skin, and it ruled over the other moose. Most tellingly, this über-moose had *"une manière de bras, qui lui sort de l'épaule,"* "a sort of arm growing out of its shoulder," which "it used as we use our arms."

Charlevoix's tantalizing account echoed in the tales recorded by a long list of travelers and researchers over the next two centuries. The anthropologist W. D. Strong collected many, including another Algonkian account of a giant moose with a fifth leg between its shoulders, which it used to prepare its bed. The Iroquois described a buffalo so big it trampled the forest. Maine's Penobscots told how their hero Snowy Owl came upon "great animals with long teeth," which could not rise if they lay down, and so were obliged to lean against trees to sleep. Snowy Owl killed these giants by cutting nearly through their trees; they toppled over, helpless. The Puritan preacher and Salem witch-hunter Cotton Mather — also an aspiring science buff and the first native-born American elected to the Royal Society — reported hearing a similar account from the Ohio Indians. These tales eerily parallel a European misconception that lasted two thousand years after Aristotle propounded it: that elephants have no leg joints and so must sleep standing up. They parallel even more closely Caesar's account of how the Germans would trap certain stiff-legged "elk" by sawing partly through the trees they leaned against.

Elephantine legends were not confined to the chilly North. The Chitimacha near Charenton, Louisiana, recounted that "a being with a long nose" once rose out of the sea and commenced killing people, rooting up trees with its nose to find those who tried to hide. When the people got guns, they hunted the monster but could not find it. Louisiana's Atakapa believed an enormous beast had perished in a local water body; an elephant skeleton was subsequently found in Carancro Bayou.

In 1934, Strong himself reported hearing from the Naskapi, isolated caribou hunters in northern Labrador, about a huge, murderous monster with "a big head, large ears and teeth, and a long nose with which he hit people." The hero Djákabish slew the monster and, in accordance with its dying wish, made blankets of its ears and had his sister cook its head. But the head jumped out of the pot and pursued Djákabish, evidently walking on its "long nose."

Native Americans were not alone in surmising that the giant bones and tusks they uncovered were left by bloodthirsty monsters. Even after the French naturalist Louis Jean Marie Daubenton identified them as ancient elephants, the English naturalist William Hunter maintained in 1767 that "this animal was indeed carnivorous." Luckily for Hunter's successors, no living mammoth appeared to contradict the lurid fantasies of their "natural histories." In 1797, George Turner inferred that this bygone giant clearly preyed upon "the largest and swiftest" quadrupeds. Since its "immense volume" prevented it from chasing through thickets and woods, it doubtless possessed the "power of springing to a great distance," taking its prey "by a mighty leap." In fact, elephants cannot jump at all.

"With the agility and ferocity of the tiger, with a body of un-equalled magnitude and strength, this monster must have been the terror of the forest and of man," Thomas Ashe wrote in 1801. He noted "that the creature to whom [some newly discovered remains] belonged was nearly sixty feet long and twenty-five feet high."

Naive as such views seem today, they persisted well into the nineteenth century, as did the tales of ancient humanoid giants. The self-titled "Dr." Albert Koch, a flamboyant paleontological showman, misassembled a mastodon skeleton — with extra ribs and vertebrae and tusks arcing out to the side, supposedly for anchoring to trees — dubbed it "the Missourium," proclaimed it the lost Leviathan of Job, and sold it to the British Museum. In 1846 another mismounted mastodon skeleton was exhibited in New Orleans as a human giant, complete with certificates of authenticity from many learned professors.

When all the hype faded, one tantalizing question remained: whether the many vivid, far-flung tales of elephant-like creatures meant that Native Americans had passed down actual recollections of living mammoths and mastodons. Not likely, the anthropologist Loren Eiseley contended in several influential 1940s articles: the whole inquiry had been tainted by the preceding two centuries' overpowering interest in fossils and zoology and belief in the indestructibility of species. As for the Indians who told of long-nosed monsters off to the north, "it is quite likely that they responded to these myriads of questions with elaboration and desire to please."

Some informants at the least did respond that way, as when the naturalist Charles H. Townsend sketched a mammoth for Alaskan Eskimos and, lo and behold, the Eskimos told other visitors about creatures that looked like mammoths. But as Ludwell H. Johnson noted in 1952, it is presumptuous to dismiss the myriad tales of elephant-like monsters, reported everywhere from the Arctic to the Gulf of Mexico, as concocted to please. Charlevoix recorded such tales before Europe discovered buried mammoths, and Mather, who credited the bones to biblical giants, wrote just as Europe was starting to learn about mammoths.

But might the natives' tales be especially acute "myths of observation" contrived to explain the cryptic bones uncovered at places like Saltlick? It is doubtful that they would construe "fifth legs" and swinging noses unlike anything they'd seen; trunks leave no fossil traces. The mystery, or delusion, still lurks somewhere between paleontology and anthropology, tweaking the assumptions of both.

If Native American elephant myths weren't all planted or induced by Europeans, they present three nettlesome alternatives. One is that American proboscideans survived far longer than believed — as on Siberia's Wrangell Island, where mammoths perished less than four thousand years ago. But no paleontological evidence of such survival has surfaced. Or we might reconsider the persistence of oral traditions. If Native Americans passed down accounts of elephants for eleven thousand years, they must have been very impressed with them, perhaps even harbored remorse at exterminating them. Or the third alternative: forgotten Asian immigrants brought the idea of elephants across the sea.

That last notion has made elephants touchstones for the oft-ridiculed, sometimes cultlike, but resilient historical heretics called *diffusionists*. These passionate scholars and amateurs argue that sometime between the flooding of the Bering land bridge and Leif Ericson's Vinland visit, other voyagers or migrants passed between the Old and New Worlds. One diffusionist school rests not on northern legends but on images carved in Mesoamerican stone that strangely resemble elephants.

A few decades after Lewis and Clark crossed the continent, another generation of explorers hacked their way into the jungles of Yucatán and Central America — and marveled at apparent signs that elephants, or people who knew them, had already been there. The first to record his surprise was John Lloyd Stephens, who in 1843 described what would become one of the most celebrated and controversial of ancient American monuments, Stele B at the Mayan temple at Copán: "The two ornaments at the top appear like the trunk of an elephant, an animal unknown in that country." Later scholars ran with the point, citing Stele B and elephantine details in other Mayan works as principal evidence that "native" American cultures did not evolve in isolation but were contacted and influenced by overseas peoples — in this case, Indian and/or Southeast Asian emissaries — centuries before Columbus.

And so the long, drooping nose of the rain god Chac was taken for a short, drooping trunk. The resemblance may be slight, but Chac rules the rains, and various Asian traditions associate elephants with rain and water — enough for some diffusionists. Another, Hyde Clark, claimed that resemblances between some Asian and African languages' words for "elephant" and Central American names for "tapir" proved crossover between the continents.

But Copán's Stele B remained the centerpiece of diffusionist claims and of ingenious zoological interpretation. Some observers saw elephants in the stele's top corners, others macaws or tapirs, or tortoises. Then, in 1916, as war raged in Europe, Grafton Elliot Smith of the University of Manchester opened a new battleground with a letter to *Nature* declaring that the best-preserved side of Stele B showed an Asian elephant *and* a rider wearing an Indian-style turban. Smith explained various shortcomings in elephant depiction — such as a bubbly geometric pattern that resembles a macaw's bare cheek — as evidence that the Mayan artist hadn't actually seen an elephant but worked secondhand from depictions shared by Asian visitors.

Smith cited other American elephantiana — Chac figures at Uxmal and Palenque, the Wisconsin "Elephant Mound" and Iowa "Elephant Pipes" — as further evidence of transoceanic diffusion. But the leading experts leaped to the letters-page ramparts to rebut him and debunk what one called "the hydra-headed fallacy of Old World origins for New World civilizations." Smith fought back with a vertiginous polemic, *Elephants and Ethnologists*, comparing various pre-Columbian figures with stylized elephant depictions from India, Cambodia, medieval Scotland, even an English bestiary.

Smith's multicultural symbol crunching is excruciatingly ingenious. Much of it turns on the *makara*, a composite sea dragon with a long snout (or short trunk) that guards portals across South India. Smith claims that the makara derives from a Babylonian sea-goat figure, that it was adopted and given a trunk in India, and traveled to Cambodia and thence to Central America, where it became the sacred rain serpent accompanying the Mayan Chac and Aztec Tlaloc. The visual parallels are striking; spend enough time with makaras and you start seeing elephants everywhere in Meso-american art.

But coincidences do not a crossover prove. In academic circles, Smith's argument for the transoceanic diffusion of elephant worship sank like a stone idol. Recent textbooks on Mayan art describe the Copán figures as merely the most stylized of various Mayan depictions of the familiar macaws; one even calls Stele B "Macaw Mountain." This makes more sense than a trickle-down theory of images of Asian elephants.

But that "macaw" with a turbaned man riding its giant head still *looks* more like an elephant than a bird. And the phantom elephants refuse to go peaceably from the diffusionist debate. In 1940 one W. Balfour Gourlay wrote to England's Royal Anthropological Institute about "a very primitive and almost life-sized representation of a strange animal" he'd seen outside a museum in San Salvador, "carved from a block of black lava [with] a trunk too long for a tapir and too short for an elephant. If this was intended to represent an elephant, the artist plainly had never seen one and did not understand its anatomy; the eyes were placed in the middle of the earlobes" — as were the eyes of the Copán macaws/elephants. Unlike Smith, who used only woodcuts, Gourlay included a photograph; the San Salvador carving looks distinctly elephantine.

North American diffusionists have also tallied a number of old petroglyphs, earthworks, and ceramics that bear varying degrees of resemblance to elephants — and also, in some cases, to bulls and pigs. But the most striking North American elephant artifact is the "Georgia Elephant Disk" discovered by one Tom Hill "Bubba" Davis while dragging for crayfish near Ludowici, Georgia, in 1973. Pressed into this coin-size clay disk are eight tiny elephantine figures with a hexagram-like rectangular character repeated above and between them and a double zigzag — the "universal symbol for water" — in the disk's center. Like Smith, Davis and his co-author, Clyde Keeler, note the correspondences between elephants and rain in Hindu myth and Chac the "watergod."

Like the overkill hypothesis, this alleged pre-Columbian elephantiana comes freighted with ideological implications. For Vine Deloria, elephant images help disprove the loathsome overkill hypothesis by showing that Native Americans knew, and so coexisted with, mammoths and mastodons. But other stalwarts of Native American pride find diffusionist claims as offensive as Deloria does overkill because they seem to suggest that the American civilizations needed cultural leavening from the Old World to rise. "Why are we so reluctant to acknowledge the accomplishments of indigenous Americans as just that, unique and ingenious accomplishments?" one op-ed writer asked, after arguing that the Mayan "elephants" were really tapirs.

The impulse to locate elephants in America doesn't merely reflect patronizing Eurasia-centrism. It reveals a more innocent, even naive, longing to *see* elephants in America again. That longing underlies an audacious idea advanced by overkill-hypothesis author Paul Martin and Fordham University biologist David Burney in a 2000 article, "Bring Back the Elephants." They propose "the ultimate in rewilding": introducing free-ranging Asian and African elephants to the American West — say, the lower Colorado or Rio Grande Valley — and to South American savannas now consigned to grazing.

Wild as this rewilding sounds, it doesn't come quite out of the blue; "Pleistocene Park" booster Sergei Zimov likewise proposes restoring Siberia's "mammoth steppe." One American supporter of that idea suggests introducing Asian elephants and African rhinos (if they could adapt to Siberia!), on grounds that nothing else could trample down the tundra and taiga so well. Kansas seems more promising elephant country than northern Siberia. And Martin's and Burney's scheme is a logical successor to such restoration efforts as letting patches of the Great Plains return to prairie and re-introducing bison, wolves, and grizzly bears to slivers of their former ranges. Whereas bison came to America only a quarter-million years ago, proboscideans dominated this landscape for some 15 million. If we want to understand what that landscape was like before humans intervened, Martin and Burney argue, we should start by restoring these "animals as potent as fire in their dynamic influence on ecosystems. . . . In the absence of elephants, inferences made on the dynamics of American vegetation types could be as one-sided as those made in the absence of fire."

Above and beyond the obvious response ("You've got to be kidding!"), the proposal draws serious objections. Today's elephants would be jumbo-sized exotic imports in America, whose plant communities have had ten thousand years to evolve away from what they were under elephant "management." Reuniting them might be unfair to elephants and ecosystem alike. Better, argues the environmentalist John Davis, to bring back the species "we European Americans have extirpated during our misspent youth in North America."

Martin and Burney anticipate the first objection. Modern elephants, they insist, would be close surrogates for America's vanished gomphotheres, mastodons, and mammoths. Perhaps they would re-evolve toward some of those forms as they re-adapt to America. "We have the opportunity to restart the evolution of proboscideans," Martin and Burney declare, "along with horses, camels, and other extinct groups native in the Americas for millions or tens of millions of years." They concede that animal rightists might object to such introductions but don't doubt the idea's feasibility: "If we can put a man on the moon, we can put an elephant on the prairie."

But we can only guess how ranchers and other rural westerners, who despite compensation fume at losing the odd sheep to reintroduced wolves, would feel about having pachyderms ambling among their herds. Martin and Burney insist that elephants need not be walking disasters: electric fences could contain them; newly developed birth control darts could limit their numbers; and they breed slowly anyway. They could eat the alien *Tamarix* and Bermuda grass that are choking southwestern riverbanks and depleting scarce waters. And who knows where it might lead? "In the New World, we can substitute bison for cattle to see if bison, too, will dance the languid ecological minuet with African elephants, to the benefit of the American range!"

SEE THE KING: To be very experienced, knowing, wise . . . An English modification of the orig. U.S. *to have seen the elephant*.

— Eric Partridge, *A Dictionary of Slang*

II. Worship and Delight

5

Dances with Elephants

They say all other elephants do feare them, and none dare fight with them.

— Ralph Fitch, Elizabethan merchant in Ceylon, ca. 1590

"Or why not leave the elephant out?"
"Impossible. What's a procession worth without an elephant?"

— R. K. Narayan, *The Man-Eater of Malgudi*

MODERNITY and old ways butt up against each other everywhere, especially in South Asia, where they collide like speeding trains. I started the new millennium wandering what Douglas Chadwick calls "the elephant trail," from Sri Lanka through India, Thailand, Burma, and Malaysia. In one small town in the southwestern Indian state of Kerala, I ducked into one of the common (though coffeeless) "cyber-cafés" to check e-mail. A gnarled old man in a white loincloth and turban, with a wide, covered wicker basket in one hand and a squirming gunny sack in the other, followed me in, hoping to earn a few rupees. There he stood, oblivious to the humming machines around him, the snake charmer in the Internet café. The proprietor shooed him away.

Even that moment did not leave me feeling so unstuck in time as the *peraheras* and *poorams,* great ceremonial processions that sweep across South India and, to a lesser degree, Sri Lanka like a celebratory monsoon in late winter and early spring. This festival season is also the elephant season; with traditional logging work fast disappearing, along with the forests the elephants help log, festivals are a major source of employment for India's 3,000 or so captive elephants and Sri Lanka's 480.

When I arrived, a substantial share of the Lankan elephants were parked in Vihara Maha Devi Park, the lush greensward at the heart of the traffic-clogged, exhaust-clouded, war-worried capital, Colombo. They loomed like upright shadows under the canopy as thousands of fruit bats snoozed in the branches above. Mere humans were barred from the park that these grander guests might graze there. Fifty-one elephants had trudged or ridden, some for many days, to join in the Navam Maha Perahera, the February full moon festival. Full moons are Sri Lanka's prime occasions for celebration, and the Navam Perahera was the biggest, loudest, merriest such occasion in a city whose peace was too often broken by suicide bombs. As day's end neared, the mahouts, who'd camped in improvised lean-tos, shooed away the gawkers and draped gold-trimmed robes, as big as tents but finely fitted to cover even trunks and ears, over their charges. The robes were cut from a rainbow of colors, from regal reds and purples to nursery pastels that made their wearers look more like giant stuffed toys than regal bearers. When people dress up elephants, the line between the sublime and the ridiculous begins to blur.

Even Colombo's traffic parted when the giants marched off to the Gangarama Viharaya temple, the perahera's sponsor. There they joined eight thousand musicians, dancers, and other marchers assembled from around the nation. The tropic night fell fast and hard as the combined force turned to march back toward the park — and past my guesthouse. It sat strategically where the parade would pause, between a giant banyan supposedly planted by early Portuguese conquerors and an equally impressive bodhi tree credited to the monks who, nearly 2,300 years ago, first brought Buddhism to the island of Lanka, whence it spread throughout Southeast Asia.

Imagine circus, saint's day, Fourth of July, and Mardi Gras parades all in one — with elephants. Imagine this spectacle inching along a dark street lit by handheld braziers casting tentacled shadows and reeking fumes. Imagine thousands of dancers, acrobats, pantomimists, and musicians, hundreds of troupes clad in enough costumes to fill a museum. One platoon of turbaned dancers from the old royal capital, Kandy, pounded booming *geta bera* drums; another tooted tiny brass oboes. A golden Buddha and a rotating electric mandala passed on a rainbow-colored float. A pack of ghost tigers — dancers in fierce wooden masks, draped in billowing white fringe like Christmas tinsel — cavorted past; demon wolves in purple fringe, clattering immense wooden jaws at the shrinking onlookers, followed. Other dancers, dressed as elderly peasants in sweetly grotesque masks, hobbled on canes, merrily mocking time's ravages. Others caromed like giant monkeys and clanged swords in alarming mock combat. Fire dancers swung blazing hoops of the sort circus tigers once jumped through — and leaped through themselves, rolling and break dancing on the pavement while holding up the hoops. Stilt walkers hopped and pranced on impossibly long poles strapped to their feet; one kicked a seven-foot stilt up behind his head and hopped blithely on the other, as though gravity had just been repealed.

Before, between, nearly on top of the human paraders strode the elephants, lending grandeur to what would otherwise have been just a show. Three imposing tuskers led the march, and the grandest bore the bejewelled coffer containing the golden Buddha and relics that is the centerpiece of the perahera.

The stars must have tusks: only tuskers are deemed worthy of honored places in Lankan peraheras and Indian processions. Tuskless *makhnas* are viewed as freaks in South India — where most males have tusks — and are commonly called "not-male-not-female." But they are anything but gender benders. Freed of the metabolic burden of tusks, they tend to grow big and vigorous and often overcome their toothy counterparts; strength and agility compensate for goring ability. The Thai elephant-camp operator Phairat Chaiyakham speaks for many trainers when he calls them "more cranky and dangerous" than tuskers. Perhaps that's why Ceylon's bulls were long celebrated as the mightiest elephants and exported at considerable profit: more than 90 percent are tuskless. Some authorities believe that tusklessness is intrinsic in Lankan elephants and any tuskers there descend from elephants imported from India, probably for ceremonial uses like this perahera. Others think that selective hunting eliminated the island's tuskers. That process is now under way in parts of Africa and in tusk-fixated India, where a growing share of bulls — 40 percent in the north — are makhnas. As ivory poachers deplete the tuskers, tuskless males get more chance to pass on their genes.

In Sri Lanka it is getting hard to round up enough tuskers to put on a good perahera. In 1984, the Navam Perahera's peak year, three times as many elephants — 157 in all, 27 of them tuskers — marched as in 2000. War and rising costs have made it more difficult to truck them in from distant parts. And not only that, as the Venerable Galboda Gnanissara, the *thero* (chief monk) who heads Gangarama and founded this perahera, told me sadly: "We don't have more than twenty tuskers left in the whole country." To ensure suitable bearers of the Buddha's tooth in future Kandy Esala peraheras, Thailand's Queen Sirikit had recently given Sri Lanka two "perfect" young tuskers. It was big news and a diplomatic coup.

The thero wears a monk's orange robe but otherwise seems decidedly un-monklike. With his wry expression, almost-shaved head, and incipient goatee, he looks from the neck up like a hip urbanite at the local Starbucks. Pacing, gesticulating, slapping shoulders, declaiming in a gruff but genial growl, he sounds like an old-time politician or football coach. I dropped in on him at day's end, thinking he might be done with his duties. Wrong; he was going at full tilt. He heard a tearful recitation from a middle-aged woman, who prostrated herself on the floor in thanks when he dispensed a few words, and gently waved her off. He read mail and signed papers even as we talked, hardly pausing when aides glided in and whispered in his ear, multitasking like the busy executive he is.

The Venerable Galboda is a stellar example of a new breed of worldly, politically engaged or enmeshed Buddhist clergy and the center of a web of religious, social service, and entrepreneurial enterprises that often shade one into another. In the tradition of Billy Graham, Pat Robertson, and Jerry Falwell, he attached himself to the Sri Lankan equivalent of the Republican Party — the pro-business, Sinhalese-nationalist-tinged United Nationalist Party, whose symbol is an elephant. In a nation as riven as Sri Lanka, even good works and sacred elephant processions occur in a tangled political and ethnic context. Prominent Buddhist clergy have whipped up nationalist sentiment in its Sinhalese Buddhist majority, and attendant resentment in its Hindu Tamil minority. Pogrom-like anti-Tamil riots erupted in the 1950s and 1970s, and in 1983 some Tamil factions took up arms for an independent homeland and the grinding civil war began.

Galboda's influence declined after his hard-liner patron, President Ranasinghe Premadasa, was assassinated and the UNP lost office. But Colombo residents still whisper of his power, and Gangarama remains the establishment's temple. Even skeptics dismayed at its wealth and political entanglements salute the schools and charities the thero funds, often with donations from Japanese and Taiwanese patrons. His last visitor of the day was an industrial executive who told me his firm supported Gangarama because of all its good works.

While waiting to see the worldly-wise monk, I perused his treasures — gifts from followers, he says. Three classic cars, one a gleaming '30s-vintage Mercedes, sat in the courtyard. Glass cases filled a large anteroom, crammed with a museum's worth of knickknacks: exotic shells and rocks, scores of statues of Buddha and the elephant-headed Hindu god Ganesha (whom Buddhists also esteem), and nine pairs of elephant tusks, some lavishly mounted. These offer a clue to the thero's dual spiritual and worldly status. Like the kings of old, he is a "lord of elephants," displaying his stature in his custody and mastery of the mighty animals.

Three live on the temple's grounds, including one who is its de facto mascot, Ruan Rajah (the biggest Lankan elephants are named Raja or Rajah), a giant with enormous, mammoth-like crossing tusks. Rajah was sent from Kandy after he became unmanageable and, by various accounts, killed anywhere from two to seven people. In 1998, one week before Colombo was to host a South Asian summit, he broke loose from Gangarama and rampaged through downtown, chasing office workers and paralyzing rush-hour traffic. While SWAT forces stood by, Galboda calmed him with sweets and mild words. "Now he's in musth all the time," says the thero. So Rajah stays tightly chained — the traditional fate of bulls seized with the raging hormonal condition called musth — in the front courtyard, just off the street, balefully eyeing the nervous passersby. The brick pavement has collapsed into muddy rubble beneath him.

Rajah will not abide anyone save one young attendant and the Venerable Galboda himself. Love — laced with firmness — makes the difference, the thero growls in choppy but expressive English. "Elephants have a transmission system. They can *understand*. They can recall evil." Hurt them and they will remember and pay you back. Treat them well and they reciprocate. "They love me," he says with a that's-how-it-is shrug.

But, the thero continues indignantly, life's not so good for other Sri Lankan elephants: "They eat very nasty. Don't get good water, animal always upset with stomach. We give them medicine, but the mahouts don't use it. Before, they give elephants tropical herbals, but now no such system. They cannot find leaves — father not passing information on to son. Mahouts are nasty people in this world." That may not be fair to Asia's mahouts, elephant handlers who work cheap and often die suddenly serving owners who value their elephants far more than them. But it's a lament you hear often across South and Southeast Asia, even from some mahouts. One white-haired veteran I met in Sri Lanka seemed relieved that his children wouldn't follow in his and his elephant's footsteps: "The young people want to learn computers, not elephants," he said with a smile.

The decline in mahoutship also worries the self-described "elephantologist" Richard Lair, author of an encyclopedic United Nations study on "the Asian elephant in domesticity." Lair has set about trying to stem that decline by establishing the first formal school for mahouts, in Thailand. He has received backing from the Ringling Brothers and Barnum & Bailey Circus, an enterprise

American animal advocates scorn as part of the problem rather than the solution to the captive elephants' plight.

The Venerable Galboda told me he used the perahera itself to help elephants by depositing 5,000 rupees ($62 U.S.) for medical care for each elephant sent to participate. He extolled the procession and the elephants themselves as vehicles of cultural revival and morale boosters for a battered nation. In 1978, when Gangarama launched its perahera, he said, "country was going down very badly. Economy very bad. People never support temple. Everything going down. Then new government come with new economy [under President J. R. Jayewardene, Premadasa's successor, who undid Sri Lankan socialism and privatized many state operations]. People wake up, start to support country and temple." The new perahera was meant to bolster this new spirit, but "we couldn't find dancers — they all sell their dancing equipment to tourists. So we train dancers. We get more than five thousand." The temple gave dancers and elephants costumes and tried to get other, paying gigs for both.

It's a moving story, but it betrays a common presumption underlying Sri Lanka's civil strife: that this multiethnic, multifaith nation belongs to its majority group. The "national revival" signaled by the perahera is a Sinhalese Buddhist revival. No paraders wore Hindu costumes or bore Hindu, Christian, or Muslim symbols, save those Hindu emblems that Buddhism has absorbed in the long exchange between the two faiths.

The anthropologist Stanley Seneviratne suggests another motive for Colombo's perahera: to show up the Buddhist establishment at lofty old Kandy. He recounts how the dynamic young Galboda was pushed away by Kandy's "sedate hierarchy" and so "brought Kandy to Colombo" by launching a perahera to rival Kandy's own. It wouldn't be the first time elephants and folk dancers have been used to serve personal ambition and cultural hegemony. But hegemony ain't what it used to be: the 2000 perahera, which so impressed me, was only half the size of some in past years. For Galboda, the plight of old Rajah, chained in the courtyard, mirrored that of the nation. Once he was a national standard-bearer; now he's a pariah and a criminal. "A few years ago," he said, "this one ready to die. Big wounds. The owner gave up on it. With medicine and caring we save it. I take care of elephant. Don't let mahout do it. If driver wash your car, no good. If you wash your car, you do good job!"

A tropical downpour had begun, and the thero did not take me outside to meet Rajah. Instead, the mountain came to Muhammad. An attendant led another elephant — a one-ton, four-year-old male with dagger-like incipient tusks — into the thero's office. He stood calmly, dripping rainwater amidst the glass cases. "This one sick," Galboda explained. "Time for medicine." He lightly touched one tusk, signaling the patient to raise his trunk, and popped crackers into his mouth, occasionally sneaking in a sulfa pill the size of a filbert. The thero insisted I do the same. When all the crackers and pills were downed, the power-broker monk kept playing with the pachyderm child, hopping about and slapping his trunk — shadow-boxing with the elephant.

Kumudu Kumara, a sociologist at the University of Colombo, told me of a poem about a mother who, as a perahera passes, explains its meaning to her child, who in turn points out something she missed: the tear falling from a parading elephant's eye.

Experts insist that elephants' eyes tear for irrigation, not from sorrow, but I wonder . . . I saw tears falling from several of the costumed, trudging tuskers that are fixtures of the streetscape during the spring festival season in the Indian state of Kerala. Towns and temples vie to secure the best elephants and stage the most lavish poorams, just as American cities vie to build stadiums and lure star athletes. The five-ton entertainers trudge alongside the roads on their way to or from festivals, or lounge about, munching palm leaves, in temple yards and empty lots, awaiting the next parade muster. They're especially numerous around Thrissur (Trichur), Kerala's wary, conservative "cultural capital" — a city of lore and relics, temples and elephants. North of Thrissur, the famous Guru-wayar Temple keeps a herd of fifty on an old maharajah's estate, whose palace is now the mahouts' bunkhouse.

Each January, Thrissur's tourist board stages a "Great Elephant March" with one hundred–plus tuskers, boat races, martial arts performances, "cultural shows," "elephant feeding," and elephant rides for the kiddies. And in April or May, columns of elephants from temples around the region march to the imposing Vadakkumnathan Temple in the center of town for the likewise well-publicized Thrissur Pooram festival. But tourism hasn't yet touched the great pooram held in March at the Arattupuzha Temple ten miles south of Thrissur, the oldest and, locals say, grandest of Kerala's elephant festivals.

When I arrived with Joshe George, a local artist who played Virgil to my stumbling Dante, I was nearly the only foreigner among the tens of thousands of bodies milling around the temple grounds. Arattupuzha's vast grassy field recalls Washington, D.C.'s, National Mall, save that it's gridded by raised roadways, like a giant rice paddy. These paths were lined with huts and booths like those that clustered around Indian temples or European cathedrals a thousand years ago, where merchants sold tea and sweets, incense and jewelry, gaudy pinwheels and the same fluorescent plastic tubes hawked at American circuses.

Joshe and I wandered into a "toddy shop," a darkened, low-slung hut serving plastic pitchers and recycled beer bottles filled with fermented toddy-palm sap, a pleasantly tangy, viscous, moderately potent brew that looks like skim milk. The bar was filled with tough-looking but extremely gregarious drunks. A gaggle of them immediately descended on our table, shook hands till my arm felt like the crank on an old Model T, and insisted on buying us toddies. "Let's get out of here," Joshe murmured after eavesdropping on them. "They want to attack us. They were testing how strong we are." No wonder they'd nearly shaken my hand off. We dashed for the door and down the midway, and ducked into the next open tent.

Inside, a magic show was about to begin: no fakir or snake charmer, just a familiar sleight-of-hand routine. The young prestidigitator, in white gloves, top hat, and a shabby black cape, made ropes slither free, bound and unbound solid-looking rings, conjured doves and roses from a scarf, and plunged sabers through the cabinet in which his female assistant stood. The effect was disorienting: Was this a temple festival or a county fair?

I stepped outside, back into a world at once ancient and luridly new. Atop a long pavilion glittered a colored-light tableau to shame the gaudiest rooftop Santa. It showed the warrior Arjuna, the Hamlet-like protagonist of the Bhagavad-Gita, bow drawn for the final battle, riding a chariot done up like a steam calliope, while blue-skinned Krishna drove his team. The lights blinked, the horses galloped, Krishna's whip cracked, and an arrow leaped from Arjuna's bow.

Electric pinwheels glimmered along the pavilion. The roof of the temple itself was a fountain of red and yellow lights. In the darkness below, thousands of sarong-clad male worshippers milled and gyrated while the women, brilliant in their go-to-temple saris, watched from the sidelines. *Chenda melam,* Kerala's traditional festival music, wailed across the crowded courtyard, sinuous and insistent; imagine Eric Dolphy and Ornette Coleman jamming over tabla polyrhythms. A hundred-odd musicians, stripped to the waist and sweating like boxers, clanged cymbals, beat hard-skinned *chenda* drums, wailed on snake-charming-style oboes, and keened on oversized round posthorns. At first it sounded like a lunatic cacophony, or a hundred maddened elephants stamping and trumpeting. Then my ears adjusted, like eyes emerging from darkness to bright light. I heard the underlying order and was swept up in the music's hurtling momentum.

Inside the temple's open door, through the smoke and flicker of coconut-oil braziers, loomed the strangest sight of all: a ten-foot-tall pillar of embossed gold, studded with jewels and ringed with rainbow-colored fringe, swaying in the firelight. I wondered how much toddy I'd drunk. My eyes adjusted again and I saw that the tower was an elephant, a grand tusker with pink-flecked ears and trunk. Atop his head stood a door-sized, bejewelled shield with the gilded bas-relief figure of Sree Ayyappan, Arattupuzha's patron goddess; the pooram celebrates the annual visit of 101 neighboring temple and village gods to honor her.

A priest standing below gave a signal, the police pushed us rubberneckers back from the door, and the golden pillar strode slowly toward it, and us. The shield, which was too tall to clear the arch, folded up like a theater seat, and the tusker marched out of the temple and into the crowd, followed by three more that were similarly caparisoned, minus the gilt shield. Each bore three bare-chested Brahmin riders in white sarongs, bearing the traditional sacred emblems of royalty. The first, sitting on the elephant's shoulders, held a tall, gold-fringed red parasol. The next would periodically stand and wave two giant whisks of cream-colored yak hair. And the third brandished two large white fans painted with mandala-like patterns.

The elephants inched forward through the crowd, as poised as runway models, during the first and slowest of the four escalating tempos that characterize *chenda melam*. Four more tuskers joined them from the shadows, and they stood stoically as the music rose to a brain-burning fever and the riders flaunted their stuff. A line of attendants faced this wall of elephants, each holding a massive crosslike iron brazier capped with six brass oil lamps. Coconut oil dripped down their bodies and splattered the ground, perfuming the air. The crowd surged toward the elephants as though hypnotized, only to be pushed back by more attendants. The musicians followed behind, blaring full-blast; twenty-six horn blowers threw their heads back and their horns up, wailing to the heavens, then hunched down and arched back, again and again, as synchronized as a Temptations stage routine.

The men (only they entered the melee, while women watched from the sidelines) were by now dancing feverishly or, if they had no room to dance, jumping in place and waving, fingers pointed disco-style in the air. They seemed by turns to be supplicating and defying the looming elephants, like demonstrators taunting a police line. Through it all the elephants stood impassive. I was pushed forward by the reveling throng, almost into their tusks. What a way to go, I thought: crushed between a maddened crowd and a six-ton wild animal turned into a living temple statue.

My senses reeled, and I wondered why the elephants' did not.

Perhaps they too were dazed, suggested N. Balan, a celebrated Keralan filmmaker and radio host, whom I happened to meet when I retreated to the dais to catch my breath. Balan's latest film, *The Eighteenth Elephant*, depicted the plight of Kerala's vanishing wild elephants and suffering captive ones, and the subject clearly obsessed him. He recounted a famous poem by Kerala's Vailoppili Sreedhara Menon: A temple elephant hallucinates during a procession, believing he is back home, free, in his native land. He interprets every detail — crowds, lights, music — as sights and sounds of the forest and sets off walking, blazing a path as he would through the brush, oblivious to the people he tramples.

Before they march in the poorams, elephants are inoculated with loud noise. But they still occasionally run amok, and some authorities fear they will more often as their circumstances and their mahouts' skills decline — in India as in other countries. Mahouts have it best in Kerala, India's most unionized state. During the pooram I met two educated brothers — the only mahouts I've heard speak excellent English — who said they were fulfilling their life's calling as mahouts at Guruwayar Temple, where they had pensions and collective bargaining and earned a relatively generous hundred dollars a month. But private owners may pay much less and, worse, provide as little as a dollar a day to fill an elephant's enormous food needs. A hungry elephant and a bitter mahout are a dangerous combination.

Even Guruwayar mahouts would say, in the words of one, "I don't like my sons to be mahouts." And so, like elephant herds that lose their wise old matriarchs, the profession gradually loses its store of traditional knowledge; some mahouts even fail to learn essential commands. One at the renowned Thepakkadu camp was crushed to death when he mistakenly commanded the elephant he was bathing to lie down.

And corruption and favoritism, perennial curses, take their toll. "Trained people are not getting the [mahout] jobs," the longtime Trichur elephant veterinarian K. Radhakrishna Kaimal told me. "Untrained people get them because of political connections. The

government should stipulate a certificate for a trained mahɩ
like driving a car."

Beside each tusker at Arattupuzha stood a visibly nervous mahout,
watching his animal and the crowd for trouble. I recalled the nail-
biting culmination of *The Man-Eater of Malgudi,* by the great
South Indian novelist R. K. Narayan. A ravening poacher-taxidcr-
mist descends on an unsuspecting town, bullying, battering, and
corrupting everyone in sight, emptying the surrounding forests of
wildlife and turning the hapless narrator's attic into a reeking char-
nel house. To all this the cowed or tolerant townspeople submit.
Finally this demon incarnate goes too far: he plans to shoot the
temple elephant during a celebratory procession, after provoking it
to turn "mad." This final outrage finally stirs the most unlikely vigi-
lantes — the milquetoast narrator and a terrified temple dancer —
to act, even to attempt murder. Saving the elephant is an end that
justifies any means.

The pooram action seesawed back and forth across the temple
courtyard, the elephant lines advancing and retreating, the crowd
writhing and jumping, both seeming inexhaustible. Around 4 A.M.,
fireworks lit the sky, as though to ignite the dawn. The elephants
stood unfazed — they'd seen fireworks before — and then, suddenly, they were gone. More fireworks, and the crowds seemed to
drift away — but instead thronged to the middle of the field, a
quarter-mile off, where the grandest spectacle of all had material-
ized. More than seventy elephants, Brahmin cheerleaders on their
backs, had sneaked around and massed in a single vast line by the
ornately illuminated tall gate that marked the entry to the temple
precinct.

I imagined how Alexander's Macedonians felt facing India's war
elephants, imagined that this invasion would sweep away us puny
celebrants and the temple itself. The elephant phalanx advanced,
musicians following behind, and stopped gravely as the sun and the
music rose.

The sun warmed, and the elephants passed through the crowd

like the ghosts of a bygone mania and disappeared. But not without a trace; the celebrants stepped adroitly around the many large offerings the elephants had left on the temple grounds. They followed the lead elephant down to the nearby river for the festival's culmination: the ritual bathing of the goddess, a participatory rite. The celebrants joined in the purifying bath; adults stood praying in waist-high water, while young boys splashed and practiced their crawl strokes. Worship and play seemed inseparable in the pooram, at least for human participants. For the elephants, the ceremony's end just meant more trudging. Already they'd set out on the long walks back to their home temples.

> SEE THE ELEPHANT: To gain worldly experience or to learn a hard lesson from experience; to lose one's innocence; (hence) to see remarkable sights.
>
> — *Random House Historical Dictionary of American Slang*

6

The Elephant Treasure

Rarely is the elephant treasure revealed in the world.

> — the Buddha, in *Anguttara-Nikāya* (The Book of the
> Gradual Sayings)

The creation of elephants was holy, and for the profit of sacrifice
to the gods, and especially for the welfare of kings.

> — Nilakantha, *Matangalila*

Who dares say Mr. Elephant blows a fart?

> — Baule proverb, cited by Donald J. Cosentino

WHAT WE DO NOT destroy in nature, we come to worship —
though we may yet destroy it. And so, as human tribes conceived
their mythologies and religions, they elaborated them around the
greatest creatures they knew — elephants, in those lands where elephants still survived. Prehistoric painters invoked them on the
walls of their inner cave sanctums. The Hindu and Buddhist traditions exalted elephants as incarnations of nearly all virtues. Many
animals were credited with one or another good quality, but only
elephants were brave, gentle, compassionate, patient, temperate,
loyal, reverent, regal, immortal, unforgetting, clever, wise, and auspicious, though occasionally stupid and gullible, and, as in real life,
unpredictably violent.

Perhaps no other beast enjoyed as exalted a mythic origin as the Hindu elephant. Nilakantha, the shadowy author of the ancient Sanskrit elephant treatise the *Matangalila,* recounts it thus: Brahma, the supreme creator, split the cosmic egg in two, releasing the sun, then held the two shells and chanted. From the shell in his right hand emerged Airavata, the elephant of the East, followed by the "noble elephants" of the seven other "quarters," or directions. From the other shell eight elephant cows were born, the eight bulls' consorts.

The eight noble elephants then marched to the great battle between the gods and demons, bearing Indra, Agni, and the other "lords of the quarters" upon their backs. But, frightened by the din, they ran back to Brahma, who infused them with "the Spirit of Must" (or musth) — the state of surging testosterone and raging temper that periodically seizes healthy adult bulls, most often in spring. And they annihilated the demon host.

Around the world, musth is a time to be feared and deplored, when elephants are kept tightly chained and nearly starved until their testosterone production ebbs. To avoid dealing with it, most American circuses and zoos exclude male elephants; in the past they even put them to death. Only in southern Asia was musth celebrated as an "excellence," the apex of bravery and warrior spirit. An early Tamil poet lauds "the sweet-smelling rut and unapproachable valour" of an elephant in musth. Nilakantha writes that those born in spring are especially prone to musth. Their odor drives other elephants to musth as well, making them fearless. And so these "scent elephants" are "bringers of victory to kings."

Not until 2000 did the United States approve "testosterone therapy" to restore the vigor of middle-aged men. But the Indian writer Ramesh Bedi notes that testosterone-rich musth fluid was sold in ancient markets to stimulate hair growth (though elephants have little hair) and for "disorders of bile, phlegm and wind, and [as] an antidote to poison and an effective healing agent." It was lately used in the Andaman Islands "for massaging genitals." Bedi adds that the ancient sage Chakara prescribed a concoction of rendered butter, honey, sugar candy, and wheat flour, "placed on the back of an elephant first," to "make a man as virile as an elephant" — a scary notion.

Even without benefit of musth fluid or aphrodisiac pancakes, men who were healthy and long-lived were called *gajaprana* — "elephant-like." The might of mythical warriors was measured in elephants: Bhimasena in the epic *Mahabharata* had "the strength of ten thousand elephants."

To Westerners nursed on monotheism, Hindu theology can seem a head-spinning blur of comic book gods and monsters. To approach it, we must set aside our Judaeo-Christian-Muslim notions of a unitary, unchanging desert god and a stark, consistent account of creation. The forest and mountain gods of the Hindu canon appear in multiple, even manifold, guises and incarnations, constituting by various accounts 300,000, 3 million, or 300 million gods, demons, and godly personas. Perhaps this early indoctrination in intricacy is one reason why India produces so many mathematicians and computer scientists.

The stories about those gods, even the accounts of their origins, go now this way, now that. In one version, the world rests on the shoulders of the giant elephant Muhapudma, Asia's Atlas, who stands on the tortoise Chukwa. In another it rests on Nilakantha's eight noble elephants, who guard its cardinal directions. These accounts may reflect an ancient Sumerian belief that the elephant guards the celestial "tree of life," which fulfills all wishes.

Even the monotheistic Muslims who conquered most of India imbibed these notions. Abu L-Fazl, chronicler to the great Mughal emperor Akbar, declared that each of the eight noble elephants is in fact "a heavenly being in the shape of an elephant." (Evidently he could not imagine an actual beast in such an exalted role.) "When occasions arise, people read incantations in their names, and address them in worship. They also think that every elephant in the world is the offspring of one of them." White-skinned, white-haired elephants descend from the noble elephant of the East; fierce elephants with large heads, long hair, and "eyelids apart" belong to the Southeast; and so on.

In the old days, the descendants of the eight noble elephants lived a much grander life. They could "assume any shape," the *Matangalila* recounts, and could even fly like birds: "They roamed as they liked in the sky and on the earth." One day the winged elephants lit on the great banyan that grew above a famed hermit's retreat. The branch broke and fell on his disciples, and the furious sage hurled a curse: the elephants would lose their wings and be bound to the earth, bearing mortal men upon their backs.

Thus were the elephants cast down like Satan for their presumption and forced to labor like Adam. The noble "Elephants of the Quarters" begged Brahma's mercy for their poor kinsmen, who would now be prey to such ills as disease, bad food, and overeating. Brahma told them not to despair, for "there shall appear a certain sage fond of elephants, well versed in medicine, and he shall right skillfully cure their diseases" — an elephant messiah. Sure enough, such a sage was born, of a lovely nymph who was turned into an elephant cow by a hermit's curse. She conceived a son, then regained human form by "drinking the seed" of another hermit. That son, Palakapya, went on to spend "twice six thousand" years learning all there was to know about elephants (clearly a subject demanding patient study). He then bequeathed the science of elephant care that Nilakantha presents in the *Matangalila*.

Much of the advice Nilakantha offers is on elephant care as we understand it today. But he also explains at length how to classify elephants by type and (as for humans) caste. First comes the elephant "that is beautiful, has an odor like the white water lily, sandalwood, orange tree, lotus . . . whose face beams, who always retains the enthusiasm of a young elephant. . . . He is to be honored as having the character of a god." Next come the elephants with the character of a demon, "divine musician," sprite, ogre, goblin, serpent, Brahmin, and warrior — and finally the lowly "artisan" and "serf" elephants.

The Sri Lankan scholar Merlin Peris laments that this "charlatan science," raised to even "more fantastic" heights in ancient Sinhalese elephant lore, is "still held in dumb admiration by a credulous public." He presents the Sinhalese *Atunge Lakshana*'s horoscope-like scheme for predicting events, usually dire ones, from elephant traits:

> O King, the elephant that casts no shadow will cause trouble to your friends. . . .
> Any elephant with a rough scrotum will ruin its owner's tribe. . . .
> A deaf elephant will cause loss of wealth and induce fear through enemies.

Perhaps the Thais should worry more about the itinerant beggar elephants who are losing their hearing in Bangkok's roaring traffic.

The interchange between the divine and elephant realms does not end with pachyderms displaying divine or demonic attributes. The gods themselves take on the qualities of elephants and are distinguished, even defined, by their relationship to them. The supreme example is Ganesha, the elephant-headed god of obstacles and beginnings, the most popular and, in daily life, most ubiquitous of the Hindu divinities. But Ganesha is so singular he requires his own chapter.

The maternal Lakshmi, or Shri, is also extremely popular, no surprise when you consider the principles she embodies: fertility, abundance, prosperity, wealth. Her image hangs in many homes and, especially, businesses, always emerging like Venus on the half-shell from a giant floating lotus, holding smaller lotus blossoms. Sometimes she showers gold from one or more of her hands. On either side of her stands a white elephant, merrily showering her with water from a golden pitcher. And so she is called Gajalakshmi, "Lakshmi of the Elephants," and "Lotus-born" and "Lotus-bearer." The connection between the elephant and cosmic lotus, which contains the seeds of creation, runs deep and wide in Hindu myth.

There is something strangely but inescapably erotic in this tableau, as there is in the modern spectacle of an elephant swinging a prostrate, half-naked circus acrobat. Several authorities note that the river on which Lakshmi floats represents the female principle, and that rain, which the lustrating elephants mimic, represents the male. In a similar vein, Kama, the god of love (as in *Kama Sutra*) sometimes rides an elephant whose body is ingeniously formed of sensuous young women. Krishna, the playful avatar of Indra, sometimes rides an elephant composed of the milkmaids with whom he famously frolicked. A popular variation on this theme shows an elephant containing all the other beasts and flowers — a biosphere packed into a single four-legged frame.

The association of elephants with rain and clouds extends far beyond the Lakshmi tableau and may predate full-fledged Hindu worship itself. Years ago, watching the elephants at the Woodland Park Zoo lumber through the misty gray of a Seattle autumn, I imagined them as low clouds gathered around tree-trunk legs. I had stumbled on the hoariest of elephant similes: the image of elephants as clouds and bringers of rain runs through Asian religious lore and secular poetry, ancient and modern.

The rain connection is most potently expressed in the great elephant Airavata, the mount of Indra, king of the gods and god of rain and war. Airavata first emerges from the ocean when the gods and demons churn the waters to determine who will have mastery. He stretches his trunk back down to the watery underworld, sucks up its waters, and sprays them into the clouds so Indra can make them fall as rain. Thus the great sea elephant joins heaven and hell, or rather turns the latter into the former, and makes life possible on the earth that lies between them.

To associate elephants with rain shows deep reverence among the dwellers on the drought-plagued Indian subcontinent, who wait each spring for the summer monsoon to bring water and life. And it prompts another association — between elephants and good fortune. From India to Thailand, supplicants receive an elephant's "blessing" — a trunk-pat on the head — for good luck. The elephant giving the blessing is not always so fortunate; by the great Shiva temple at Nanjangud, south of Mysore, I saw a female elephant kept in a metal pen like a baseball batting cage, giving blessings to anyone with a few rupees to spare.

In Burma and especially Thailand, earnest Buddhists leave carved elephants at shrines and temples. Thousands of Bangkok urbanites seek good fortune by placing them at the famed Erawan shrine — Erawan being the Thai version of Indra's three-headed Airavata, his heads representing the Brahma-Vishnu-Shiva trinity. Pregnant Thai women duck under an elephant's belly three times to ensure an easy delivery. In Sri Lanka, mothers pass their infants under three times for strength and good fortune. In one old Indian tale, a king despairs when the royal elephant is too indisposed to lead his daughter's wedding procession and assure an auspicious union. "The prestige of the kingdom was at stake," writes the scholar V. S. Naravane. But the wise vizier waves a lotus blossom under the unhappy elephant's trunk, making him "cheerful and majestic as ever," and all's well in the land.

The link between elephant and lotus endures in another religion out of India, Buddhism. Buddhist teachers discarded much of Hinduism's imagery and idolatry but preserved two sacred figures: the lotus upon which the Buddha sits and meditates, and the elephant. These even figure in the Buddhist answer to the Virgin Birth: Before he was born in human form, the Buddha appeared as a splendid white elephant and approached his future mother, Queen Sirimahamaya, bearing a white lotus. After bowing (or tapping her) three times, he entered her womb, to emerge nine months later as the infant Siddhartha. His mother is shown delivering him in a lotus grove as she is showered, Lakshmi-style, by elephants. This incarnation comes full circle in the scriptural prediction of the Buddha's final coming, as a perfect white elephant "with a head the colour of cochineal, with tusks shining like silver sparkling with gems."

Elephants — and the Buddha as elephant — also figure prominently in the Jataka tales, popular stories of the Buddha's earlier incarnations. In one particularly Aesopian tale, he is reborn as a noble tusker leading a herd of eighty thousand elephants in the Himalayas. A quail whose nest sits in the herd's path begs him to protect her flightless chicks. This he gladly does, directing his followers to step around. When one rogue defiantly tramples the chicks, the quail gets her revenge: she induces a crow to peck out his eyes and a fly to lay eggs in the sockets. Gnawed by the maggots, the blind elephant seeks water for relief. A frog lures him to a precipice, and he falls to his death.

The tale handily summarizes the elephant's dual nature, by turns gentle and protective — the kindly Buddha-elephant — and rampaging and deadly. The theme recurs in another tale, in which the Buddha, born as a Brahmin seer, warns an anchorite to give up his beloved pet elephant because "when elephants grow up they kill even those who foster them." But the anchorite can't bear to lose his giant companion, who, sure enough, goes mad when the south wind rises (indicating spring, the musth season) and kills him. So work the snares of desire and attachment.

In another Jataka tale, the Buddha-elephant resolves to catch the giant crab that seizes elephants who drink at a Himalayan lake. But the crab grabs him and starts dragging him down. He trumpets to his elephant wife for help. She flatters and beseeches the crab, who, like Aesop's vain crow, forgets himself and releases his prey. The Buddha-elephant then stamps out the crab. Buddhist notions of mercy apparently do not extend to killer crabs any more than to killer elephants.

Other tales convey a more altruistic message. In one, the Buddha is a king whose sacred white elephant brings rain to the land. When a neighboring kingdom suffers grievous drought, the Buddha-king gives it his magic elephant. His people are aghast, and he goes into exile as a wandering hermit.

One especially cherished tale recounts a supreme self-sacrifice. Again, the Buddha is born as the six-tusked elephant king of the Himalayas. His second wife, obsessively jealous of his first, wastes away and dies, after persuading the gods to reincarnate her as a human queen so she can seek revenge. Thus reborn, she sends the greatest hunter in the land to kill the elephant king and retrieve his tusks. The hunter wounds the Buddha-elephant and begins sawing off his giant tusks but isn't strong enough to sever them. The dying elephant graciously takes the saw and finishes the job. When his ex-wife receives the tusks, she falls dead from remorse.

In other Jataka tales, Buddha's enemies try to harness the elephant's strength against him. The demon Mara rides the 150-

league-tall elephant Girimekhala in a futile attack on the meditating master. The envious Devadatta gets a great elephant drunk "on a thousand pots of toddy" and sends him to trample the Buddha, but the elephant instead bows down before him.

This last story has its Islamic counterpart in Book 105 of the Koran, al-Fil, "The Elephant," which reads in its entirety:

> In the Name of God, the Compassionate, the Merciful
> Have you not considered how God dealt with the Army of the Elephant?
>   Did He not confound their stratagem and send against them flocks of birds which pelted them with clay stones, so that they became like the withered stalks of plants which cattle have devoured?

A legend-limned incident underlies this invocation. Shortly before the birth of Muhammad, the Christian King Abraha of Abyssinia marched on Mecca to destroy the Kaaba, its holiest shrine. But Abraha's elephant stopped at the Meccan frontier, knelt down, and, like the drunken elephant dispatched against the Buddha, refused to advance farther. Abraha and his troops halted, and the birds pelted them to death. And so the elephant is honored in Islam as well. The year the Prophet was born is still known as "the Year of the Elephant."

The same reverence underlies another Jatakaesque tale recounted by the fourteenth-century Cairoan scholar ad-Damiri. A certain Abu-Abd-Allah, shipwrecked with his companions, refused to join in eating a baby elephant they had killed. That night the mother elephant trampled all save the good Abu, whom she bore on an eight-day trek back to civilization.

Ad-Damiri devotes more space to elephants than to any other entry in his treatise on all the animals mentioned in the Koran. He offers a pharmacopia of elephant-derived remedies, dream interpretations, and the odd spell or two. For example, you can ward off evil by silently reciting the Book of the Elephant, repeating aloud two key phrases, and folding and unfolding your fingers. But if you want to destroy someone, recite it one hundred times a day for ten days, then sit over flowing water and invoke God's wrath upon him.

On a kinder note, ad-Damiri recommends ivory shavings with water and honey to improve the memory and make sterile women conceive. But slipping a woman a mickey of elephant urine, or hanging elephant dung on her person, will prevent her conceiving. Burning elephant dung restores lost eyebrows. Elephant bile removes leprous sores. Wearing elephant skin cures ague; burning it cures piles. Elephant bone protects children from epilepsy and plants from pests, but ivory stops trees from bearing fruit.

Whoever drinks "the wax out of an elephant's ear, will sleep for seven days." Whoever dreams of riding or obtaining an elephant will live long and win a high position from the sultan. But a dream elephant can also represent "a covetous stout foreigner" — a crusader. Dream of riding the elephant and you'll overcome the foreigner. Milk an elephant in a dream and you'll "deceive a foreigner and gain wealth from him." But a king who dreams of riding a war elephant will die, just as King Abraha did.

Ad-Damiri reports that the Jews by contrast believe that "an elephant in a dream indicates a noble or generous, gentle, courteous, and patient king." And the Christians believe that anyone who "sees an elephant in a dream, but does not ride it," will lose health or wealth.

Although the Hebrew poet-kings celebrated ivory and the prophets decried it as the essence of sensuous luxury, the Bible is the rare scripture in which elephants themselves do not appear (the cryptic "behemoth" aside). The Hebrews surely knew the animals, which ran wild in Syria and were kept by the Egyptians and Persians, but evidently scorned them as mascots of foreign conquerors. Thirty-two war elephants do appear, "roused for battle with the juice of grapes and of mulberries," leading a Syrian invasion in the apocryphal 1 Maccabees. The hero Eleazar Awaran wins "everlasting renown" when he kills the mightiest elephant, which falls and crushes him — an apt image of the heroic but suicidal Jewish resistance.

The exaltation of the elephant rose to erotic rhapsody in the secular poetry of South Asia. The classic verse of India's Tamils, reviewed by E. S. Varadarajaiyer in *The Elephant in the Tamil Land,* suggests the range of imagery that can be conceived from the elephant's parts, and the central role the beast played in courtly custom.

The Tamil poets praised chieftains first for their wealth, depending on how many elephants they owned, and second for their generosity, according to how many they gave away. They must have especially appreciated one chief, Ay Eyinan, who "gave away as presents to the singing bards and minstrels high-class white-tusked elephants." Ay Eyinan followed in illustrious footsteps: giving elephants as gifts has long been a hallmark of greatness, celebrated even in the Vedas, India's oldest literature. The Vedas warn that it is less auspicious to receive than to give elephants, anticipating both the sardonic Thai curse "Give your enemy an elephant" (and saddle him with the upkeep) and the Western term "white elephant." In the *Mahabharata* (where all numbers run high), King Janmejaya regularly makes sacrificial offerings of ten thousand elephants. Krishna gives fourteen thousand to honor the hero Arjuna.

Elephants were poetic beasts in other ways. The elephant-headed Ganesha was credited with transcribing the *Mahabharata,* breaking off a tusk for a pen and never stopping until the bard Vyasa finished reciting. Later poets made elephants touchstones of human excellence. A king was lauded as striding with "the gait of the elephant" across a battlefield. "That splendor that resides in an elephant, in a king," one Aryan poet wrote, "with that same splendor make me splendid, O Lord."

The elephant's trunk and tusks afforded an especially rich field of similes, and not just of the obvious phallic sort. One Tamil poet celebrated a trunk hanging down "like the braided hair of a maiden." The Sanskrit poet Bhartrihari compared a woman's thighs to an elephant's undulating trunk and sighed that her breasts "swell like elephants' temples." To the Tamil poets, the trunk evoked both graceful female legs and fertility and abundance in general: "the long ear of the millet with the head bent down like the trunk of the mating elephant." The "ripe," white tusks of mature elephants were said to contain precious pearls, or resemble a bubbling mountain stream. Bloodshot eyes were a mark of beauty in southern India —

Kerala's Kathakali dancers still redden theirs by placing tiny seeds under their eyelids — and one poet rhapsodized that the "reddened eyes" of his beloved recalled "the budding tusk of an elephant." Imagine what a central role elephants played in daily life for that image to resonate. Where we say "fighting fire with fire," the Tamils said "using elephants to capture elephants."

As the religious scholar Paul B. Courtright notes, other animals — stallions, mares, bulls, cows — are one-dimensional sexual symbols, always clear in their gender and meaning. But the elephant is a protean and versatile figure, by turns male and female, wild and tame, "containing all dichotomies within his more than ample form." Nevertheless, the *Kama Sutra*'s erotic bestiary uses "elephant" only to designate a class of woman, one with an especially deep *yoni*. Such a woman can mate equally only with a man of the "stallion" class; with a "hare" or "bull" she will achieve but "low union."

Various African peoples have seen elephants as both quintessential male and female figures. The Samburu of northern Kenya call them "old women," supposedly because of the resemblance of their breasts and pudenda (not to mention their matriarchal society). The "old women" are masters of the natural (female) world, as opposed to the divine realm, which is male. For the Yoruba of Nigeria, the god of the bush, the realm outside human control, is Erinle, "Elephant of the Earth," a hunter who became an elephant.

The Mende of Sierra Leone believed that elephants could change into men, and that they bequeathed their territory to the Mende. But humans could also become elephants, a transformation that the folklorist Donald J. Cosentino explains "is also the move from life to death. Elephants are the physical form assumed by the spirits of the dead." The Bambuti pygmies Colin Turnbull studied believed that their larger, "trickier" Bantu neighbors would "frequently turn into elephants, and take advantage of their great size to make war on the pygmies, destroying the forest as they do so."

Many African tribes invoke elephants as ancestors or patrons in their creation myths, intuiting perhaps the animals' contribution to human evolution through their transformation of the landscape. In a Nganbi myth recounted by Jan Knappert, Elephant descends from heaven but dies in a noisemaking contest with Lightning. From his fermenting guts spill "the seeds of all the good plants that Elephant had been eating in Heaven. That is how vegetables came to the earth." A man emerges from one seed and collects others in a box. "When this was opened, innumerable children flew out in all directions, like young ants in the rainy season."

In this delightfully earthy creation myth, elephant is a Prometheus-*cum*-greengrocer, a Jesus-like sacrificial figure who gives himself, albeit unwittingly, so that humankind may live. The way he does so, by splitting a gut, uncannily matches the tale told of another elephant god on another continent — the beloved and equally down-to-earth Ganesha.

SEE THE ELEPHANT: To be seduced.

> — Cary, *Venery,* cited in *Random House Historical Dictionary of American Slang*

7

The Elephant-Headed God

Son of Parvati, re-created by
Shiva, blessed by Brahma,
cherished by Vishnu, your
elephant head a gift from Indra. . . .

Beloved of the gods, you are all
things to all men

— ancient Sanskrit prayer

IN THE DISTRICT of Edappalli, just outside the fabled South Indian port of Kochi (Cochin), at the end of an unmarked footpath
off the main thoroughfare, sits a curious temple with a very loyal
following. From the outside it is nondescript, a rundown wooden
veranda pocked with dark doorways. No writhing gods or demons
grace its facade; the only clues that this is a temple are the sandals
and shoes lined up like pilgrims on the veranda, and the scores of
barefoot worshippers filing in and out. Some smash coconuts as offerings; some prostrate themselves in prayer before entering the old
stone sanctum that lies behind the wooden facade; others step
briskly out, glancing at their watches. The time is 7 A.M., and the
temple is about to close. It opens to the public for just two hours,
before dawn each morning, courtesy of the maharaja of Cochin's
family, who own the temple and much of the rest of Edappalli.
They gave the land for the large Catholic church nearby, and live in
the mansion in back.

Why, out of all the local temples, is this unassuming one famous, and why do people flock to it at this ungodly hour? I put the questions to Padmanabha Menon, a gracious fellow who'd just finished his prayers. "Maybe because it's very ancient," he replied. "Maybe because it belongs to the maharaja's family. And because it is a temple to Ganesha. I come here every morning to pray, to make a good beginning, because Ganesha is lord of the world, very powerful. For things to start well, you need Ganesha."

You hear this refrain again and again from practicing Hindus. They may not stand in awe of Ganesha as they do of Brahma, the invisible creator and closest counterpart to the West's God the Father, or the dancing, world-destroying and renewing Shiva, or the fearsome Kali and Durga. Not so many or such grand temples are dedicated to him as to Shiva and Vishnu the Preserver. Ganesha is a latecomer to the Hindu pantheon, a humble village god elevated to the big time long after the Vedas were written and the other divine forms enshrined. Even amidst the rainbow of skin hues, the multiple heads and arms of the Hindu gods, Ganesha is the odd man, or elephant, out — comic and ungainly, a potbellied fellow with a broken-tusked elephant's head plopped on his pudgy shoulders, a tropical version of Shakespeare's Bottom.

And yet he is generally accounted the most popular and widely worshipped of the Hindu gods. His statues, shrines, and images are everywhere, in every home and business and at the entrances to the other gods' temples. Sometimes his is an elaborate, flower-laden altar with its own priest, or an immense statue like the one made "of 450 *saligramas* (sacred black stones) brought from 300 sacred *kshetras* (spots)" in the Atmavilas Ganesha shrine at the great Mysore Palace. Sometimes it is just a glazed tile set in a doorway, as at another of the palace's temples. In whatever form, Ganesha is the first god people pray to when they enter the temple and the last one they bow to as they leave. They make a shrine where they find him. Amidst the artworks displayed in the Mysore maharaja's residence are two blood-red Ganeshas from Maharashtra, the heartland of his worship; visitors, loath to pass without honoring Ganesha, pile forests of burning incense around the statues. Across town, in the "Temple of One Hundred Ganeshas," a mountain of black figurines — stacked like prizes in a carny ring toss — greets the worshipper. You can't have too many Lords of Auspicious Beginnings on your side.

In Tamil Nadu, students, correspondents, even publishers and official clerks inscribe the *pillayar soozhi* (Ganesha whorl), a cross between a numeral 2 and Greek capital omega, atop every book, letter, and document to invoke the god and ensure a good beginning; he is the special patron of writers and merchants. His worship has also been adopted by Buddhists and Jains, and spread to Afghanistan, Borneo, Japan, and all lands in between. With his elephant head and weirdly hybrid demeanor, Ganesha, rather than the legion of human-shaped deities, is the god people trust, the one who's there for them, whom they turn to in need and gratitude. "Oh, Elephant-faced One! You are so near," one Hindu prayer begins. The chubby guy with the elephant's head fills the same role as the Catholic saints.

On September 21, 1995, everyone else discovered just how vital a figure Ganesha is for Hindus when the sensational "milk miracle" erupted in temples and on front pages around the world. It supposedly started when a young woman or a wandering pilgrim dreamed that Ganesha wanted milk, went to the nearest temple, and gave him some — which he drank. The word spread like a monsoon flood, and millions of the faithful — not just in Delhi and Mumbai but in Kathmandu, Kuala Lumpur, London, Rome, Hamburg, Los Angeles, Toronto, and of course the international crossroads of Queens — rushed to ladle milk to Ganesha statues. And the idols sucked it up. The faithful were not discouraged at finding that, as Lavina Melwani reported in the Pennsylvania-based magazine *Lit-*

tle India, "Ganesha seemed to be in a whimsical mood; sometimes he spurned the offerings of devotees and slurped up that offered by non believers." Worshippers offered milk to other statues — Shiva, Nandi, Vishnu — and saw them drink, too. India's dairy board warned of looming milk shortages, and its welfare minister lamented the waste of milk that could feed thousands of poor children. Melwani suggested that America's dairy board hire Ganesha for "milk moostache" ads. A report spread of "a baby born with the head of a Ganesh . . . to help us, to make the world a better place," but this reincarnation was never located. Nevertheless, religious leaders and ordinary believers alike celebrated a return of miracles, betokening a new age of faith and harmony — "the Hindu millennium," as Melwani put it.

India's secular newspapers were more wary, even alarmed. One lamented the "mass upsurge, bordering on unhealthy hysteria, which virtually brought many parts of the country to a standstill." The "hysteria" soon petered out, as the idols grew sated and the offerings dribbled down their clay chins. Already, skeptics had begun chipping away at the miracle. Scientists and political mavens alike offered other explanations for Ganesha's thirst. Capillary action, said the scientists, demonstrating by dipping statues and flowerpots and showing how liquid spread through porous, unglazed clay. Even on glazed ceramics, small unglazed patches — say, in a mouth, or under a trunk — could still absorb liquid. One skeptic reenacted the miracle with a Mickey Mouse figurine. (I tried it at home and found that my flowerpots and knickknacks absorbed some milk, but not nearly the tablespoonfuls reported by the faithful.) What about the brass and other nonporous statues that also seemed to drink? "Surface tension," replied the scientists: many idols had been ritually washed and were still damp; the milk clung to the watery film and spread rather than running down, on the same principle that makes droplets cleave together.

As if all these processes weren't enough to whet an idol's thirst, skeptics claimed that some statues were hollow and packed with absorbent materials, making them even thirstier. The milk miracle became a focus for all the divisions of religion and secularism, tradition and modernity, wracking Indian society. The Indian Rationalists Society offered 100,000 rupees to anyone who could demonstrate the miracle under controlled circumstances; apparently no one collected.

Indian journalists began bruiting more conspiratorial explanations. The miracle came at a convenient time, they noted, just as the Hindu Nationalist Party was ascending to power and the investigation into former prime minister Rajiv Gandhi's 1991 assassination had turned to the well-connected "godman" Chandra Swami, sometimes called "India's Rasputin," reputed spiritual adviser to the prime minister, Elizabeth Taylor, and the sultan of Brunei. News surfaced that priests around India had received mysterious phone calls the night or morning before the miracle, telling them to go to their temples and "feed Ganesha"; word passed worldwide over the Internet. Chandra Swami admitted "dreaming" of the miracle the day before, but said that credit went to Ganesha, not him.

The miracle's defenders likewise charged the debunkers with underhandedness. "In India, which has taught mankind so much about religious tolerance, it is a surprise to see such an anti-Hindu bias," *Hinduism Today* declared. "Years of British 'divide and rule' policy, Christian missionary attacks and Marxist influence [have] created this atmosphere of bias. Lord Ganesha, Guardian of Dharma and Remover of Obstacles, has now revealed this anomalous situation to the entire world." And, as Melwani noted, "He is a savvy God who understands the power of the press." One would expect nothing less from the god of scribes.

Ganesha's story is not told in Hinduism's original scriptures, the Vedas. It unfolds in the Puranas, eighteen later epics written down in the first millennium of the current era, and in innumerable folktales and local legends. In the most familiar account of his origin, Parvati, also known as Uma and Devi, Shiva's consort, craves a child — as befits her role as mother goddess — and also a guard to block her husband from barging in on her. But Shiva, wild and ascetic at once, wants nothing to interfere with their nonprocreative couplings and his yogic retreats. So Parvati gathers the residue from her bathwater (or, in another version, smears herself with sandalwood paste and scrapes it off) and molds a beautiful boy — a son entirely her own. She sets this lad, Ganesha, to guard her bath.

Shiva returns from his austerities, eager as a sailor on shore leave, but Ganesha, wielding a spear invested with his mother's power, blocks the way. They fight, until Shiva goads Ganesha into throwing the spear, catches it, and chops off his new stepson's head. It's the mirror image of the Greek myth in which Oedipus kills the father he never met in an anonymous road-rage encounter.

Parvati emerges, her fury rising till it threatens to destroy the world. Shiva tries to undo the damage, but the boy's head is lost. So he sends the sacred bull Nandi (or "one thousand goblins," in one telling) to take the first head they see. In one version Nandi finds a baby elephant snuggling with its mother, waits till it turns its head, then lops it off. In another, he kills Airavata, the elephant steed of the rain god Indra. This gives the story a new historical dimension: Shiva and Ganesha supersede Indra, the original king of the gods, just as their worship has superseded his in daily life.

In a kinder, gentler version — recently concocted, I suspect, to placate modern sensibilities — Nandi meets an aged elephant who gladly offers up his head. One way or another, Ganesha gets an elephant's head.

Already the tale has enough psychosexual and gender-conflict implications to fuel a shelf full of dissertations. But the best is yet to come. After what would seem the ultimate dysfunctional family saga, Shiva, Parvati, and their sons Ganesha and Skanda (whose birth story is also bizarre) become the definitive icons of familial bliss, a favorite subject for popular paintings and prints, the equivalent of the Holy Family, or Ozzie and Harriet and their sons. The only odd note is little Ganesha's pink elephant's head, with adult tusks and a preternaturally wise expression. Popular art never seems to depict Ganesha's bloody origin, though it is hardly reticent about other gory images.

That's the common tale, but countless other versions are told. In one, Shiva withholds his seed from Parvati, but it mixes in the bathwater and generates their son. In another, Parvati prays for a son and a beautiful baby appears. She is so proud, she insists that even the planet Sani (Saturn), whose gaze is malevolent, look on him. Sani does, the babe's head falls off, and the god Vishnu finds an elephant's head to replace it.

In a South Indian myth recounted by Paul Courtright, Shiva and Parvati see a pair of wild elephants copulating and, aroused, become elephants and reenact the act (one position not found in the *Kama Sutra*). Or they are inspired by the sacred letters *a* and *u* painted in the audience hall of the gods, which together form the incantatory sound *aum (om)* and visually resemble "two elephants in embrace."

These examples, in which Ganesha is born of the actual union of Shiva and Parvati, are rare exceptions. And even then, as Courtright notes, the divine couple never conceive while in their human forms. They must first become elephants, entering into the prehuman natural sphere, where a wild redemption — Ganesha's role as intermediary and protector of humankind — can be found.

Another version evokes the same return to nature in ingeniously grotesque fashion: Parvati offers her bodily scrapings to the elephant-headed demoness Ganga (identified with the Ganges River), who swallows them and gives birth to a boy with five elephant heads. Shiva clarifies the situation by cutting off four of the heads and declaring the now single-elephant-headed child to be Parvati's. In another version recounted by Courtright, Parvati herself molds an elephant-headed lad and "playfully" throws him in the sacred Ganges, "where he became so large that he extended himself as big as the world." (Ganesha's rotund belly is often said to contain the entire world.) Or she runs out of paste before finishing the head and sends her other son, Skanda, to find more. Instead, he cuts off an elephant's head and plops it on the headless body. The result is something wiser than man and wiser than swaggering man-gods like Skanda: the god of prudence, the philosopher god.

Not that Ganesha is always kindly; the elephant is only the gentlest of creatures some of the time. He is a walking, talking duality: he is best known as the "Remover of Obstacles," who smoothes the path and lifts the burdens from suffering humankind's shoulders. But in his Vinayaka guise he is the "Lord of Obstacles," who blocks and frustrates every effort, sometimes to steer us from the wrong path. As Ganapati he leads the *ganas*—impish, bestial demigods who can be malevolent, mischievous, or benign.

As Courtright and A. K. Narain note, Ganesha's protean, unpredictable character is in keeping with his elephant aspect. It also reflects the obscure and varied roots of his worship, a source of wide-ranging interpretation and debate among Indian scholars. Ganesha came late to a Hindu pantheon that had already been evolving for two millennia. Indian mythology and art are not otherwise given to therianthropic (hybrid animal/human) figures. But these run rife through Greek mythology, which M. K. Dhavalikar credits with helping inspire the elephant-headed god. Ganesha worship first appeared in northwest India, in the Greek-influenced Kusana Empire, a legacy of Alexander's conquests. "Greek artists were adept at fashioning therianthropic representations such as centaurs," notes Dhavalikar, "and their experience must have come in handy for carving the first images of the elephant god." A first-century Indo-Greek coin appears to be the first representation of Ganesha, and Narain suggests that it may derive from the familiar coins showing Alexander and his heirs in elephant headgear. If so, Ganesha represents a tidy cross-cultural exchange: Alexander took elephants and elephant warfare back from India to the Mediterranean and gave India its elephant-headed god.

Other scholars trace Ganesha worship back further, to the Dravidian cultures that preceded the Aryan invaders and their Hindu pantheon. Still others suggest that the beloved remover of obstacles evolved out of an earlier malign figure who thwarted hopes — what Alfred Foucher calls the "Demon of the Jungle." The elephant's head caps this transformation; the new god removes obstacles just as the wild elephant smashes through thickets and the tame one moves boulders and logs. But Narain argues that Ganesha's roots go back further yet, to the worship of the sacred elephant in the Harappan culture that flourished more than four thousand years ago in the Indus Valley, the same northwest region where Ganesha later appeared. In the tales of Ganesha's creation, northwest is also the direction in which Shiva sends his attendants to find a new head.

Foucher notes that if Ganesha evolved in history as he develops in the tales — starting out human and adopting another animal's form — he would be unique. Hybrid gods worldwide start as animals and evolve toward humanness, shedding their animal heads last of all, just as indigenous peoples cling longest to their headgear when they adopt Western dress. If Narain is correct, Ganesha evolved along the usual lines: the sacred elephant came first, and then took on human form.

Certainly elephant attributes persist in the chubby god. Like an elephant, Ganesha is always eating; he craves a type of sweet called *modaka,* which according to one Puranic tale grants immortality, and is commonly shown holding a heaping plateful. (He often holds an ax, elephant hook, and rope in his other hands.) This craving leads to one of the most popular Ganesha tales. He is riding his steed — a rat — after stuffing himself on modaka. A snake frightens the rat, which throws Ganesha, whose bloated belly bursts. Unfazed, he gathers up the scattered modaka balls and uses the snake to tie up his belly. The moon laughs, annoying Ganesha. He breaks off his tusk and hurls it, puncturing the moon and turning the night black. Either he takes pity or the other gods persuade him to relent; in any event, he ordains that the moon may shine again but must henceforth wax and wane.

The Czech scholar Karel Werner sees nothing less than the creation of the universe in this tale: "The scattering of the sweetmeat balls from his burst belly represents obviously the emanation of the world systems from the divine source and the act of collecting the balls and stuffing them back into his belly stands for the reabsorption of the worlds into the divine." On a more mundane level, Ganesha's showdown with the moon points up his role as a god of the day, just as elephants are mainly diurnal. His making the rat, which sneaks about at night, his steed marks the triumph of day over night and light over darkness. The scholar Alice Getty, in a monograph on Ganesha, argues that this reflects the fact that Ganesha first appeared among the sun-worshipping Dravidians. And since he began as a harvest god and farmers still invoke him to protect their crops, it is apt that he should conquer the pest that spoils them.

In the *Garuda Purāna,* Ganesha faces the giant Gajamukha, whom neither god, demon, man, nor beast can best. Ganesha, who is none and all of these, throws his tusk, turns Gajamukha into a rat, and tames him. Ganesha and Gajamukha become even mightier together because they embody both ways of overcoming obstacles: the elephant crashes through and the rat sneaks around.

A two-way street runs between the worship of Ganesha and the adoration of elephants. Elephants inspired his worship, and their mystique continues to inform it. Ganesha enriches and perpetuates that mystique. In 1879, G. P. Sanderson noted that elephants that grow only one tusk "are known as Gunésh (the name of the Hindoo god of wisdom) by Hindoos, and are reverenced by them if the tusk be on the right side." Today the name is not reserved for single-tuskers. "At every elephant camp in the forest, we have a calf named Ganesha," says Dr. Vaidyanathan Krishnamurthy, India's most celebrated elephant veterinarian. "Ganesha is one of the reasons we have great respect for the elephant. Otherwise the elephant would have disappeared some time ago." Raman Sukumar, director of the Indian Institute of Science's Asian Elephant Conservation Centre, suggests that early kings promoted Ganesha worship to encourage people to spare and protect elephants.

The boundary between beast and god still gets blurred when elephants are draped in gilt finery and paraded before the temple throngs, or trained to perform prayer *pujas* before the candlelit shrines like oversized priests. In the graffiti argot of the sixties, Ganesha Lives! But it will be a lonely life if, despite all his good offices, Asia's shrunken elephant population is pushed to extinction. A billion people, whose favorite god is modeled on the animal they cherish above all others, will have only the god in his shrines to remind them of the giants who once walked the land.

8

The Land of
the White Elephant

> The reality is that while history still colors people's perceptions, traditional values no longer have much effect on people's motivations and actions. . . . Teenagers know all of the rock stars on MTV but none of the lovely elephant stories found in the Jataka tales. Thai teenagers are only slightly more familiar with elephants than Western teenagers, having seen a few more elephants on television.
>
> — Richard C. Lair, *Gone Astray*

> The SUV is to Dallas what the elephant is to Thailand: a sainted, mythical beast.
>
> — Rawlins Gilliland on *All Things Considered*, May 22, 2001

HOWEVER OTHER nations' priests and poets may celebrate elephants, nowhere else are they as central to a nation's myths and mystique as they are to Thailand's. The earliest known depiction of Thai people, a frieze at Cambodia's Angkor Wat, shows soldiers marching beside an enormous war elephant. The oldest known specimen of Thai writing extols King Ramkamhaeng "the Brave" for his battle exploits on elephant-back. The elephant was not just the bearer, defender, and servant of sacrosanct Thai values but their very embodiment — if it happened to possess the highly specific, carefully calibrated features summed up in the term commonly translated as "white elephant."

That misnomer has caused no end of mischief and confusion. The official title is *chang samkhan*, "illustrious" or "auspicious elephant," though ordinary Thais now say *chang pheuk* — "white elephant." Not all albino elephants are illustrious, but chang samkhan are strategically adorned with pink or cream eyes, palate, nails, hair, and tail tuft. They are not "smooth and spotless and white as the driven snow," as one imaginative nineteenth-century writer claimed. Indeed, one illustrious class, the "short-tusked," has black skin and nails and "tusks shaped like banana flowers." Another, the "strange-colored elephants," can have any of seven non-albino "illustrious features," including sweet-smelling feces.

Stranger lore than this is preserved in the Royal Elephant National Museum, tucked away in the former royal elephant stables of the Dusit Palace, across the street from Bangkok's zoo. Its centerpiece is the gold-tipped tusks of the chang samkhan of King Rama I, who, at the same time other founding fathers were uniting the American states, established the modern Thai monarchy and its capital, Bangkok. Behind these tusks stand those of other royal elephants, plus the instruments — drum, conch, horn, and a sort of trombone — played when they are invested, ivory-handled whips used to goad them, ivory-handled brushes made from their tail hairs, and the "magic knives" of the elephant-hunting Sui people, whose ivory handles are carved into images of Ganesha.

Intensely colored illuminations from the old elephant manual *Gaja-Laksana* illustrate the taxonomy of royal elephants, as elaborate as the genealogies of the old royal houses. The three classes each divide into four "families," which themselves divide into dizzyingly diverse groups. Each family is named after the god who created it. Elephants from Brahma "bring wealth and knowledge to the king." Shiva's bestow "royal properties and power." Vishnu's give rain, "fertility in nature," and victory over enemies. Those from Agni grant "fertility in animals" and prevent "war and inauspicious events." Peace and prosperity demanded that the king receive any such elephants discovered in Thailand; their presence legitimized his rule, and the Elizabethan traveler Ralph Fitch noted that envious potentates sometimes battled to possess them.

That belief proved a fatal lure for a regent who attempted to usurp the throne in 1548: conspirators spread a false report of an auspicious elephant sighted in the woods, then ambushed the usurper when he rushed out to catch it. The same belief dragged the nation into disastrous war on one of those occasions when events align into better fables than any fabulist could conceive. King Mahachakrapat, who ascended after the would-be usurper's murder, did not heed the example of the Jataka tale in which the reincarnated Buddha gives away his country's auspicious elephant to relieve a drought-plagued neighbor. When Mahachakrapat's reign was "blessed" with the discovery of a record seven such elephants, Thailand's rival Burma demanded two as peace tokens. He refused; the Burmese attacked, won, and took not two but four of the cherished beasts. The Burmese eventually conquered and razed the Thai capital, though Mahachakrapat's successor Naresuan managed to delay that fate by killing Burma's crown prince in an elephant-back duel after his tusker gored the prince's elephant. Thailand still celebrates that duel's anniversary.

The Royal Elephant National Museum is a small hall, but it packs a large load of incongruity. On one side, elephants are celebrated as divine proxies bearing the gods' gifts to humankind; in a glass case on the other lie the leather ropes, harnesses, and other tools that the Sui used to capture and break wild elephants, including royal elephants. One can't help thinking that heady and poetic as all this exaltation of the sacred elephant is, it has little to do with real elephants trying to live their elephant lives, who couldn't care less about royal iconography. It also seems to have less and less to do with life in the roaring streets and high-speed economy of the metropolis that lies outside the palace gates. Perhaps the ambivalence I felt there has also infected the museum's overseers; they seem at once to cherish this rare gallery and hide it from public view. Other Dusit Palace attractions — including the royal Decorative Arts and Old Clock museums and two museums displaying the photography of the reigning King Bhumibol Adulyadej — are blazoned in maps and guidebooks and on the signboard directory at the entrance to the grounds. The elephant museum, though arguably more interesting than any of these, is accessible only to the lucky and persistent. Tourist information clerks, guards at the current royal palace, and nearly everyone else I asked had never heard of it. No one else entered while I visited, save a watchful attendant. Exquisitely appointed and maintained, it seems almost a private shrine — or maybe a guilty secret.

Thailand is a nation ardently — desperately, it sometimes seems — dedicated to preserving its heritage in the forms of art, dance, monuments, and, above all, its constitutional monarchy. But it is weirdly ambivalent about the large share of that heritage that is tied up with elephants. In 1782, Rama I chose a suitable flag for the Land of the White Elephant: a white elephant against a red field. But by 1917 such a symbol seemed quaint for a nation rapidly modernizing under a British-educated monarch: "Rama VI was a brilliant king," Tuchpong Tulyayom, an aide in the Bureau of the Royal Household and an eager exponent of Thai traditional culture, explained to me as we chatted outside the Grand Palace while sunstruck tourists trooped past. "But he felt the image was too exotic. No other countries had animals on their flags." So he substituted streamlined red, white, and blue stripes.

Tuchpong shook his head sadly, lamenting both that change and the later changing of the country's name from Siam to the more generic and colonial-sounding "Thailand." "Really, it's so perfect for our country to have [the elephant flag]. Thailand *is* the land of elephants, but people forget that. What's going on now, elephants becoming beggars in the streets — if they still had the picture of the white elephant on the flag, no way would they do that. No way!"

This lament is shared by Dr. M. L. Phiphatanachatr ("Pony") Diskul, the royal veterinarian who watches over the health of the king's elephants and vouchsafed me a brief visit to their stables at the king's official residence. I asked whether the Thais still understood the traditions that royal elephants embody. "No, not many," he replied sadly. "The old ones do, but the young ones don't understand."

Even within the royal circle, preserving memory and upholding tradition are a struggle. Tuchpong introduced me to the man who, perhaps more than anyone else, embodied his nation's institutional memory: ninety-year-old Khun Sawet Thanapradit. Khun Sawet served four kings, caring for royal elephants and overseeing official ceremonies. When he retired, the king's staff realized how much lore would be lost with him. Who else could verify the authenticity of any newly discovered auspicious elephants or uphold forgotten palace protocol? So he remained a "Special Consultant to the Bureau of the Royal Household," which each morning sent a car for him. He looked frail, almost ethereal, but his mind was undimmed: like the fabled elephant, he never forgets. "He corrects every ceremony we do," said Tuchpong. "If we leave something out from an old ceremony, others won't notice, but he will." Such recall is especially useful at state funerals.

In a side building off the palace, amidst dark teakwood cases piled high with mysterious memorabilia and faded documents, Tuchpong interpreted while Khun Sawet regaled me with photos and tales. He explained how royal elephants become actual titled members of the royal household and showed photos of the last three being invested; they stood on a dais as the king fed them sticks of sugar cane incised with their new names. He explained that once they have received these titles, the royal elephants won't stand for anything less. If you say, "Hey, you!" they will "kick and swing their trunks." Even if they are young and untrained, the royal elephants turn placid and obedient before the king, as though they recognize him. Seeing the amazement on my face, Tuchpong and Sawet's assistant, Kamal Sangpreecha, swore they'd witnessed exactly the same phenomenon.

But times have changed. "In the old days," Khun Sawet recounted, "the king would have to be able to ride elephants really well." He would ride into battle in the mahout's place, behind the elephant's head, with his spear-bearer taking the less exposed seat behind. But the military hadn't used elephants since the 1932 coup in which it overthrew the absolute monarchy. Rama V was the last king to ride his elephants. Now, said Khun Sawet solemnly, the king "just has to know how to drive a car."

Literally as well, the illustrious elephants no longer hold the place they did. Until the late 1980s, all the royal elephants (now eleven) lived here with the king, as tradition dictated they should for the nation's sake. But, Dr. Pony explained, Queen Sirikit grew concerned at their being confined in tight urban quarters far from fresh food sources. She instigated a trial relocation, and by 1996 nearly all the royal elephants had been moved to forest camps up north, where they can stroll, browse, and live more as elephants. Dr. Pony said they were thriving — though it was unnerving to consider that the next year, Thailand suffered a sudden financial collapse which triggered an Asian recession and global panic.

Perhaps that crisis would have been even worse if the grandest royal elephant hadn't remained at the palace. He was a fifty-year-old tusker named Prasawet Aduntdet Paho Puni Pom Nam Nata Balami Tudiya Sawekali Khamotpan Nophat Belom Khamala Satnat Wisutamon Sapatbonkon Laksinat Khatchien Katradtad Soyamrasdaon Suwadipratsit Pratanagundshon Nitnitbunyatikan Patratmintatrat Bhapitratsan Sakhundpha — Prasawet Yai ("Biggest White Male") for short. I'd read the disparaging remarks about not-so-"white" elephants of early European visitors, and of the disappointed viewers when P. T. Barnum brought the first such elephant to the West, but Prasawet Yai was the most extraordinary-looking elephant I'd ever seen. He wasn't tall — just 2.48 meters, a little over eight feet — but he seemed much larger, just as white cars seem larger than dark ones. His tusks were enormous and swooping and crossed in auspicious fashion, right over left. Most of his body was an ordinary gray, but his trunk was white mottled with tan, and his ears were white flecked with black spots. He had the tawny hair that is considered a hallmark of royal elephants and (this is important, as not all elephants do) a full complement of eighteen toes; twenty would be a bonus, fewer a serious flaw. Most striking of all, his eyes were white and seemed to glow — with anger or madness? one couldn't help wondering — in the shadows of his barn. Compounding the effect, he was in musth when I saw him, chained and pacing in usual musth fashion, though on a more than usually generous lead. Black ooze poured from his temples and ran down his neck and shoulders.

I remembered Douglas Chadwick's description of a royal elephant pacing in this pavilion as "very likely insane," an "obsolete" god lost in "divine madness." But overflowing musth like Prasawet Yai's indicates good health and ample food, not insanity. Dr. Pony assured me that Biggest White Male was otherwise the most placid and contented of elephants. He would wander the palace grounds (though not so much as to tan his pale skin), bathe in the nearby pond, and let his attendants ride him — with the king's permission, of course. What he could never do in his solitary confinement was what his musth signaled he was so fit for: mate. "We tried [to breed the royal elephants]," said Dr. Pony ruefully. "But this is not a suitable place for them to mate. If we let them mate here, we cannot separate them when we need to" — a recipe for disaster.

And so, like the temple elephants of India who must remain chaste even as Brahmin priests marry, Thailand's most esteemed elephant is removed from his species's ever-shrinking gene pool.

For Biggest White Male's plebeian counterparts outside the palace, life is much less secure. A century ago Thailand had about 100,000 working elephants and even more wild ones. The former were essential for logging, transport, farming, and of course ceremony. Today, by official estimates, 2,700 domestic and 2,000 wild elephants survive, and times are tough for both. In 1989 — the same year, by chance, that the international community banned ivory trading — deforestation and erosion unleashed disastrous floods. Prompted by the king, Thailand also banned logging. This did not end the cutting; soaring timber prices sent Thai buyers scrambling across neighboring Burma, Cambodia, and Laos to work the same sort of havoc in ungoverned areas where forest regulations were not even a feeble hindrance. And covert crews fanned out into Thailand's reserves, parks, and other forests to cut whatever they could steal.

Heavy machinery is too bulky and noisy for guerrilla logging, so the cut-and-runners use the animals whose habitat they pillage. Speed, like stealth, is essential, and chemical speed is one way to get it. Elephants are cranked up with amphetamines, then worked at breakneck speed under neck-breaking conditions through the night, dragging, shoving, and lifting tons of teak for far longer than the three to five hours they can safely labor. The cut-and-run loggers rent elephants from desperate owners and have no compunction about burning them out. You see the results at the Elephant Hospital, operated by the nonprofit Friends of the Asian Elephant on a site provided by the official Forest Industry Organization (FIO) outside Lampang, near the Thai Elephant Conservation Center, new home of six of the eleven royal white elephants. Patients — tall, once-splendid beasts, now gaunt and broken — stare hollow-eyed and shuffle absently under their tin roofs, like the Thorazine-blasted denizens of a human mental hospital.

Experts debate whether elephants get addicted to amphetamines as people do; Friends director Soraida Salwala and expat "elephantologist" Richard Lair argue persuasively that they do. Certainly speed kills them, as it does us. One can't help wincing as the Dusit Zoo's veterinarian, Alongkorn Mahannop, who also provides free emergency care to privately owned elephants around the country, ticks off the symptoms he has seen in amphetamine-jacked elephants: anorexia, hypertension, cardiac fibrillation, blurred vision, and painful gastric ulcers — 150 in one animal he autopsied. Lately he's seen thirty to fifty such elephants a year.

Motala, another patient at the Friends' hospital, has become the poster child for the logging elephants' travails. When I saw her in 2000, she was shifting excruciatingly on her three feet and the sling that substituted, poorly, for the fourth, which had been blown off by a land mine. Motala was one of four elephants injured by mines along the war-torn Thai-Burmese border in the summer of 1999; she became a hero after she limped for days through the jungle to find help. Media attention and Soraida Salwala's passionate pleas brought a flood of donations for Motala — about $120,000, four times the amount sought. Some experts and rival elephant groups wondered at this outpouring for one mediagenic elephant while so many others suffered out of sight. "Every Western veterinarian who's seen that elephant thinks she should be put out of her misery," Lair said then. But euthanasia is not the Buddhist (or Hindu) way, and Asian animals are allowed to linger long past what would be accepted on the other side of the world. Sometimes they pull through; wretched and hopeless as she seemed then, Motala was alive and stronger a year and a half later, though doctors still hadn't managed to fit a prosthesis to her ragged stump.

The alternatives for Thailand's underemployed elephants aren't pretty. Here, as in every part of the world with charm and color to sell, tourism is the great economic hope. And elephants play a big part. Elephant parks (or "camps," as they're called) have mushroomed around tourist centers; their residents amuse the masses with rides and circus-like shows. Hotels and resorts have long used baby elephants as greeters, a practice as grim as the little Dumbos are adorable. The infants are torn from their mothers when only six to twelve months old, depriving them of three years of mother's milk and the ten-year-long maternal nurturing and extended family bonds that are cornerstones of elephant life. Kept in jarring isolation, they have little chance to learn to be elephants, and often die young. And while Thailand forbids all capture of wild elephants, the babies slip through a legal loophole: captive elephants need not be registered until age eight, and can be freely traded until then.

Their fate recalls that of the thousands of human children sold into bondage in Bangkok's sex trade by their impoverished, often duped, families in Burma, Cambodia, and Northeast Thailand. With Thai wildlands now better protected, government veterinarian Sitthidej Mahasawangkul reports, dealers are increasingly turning to Laos, Cambodia, and especially Burma for captured baby elephants.

And of course there are the streetwalkers. Scores of elephants cruise the streets of Bangkok and the resort towns each night as, depending on how you look at it, sidewalk beggars or ambassadors of cheer and good luck. Their mahouts sell small bags of fruit for about forty U.S. cents, double the street vendors' price, to shoppers and night-lifers, who feed them to the elephants — a tidy entrepreneurial loop. Some may also pay for special gestures, such as pregnant women who step under the elephants' bellies. Virtually all Bangkok's mendicant mahouts are ethnic Sui (also called Kui, Kuy, Suai, Kuai, and Suay), from the elephant-taming mecca of Surin in the impoverished Northeast. As in Sri Lanka and Vietnam, elephant catching and training were the province of ethnic minorities on society's margins — when there were elephants to catch.

Imagine cowboys with no cows to herd or grass to feed their horses, and you get an inkling of the plight of these hereditary elephant keepers, steeped in proud and ancient elephant magic. Their work vanished when elephant catching was banned. Even the browse and forage that would feed their elephants have been depleted by livestock and a competing tree from Australia: around Surin, as in parts of India and Sri Lanka, officials have planted fast-growing eucalyptus, which even elephants cannot eat.

The elephant cowboys have their rodeo, the annual Surin Elephant Round-up, with performances ranging from battle reenactments to soccer and tug-of-war matches. Afterward they resume looking far afield for work. For the Sui, as for hundreds of millions of rural poor worldwide, the cities beckon with the prospect of catching a few crumbs that fall off the global economic table.

Those crumbs can constitute a good living, by Surin standards. Wildlife officials tried to put some of the mahouts and elephants to work patrolling national parks, as rangers do in northern India. But the mahouts turned the offer down; the pay — about one hundred dollars a month plus food for their elephants — couldn't match what they made on the city streets.

The Bangkok-based journalist Mick Elmore followed one family of Surin mahouts from their campground in a freeway-ringed vacant lot to the bustling boulevards they worked after dark. He found that they earned twenty-five to fifty dollars a night selling elephant encounters. That sum supported seven people and two elephants camped in Bangkok, plus more of both back in Surin. The elephants found forage in the overgrown lots left unbuilt when Bangkok's construction boom stalled.

The prospect of elephants getting hit by trucks on dark, crowded streets, or panicking and hitting people, creates a whopping headache for officials. But so does getting them out of the city. "If Bangkok try to catch them, they move to Pattaya. If Pattaya try to catch them, they move to Bangkok," explained Verawat Khakhay, the earnest, bespectacled young deputy mayor of Pattaya, the beach resort that is Thailand's answer to Atlantic City (serving sex instead of gambling). "It's very sensitive. If we make them go, and a truck riding back to Surin has accident and elephant dies, people will blame the government."

Bangkok banned itinerant elephants in 1995, but not until March 2000, after one went on a small rampage, did the authorities crack down. They gave many elephant families one-way rides to Surin; others just vanished from sight. Few city dwellers seemed to believe that the giant mendicants would stay away long, or even that they'd really gone. Dr. Alongkorn told me of an area fifteen miles outside Bangkok where elephants had last been seen. Mick Elmore and I headed there. It was perfect urban turf for hiding elephants, a sprawl of warehouses, shopping strips, and fast food joints punctuated by wide vacant swaths overgrown with scrub trees and head-high grass. We saw clearings where large bodies had lain and flattened the grass. But the locals said all the *chang* had just cleared out.

Media attention soon shifted to another, hotter elephant *cause célèbre:* at Nong Nooch Tropical Garden, a lavish arboretum and entertainment park near Pattaya, a performing elephant named Plai Ngern had gored to death a young British nurse visiting with her family. High officials and Thai and foreign media swarmed on Pattaya. Footage of the attack — shot by another tourist — aired day and night on TV, like Oswald's shooting and Rodney King's beating. Deputy Mayor Khakhay lamented wryly that he'd been hired to manage the city's finances, not its elephants.

The press originally quoted Nong Nooch managers as saying

that the British tourists had teased the elephant with food. Richard Lair calls such rumors preposterous. When the elephant lunged, a Taiwanese couple sitting in front of the British tourists jumped aside. "I absolutely believe," says Lair, "it was some Taiwanese or Korean guys teasing the elephant by offering food and pulling it back [that incited the attack]. I've seen it so many times. What did they expect? It's the end of the show, the elephant's tired and wants to eat. It expects to get a treat, and this happens."

The press and ministers had already decamped when, three days after the goring, I saw the elephant show at Nong Nooch. The bleachers were packed, but I was the only Caucasian in a sea of Asian faces; European tourists strolled elsewhere in the gardens but appeared to have been scared off the elephant show.

That show made your usual American circus act seem like a church pageant. The elephants were young and agile, and were pushed hard. They didn't just parade and pose; they played soccer, trotted down the field swinging their mahouts in their trunks, and ran low hurdles over fearless young men lying on the ground. At the end of the show, vendors swarmed through the crowd bearing crates of bananas, and the spectators pressed forward to feed the elephants — the point at which things had gone so wrong three days earlier.

Soon after that incident, the provincial governor had convened the local elephant park operators to work out safety standards. He told the press that they had agreed to end direct contact between elephants and spectators, who would henceforth throw bananas rather than handing them to the performers. But Sodawan Buranisiri, the congenial Nong Nooch representative I spoke to, thought that an unnecessary killjoy measure: "We think you can give the food to the elephants. Is nicer — and Thai people are so nice. People love to touch the animal, including me . . . especially baby elephants."

Nong Nooch had speedily erected a low tubular steel barrier about five feet from the bleachers. Elephants could no longer charge or stumble into the audience, but they could still take bananas from the tourists — and, if they chose, grab the tourists too. Wise guys still teased the hungry animals, dangling and withdrawing bananas. I marveled at the folly of the people and the forbearance of the elephants.

Not all elephant tourism is created equal. The Nong Nooch gardens, Sodawan explains, were a labor of love by their founder, dedicated to public enjoyment and education; the elephant shows and other auxiliary businesses help support them. But at the nearby Pattaya Elephant Village, the elephants are the point. No raucous shows here. Visitors simply ride the elephants and learn about their care. The mood is peaceful, the only entertainment a small Thai classical music ensemble. Lair, a sharp critic of the commercial camps, lauds Elephant Village as a cut above the rest.

But visitors are far fewer here than at Nong Nooch, and proprietor Phairat Chaiyakham struggles to make bank payments. Still, he's living his dream. He caught the elephant bug as a boy, growing up beside what was then the country's largest elephant yard — in Bangkok, a metropolis that still had room for elephant camps fifty years ago. Newly captured elephants were kept there for shipment overseas. Young Phairat played hooky to hang around and help out, learning the training methods and traditional elephant medicines that are fast disappearing now. His is a business with a mission. He bought his seventeen elephants out of illegal-logging servitude up north; taking them out of action, he calculates, "saves seventeen, twenty, maybe thirty trees a week." He has eschewed training one tusker he hopes to release into the wild.

From 1973, when Phairat took the money he'd saved working for the U.S. government in Thailand and Laos and plowed it into elephants, until the mid-nineties, his was the only elephant camp hereabouts. Pattaya was just beginning to grow from fishing village to resort, and forage was ample. Now, he says, over two hundred tourist park elephants compete in an area that can grow fodder for sixty. He brings in two seven-ton truckloads a week. Though sympathetic farmers charge only half-price, "there's no limit what you can spend to feed elephants." Other owners stint, he claims; they blame their managers for the lack of food, the managers blame the owners, and the elephants go hungry. And as logging and wild forage continue to decline, more and more elephants are squeezed into crowded areas like this, chasing the tourist dollar.

Phairat's laments echo across elephant country, in Africa as well as Asia, for wild as well as tame elephants. Gone are the days when owners could just let their ellies browse the woods out back. From Colombo to the overcrowded national elephant orphanage, Sri Lankan elephant owners must likewise transport palm fronds and *kitul* trunks ever farther, at ever-higher expense. In southern Africa, poaching, farming, and fencing have forced elephants into narrow protected areas. There they find year-round artificial water holes, dug so that tourist safaris can be assured of finding and photographing them. Trouble is, as University of Washington reproductive biologist Sam Wasser explains, elephant birthrates are self-regulating according to water supply. A steady supply triggers a population boom which depletes plant resources, causing erosion, starvation, and conflicts with humans. Governments respond by culling herds, and then clamor for a resumption of ivory exports so they can sell the fruits of that culling.

Back at fun-loving Pattaya, the elephant parks did not rush to implement the governor's safety measures. Some installed steel barriers. Some talked of sending their tuskers away but, according to Lair and Phairat, hadn't done so by winter. Three months after the first fatality, a young bull at another elephant camp fatally gored a man who took food away from him to give to another elephant. The papers also reported that, contrary to earlier avowals, Nong Nooch would put Plai Ngern back in the show rather than out to pasture. Managers said he was not a problem and, yes, Asian tourists had been taunting him when he attacked the British nurse.

Meanwhile, the elephant buskers returned to the streets of Bangkok.

Beyond all the other ills threatening Thailand's beleaguered elephants, a few activists in mid-2000 alleged a particularly gruesome new trend: that surplus elephants were being butchered for their meat — in particular penises, trunk tips, and other delicacies to be sold as natural Viagras. This claim was a predictable sequel to the very real alarm over the slaughter of tigers and other endangered creatures to feed the ceaseless quest of aging men for potions to preserve their potency. Sure enough, it found a ready audience in the local and world press. Northern Thai villagers protested that while they had long butchered elephants that died naturally, they never killed any for their meat. The claims were speedily dismissed as attention-getting hype.

Still, the hype did highlight two real trends that might someday converge: the growing desperation of elephant owners who, unless they have the cute babies craved by tourist resorts, will be increasingly tempted to dispose of their burdensome beasts; and changing consumption patterns across South and Southeast Asia. Many tribal minorities have always been avid meat eaters, even elephant eaters: the Nagas of northeastern India are famous for hunting elephants whenever they can get away with it. But the ethnic majorities have traditionally shunned elephant meat, reflecting both a special regard for elephants and general Hindu and Buddhist adjurations against killing. Hindus tend to uphold vegetarianism much more strictly than Buddhists — avoiding meat in Thailand or Vietnam can be as difficult as finding it in India — but even they are straying more now.

The mystique of elephant meat may be crude superstition, but it has even attracted citizens of sophisticated empires. Lamenting the lust for ivory in first-century Rome, Pliny noted, "Luxury has also discovered another thing that recommends the elephant, the flavour in the hard skin of the trunk, sought after, I believe, for no other reason than because the epicure feels he is munching actual ivory." The Burmese logging supervisor U Toke Gale writes that he tried for years to obtain an elephant trunk tip, the first part that camp workers took from each elephant that died, in the belief "that it possesses potent aphrodisiac properties." And Ramesh Bedi reported that hosts at the 1964 Democratic convention in Atlantic City attempted to serve elephant (i.e., Republican) meat. An eligible elephant — a "killer" marked for disposal in Southwest Africa — was shot and butchered. But the political steak-seekers discovered that even then, the U.S. Agriculture Department forbade importing elephant meat.

Was roast elephant really planned for Atlantic City? I couldn't find any confirmation in the records, and Jack Germond, who covered the 1964 convention, did not hear anything about it. Perhaps the story is just too good — or bad — to be true. No one has accused the Republicans of trying to serve donkey meat. Somehow, the effect just wouldn't be the same.

> People went down to Coney just to see the Elephant [Hotel]. Indeed, the phrase "seeing the elephant" passed into the language . . . The bucko who arose, stretched, and announced that he was off to see the elephant was understood to say that he was up to no good and looking for a complaisant young lady who would second his motion.
>
> — Edo McCullough, *Good Old Coney Island*

III. In War and Pieces

9

Warriors and Giants

Many believe that elephants have a great effect in war; this is undoubtedly true, but not always in the way which is imagined.

— Jean Baptiste Tavernier, *Travels in India*

They faced about, at "double-quick," and run with all their might
For they had seen the "elephant," and did not like the sight.

— Francis Allan, *Lone Star Ballads*

FORGET THE SO-CALLED HERO who first ate an oyster. Consider
the first who thought to tame a living mountain that could crush
him with one footfall or snap him with a flick of its trunk. The first
domestication of elephants is, in the way of seminal innovations,
an event lost in prehistory. A soapstone seal showing a roped elephant survives from the Harappan civilization that flourished in
the Indus Valley, about 3,500 to 5,000 years ago; Egyptian depictions date back more than 3,500. The Indian scholar D. K. Lahiri-
Choudhury suggests that elephant keeping might stretch back "up
to 8,000 years," and Richard Lair argues that it "undoubtedly" occurred when "a lost or orphaned calf attached itself to a tribe of
[Paleolithic] hunters; young elephant calves have no instinctive fear
of man and are well known for seeking out humans if bereft of elephant society."

Or perhaps early hunters retrieved the young of mother elephants they had killed and, like so many zoo and circus visitors since, delighted in the antics of baby elephants, the most irrepressible creatures on earth, with no instinctive fear of anything. These antics might have suggested tasks elephants could perform: lifting, hauling, pushing. Perhaps the labors that elephants would perform for humans began as childish play between the two species.

Later, but before the advent of Tarzan flicks and nature shows, children in much of the world first encountered elephants in the parades and sawdust rings of traveling circuses. (Zoos were an amenity for the minority who lived in cities big enough to have them.) Few would have given any thought to the origins of the circuses' rituals and regalia — that their stately elephant walks derive from temple processions that began more than two thousand years ago in India and much earlier in Egypt. Or that the pageantry also harks back to the elephant's other great historical role as an engine of destruction, the original tank and high explosive, used in wars from Spain to the South China Sea. Mirth and slaughter, cruelty and awe meet in a circus elephant, caparisoned in a show business version of ancient battle armor.

The demands of war and pageantry weren't just related; they were in large measure the same. Devastating though they could be in the right battle, elephants were not the most reliable or efficient weapons even in their military heyday; they often panicked and were nearly as likely to trample their own troops as the enemy's. They were touchy if pushed too hard and troublesome to feed and, when seas and rivers intervened, to transport. But an elephant's essential value, on the field as in the ring, derived less from what it did than from what it was — the sheer marvel and immensity of it, enough to enchant or terrify the masses as peace or war demanded. The notion of dressing elephants in glittery costumes and forcing them to perform tricks both majestic and ridiculous reflects a stew of motives: our sense of humor, our craving for mastery over what is greater than us, our twin impulses to exalt and to desecrate.

*   *   *

Pageantry came first. Elephants were probably used in spectacles and entertainments long before they were sent into battle. The circus has its roots in the pharaohs' menageries and the human acrobatics the Egyptians staged 4,500 or more years ago. Master animal trainers, they employed lions, leopards, and even hyenas in the hunt, but no sure evidence survives that they ever thought to train elephants. Not until a backwater prince named Alexander of Macedon got the itch to conquer would the Mediterranean world learn how forbidding a weapon an elephant could be.

But Egypt was certainly hungry for ivory. Its own elephants vanished five thousand or so years ago, through a one-two punch of climate change and hunting, but that didn't dampen the hunger. Egyptian soldiers and traders ventured south to Nubia and east to Syria to find it. Around 1500 B.C., Queen Hatshepsut even sent expeditions down the Somali coast. Ivory fever led the Egyptians, as it later would the Europeans, to import and display the animals that produce it. Hatshepsut's husband, Thutmose III, an early natural historian, hunted elephants in Syria and brought them, with other living prizes, back to his private zoo, the world's first. A painting in the tomb of his vizier Rekhmire shows a collared Asian elephant led by a rope. Its keeper bears a tusk over his shoulder. Though it is an adult with tusks, this captive stands only to the man's waist — suggesting the mastery that the pharaohs of the New Kingdom claimed over the natural world.

Around 500 B.C., a coin issued by the island of Aegina hinted tantalizingly that the Greeks too were at least aware of elephants. It shows the Aeginan emblem, a sea turtle, with an elephant's head stamped (perhaps later) on the obverse. Soon after, the Carthaginian navigator Hanno — namesake of two later elephant warriors — sailed past the Pillars of Hercules and down Africa's west coast and observed "elephants and multitudes of other grazing beasts." The Punic settlements Hanno founded would later round up elephants for Carthage's wars against Rome.

In the mid-fifth century B.C., Herodotus, the granddaddy of historians and travel writers, reached the Egyptian city of Elephantine and reported that elephants and other fabulous creatures dwelt to the west in Libya. Around 400 B.C., Ctesias of Cnidus, a Greek historian serving at the Persian court, described two illustrious elephant battles. In one, Scythians from Central Asia used elephants obtained from their Indian allies to ambush the Persian cavalry. In the other, the semi-mythical Queen Semiramis of Assyria faced India's mighty elephants with none of her own. She supposedly mounted dummy elephants made of straw and hide atop camels; these scared off the Indian cavalry until India's real elephants smashed them.

True or not, the story bequeathed one more name to the surprisingly long roster of women elephant warriors. The Trung sisters, who led Vietnam's first great uprising against foreign domination in 40 A.D., are commonly shown riding into battle, swords drawn, on mighty elephants. In 1548, Thailand's Queen Suriyothai and Princess Tepastri rode with King Manacharapad — all of them on war elephants — against Burmese invaders. When the king was surrounded and apparently doomed, his wife and daughter raced into the fray, sacrificing themselves to rescue him.

These elephant queens recall the association of the most cherished Hindu goddesses and the Buddha's own mother with elephants. And they foreshadow the current generation of women elephant warriors, researchers and activists who have spearheaded the fight to understand and protect the elephant before it is too late. Some who work in Africa have become celebrities: Cynthia Moss, Joyce Poole, Daphne Sheldrick, Oria Douglas-Hamilton. Others are becoming prominent in this country: pioneer elephant communications engineer Katy Payne and two trainers who renounced using elephants in performance and founded innovative refuges for them, Pat Derby and Carol Buckley. Little known outside their own countries, but perhaps even more remarkable, are three homegrown elephant defenders: Soraida Sawala, the feisty founder of Friends of the Asian Elephant and Thailand's most outspoken advocate for the animals; the housewife Sagarica Rajakarunanayake, who launched Sri Lanka's first successful animal rights campaign when the national zoo blithely tried to sell off a problem elephant; and an indefatigable young lawyer in Kochi, India, named Daisy

Tambi, who defies death threats and big money to fight for the forests and wildlife of the Western Ghats.

However embroidered Queen Semiramis' 2,800-year-old legend may be, it points up the antiquity of elephant warfare. In ancient India, the elephant corps composed one of the four essential armed forces, together with infantry, cavalry, and chariot units, and was especially glorified. No king's or sultan's complement was complete without an imposing elephant troop, risky though it might be to field in battle.

The strengths and shortcomings of war elephants became clear in the first full-scale Western collision with them, when Alexander the Great's undefeated Macedonian shock troops met the elephants of the Punjabi king Porus at the river Hydaspes in 326 B.C. The Macedonians had already captured some fifteen elephants when they defeated the Persians in their first big showdown, but they got no baptism in elephant battle then; King Darius III did not deploy his elephants. If he had, the historian W. W. Tarn writes, "they might have prevented Alexander charging, as untrained horses will not face them. Probably they could not be put in line, the Persian horses not being trained to them either." How different might history have been if Alexander — who sowed the seeds of both absolute despotism and modern governance, laying the ground for both the Roman Empire and American Revolution — had been stopped then!

Alexander was likewise not ready to deploy his elephants when he reached India; he used them only for hauling and other support. But he had readied a defense against Porus' two hundred–odd armed elephants. These frightened off the Greek horses and, as the Greek historian Arrian writes, smashed through the infantry, "dense though the Macedonian phalanx was." But the Macedonians cannily stepped aside and then swarmed the retreating elephants. While archers and javelin throwers picked off their mahouts, Alexander's premier troops hacked at their trunks with scimitars and their legs with axes. Finally, records Arrian, "the elephants were crowded into a narrow space, and their own side were as much

damaged by them as the enemy, trodden down in their manoeu-
vrings and their chargings." The Indians "were retreating among
the elephants and already were receiving the greater part of their
damage from them." Backing up "like ships," the weary, wounded
animals began trumpeting as though signaling the battle's end.

Porus, riding the largest elephant of all, fought while his troops
did and then, wounded, turned to flee. The more romantic ancient
accounts say that his elephant, fearing his master would fall and be
further injured, gently lowered him to the ground and plucked
each javelin from his body; the other elephants, taking the cue,
knelt and surrendered. Arrian merely reports that after Alexander sent many emissaries urging he surrender, Porus finally dismounted.

Alexander, in his most famously gallant gesture, spared Porus
and gave him back his kingdom, but kept his elephants. He pushed
on to the river Beas, across which an even larger force of even
more powerful elephants reportedly waited. The Roman historian
Quintus Curtius writes that Alexander tried to urge his men on, arguing that elephants weren't really much of a threat except to the
side that had them. But the Macedonians, the world's toughest
warriors, who had faced other obstacles unwavering, were unper-
suaded. Shaken and bloodied after narrowly surviving their first
battle with elephants, they refused to face another. They mutinied,
and Alexander finally relented and turned back. Porus had lost the
battle, but his elephants had won the war against the Hellenic wave
that had until then swept unchecked across Asia. The unification of
the Eastern and Mediterranean worlds had been forestalled.

Stymied in his dream of reaching the fabled "Eastern Sea," Alexander settled into the ways of an oriental potentate — which meant
displaying his power through elephants. He brought two hundred
back to his new capital, Babylon, and assembled them in full regalia
in a circle around his throne tent. Even after he died, he was es-
corted by figurative elephants; the lavish carriage that bore his
young body to Egypt, though drawn by horses, was painted with elephants striding to war, bearing Indian mahouts and flanked by
Persian and Macedonian troops.

Three hundred and fifty years later the legend of Alexander and his elephants still lived in India. When the Greek seer Apollonius of Tyana visited Taxila, "the largest city in India," according to his biographer Philostratus, he found the residents lavishing care on an elephant they claimed had "fought for Porus against Alexander," and whom Alexander had subsequently named Ajax after the giant of the *Iliad*. They kept it "anointed with unguents and wreathed with fillets," writes Philostratus. "It had gold bands welded around its tusks, and inscribed in Greek letters 'Alexander son of Zeus dedicates Ajax to the Sun.'" Assuming that the same Ajax wasn't still alive after four hundred years, and that Philostratus (who did tend to embroider) didn't invent this tale whole, then Ajax had established an elephant dynasty that was still revered three centuries later. If so, his heirs fared better than Alexander's did.

After Alexander's death, his generals carved up his overextended empire and fought over the pieces. Elephants were often decisive in these internecine "successor wars." When the aristocratic horsemen who supported Alexander's unborn child as his heir faced down the common soldiers who backed his half-brother, they had thirty of the commoners' leaders trampled by elephants to make sure they knew who was boss.

This cavalry, under the brutal Perdiccas, next besieged another general, Ptolemy, in the Egyptian Fort of Camels. Perdiccas' elephants began tearing down the fort's walls, but Ptolemy rallied his quavering forces by stepping atop the outwork and putting out the lead elephant's eyes with his spear. Perdiccas was finally beaten when he tried to ford the swift-flowing Nile by setting a living breakwater of elephants across it. The elephants and horses stirred up the sandy riverbed, making the water too deep for Perdiccas' soldiers, who were washed downstream and eaten by the waiting crocodiles.

The battles and betrayals continued, until the brutal Antigonus Monophthalmus won the first elephants-versus-elephants showdown of the successor wars and seemed poised to reassemble Alexander's empire. His troops outnumbered all the other successors' together, but one, the eastern general Seleucus, held a secret weapon. Seleucus had traded vast lands for a mighty force of elephants — 150 by one account, 500 by another. These elephants turned the day, and Antigonus fell; elephants had stymied another would-be master of the world. And there the tale runs dry; as H. H. Scullard writes in his exhaustive study *The Elephant in the Greek and Roman World,* "The greatest of all the Hellenistic elephant corps mysteriously disappears from history."

But more corps would appear soon enough, and bring the terror of elephant warfare west to Rome — which, in the third century B.C., was still a target rather than a universal conqueror. Early in the century, Alexander the Great's cousin Pyrrhus of Epirus (the land just west of Macedonia) set off like an Alexander of the West, boldly if erratically attacking one Mediterranean power after another. After subduing his homeland, he tried and failed to take Macedonia, then saw another opportunity when the Italian Greek colony of Tarentum sought protection against Rome. Off Pyrrhus sailed, with elephants left from Alexander's eastern conquests, in perhaps the longest sea journey yet taken with the animals. The Tarentines celebrated his arrival with a coin showing his emblem, an elephant, beneath theirs, the hero Taras riding a dolphin.

The Roman horses fled at the sight of the first elephants ridden in Italy, and Pyrrhus advanced to within thirty-seven miles of Rome itself. Rome's legions crumpled before the elephants, Plutarch writes, "overthrown as it were by the irruption of a sea or an earthquake." But Pyrrhus also suffered terrible losses, and grumbled that one more victory like that would undo him, thus bequeathing his one enduring memorial, the phrase "pyrrhic victory."

Aelian records that the Romans won a "glorious victory" by sending in swine, demonstrating elephants' supposed fear of squealing pigs. One way or another, the Romans drove Pyrrhus' elephants to panic at Beneventum; they charged into their own army, spreading the usual havoc and dashing his Italian hopes.

The indefatigable Pyrrhus turned homeward and attacked first Macedonia, then Sparta. With uncharacteristic luck and freshly captured elephants, he won some less pyrrhic victories, but as usual failed to hold his gains. He turned next upon neutral Argos, and made a fatal discovery: elephants aren't suited to stealthy entrances and cramped street fighting. As his force slipped into Argos by night, the elephants' howdahs caught in the city gate. In the delay and confusion, the Argives woke and fought furiously. The largest elephant fell in the gate, blocking the retreat. Another trampled the fleeing troops as he sought his fallen mahout, whom he picked up and bore away. In the melee, Pyrrhus was felled by a roof tile thrown by an old woman. *Sic transit gloria elephanta.*

This pyrrhic swashbuckler was scarcely gone before Rome faced another, more determined elephant-borne adversary. The contest between Rome and the North African city-state of Qart Hadasht (better known as Carthage — to the victors goes the orthography) spanned three wars and 128 years. It was one of history's great grudge matches, a showdown for supremacy over the Mediterranean, the closest thing yet to a world war. And Carthage's elephants were pivotal.

Modern depictions tend to show Hannibal's elephants as Asian, and one of them apparently was: Hannibal's personal Surus ("Syrian"), the strongest of the lot. But most were surely African; the Carthaginians scoured North Africa and the Atlantic coast for more, and minted a coin with a conspicuously African elephant. Ancient chroniclers describe these now-extinct "Libyan" elephants as smaller and more timid than "Indian" ones, and modern scholars surmise that they were of the forest elephant type. A tantalizing stone carving from Meriotic Egypt in the Seattle Art Museum shows an elephant with big African ears and brow and a distinctly Asian sloped back.

Whatever the elephants, the Carthaginians made devastating use of them. They repeatedly routed the Romans, destroyed an invading army, and spooked Rome itself in the First Punic War. The historian Polybius records that Rome's generals were "in such terror" of Carthage's elephants that for two years they avoided not just direct battle but open ground. But Carthage's elephant jockeys grew overconfident, and a Roman commander named Caecilius broke the spell. He had his infantry blanket the elephants with volleys of javelins and arrows, then flee into a ready moat that the beasts could not cross. The elephants panicked and, for the first time under the Carthaginians, trampled their own side. Rome, its confidence restored, won a favorable peace.

Two decades later both sides broke that peace, and a brilliant new Carthaginian commander set out on the most celebrated elephant odyssey and one of the most audacious military campaigns of all time. From Spain, Hannibal, his army, and thirty-seven elephants fought through 1,500 miles of hostile territory, crossing the icy Pyrenees and enemy-lined Rhône without mishap. At the rushing river Hannibal had rafts lashed together two hundred feet long and covered with dirt to resemble solid ground. Once the elephants were lured on, sections were broken away and towed across, leaving the nervous animals no choice but to stay put or jump and swim the rest of the way.

Then came the feat for which Hannibal is forever remembered: leading his army, subtropical elephants and all, over the Alps in November. With their great bulk, elephants can stay warm for a while; a Buffalo zookeeper once told me his elephants frolic in that city's famous snows. But once they get chilled, they're terribly hard to revive — and Livy says the Alpine crossing took fifteen days.

The sure-footed elephants fared better than many of Hannibal's pack animals, which slipped off the precipices. And they proved Hannibal's best protection against ambushes by the fierce mountain tribes: "On whatever parts of the line [elephants] were placed the enemy never ventured to approach," writes Polybius, "being terrified at the unwonted appearance of the animals."

Somehow, the sometimes-questioned chronicles say, Hannibal got all thirty-seven across alive. This feat, coupled with the elusiveness of his route, has infected generations of adventurers and publicity hounds with *Kon-Tiki* syndrome — the irresistible urge to reenact legendary ancient journeys. In 1775 a British general tried but turned back because, he lamented, "I cannot get my elephants over the rock." In 1959 some Cambridge grads tramped across with a single elephant from the Turin zoo and got a book out of the jaunt.

In 1979 another British team proposed making the crossing, and an American team made it with two rented elephants. In 1988 the cricket star Ian Botham set out to raise funds for leukemia research by walking from Perpignan with three elephants. But he reverted to trucks after one went lame on the first day and animal rights groups protested.

These latter-day imitators enjoyed many amenities that Hannibal lacked, from supply vans to summer weather. And no barbarian tribes threw rocks at them.

Once in Italy, Hannibal's elephants soon justified the trouble of bringing them when they smashed the Roman army at the Trebia River. Hannibal was more elephant-savvy than most commanders: when the main Roman legion held and his elephants started to panic, he pulled them back before they turned against his own side and had them attack Rome's Gaulish auxiliaries instead. But winter in the Apennines wore harder than November in the Alps, and cold and hunger soon caught up with the stoic giants. All succumbed save Hannibal's own Surus.

Hannibal fought on for thirteen years, to the edge of Rome: "Hannibal is at the gate" became a watchword for alarm. But he was finally undone by Rome's resources and his pampered countrymen's refusal to send support. Victorious Rome made Carthage renounce its key deterrents — its navy and elephants. When Carthage, like postwar Japan, nevertheless prospered as a trading rival, Rome provoked a new war. Disarmed and dis-elephanted, the Carthaginians resisted unto annihilation. Rome, which absorbed all other rivals into its empire, feared Carthage too much to let it survive.

TO SEE THE ELEPHANT is a South-western phrase, and means, generally, to undergo any disappointment of high-raised expectations . . . Men who volunteered for the Mexican war, expecting to reap lots of glory and enjoyment, but who instead found only sickness, fatigue, privations, and suffering, were said to have "seen the elephant."

— John Russell Bartlett, *A Glossary of Words and Phrases Usually Regarded as Peculiar to the United States* (1860)

10

Blood and Circuses

What pleasure can it possibly be to a man of culture, when either a puny human being is mangled by a most powerful beast, or a splendid beast transfixed by a hunting spear? ... The last day was that of the elephants, and on that day the mob and crowd were greatly impressed, but manifested no pleasure. Indeed the result was a certain compassion and [a] feeling that that huge beast has a fellowship with the human race.

— Cicero, letter to Marcus Marius, 55 B.C.

... as though elephants had not got bad habits of their own, without teaching them ours as well.

— W. A. R. Wood, *Consul in Paradise*

WITH THE FALL of Carthage and the Syria-based Seleucid Empire, Rome was no longer threatened by elephant-borne rivals. It used the elephants it had captured in its own expeditions against the Gauls and Britons and the Celtiberians in Spain, and like the potentates they superseded, its triumphant generals employed elephants to display their grandeur. One, Domitius Ahenobarbus, celebrated his conquest of what would become Provence with a ceremonial elephant ride through it. Julius Caesar issued a coin showing an African elephant, representing himself, trampling a serpent, representing his foes. One expert, William Hayes, writes that the coin commemorated Caesar's triumph over the Gauls, but another,

Tom Cederlind, thinks it could as easily be a warning to his domestic enemies: "The message is, 'Don't mess with Caesar.'" When another general, Pompey, put down an uprising in what is now Algeria, he captured more elephants and sent them back to Rome. He tried to commemorate his victory with a triumphal entry in a chariot drawn by four elephants. But Rome's gate was too narrow, and Pompey the Great had to switch to mere horses.

Elephants were key in a much bigger conflict, one that spelled the death of the Roman republic and the rise of the empire and, perhaps, the Christian religion which emerged within it. This was the showdown in 49 B.C., near the ruins of Carthage, between the republican strongman Pompey and his erstwhile ally, the would-be emperor Caesar. Pompey had the elephants, since Africa was his stronghold. Caesar sent to Italy for his own, perhaps drawn from circuses, which he used to train his men and accustom his horses to the giant beasts. This preparation worked: Caesar's slingers and archers drove the enemies' elephants back on them. Returning to Rome, he wisely declined to ride Pompey-style in an elephant-drawn chariot. But when he later celebrated his Gallic victory, forty elephants holding torches in their trunks lined the way up the Capitol. After his famous assassination Caesar received one final honor, a funeral couch of ivory.

Caesar's victory marked the end of the elephants' military service; Rome would not send elephants into battle again for nearly three hundred years. But that did not mean the animals did not labor or suffer for the new empire. They simply became vehicles of spectacle rather than war.

The Romans were far from the first to realize what a showstopper an elephant can be. Ptolemy Philadelphus, Egypt's second Macedonian king, staged a magnificent all-day procession that presaged every circus parade to come. To honor the god Dionysus, who was said to have tamed even the fiercest beasts, a grand menagerie marched down the route — led, naturally, by a caparisoned elephant crowned with ivy and ridden by a satyr.

India's rajahs conducted not only holy processions but thunderous fights with their elephants — preferring contestants inflamed with musth and inciting them further with taunting, drugs, and distilled *arak*. The seventeenth-century traveler François Bernier, a guest of the Mughal emperor Jahāngīr, gave a grim account of these ultimate heavyweight bouts: two war elephants, each bearing two mahouts in case one should fall, would square off across a six-foot earthen wall. When they charged, Bernier wrote, "the shock is tremendous, and it appears surprising that they ever survive the dreadful wounds and blows inflicted with their teeth, their heads and their trunks. . . . The mud wall being at length thrown down, the stronger or more courageous elephant passes on and attacks his opponent, and putting him to flight, pursues and fastens upon him with so much obstinacy, that the animals can be separated only by means of cherkys, or fireworks." By then the riders had often been trampled, along with some spectators. "So imminent is the danger considered, that on the day of combat the unhappy men take the same formal leave of their wives and children as if condemned to death." They were assured, however, that in the worst case, their families would be provided for.

However lurid the Indian bouts, the Romans brought spectacle to a new height. In the Circus and in rich homes, their elephants performed tricks that even today sound remarkable. One was trained to write a dedication in Greek. Others, Pliny recounts, would walk through crowded banquets "planting their steps carefully so as not to touch any of the drinking party." In the Circus they would dance, hurl weapons straight and true, and "perform gladiatorial fights with one another." One that had been beaten because it was slow to learn its stage moves was found practicing at night. Pliny claimed that elephants even walked on tightropes, sometimes "carrying in a litter one that appeared to be lying in," and walked back down an inclined rope. Suetonius confirms this incredible report, and circus trainer Dave Whaley says he finds it entirely plausible. For all their ungainly bulk, elephants are famously sure-footed climbers; I've seen one escape up an almost vertical slope.

The elephant "understands the language of its country and

obeys orders, remembers duties that it has been taught, is pleased by affection and by marks of honour," Pliny rhapsodized. When ill, the noble creatures "throw grass up to heaven, as though deputing the earth to support their prayers." (In fact, they toss it on their backs to ward off sun and insects.) They "understand the obligations of another's religion" and refuse to board ship till their mahouts swear upon their own gods that they will return safely home. A century and a half later, the elephant-loving (but otherwise vicious) emperor Caracalla urged his Mauritanian officials to guard the "forests that nourish celestial animals."

But all the Romans' admiration and genius at animal training did not translate into gentle treatment. J. M. C. Toynbee calls it "one of the outstanding paradoxes of the Roman mind — that a people that was so much alive to the interest and beauty of the animal kingdom, that admired the intelligence and skill to be found in so many of its representatives . . . should yet have taken pleasure in the often hideous sufferings of quantities of magnificent and noble creatures."

Pliny credited, or blamed, Rome's nemesis Hannibal as the first to stage a duel between a man and an elephant. The Carthaginian general supposedly promised a Roman prisoner his freedom if he could kill the elephant. When the Roman succeeded, "Hannibal realized that reports of this encounter would bring the animals into contempt," and so had him followed and killed. The story seems doubtful; the famously determined and disciplined Hannibal was hardly the sort to risk a valuable elephant at such sport. This may have been one more piece of disinformation from the Romans, who also spread false tales of Hannibal wallowing in luxury and lechery.

Amidst all the carnage in the Circus, it took the sufferings of elephants to arouse the jaded Romans' sympathy and outrage. In 55 B.C., Pompey the Great commemorated the dedication of his theater with a gladiatorial display such as the republic had never seen. "The world was ransacked for animals," writes H. H. Scullard; Dio Cassius records that five hundred lions alone were massacred.

Then, on the games' last day, came the crowning touch, never staged before: somewhere between seventeen and twenty elephants were sent out to battle Gaetulian prisoners armed with javelins. One of the elephants put up "a marvellous fight," writes Pliny. "Its feet being disabled by wounds, it crawled against the hordes of the enemy on its knees, snatching their shields from them and throwing them into the air, and these as they fell delighted the spectators . . . as if they were being thrown by a skilled juggler."

But then Pompey's show of shows went awry. The elephants stampeded and tried to break down the iron palisade containing them, terrifying the crowd. "After being wounded and ceasing to fight," Dio Cassius writes, "they walked about with their trunks raised toward heaven, lamenting so bitterly as to give rise to the report that they did so not by mere chance, but were crying out against the oaths in which they had trusted when they crossed over from Africa, and were calling upon Heaven to avenge them."

The elephants' pleas did not go entirely unheard, writes Pliny: "When they had lost all hope of escape, they tried to gain the compassion of the crowd by indescribable gestures of entreaty, deploring their fate by a sort of wailing, so much to the distress of the public that they forgot the general and his munificence carefully devised for their honour, and bursting into tears rose in a body and invoked curses on the head of Pompey for which he soon afterwards paid the penalty." Scorned by the people, defeated by Caesar, Pompey was later assassinated. The tragedian Seneca saw this as poetic justice for one who "thought himself above nature's laws . . . when he was setting such disparate creatures against each other."

But the carnage did not end with Pompey. As Seneca feared, the emperors who followed his and the republic's fall vied to outdo their predecessors in gory showmanship. Toynbee notes that 3,500 beasts were slaughtered in Augustus' twenty-six "African animal hunts"; nine thousand in the spectacles Titus staged in A.D. 80; and eleven thousand in those that Trajan, an emperor not generally noted for cruelty, held to celebrate his conquest of what is now Romania. Commodus, the licentious villain of the film *Gladiator,* delighted in personally killing elephants, rhinos, and bears by the score and decapitated ostriches with crescent-shaped arrowheads so their headless bodies would continue running.

Nevertheless, elephants "fared better under imperial [than republican] rule," the circus historians Rupert Croft-Cooke and Peter Cotes write, "for then they were rarely killed in the Circus and were used instead to pull the imperial chariot or exceptionally heavy loads." This may explain why no later circus offended the public as Pompey's elephant show had; suffering bulls and lions did not arouse the same sympathy. Also, Caesar had ensured against future victims escaping and alarming the public by installing a moat around the arena floor.

By the fourth century, the increasingly Christian empire took less pleasure in watching men and beasts rip each other apart. Constantine abolished gladiator contests; the bloody staged "hunts" declined; and the circuses crumbled into the weedy, benign-looking ruins that enchant tourists today. But fourteen centuries later, circus horse shows revived in England and France, modeled on the ancient Roman hippodrome. A century after that, American showmen reintroduced exotic animals — in particular elephants — to the circus ring. They stopped short of reviving the full Roman tradition, but a new generation of animal defenders would nevertheless assail these circus operators as modern Pompeys and Commoduses.

Even as the Roman circus followed elephant warfare into the sawdust bin of Western history, captive elephants continued to strut and fight in India and Southeast Asia. Like the Romans, Asia's kings and rajahs celebrated the animals' gentleness and docility — and set them to gruesome tasks, most notably the execution of prisoners. P. E. P. Deraniyagala describes the especially imaginative training given Lanka's executioners. Elephants with sharp irons on their tusks would tear prisoners to pieces. Others would slowly crush the victims' limbs, then finish the job with one foot on the abdomen and one on the head. Two elephants would bend together suitably spaced trees: "To each tree was fastened a hand and a foot. . . . Upon a given signal the elephants released the trees which sprang back tearing the felon into two."

John Balaban notes that executioner elephants were also put to emphatic use in conservative seventeenth-century Vietnam: "For an upper-class woman, pregnancy out of wedlock could be punished by being forced to lie down while an elephant trod on her stomach, killing both mother and unborn child." The English merchant-adventurer Ralph Fitch observed likewise excruciating procedures in Burma nearly four hundred years ago. Special elephants were trained first to toss prisoners about with their trunks, then pierce them with their tusks, and finally crush them underfoot. This tradition echoed, much more benignly, in 1999, when, to publicize a crackdown on software pirates, authorities in New Delhi had an elephant trample hundreds of counterfeit computer disks.

The old potentates did not just train their elephants to kill; one, in Burma, sought to make his literally bloodthirsty. After taking a rival city in a lethal siege, he had its dead children chopped up fine, mixed with rice and herbs, and fed to his war elephants.

As one invasion after another swept in from the west and north, the kings of India, Burma, and Sri Lanka fought back atop elephants — with mixed results. In the late twelfth century, India's elephant corps repelled horse-riding Turkic invaders. But a later Turkic chief, Tamerlane, devised elephant-proof barriers and other elaborate measures that evidently worked. India's elephants succumbed to the Turks' bows, armor, and, later, guns. In 1526, Tamerlane's descendant Babur, India's first Muslim Mughal emperor, pressed further, defeating the elephants deployed against him with the sort of ruse Alexander worked on Porus: his soldiers spooked them so they trampled their own side. Babur's grandson Akbar seized 1,500 elephants from a Hindu rival.

The Muslim conquerors wondered at the Indians' attachment to elephant warfare: "What strange practice is this that the rulers of Hind have adopted?" asked one quoted by the historian Simon Digby. "In the day of battle they ride on an elephant and make themselves a target for every one." Disaster befell when Indian commanders fell from atop their elephants, or merely dismounted. In 1658, Prince Dara, finding his elephant targeted at Samugarh, switched to a horse; seeing his howdah empty, his troops panicked and fled. But the invaders were soon won over — or, as the Indian historian A. L. Bashan puts it: "The pathetic Indian faith in the elephants' fighting qualities was inherited by the Muslim conquerors, who, after a few generations in India, became almost as reliant on elephants as the Hindus and suffered at the hands of armies without elephants in just the same way." Akbar himself became a Lord of Elephants. By the time Captain William Hawkins visited it in 1608, the Mughal court owned twice as many elephants as horses — twenty-four thousand, twelve thousand of them calves.

Imagine the allure for these conquerors from the austere steppes to the north. A decked-out war elephant must have been an irresistible sight, made even larger than life by its thickly padded armor, with plumes fluttering and head plate gleaming fit to blind, sharp, poisoned metal tips on its tusks and knees, and a howdah full of archers and spearmen on its back, swinging a slashing scimitar in its trunk or, worse, snatching up foes and tossing them over its shoulders. The Mughals even mounted swivel guns atop their elephants.

All that was not enough when the great Muslim emperor Aurangzeb, with forty thousand men and two hundred elephants, besieged eight hundred Portuguese at Daman. The Portuguese attacked at night and threw fireworks at the elephants, which "turned against the besiegers with such fury," noted one witness, Jean Baptiste Tavernier, that within three hours, "half the army of Aurangzeb was destroyed."

Finally, in the Indian civil wars of the eighteenth century, firepower conclusively displaced elephant power. One commander after another rode his elephant into battle and was picked off by musket fire. In 1756, Nawab Sirajuddaulah brought elephants when he attacked the British at Calcutta, but did not use them.

Although elephants were now obsolete as weapons, they remained inseparably associated with war, even in American slang. Soldiers in the Mexican-American War would refer to going to war, and all the danger, disappointment, and worldly education that entailed, as "seeing the elephant." "I came to Mexico to see the 'Elephant,'" one soldier wrote. "I have seen him & am perfectly willing to see him again." The phrase filtered into the California Gold Rush and became pervasive during the Civil War. It even persisted till the Vietnam War, after which J. M. G. Brown wrote, "Those of us who were there and 'saw the elephant' know what America is."

Though superseded by cannons and later engines of destruction, elephants remained conspicuous in the parades of Asian warlords, and sometimes in the fevered dreams of Western ones. In 1815, when Field Marshal Blücher, the Prussian commander who saved the duke of Wellington at Waterloo, was appointed to his command, he suffered a "mental disturbance" and believed himself pregnant with an elephant. By one account, he thought the father was a French soldier. Perhaps the steadfast marshal's delirium was prophetic: he helped deliver Napoleon a great defeat.

A century later, in the First World War, Blücher's countrymen employed at least one elephant, drafted from Hamburg's Hagenbeck zoo, to haul supplies and timber on the Western Front. In Asia's jungle wars, elephants continued to serve through the twentieth century as trucks, tractors, and occasionally fighting platforms. In the three Anglo-Burmese wars, the elephants on which the Burmese relied proved no match for British firepower. But the British themselves readily adopted elephants for military transport and construction in India and Afghanistan as well as Burma. The Japanese used them successfully to overtake the British in their lightning 1941 invasion of Burma and again in 1943, when they dispatched 350 elephants to attack India. British and Burmese refugees fled the Japanese invaders in an elephant caravan led by "Elephant Bill" Williams, and the Allies used elephants to haul supplies and build roads as they returned to push out the Japanese.

Elephants also provided jungle transport where no vehicles would go for various ethnic groups resisting the government of Burma/Myanmar. In the 1960s, elephants ferried supplies along the Ho Chi Minh Trail through Laos and Vietnam, and the Cambodian army undertook a halfhearted campaign on elephant back against the Viet Cong. The long-suffering animals met new destruction from the air; both the RAF in Burma and U.S. pilots in Indochina made a point of bombing and strafing them to prevent their being used for transport. Williams reported that his own countrymen killed forty in just one bombing raid, and many more received "gaping wounds." He established what he believed was the first elephant field hospital to treat them.

Though lacking India's long tradition of elephant warfare, African fighters have continued to invoke the mighty elephant when they go to war — even in crowded Nigeria, where few actual elephants remain. In 1976, Nigeria's military chief, General Murtala Ramat Muhammed, was killed in a coup attempt. "The elephant has fallen, the elephant cannot get up," mourners declaimed. "See how the elephant lies down like a mountain." Six years earlier, Ibo rebels in Biafra opposing Murtala's regime had summoned the elephant's power for their own cause: "Trample, trample / Elephant herd, elephant / Trample, elephant herd."

Like the star-crossed creatures they invoked, the Biafrans suffered badly.

SEE THE ELEPHANT: To see combat, esp. for the first time . . . **1985**
J. M. G. Brown, *Rice Paddy Grunt* 242: Those of us who were there and "saw the elephant" know what America is.

— *Random House Historical Dictionary of American Slang*

11

Ambassadors from the East

So geographers, in Afric maps,
With savage pictures fill their gaps,
And o'er uninhabitable downs
Place elephants for want of towns.

— Jonathan Swift, "On Poetry: A Rhapsody"

I was full of dreams. I saw myself marching into Asia, riding on an elephant, a turban on my head and in my hand a new Koran.

— Napoleon Bonaparte, upon conquering Egypt

AS ROME COLLAPSED and Christendom looked inward, elephants, like so much else, were lost to Europe. But still its cloistered Christians dreamed of the pagan world's elephants, spinning fine fancies and exemplary legends of distant giants, hazy intimations of the world beyond their hedgerows. They associated elephants with Adam and Eve and the Virgin Mary because of their supposed enmity with snakes, believing that they, like Mary, trampled the serpent fiend. They accounted them paragons of piety and propriety, believing that some even crossed themselves with their trunks when they passed a church. "Each of them has only one spouse like the most moderate men, and when one commits adultery among them, it is killed by the others," the fifth-century poet Timotheus of Gaza declared. "They are modest and shamefast" about procreation, wrote the Elizabethan bestiarist Edward Topsell (who never saw a mating pandemonium), "for they seek Desarts, Woodes, and secret places . . . and sometimes the waters because the waters support the male in that action. . . . When they goe to copulation, they turn their heads toward the East, but whether in remembrance of Paradise . . . or for any other cause, I cannot tell."

A real creature was reimagined in the image of a mythical one: "Singing women enchant it and lead it to the hunt, in the same manner as a virgin also leads out the unicorn," Timotheus wrote. Such tales were scarcely more fanciful than medieval drawings of the now fabled beasts, resembling by turns pigs, rats, and woolly bears, with fangs for tusks and trunks like brass trumpets. Some of the most outlandish visualizations uncannily resemble modern reconstructions of vanished proboscideans that seem as strange to us now as the fabled elephants of Inde and Afric did to our predecessors. Perhaps the cloistered scribes were blessed with paleontological visions.

In the seven centuries between Rome's collapse and the Crusades, only one elephant is known to have reached Europe. In 797, Harun al-Rashid of Baghdad sent Charlemagne a tame one named Abul Abbas, after the elephant that bowed to Mecca in the Koran. It was a fitting gift from the greatest of the Abbasid caliphs to the greatest Holy Roman emperor. Each was an internationalist who extended the horizons of the parochial world he inherited; Harun's diplomatic ties stretched from Spain to China. And each appreciated a good elephant; Charlemagne had Abul Abbas marched from Lombardy across the Alps to Germany (reversing Hannibal's epic crossing) and kept as a royal mascot and companion until death.

The Crusades brought elephants — as well as science, philosophy, fashion, and spices — back into Europe's view. Another Holy Roman emperor, Frederick II, was forced to undertake a crusade but smart enough to avoid fighting a wasteful religious war. Instead, he seized the opportunity for diplomacy and shopping. One of his prize purchases was an elephant, which, though overlooked in most modern accounts, had a rare military career: Frederick had a castle-like howdah manned by Sicilian Saracens mounted on its back and deployed it in a successful attack on Cremona. Afterward, A. E. Popham recounts, the elephant led a Roman-style triumph through Cremona's gates, "drawing behind it a wagonload of distinguished captives, amid the cheers of the population." After nearly a millennium in remission, elephant processions had not lost their appeal.

Around 1254, France's sainted Louis IX, returning from his own disastrous crusade, sent a gift elephant to his cousin Henry III of England. Saint Louis may have been trying to divert attention from the ignominy of his return as a ransomed captive. Or perhaps he sought to soften up Henry with this most regal of gifts, preparatory to negotiating their territorial disputes. (Memo to Israelis and Palestinians: Send elephants.) The elephant was well received, and became one of London's prime attractions.

Able at last to *see* elephants, Europe's artists and scholars quickly set about correcting their predecessors' mistakes in depicting them. The monk Matthew Paris painted the most accurate European representation of an elephant in nearly a millennium. The great German scholastic Albertus Magnus acutely punctured some longstanding myths. He noted that the "fabulous tale" about dragons grappling with elephants and drinking their blood was unverified. Likewise those about elephants fearing mice, detesting pigs' grunts, and loathing wild oxen were unverified. And though elephants' legs might appear stiff, Albertus argued, they could hardly be jointless: "If the elephant had no such flexibility, it would be unable to walk with a coordinated gait." Fortunately Shakespeare and Donne appear not to have read this as they spun their fine images of jointless elephants.

A tradition was set, mirroring that of India: the giving of elephants, first to potentates, then to cities and parliaments, as a dual gesture of homage and ostentation. The most celebrated such pachyderm diplomat was bestowed on not just another prince but a pope — albeit a very worldly one.

By the early sixteenth century, Portugal's kings ruled the world's first transoceanic empire — and a stable full of African and Indian elephants. Sylvio Bedini, in *The Pope's Elephant,* writes that Manuel I, showing "all the characteristics of an oriental potentate," marched them from palace to cathedral for ceremonies. Renaissance princes strove to revive not only the ancients' culture but also their blood sports. Bullfights were held in the Vatican piazza, where tour bus pilgrims now hear the pope's Christmas greeting, and Manuel set out to test the ancient reports of mortal enmity between elephants and rhinoceroses by staging a Circus-style combat. The elephant chosen was too timid, or too smart, to play gladiator; it smashed a grille in the palace wall and fled trumpeting down the street.

Empires can be costly, and Manuel sought church aid for his wars with the Moorish infidels. To sweeten his plea, he dispatched an extraordinary mission to the newly elected Pope Leo X, bearing bejeweled gifts and an exotic menagerie. Its centerpiece was a young elephant with the old Carthaginian name Hanno. Hanno arrived in Italy to the 1514 equivalent of a tickertape parade. Swarming gawkers collapsed the roof of one inn and stormed the cardinal's villa where he berthed in Rome, tearing down walls to get a glimpse of this living marvel. Even the Swiss Guard could not stop them.

King Manuel clearly got his elephant's worth from this mission; the papal court fell for Hanno just as the towns along his path had. Poets composed effusive verses to his virtue and grandeur. One reported that Hanno genuflected three times before the pope — a gesture that must have seemed even more miraculous to those who still believed that elephants could not bend their legs.

Leo and his courtiers also noted the animal's comic potential. They had the vain poetaster Giacomo Baraballo, self-styled successor to Dante and Petrarch, paraded on Hanno to his mock coronation as "king of the poets." Only Baraballo seems to have missed the joke. A contemporary woodcut shows him as an ass, preceded by a retinue of lions, riding elephant-back with an ape attendant. But Hanno bowed out of the cruel joke, dumping Baraballo at the bridge to the Castel Sant'Angelo and returning to the papal palace.

Meanwhile, humanists in the north and apostate reformers in

the church condemned the extravagance Pope Leo's giant pet
represented. One, the "Angelic Pope" Fra Bonaventura, descended
on Rome in 1516 preaching an alarming prophecy: within four
months, the pope, five cardinals, Hanno, and his keeper would all
die. Leo, already stricken with melancholy and malaria, was in
no condition for such omens — especially when, the next month,
Hanno suddenly fell ill for the first time since arriving in Rome.
Bedini recounts that Leo summoned Rome's finest physicians, who
were worse than useless; they gave Hanno a "strong purgative" that
purged the life right out of him. According to another account,
Hanno declined after nearly suffocating when he was covered in
gold for a celebration.

Pope Leo, heartstruck, composed Hanno's epitaph himself, declaring that Fate had stolen the elephant away because it envied his
"residence in the blessed Latium." He commissioned the great Raphael to paint a vast fresco of Hanno at the Vatican's entrance,
which Popham reports Raphael delegated to his favorite pupil,
Giulio Romano. It does not survive, but Giulio's meticulous drawing of Hanno and other sketches attributed to Raphael do. Bedini
exhaustively catalogs the many ways in which later artists copied
these in compositions ranging from the Creation and the Adoration of the Magi to a horoscope and fountain design.

Rich as Hanno's legacy was for artists, it was not so auspicious
for his adoring patron Leo. "For years after his death," writes
Bedini, Hanno remained "a telling symbol of Leo's irresponsibility
and negligence," of a papacy that squandered its wealth on luxury
and cultural largess while Christendom crumbled. This association
was reinforced by the elephantine figure the jolly, generous, slow-
moving pope himself cut. To meet his debts, Leo sold papal offices
and indulgences, provoking further denunciations of corruption
and simony — especially from a Wittenberg theology professor
named Martin Luther. In his last and most fiercely antipapist tract,
Against the Papacy of Rome, an Institution of the Devil, Luther portrayed Pope Leo as "indolently catching flies while his pet elephant
cavorted." The rest is history.

*   *   *

Despite all the condemnation Hanno brought Leo, the diplomatic tradition of elephant giving continued. In 1552, King Manuel's son João III sent Maximilian of Bohemia, the future Holy Roman Emperor, a thirteen-year-old elephant that reportedly ingratiated itself just as Hanno had, by genuflecting to the archbishop of Milan. More touching yet, when a dumbstruck mother dropped her baby in the passing monster's path, it stopped short, gently picked up the babe, and returned it to its mother. Popham notes that a more cynical age might write off such an account as a publicity stunt. But other elephants have been reported to rescue human children in the same way, as did a gorilla at Chicago's Brookfield Zoo in 1996.

This elephant's Bohemian rhapsody was brief; two years after its arrival, Maximilian gave one of his subjects an armchair built of its bones. In 1563 another elephant unpacked its trunk in Maximilian's stable, a gift from Portugal or Spain. Popham reports that it caused the usual sensation among the common folk but was derided by intellectuals at pains to show they'd already seen the elephant. "One doesn't see such singular or rare qualities in this animal as the ancient authors attributed to it," one Guicciardini wrote in French, the language of disdain. "It is as gross in mind as in body and proportion; it follows naively the nature of a pig, taking pasture and eating and drinking everything that it meets; once it drank so much wine that it seemed for twenty-four hours to be dead." Justus Lipsius dismissed the elephant as "puny, young, good for crude work" — impressive to the ignorant unwashed, perhaps, but hardly matching the ancient hype.

This cycle of expectation and disappointment recurs in today's debates over conservation and animal rights. Maximilian's second elephant affords a caution to those who advocate for charismatic megaspecies such as elephants, whales, and dolphins. Sometimes such advocates extol their chosen creatures as superhuman natural philosophers, wise and knowing beyond our ken. Along come the hunters, lab operators, and other debunkers harrumphing, "Wait a minute, these are just *animals*. They get hungry, scared, and horny like any others. Why shouldn't we use them as we do the others?"

Exalters and debunkers alike forget how marvelous whales are as whales, and elephants as elephants.

Maximilian for his part paid his second elephant a peculiar thrifty homage: he had its image painted over John the Baptist's in an old tableau. Despite such saintly associations, the elephant died a few months later from, according to one contemporary account, "lack of female companionship."

Still the elephants kept coming — one to England's Queen Elizabeth from France's Henri IV, another, which Rembrandt sketched, to bourgeois Amsterdam. But thousands of imported elephants later, familiarity still has not effaced the fascination of the beasts, as anyone knows who has seen the families jostling to view them at a modern zoo, like tourists lining up at the Louvre's Mona Lisa — especially if that zoo happens to have a baby elephant. As more elephants reached Europe in the eighteenth and nineteenth centuries, and as royal menageries evolved into public zoos, seeing the elephant became an everyday diversion. The Eastern practice of flattering the Western powers with these grandest of living gifts survived into the mid-nineteenth century, though royal recipients were not always so receptive as before. In 1840 the *Lady Flora* bore an unsolicited gift from Calcutta for Queen Victoria — what *The Times* described as "a magnificent male elephant . . . docile, and good-tempered." The unidentified benefactors even named this magnificent specimen "Prince Albert." The queen was unswayed: "Having no accommodation for so giant a *protégé,*" *The Times* sniffed, Her Majesty presented it to the London Zoological Society.

Twenty-one years later, Siam's King Rama IV, also known as Mongkut, sent U.S. President James Buchanan a remarkable letter. Mongkut is remembered in America as the king of *Anna and the King of Siam* and *The King and I,* but he was a notable leader in his own right, the first of the great Thai modernizers who imported Western learning and technology while deftly staving off Western domination. Mongkut evidently wished to reciprocate with a gift of traditional Thai technology. He wrote Buchanan that he had lately learned that even though Americans regarded elephants as "the most remarkable of the large quadrupeds" and marveled at their tusks,

> on [your] continent there are no elephants. . . . If on the continent there should be several pairs of young male and female elephants turned loose in the forests where there was an abundance of water and grass . . . they will increase till there be large herds as there are here on the continent of Asia until the inhabitants of America will be able to catch them and tame them and use them as beasts of burden making them of benefit to the country.

He even offered to send some breeding stock, and included as a token a fine pair of tusks. But Abraham Lincoln, who had succeeded Buchanan as president, regretfully declined, explaining that the United States did not "reach a latitude so low as to favor the multiplication of the elephant, and steam on land, as well as on the water, has been our best and most efficient agent of transportation."

Mongkut was merely ahead of his time: 139 years later, Paul Martin would propose restoring America's prairie ecosystem by reintroducing elephants. Just imagine. If America *had* become elephant country, its vast forests exploited with elephant-powered selective logging rather than mechanized clear-cutting, the devastation and bitter old-growth battles of the twentieth century might have been avoided.

In Mongkut's Siam, even a few hairs from a white elephant were considered a gift worthy of kings and queens. In 1865 the British diplomat John Bowring recounted how, "after the treaties were signed," he left Bangkok laden with "handsome presents" and royal letters "engraved on golden slabs for the Queen of England, and placed in a gold box, locked with a gold key." But "one offering was placed in my hands with the assurance that it was by far the most precious of the gifts to be conveyed . . . a bunch of hairs from the white elephant's tail tied together with a golden thread." Although ordinary elephants were now familiar in the West, the fabled "white" ones continued to fascinate — at least until P. T. Barnum imported one that proved not so white after all. This fascination jibed with and perhaps reflected the hardening racial attitudes of the Enlightenment and colonial eras: Bowring described Siam's royal white elephants as "not wholly brown or pale black, with pendent ears of a lighter colour and spots on the skin, which showed some affinity to a purer and diviner race."

Times change, but one strain of the courtly elephant tradition survives in a nation synonymous with tolerance and streamlined modernity. Denmark's monarch still heads the Order of the Elephant, one of the oldest and most illustrious of Europe's surviving chivalric orders, which King Christian I founded in the 1470s. Its knighthoods are still bestowed upon other royal Danes, foreign heads of state, and the rare exception who is neither, such as Winston Churchill and Niels Bohr. Why an elephant for this exalted order? "The battle elephant was used as a symbol for the champion of Christianity, roused by the sight of Christ's blood," the Danish government explains. "Also the elephant was the symbol of chastity and purity."

In Asia, elephants continued to play a part in official ceremonies right up to the atomic age. In Thrissur, India, I heard the elephant veterinarian Radhakrishna Kaimal recount the proudest and most difficult task of his career: transporting thirty-four elephants in open train cars to distant Delhi, over a period of eight days, to inaugurate the 1972 Asian Games with a proper procession. "Indira Gandhi was very fond of elephants," Dr. Kaimal recalled.

But already this elephant caravan on wheels seems a quaint rite of a bygone era. Today, missile systems, jets, and billion-dollar contracts take the place of elephants as tokens of international intercourse. Elephant diplomacy followed elephant warfare into history's afterglow. But in the intervening centuries yet another, bloodier use of the beasts came to play an even bigger role in trade and conquest: slaughtering them for the precious ivory that grows from their gums. Men had found another way to cherish elephants to death.

12

White Gold

I turned away from the spectacle of the destruction of these noble animals, which might be turned to so much good account in Africa, with a feeling of sickness. This was not relieved by the filthy lucre propensity, though the ivory is all mine.

— David Livingstone, *African Journal, 1853–1856*

Every pound weight has cost the life of a man, woman, or child; for every five pounds a hut has been burned; for every two tusks a village has been destroyed; every twenty tusks have been obtained at the price of a district with all its people, villages, and plantations.

— Henry M. Stanley, *How I Found Livingstone*

THE RETAIL BOOTHS outside Tokyo's Asakusa Kannon Temple aren't usually where shoppers go for exotic or expensive goods. Far from the flashy Ginza, Asakusa is, like the nearby Ueno Zoo, a haven for the capital's ordinary folk, a favorite spot for a weekend stroll and inexpensive shopping. Its hundreds of booths offer all manner of quintessentially Japanese gifts, garments, and knick-knacks, from cotton kimonos and paper fans to costume samurai hairpieces. But one shop specializes in smaller items with much larger price tags. Its glass cases are filled with netsuke — tiny figurines originally designed as clasps for the pouches that serve as pockets on kimonos — and other carved ivory *objets*. Some are

plain and utilitarian but exquisitely finished: hairpins, letter open-
ers, and, costing 12,000 yen ($115) in spring 2000, shoehorns. Spat-
ulas for hand-dyeing kimonos cost 50,000 to 75,000 yen. Minia-
tures of Noh theater masks cost 8,500 to 27,000 and the cheapest
crude trinkets 3,000.

The proprietors, an elderly couple with merry eyes, sweet smiles,
and rudimentary English, were especially proud of a certain artist's
miniature Noh masks. His carving was indeed several cuts above,
but the effect was nonetheless deflating, more Halloween than hallowed legend; their favorite mask had a joker's leer, devil's horns,
and Dracula-style hood. If it were plastic rather than ivory, you'd
expect to find it in a gumball machine — a far cry from the exquisite old netsuke, box after packed-away box of them, that I'd viewed
in the basement of Seattle's Asian Art Museum.

I'd already checked out netsuke at a much larger, more fashion-
able store that sold Japanese handicrafts to an international clien-
tele. Its pieces were finely detailed figurines of animals (no elephants), peasants in traditional dress, genre scenes, and the odd
divinity. Prices ranged higher, from 12,500 to 56,000 yen ($119 to
$533). Many were supposed to be of mammoth ivory, which, unlike
elephant ivory, is not restricted. I scrutinized and stroked these and
pieces labeled as modern ivory, trying (with a naked, untrained
eye) to tell the two types apart, and often could not. The very pur-
est white material with the finest grain always proved to be modern
ivory, but so did some of the darkest and most deeply grained
(ivory absorbs oils, developing patinas that vary from glowing gold
to deep, almost smoky sienna and umber). On the lowest shelves
sat inexpensive, cruder pieces in soaplike cow bone.

The helpful clerk, who seemed to enjoy my ivory guessing, explained that animals and boxes could be carved from bone, but
only ivory was suitable for human figures. She added that the international trading ban had made elephant ivory more expensive than
mammoth. It was hard to see the effect here; comparable pieces in
new and ancient ivory were comparably priced. One way or another, fresh ivory was getting to the Japanese market.

The legal trade in mammoth ivory provides cover for contraband elephant ivory, even in elephant-range countries. In 1986, India banned sales of domestic ivory but not of African and mammoth ivory. So traders "continue the business as 'imported ivory,'" says Daisy Tambi, the crusading public interest lawyer in the poaching hotbed of Kerala. The battle over this loophole has gone all the way to the Indian Supreme Court. Meanwhile, the Indian government vehemently opposes letting the southern African nations sell their burgeoning ivory stockpiles (the fruit of effective anti-poaching protection and official culling) on the world market, on the grounds that this would stimulate yet more poaching of its own elephants.

In 1999, ten years after the international ban on ivory trading was instituted, Botswana, Zimbabwe, and Namibia were allowed a one-time sale of 59.1 tons to Japan. But that windfall was less than one-eighth as much as Japan, then by far the largest ivory consumer, imported each year in the early 1980s. The difference, complain conservationists and officials of countries whose elephants are still being decimated by poachers, is made up by smuggling, made easy by lax enforcement.

I asked the friendly clerk at the upscale Tokyo boutique about the sources of the ivory in the netsuke she sold. She assured me it was all legally imported and properly certified, but showed me no certificates. When I asked the elderly vendor at the little Asakusa shop the same question, he just exclaimed again and again, "All ivory, genuine ivory!"

It is hard to imagine such cute little trinkets presenting a major threat to the largest animals walking the earth. But according to estimates presented to the Conference on International Trade in Endangered Species, between 1977 and 1987 (shortly before the ban on ivory imports), 170 tons of ivory, the take from 17,000 elephants with an average tusk weight of ten pounds, went into the production of netsuke and other sculpture in Japan. Of course that was only 6 percent of the 2,832 tons Japan imported during those years. Nearly two-thirds of it went into *hanko* ("chops" in China, which is expected to overtake Japan as an ivory buyer), the carved seals whose imprints are still required on contracts and official documents. Japanese typically keep three different hanko and register the foremost one with the police. Hanko are also made of stone, wood, bone, plastic, even water buffalo horn, but Japan's hanko dealers — who number nearly fifty thousand — insist that none of these can be carved as fine, make as good a print, or satisfy their customers as ivory can. I suspect that the appeal stems not just from ivory's capacity for fine carving and crisp printing, but from the intrinsic allure of the material itself. Ye Htut Daw, warden of Burma's Alaungdaw Kathapa National Park, who passionately opposes lifting the ban on African ivory exports, tells of a Japanese colleague who "says he can't afford ivory hanko — but if he could afford it, he'd buy ivory." Daw shakes his head. "And he's a forester!"

Indeed, the demand persists despite prices that have risen steadily as ivory stocks have dwindled. According to the ivory art vendor, just the block for a hanko now costs about $380. Even at that price, however, old hanko are not ground clean and re-carved, though doing so would save many elephants; the Japanese abhor recycling personal items. "It would risk bringing bad fortune from the previous owner," explained the Tokyo clerk. "Like wearing old clothes."

I asked her whether ivory was preferred because (as many other Asians believe) it brings good fortune. "Maybe in South Asia, but not here," she replied. "People like it here because it's rare, and not everyone can have it." Indeed, status and connoisseurship count for much in Japan. But some offerings at the little Asakusa shop suggested another motive: the actual tips of elephants' tusks with cords running through holes drilled in them, giant organic versions of the little gold horns that tough Italian guys used to wear around their necks. They've been polished till they gleam, but they're palpably, viscerally, unmistakably *pieces of the elephant,* the leading edges of once-living creatures. To hold them is to hold the elephant itself in your hand — a feeling both hypnotic and unsettling. They are incantatory objects, natural fetishes, trophies at once elegant and brutal. To possess them is to possess the beast.

And there, in part, lies the appeal of ivory itself. It entrances even in this squeamish age because it is so nearly a living thing — not in spite of but because of the fact that it is ripped from an elephant's mouth. The inner mammoth hunter still claims his trophy.

Africa's peoples made wide artistic and practical use of ivory, carving it into objects of surpassing beauty and ritual gravity. Some cultures made ivory ownership a royal prerogative, forbidden to commoners without special dispensation. And yet the Africans marveled at the European appetite for it, as the Scottish explorer Mungo Park noted nearly two hundred years ago:

> Nothing creates a greater surprise among the Negroes on the seacoast, than the eagerness displayed by the European traders to procure elephants' teeth — it being exceedingly difficult to make them comprehend to what use it is applied. Although they are shown knives with ivory hafts, combs, and toys of the same material, and are convinced that the ivory thus manufactured was originally parts of a tooth, they are not satisfied. They suspect that this commodity is more frequently converted in Europe to purposes of far greater importance; the true nature of which is studiously concealed from them, lest the price of ivory should be enhanced. They cannot, they say, easily persuade themselves, that ships would be built, and voyages undertaken, to procure an article which had no other value than that of furnishing handles to knives, &c, when pieces of wood would answer the purpose equally well.

Unlike useful meat and hide, ivory holds largely aesthetic and symbolic value. Although it has been used throughout the ages to make utilitarian objects ranging from arrowheads and fishhooks to spoons and horns, it is not the only or even the best material for any. It is harder, and much harder to work, than clay or wood, but not so hard or readily sharpened as stone and metal. It cannot be molded, bent, cast, or flaked into shape; it must be painstakingly carved. But for carving it is matchless, taking detail like no other substance, glowing with an inner luster that deepens with age, warm as wood and fine as metal. Even in death, it seems to hold the light of life.

Ivory both liberates and constrains the carver, spurring creativity on both counts. The tusk's diameter limits a piece's size, obliging carvers to work small. But unlike wood, ivory does not split when cut the wrong way or worked too fine; it can be (and, in the finest Chinese and Japanese openwork, is) worked so freely and delicately as to seem spun from milky gold. The body of an eighteenth-century Qing dynasty box — one of many ivory treasures stored out of sight in the Seattle Art Museum's and Asian Art Museum's basements — is cut in a cross-shaped openwork pattern nearly as fine as the woven wire of its top. An exhilarating nineteenth-century Chinese carving of a humble crab-trap basket is a symphony of negative space, enclosed by intricate lattice that is by turns geometric — the weave of the basket trap — and fluid — the ropes and bamboo boughs that twine around it and the crabs that scamper over it. And it is a relatively large piece, two by nine inches. Netsuke compress vivid tableaux into the space of a walnut.

Sometimes natural form dictates artificial function. For Chinese officials, wrist rests — half-cylinders on which writers would steady their arms and hold back their sleeves — were essential desktop accoutrements. Split bamboo worked well enough, but the grander mandarins demanded ivory. The tusk's outer surface would be but lightly incised, to let the wrist slide. But inside, and turned facing the table unless the owner chose to display them, elaborate tableaux were carved in high relief, landscapes stacked above historical and mythological scenes, reminding their cloistered users of the wide world outside. "Devil's work balls," the most celebrated and mind-boggling Chinese masterworks, contain not just one but many worlds within worlds within worlds — intricately carved concentric globes, one within another, seemingly without end.

Such magic would be impossible without the devil's own medium, ivory. And admiring it is a devilishly dubious pleasure. In 1988, the Los Angeles Police gave the Washington Park (now Oregon) Zoo's Elephant Museum two thousand ivory carvings, with a street value in the millions, seized from smugglers in the early 1980s. Twelve years later, this white elephant windfall still sat unseen in a bank vault while zoo officials anguished over what to do with it. "We worry about encouraging the consumption of ivory if we show people how beautiful it is," says zoo director Tony Vecchio. Indeed. The zoo does show a mound of ivory trinkets, piled behind glass like the human skulls at Cambodia's killing fields, with signboards decrying the ivory trade. But the effect is almost pornographic; like anti-drug propaganda, such displays whet the very appetites they're supposed to discourage.

Humans appear to have been drawn to ivory since they first made art — certainly since the days when they hunted mammoths across the steppes. One image of a mammoth incised in mammoth ivory, found in the Czech Republic, dates from 24,000 B.C. The Egyptians may have carved figures (including elephants) in ivory as early as 6000 B.C. From westernmost Africa to northeast Asia, as cultures rose, expanded, met, and mingled, they took up the carving of ivory. It became a goad to exploration, trade, and conquest, and, in the most concrete sense, a medium of cultural exchange.

Because it is durable, compact, valuable, and widely cherished, ivory lends itself to export and exploitation like few other commodities. At the same time, the crafting of ivory became a sort of universal language, a locus of crossovers and commonalities among far-flung nations. "The Phoenecian [carving] affected the Abyssinian, the Greek influenced the Italian, and Italian affected the German," notes the ivory historian Norbert J. Beihoff. In the 1960s, Italian craftsmen still carved "Chinese" figurines that "usually passe[d] for actual Chinese" but were "superior to the genuine." Beihoff does not mention other, more surprising crossovers: the long-forgotten "Afro-Portuguese" masterpieces and the ingenious adaptations that sixteenth- and seventeenth-century Chinese artisans made for local consumption of the European religious statues that Spanish and Portuguese priests commissioned them to copy. They modeled figures of Kuan Yin, the Buddhist goddess of mercy, on the Virgin Mary, down to the baby in her arm and the rosary on her sleeve. And they copied languid, recumbent figures of the infants Jesus and John the Baptist as erotic figurines — with female genitalia and, in the way of old Chinese erotica, socks on their bound feet.

*   *   *

The passion for ivory echoed throughout the Mediterranean world, and it became as definitive a symbol of wealth and luxury as gold, a material with which it was often associated. The Greeks perfected layering the two to form *chryselephantine*, the ultimate luxury good, which the Hebrews likewise cherished. King Solomon "made a great throne of ivory, and overlaid it with pure gold." He sent Hiram's navy to Tarshish — probably in southern Spain, near North African regions still inhabited by elephants — to gather "gold, and silver, and ivory, and apes, and peacocks." King Ahab built an entire palace of ivory.

For Israel's poet-kings, ivory embodied sensuous luxury. "All thy garments smell of myrrh, and aloes, and cassia, out of the ivory palaces, whereby they have made thee glad," sang David. "His hands are as gold rings set with the beryl: his belly is as bright ivory overlaid with sapphires," the author of the Song of Songs rhapsodized. And "thy neck is as a tower of ivory, thine eyes like the fishpools in Heshbon."

The prophets who followed decried ivory as an emblem of impious luxury and indulgence. Ezekiel lamented the "benches of ivory" of the doomed city of Tyrus, whose merchants "brought thee for a present horns of ivory and ebony." Ahab's ivory palace was no treasure to Amos, who foretold that the Lord would "smite the winter house with the summer house, and the houses of ivory shall perish." And woe to them "that lie upon beds of ivory, and stretch themselves upon their couches."

The Romans had no qualms about luxury; virtuosos of excess, they hungered insatiably for ivory. Pliny lamented that large tusks had vanished from "our world," their ivory being especially favored for "elegant" representations of the gods. And so Roman epicures craved elephant trunk meat as a sort of ivory substitute — the first-century equivalent of Japanese tycoons eating gold shavings on their caviar in the high-flying 1980s.

The early Christians didn't just inherit the Hebrew and Roman passion for ivory; they converted Roman ivories to their own sacred use. Ivory diptychs commemorating the appointment of imperial consuls were reinscribed with the names of those faithful to be remembered in the Mass. The circular boxes that held Communion bread were modeled on the boxes Roman socialites used for their jewelry. Reliquary panels, manuscript covers, bishops' croziers, liturgical combs, the *situla* used to hold the holy water, the *pax* icon used to transmit the priest's kiss of peace — all were carved from elephant's teeth.

Even as European demand grew, India and China began consuming all the Asian ivory available. But vast new stocks still beckoned in sub-Saharan Africa, and Arab traders were strategically placed to exploit it. From the tenth through the sixteenth centuries, they established a string of ports along the East African coast, the "Swahili corridor," importing cloth from the East and sending dhow-loads of tusks to India and, via Egypt, to Europe. First Zanzibar, then Moçambique and Mombasa boomed as ivory entrepôts.

The Arabs came for ivory but learned to extract another commodity with it: slaves. A human captive was worth only a third to half as much as a good tusk, but could also carry tusks out; captives who survived brought additional profits at the end, and those who didn't had more than repaid their purchase price. Thus did the ivory trade help build the slave trade that eventually superseded it — a gruesome association that anti-slavery agitators exploited as they decried the twin "scourges of Africa." This dual trade introduced guns to the continent, and with them a mercenary culture that descends down to modern Africa's recurrent cycles of war.

The first Europeans to buy ivory in Africa dealt more respectfully with native suppliers than the Arab traders had — as artistic patrons rather than despoilers. For four centuries the memory of this early economic and artistic exchange was lost to history's ken, stowed away — in the form of spoons, vessels, and hunting horns — in Europe's royal attics and museums. When scholars considered these pieces at all, they took them for mere variations on the traditional carving style of West Africa's Benin civilization. Then, in 1959, the British scholar William Fagg announced an eye-opening discovery: these oddities were in fact a distinctive hybrid form, which he called "Afro-Portuguese ivories." African artists had adopted familiar European forms and motifs: deer, centaurs, wyverns, even a howdah-bearing Asian elephant. But they hadn't merely copied; they'd subsumed these elements into their own rich imagery and design. Their most spectacular creations were hollow globes divided into cup and lid, standing on elaborately figured tripod bases with further figures, human and animal, on top. Historians and critics took these for Communion chalices, but Fagg showed that they weren't, noting that one, depicting a "man whose genitals are attacked by a crocodile seems positively unsuitable for this purpose." Rather, they were saltcellars, royal centerpieces far exalted beyond today's humble shakers; the salt and perhaps pepper they held were precious commodities.

Further research has filled in some of the mystery of the Afro-Portuguese ivories. They came from three locales: the Congo River delta; the Benin civilization in today's Nigeria and Benin; and, first and foremost, the brilliant Sapi culture in today's Sierra Leone. Fagg and the Italian scholar Ezio Bassani even uncovered many of the books, woodcuts, colophons, and other European sources that the African artists evidently worked from. And, scholar Susan Vogel argues, since Renaissance Europe and the intact West African societies were at fairly similar levels of development, their terms of exchange must have been relatively equal.

But this free-trade idyll did not last. Inland wars overwhelmed Sapi society, of which scarcely a trace remains. The Portuguese, followed by Dutch, British, and French traders, began to think big. They graduated from selectively commissioning ivory craftwork to acquiring raw ivory in mass for their own booming workshops — and slaves. A new racist ideology arose; as Vogel writes, "A growing slave trade made it expedient for Europeans to view Africans as radically different from themselves."

The Industrial Revolution introduced new differences. Africans little knew what it actually cost to manufacture cloth and nails in England, and traders profited enormously. On the west coast, they might trade a cheap knife or muslin shirt for ten tusks. In 1871, when the explorer-journalist Henry Morton Stanley located the

long-absent David Livingstone at Manyuema in the Congo, he
marveled at the same spectacle Park had noted on the Niger seven
decades earlier: the villagers had so much ivory, and were "so
ignorant of the due of the precious article," that they "reared their
huts upon ivory stanchions" and used tusks as pillars, doorposts,
and eave supports, "until they had become completely rotten and
worthless." A pound of ivory worth as much as $1.70 in Zanzibar
cost "from half a cent to $1\frac{1}{4}$ cent's worth of copper" at Manyuema.

However many slave lives it cost to transport that ivory to
the coast, the margin was irresistible. "The fever for going to
Manyuema to exchange tawdry beads for its precious tusks," wrote
Stanley, "is of the same kind as that which impelled men to the
gulches and placers of California." Worse yet, the Arab and "half-
caste" traders who came to buy ivory graduated to seizing slaves,
using "indiscriminate massacres" to forestall resistance.

Stanley's eloquent outrage at the Arabs' "rapacity and cruelty"
was at least partly genuine, but also self-serving and freighted with
heavy, if unconscious, ironies. Like other European explorers and
imperialists, he conveniently blamed "Arab" procurers rather than
Western consumers for the havoc wreaked by tusk lust — just as the
same Western nations now blame foreign peasants and smugglers
for their own "drug plague." As Adam Hochschild notes in his
Congo history, *King Leopold's Ghost,* the "public idolization of African explorers" boosted ivory's exotic cachet; the more luridly Stanley recounted the horrors of the ivory trade in his best-selling
books and sensational newspaper dispatches, the more he fanned
the appetite for things African. Worst of all, Stanley signed on to
open up the Congo, Africa's last great "virgin" territory, for Belgium's insatiable King Leopold II. Under the guise of driving out
Arab slavers and establishing a "Congo Free State," Leopold created
Africa's most brutal and lucrative system of forced labor — in
effect, a slave empire. And, as Hochschild notes, "of the riches
Leopold hoped to find in the Congo, the one that gleamed most
brightly in his imagination was ivory."

In its late 1880s heyday, the Congo Free State shipped an average
of 471,000 pounds of ivory a year to Antwerp, out of a peak Africa-

wide production of 2 million pounds. At an estimated average tusk weight of nineteen pounds, that meant 53,000 elephants were killed each year — and even that widely accepted tally may be low. In 1867, Livingstone, the most seasoned African explorer, put average tusk weight at fourteen pounds and estimated that "44,000 elephants, large and small, must be killed yearly to supply the ivory which *comes to England alone*" — never mind the "enormous quantity" shipped to India, China, and America. Average tusk weight likely dropped further, and kill counts climbed, as hunters fell to taking ever-smaller elephants and more of the elusive, thinner-tusked forest elephants. And because the trade was widely dispersed, and poaching and smuggling were common even then, the actual haul may have been much greater than recorded. Compound all these factors, and Africa's first elephant holocaust may have killed one hundred thousand or more animals each year.

Even before Leopold set his eyes and Stanley's feet on the Congo, the Portuguese had wiped out elephants on the Angolan coast and begun ranging into the same heart of darkness for bright ivory. By century's end, West Africa's ivory exports dried up; in the land of Babar, elephants were largely "shot out." In the Congo, rubber supplanted ivory as the main source of wealth and, for Leopold's press-ganged laborers, misery. The ivory trade shifted back to where it had begun, East Africa, with transshipment through Bombay to the ivory-working centers of China and Japan.

In 1859, Livingstone counted eight hundred elephants in the "Elephant Marsh" of Malawi's Shire Valley, where "they sometimes formed a line two miles long." In the early 1880s, Joseph Thomson spent fourteen months in the same region without seeing a single elephant. He ruefully recalled Livingstone's accounts and predicted: "This ruthless destruction of elephants cannot continue long. They cannot be bred in a year or two, and when once destroyed in any region can never be replaced. The area in which they are still found is being gradually reduced. An iron band of ruthless destroyers is drawing around it; and it may be safely predicted that in twenty years the noble African elephant will be a rare animal."

*   *   *

What urgent need could impel such acquisition to the point of extermination? Unlike other colonial commodities — oil and rubber, tin and copper, tea and coffee — ivory did not serve to stoke the industrial machine or its workforce. Nor did the nineteenth century crave ivory primarily for the artisan work that had driven the trade for the preceding four millennia. Ivory curios and cameos remained popular but scarcely required 2 million pounds of the stuff. Instead, most of the booty from Africa's vanishing herds went to the nineteenth century's home entertainment centers, two essential fixtures of Victorian leisure and gentility: the piano, around which women and children would gather in the parlor, and the billiard table, where men carried out their social rites.

One death knell sounded in the late eighteenth century, when white keys replaced dark wood and pearl finishes on the new pianoforte. But billiards was by far the greediest consumer of elephant ivory; only the cores of the largest tusks produced satisfactory billiard balls, and only four or five per tusk. So two big elephants died (along with however many were killed to get those two) to stock a single table.

In the 1860s, a billiards craze drove ivory prices higher than a rich boozer's table losses. Phelan & Collender, America's largest billiards manufacturer, offered ten thousand dollars to anyone who could devise a synthetic substitute — and spurred a technological revolution arguably as important as those initiated by Edison, Bell, and the Wright Brothers. One of the many tinkerers who sought the prize was John Hyatt, variously described as "an Illinois printer" and an "Albany chemist." Hyatt failed to make a better cue ball but, thanks to a lucky spill, did create celluloid, the first plastic. Celluloid was too brittle and flammable to survive cue-wielding, cigar-puffing pool sharks, but it initiated the plastics and synthetics age. Bakelite, the first fully synthetic plastic, soon followed; it lacked the liveliness required of a pool ball, but it held up better than celluloid and found myriad other uses. Finally, a million dead elephants later, chemists concocted cast phenolic resin, an acceptable and nearly indestructible ivory substitute, and billiards ceased to be such a bloody sport.

Piano makers had likewise searched since the late 1700s for a cheaper alternative to ivory; glass, enamel, porcelain, and ox bone all fell short. Today most keys are plastic — but many pianists still pine for ivory's soft, warm feel and absorbency (it soaks up sweat instead of getting slippery). And we still speak of "tickling the ivories."

The switch to plastics reduced the pressure on Africa's elephants. As demand for ivory softened, hunting for sport (by rich Europeans and Americans) and meat (by not-so-rich Africans) became more important in some regions, and tusks just a bonus. Colonial regimes instituted controls on elephant hunting and ivory exports and dedicated game parks that would later become national parks and reserves. The First World War, followed by world depression and another world war, further reduced hunting pressures. European ivory imports fell from nearly 2 million pounds in 1911 to a fifth of that in 1914. Not until the 1970s would the entire world's legal ivory trade reach that 1911 figure.

Joseph Thomson's dire twenty-year prediction did not come to pass. Rather than becoming rare, the African elephant had rebounded in some areas by the mid-1900s. But extend the timeline and Thomson seems prescient. He anticipated the time bombs — soaring human population, unending agricultural expansion, and epidemic poaching — that would wait until the second holocaust of the 1970s and '80s, when more than half of Africa's remaining elephants were slaughtered.

Almost everywhere in Africa, elephants were viewed as ivory lodes to be mined, not powerhouses to be tamed and worked. Carthage's and Ptolemaic Egypt's elephant corps were distant memories, and the belief took root that African elephants were too wild or primitive to be trained, a belief echoing Europe's growing and convenient disdain for Africa's peoples. If Africans were irredeemable savages, they could be enslaved; if its elephants were incorrigible, they might as well be shot.

But even in imperialism's heyday, those who knew the animals suspected otherwise. A. D. Bartlett, the London Zoo's able director through much of the nineteenth century, conceded that African elephants "require a much greater amount of skill and attention than the more docile Asian species," but urged that they be tamed. "The interior of Africa is now likely to undergo a great change," he wrote in his posthumously published memoir, "and if the determined, bold, and reckless slave-hunters and slave-traders will turn their attention to the capture and training of the elephant in Africa, there can be no doubt they would succeed and render the country and themselves a great and everlasting good."

In fact, one of Britain's greatest colonial emissaries, General Charles Gordon, was already reported to have undertaken just this project, to little notice then and no mention in the histories of elephant training. "Gordon Pasha is trying the experiment of taming African elephants, with the help of some Indian mahouts," Frank Buckland wrote in a now-forgotten 1879 essay purportedly based on another traveler's account. These elephants had been made "quite tame at Kasala. . . . They were not made to do any hard work, but the boys used to ride them about the streets." Buckland urged schooling the Arabs who "catch calf elephants [but have] as yet no idea of taming them" in mahoutship; elephants might then "supersede slaves as beasts of burden," weakening the slave trade.

But that same year Gordon left the Sudan. When he returned five years later, elephants were forgotten amidst the Mahdist rebellion and siege of Khartoum, which made him colonialism's foremost martyr. Meanwhile, another unlikely angel had already picked up the torch of elephant taming. King Leopold, an old hand at exploiting human labor and elephant ivory, set about harnessing elephant labor in his Congo Free State.

Leopold's agents first imported Indian elephants, but these sickened and died, and their mahouts fled back to India. Native *cornacs* (handlers) next succeeded in lassoing and training local calves, often killing their mothers to catch them. They sang to their captives, were accounted much gentler than Asian mahouts, and eventually set over one hundred animals to logging, plowing, road building, and other civilizing tasks. Leopold scored a public relations bonus: in 1902, the *New York Times* reported that domestication might save the African elephant, which otherwise would be extinct in the Congo in "eight or ten years." The project also penciled out on utilitarian grounds: a 1927 review cited by Kes Hillman Smith found that elephants could plow a cotton field more cheaply than oxen or human power, and at one-seventh the cost of a tractor.

But farm work ceased after 1960, when the Congo's independence brought turmoil to captive elephants as to other residents. The remaining graduates of the elephant school in Garamba National Park still carried occasional visitors, but no new calves were captured. During the 1964 Simba Rebellion, cornacs and elephants hid in the bush. Mercenaries commandeered the elephants to hunt buffalo in the park. Garamba's hopes revived in 1984, when the British/Zimbabweans Kes and Fraser Smith took charge of the park, and the World Wide Fund for Nature (a.k.a. the World Wildlife Fund, WWF) gave money to protect its rare white rhinos and restore the elephant school. Tourism offered new hope for staving off poachers: "At current prices," Kes Smith wrote in 1992, "thirty-three people riding the elephants per year pay the equivalent of all the guards' salaries."

But Central Africa's wars and a new scheme for African conservation overturned these plans. Rebels and refugees poured into Congo and ivory and other poached booty poured out. In 1998, despite dire warnings from other conservationists, the WWF decided to replace Europeans like the Smiths with native park managers. As of late 1999, four graduates of the colonial elephant school still survived. "But the old ladies are getting older," WWF regional director Kate Newman told me. "They're dying, and no new ones are being trained."

And so Leopold's elephant dream fades into the bush. But it has inspired others. Elephant riding is now a ballyhooed eco-tourist attraction in Botswana, and other African countries seeking new ways to turn elephants into cash are trying to follow suit.

ELEPHANT (American thieves): A wealthy victim.

— Farmer & Henley, *Slang and its Analogues*

13

Brown Ivory

Elephant and Tiger saw men arriving in ships. Tiger said, "This creature coming to us must be very intelligent, to harness the power of the wind. We must run away."

Elephant said, "No, he's very small. I'm big enough to crush him. I'll stay here."

So Tiger ran away. Elephant stayed and was captured and put to work.

— Burmese legend recounted in J. H. Williams, *Elephant Bill*

A trail blazed by an elephant becomes a roadway.

— Burmese proverb, in Lu Zoe, *Myanmar Proverbs*

As THE EIGHTEENTH CENTURY shaded into the nineteenth and the European powers rushed to snatch up Africa's ivory, another saga of elephants and empire unfolded to the east — and changed the course of events across the globe. This time the treasure was not ivory but another elephant-dependent resource, one with a strategic importance that ivory lacked: the teak groves of India, Siam, and, above all, Burma. The balance of power and might of nations swung on who could control and extract this precious timber.

More and more, war was a matter of frigates and blockades rather than land campaigns. At the same time, surging global trade demanded new shipping capacity, and merchant and naval fleets competed for dwindling stocks of shipbuilding lumber. Oak was the European standard: strong, hard, rot-resistant, and previously plentiful, as important to the sailing age as steel would be to the next age. And oak was a big worry for Britain, the most sea-dependent of the European powers.

One rival, France, still had ample oak forests. Another, Spain, had the vast hardwood jungles of its New World colonies, where it had taken to building ships. But Britain's oak forests were misman-aged, overcut, and insufficient. It had lost its American colonies' vast reserves, even as the Revolution's end triggered a shipbuilding boom. In 1792, the Commission Appointed to Enquire into the State and Condition of the Woods, Forests, and Land Resources of the Crown reported darkly that without a new supply and more ef-ficient use, "this country will in all probability experience a fatal want of great Oak timber and become dependent on other powers for the means of supporting her Navy."

The solution lay in the teak-rich forests of Burma. If there is a king of woods, it is teak: matchless at resisting rot and pests, so fine a balance of lightness, strength, and beauty that its Latin name, *Tectona grandis,* means "great carpentry." Teakwood has lasted five hundred years in temple ruins exposed to the tropic elements, two thousand years in cave temples, and even longer in Baghdad's Pal-ace of the Persian Kings. Like ivory, it has been borne west by trad-ers for thousands of years. And, as Ivan Sanderson notes in his quirky but enlightening *Dynasty of Abu,* it afforded a critical ad-vantage to mariners who had to make repairs far from home. Most foreign woods expand and contract at different rates than oak, so repairs done with them split or leak. Only teak matched oak's "ex-pansion coefficient" and stayed watertight. Its oils even protected nails against corrosion. Moreover, it was one of two important tropical hardwoods (with Central American mahogany) that dried light enough to float downriver — the only way to transport timber in quantity from the inland jungles. And only elephants could haul it from its far-flung groves to the rivers.

Burma had the teak, but it was a defiantly independent king-dom. In 1795, as Britain faced a new sea war with France, a particu-larly enterprising and sharp-eyed British operative, Major Michael

Symes, arrived there from India on a strategic scouting mission. Symes reported on all he saw: politics, products, customs, and of course the great numbers and manifold uses of elephants. He concluded on an urgent note, though phrased with the delicacy of the time. "Birma," Symes explained, abounded in something Britain needed: "timber for maritime purposes." That created a "political necessity . . . for our preserving such a degree of national influence with that government, as may enable us hereafter to counteract any attempts to diminish our weight, or to erect any alien power that might eventually injure our interests, and even one day rival our authority."

Translation: Britain must do whatever it takes to keep out rivals and secure Burma's teak for its Indian shipyards. But Burma's Irrawaddy River offered an excellent natural port for shipbuilding, and foreign "artificers" — the French, who had beaten Britain to the punch — were teaching the Burmese to build modern ships. Soon, Symes warned, a "formidable navy may rise" there.

The British hurried to push out the French and lock up Burma's trees. They fought three wars with the Burmese kings, finally taking control over the entire country. Still, one challenge remained: extracting the timber they'd fought so hard for. Burma, which formerly exported elephants, became a net importer, and the British raided the still-plentiful wild herds of Ceylon and India to supply its Burma crews.

The gambit worked. Without ships built in India of Burmese teak, notes Sanderson, "the British would have been in a sorry plight in the Napoleonic wars." Thus did they consolidate their hold on the jewel in their crown and confirm their global naval supremacy — with help from their hardworking captives. Small wonder elephants grace so many colonial monuments and emblems; that was the least their colonial masters could do to recognize their contribution.

A torturous half-century after Burma's hard-won independence from Britain, timber is still essential to its economy, and elephants are still essential to harvesting it. The country, now called Myanmar by its ruling junta, still holds continental Asia's largest surviving tropical forests, with as much as 80 percent of the world's old-growth teak. It is the working elephants' final bastion, the last place where thousands of pachyderms and people labor as they have for centuries, in close if arduous partnership, hauling great logs out of the forest rather than plump tourists around ersatz camps.

"Elephant-wise, Myanmar is in a positive sense a living museum," writes Richard Lair, "seemingly frozen in time decades or even centuries ago." It has "the best surviving habitat and the highest number of domesticated elephants in Asia," "the best large-scale veterinary care," and "a legacy of superb mahouts." All true, but even in this living anachronism the old ways are besieged by the forces that have leveled forests and dispossessed elephants and mahouts in neighboring countries.

I got a taste of this living past when I headed north from Yangon (Rangoon), sitting mid-aisle in a roaring, rattling bus packed cheek-to-jowl, to the town of Taungoo on the edge of elephant country. From there I rode at dawn with two young *oozies* (mahouts) on the luggage rack (still packed cheek-to-jowl) atop a small pickup turned rural bus. At ride's end we trudged up a rutted dirt road through cut-over forest till we caught a ride on an ancient, empty log truck, along with as many local villagers as would fit precariously on its frame. One oozie and I climbed atop the cab's rounded roof, scorching in the ninety-five-degree heat, and bounced and swayed with the ruts; I imagined this was what riding an elephant bareback would be like. I made a turban of my plaid *lungi* cloth (an essential accessory in such travel) to block the sun.

Evidently this unintended disguise was enough to get us waved through a military checkpoint. After disembarking we had to pass one more checkpoint, but the soldiers here were already well into a bottle of rice whiskey (it was now late morning) and let me pass on condition I chug a glassful. I stumbled after my hosts, fast-striding young Karen tribesmen used to this commute, for six sweltering miles through the woods, till we reached their camp.

Seven oozies lived here in the logging season, July to March, in an elevated, open-sided bamboo hut, their goods stashed on a ledge

A messenger from the past: Siberian gold miners unearthed the forty-thousand-year-old baby Dima, the best-preserved mammoth ever recovered, in 1977. *Novosti*

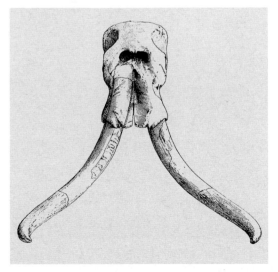

This mastodon skull was uncovered near Newburgh, New York, in 1845. *Courtesy of the American Museum of Natural History*

Most scholars see macaws in Stele B from the Mayan temple at Copán; Grafton Elliot Smith saw elephants. *Woodcut by A. Horace Gerrard and K. Leigh-Pemberton, in Smith,* Elephants and Ethnologists. *Used by permission of Kegan Paul*

A worn bas-relief in the ancient Cambodian city of Angkor shows elephants at war. *Eric Scigliano*

A star tusker in the Navam Perahera procession, Colombo, Sri Lanka. *Eric Scigliano*

The Venerable Galboda Gnanissara, the head of Colombo's powerful Gangarama Viharaya Temple, demonstrates proper elephant care in his office. *Eric Scigliano*

Midnight and dawn at the Arattupuzha Pooram near Thrissur, India, as the milling mob meets the elephant phalanx. *Eric Scigliano*

Ganesha is everywhere in southern India. Here, a float in a community parade in Edova, Kerala.
Eric Scigliano

Krishna, Vishnu's playful avatar, rides an elephant composed of the milkmaids of Gakula, with whom he cavorted. *Drawing by F. H. Andrews from an Indian painting,* Journal of Indian Art and Industry *10 (1904)*

A silver coin from the Indo-Bactrian Empire showing Alexander the Great's successor Demetrios I with an elephant-scalp headdress, a symbol of power.
Collection of Raju S. Paricherla, Andhra Pradesh, India

A silver coin showing Julius Caesar as an elephant trampling his foe, a serpent.
Courtesy of David Kaplan, Coins from Famous People in History (Web site)

A baroque elephant decorates an arch in the Palazzo Barberini, Rome.
Eric Scigliano

A painting of executioner elephants in Emperor Akbar's Mughal court, from the *Akbarnama* folios of 1597–98. *V&A Picture Library*

Above left: A leg from a sixteenth- or seventeenth-century Mughal ivory throne in Orissa, India. The mythic *gajavirala*, combining features of the elephant and lion, India's most regal animal symbols, recalls the common *makara* figures. *Seattle Art Museum, Eugene Fuller Memorial Collection*

Above right: Afro-Portuguese ivory saltcellar from the Sapi culture of Sierra Leone, late fifteenth to mid-sixteenth century. *Seattle Art Museum, Gift of Katherine White and the Boeing Company*

Opposite: Jumbo, his size typically exaggerated, on the cover of a promotional pamphlet for P. T. Barnum's circus. *Somers Historical Society, Somers, New York*

THE · BOOK · OF

JUMBO

HISTORY OF THE **LARGEST** **ELEPHANT** THAT · EVER · **LIVED.**

PONTIAC, TUESDAY, JULY 3.

A trained elephant hauls logs to a sawmill in the Karen rebels' "Free State of Kawthoolei" in eastern Burma, 1989. *Eric Scigliano*

Master showman P. T. Barnum staged elephant plowing demonstrations for publicity purposes at his estate in Connecticut. *From* Struggles and Triumphs; or Forty Years' Recollections of P. T. Barnum

Elephant Hotel, "An Old Landmark", Margate, N. J.

Lucy rises tall over Margate, New Jersey, on this early postcard.
Courtesy of the Save Lucy Committee, Inc.

Chang ("Elephant") Tower lends a touch of whimsy to Bangkok's skyline. *Courtesy of Arun Chaiseri*

Raja, star tusker at the Temple of the Tooth in Kandy, is memorialized on his own commemorative stamp.

A different Rajah, double killer and former star of Sri Lanka's national zoo, works in the woods after being auctioned off to a private owner. *Eric Scigliano*

Peaceable kingdom or disaster waiting to happen? Tourists frolic with the elephants at the Pinnawela Elephant Orphanage. *Eric Scigliano*

A neon barker for Amsterdam's leading sex club. *Eric Scigliano*

Dr. Nandana Atapattu (in hat) and his rangers use sweat, rope, and noise bombs to force a captured crop raider to a waiting truck. *Eric Scigliano*

After a two-day struggle, the captured bull is ready to be shipped to a secret location in a national park. *Eric Scigliano*

Mother Som and baby Pong, two Surin elephants who busk on the streets of Bangkok, spend off-hours in a vacant lot. *Mick Elmore*

Young fans meet a performer at the Clyde Beatty–Cole Brothers Circus. Activists decry such encounters as unsafe for both humans and elephants. *Eric Scigliano*

Elephant expert and impresario Richard C. Lair conducts the Thai Elephant Orchestra. *Thai Elephant Conservation Center*

Elephant art, human fashion: to promote conservation, Israeli designers created garments from fabrics painted by elephants at Jerusalem's Tisch Family Zoological Gardens. *Photo: Yaniv Edry; producer and creative director: Barbra Jerard; gown: Kedem Sasson; elephant: Michaela*

above their bed mats. Slinging timber for private contractors, they earned the black market equivalent of a dollar a day — eight times what oozies working directly for Myanma Timber Enterprise (MTE), the state timber monopoly, made. Now they rested. This was the hot season, when the elephants were taken far into the jungle to forage and build strength until the rains brought cooler weather and a return to work. Only two remained in the camp, a mother and her calf, who came loping in from the bush. The calf was four years old, a particularly touchy age, big enough to kill a man with a blithe body slam and as energetic and obstreperous as any tyke. He sniffed around an empty supply hut, then turned toward our platform. Playfully, or perhaps in challenge, he began feinting at charging. One oozie with a face like an angel's leaped up, grabbed a long spear with a fearsome iron point from the rafters, and pointed it at the calf, shouting fiercely. The calf, whose training had just begun, understood this much, and backed off. The Karens are renowned as Burma's master elephant handlers, especially solicitous of their animals' welfare; even elephants kept by ethnic Burmans learn commands in the Karen tongue. But their tools, elegantly handcrafted, mean business: the familiar spear and ankus, a Bowie-like knife with a handle big enough to swing like a broadsword, and a sharp curved hook rigged with rope for tugging an elephant by the ear.

For food, oozies are typically issued rice and lentils and gather or catch what meat and vegetables they can. At lunch they insisted I take the prize treat, a roasted songbird the size of a chicken wing. After siesta, I trudged on. Down the road lay the MTE division headquarters, thronging with loggers, soldiers, children, and wives. One young fellow rode by proudly on a big elephant, like a dude cruising the strip in his Caddie convertible. His destination: an elephant-height elevated hut from which a fetching girl peeked out. He pulled up on his elephant and flirted with her. She giggled. The elephant cast around for something to nibble.

Down the road lay a private ethnic-Burman elephant camp, whose headman invited me up for a cup of tea with his family. He mentioned how earnestly he hoped the MTE would raise its oozies' salary, currently a thousand kyats (a little over three dollars) a month, and was gratified when I said I'd heard in Yangon that it would be raised to five thousand. A boy of about eight rode up, bareback, on a full-grown elephant, who sniffed us, then began gathering a few rice grains spilled on the ground. A little girl reached out to pat the elephant. The headman announced that this animal was the celebrated Pan San Hla, famed for her intelligence and repertoire of stunts and a favorite of General Khin Nyunt, the feared head of the national ruling council.

Burma has maintained the system of logging and forestry established by the British, even as so much else, from roadways to democratic institutions, has eroded. It even preserves the old quaintly British elephant categories: "CH" for "calf at heel" (under age five), "TC" for "trained calf" (five to seventeen), and so on. Elephants are still classified by strength: "First class" can drag nearly two tons, second class a ton and a half, third a ton; fourth class are old or weak, fifth in training, and sixth still babies. Sustainable forestry is extolled, if not always perfectly practiced.

"The system hasn't changed," U Khin Zaw, Myanma Timber Enterprise's deputy general manager, explained after graciously receiving me in MTE's ramshackle headquarters compound outside Yangon. He wore a traditional gray collarless tunic rather than a Western suit. Trees are usable when they reach four-and-a-half-feet circumference at chest height, Khin Zaw explained, but foresters prefer to let them mature: "We usually cut at seven feet, six inches, in good forest." (Here, as in the States, the metric system hasn't caught on.) That threshold is reduced in poorer forests — "sometimes, in urgent demand," to six feet. And there's the stinger. Conservationists charge that demand has grown ever more urgent as the regime pushes timber sales to support a crippled economy and perennial wars with aggrieved ethnic minorities, at the price of precious resources and habitat.

Cutting, on a thirty-year rotation, is supposed to be highly selective; each forest acre holds only two or three suitable teak trees, plus ten or twelve other harvestable hardwoods. Trucks, bulldozers, and mechanical lifters aren't suited to such dispersed off-road duty and would wreck the landscape. Besides, says Khin Zaw, "we can't afford the fuel." Elephants by contrast are perfect for low-impact selective logging. They leave only footprints and fertilizer; for fuel, their oozies turn them loose to forage after work, hobbled so they can't stray too far. Wild foraging also ensures a more diverse diet and less need for medical care, since elephants seek out medicinal plants. "The best natural medicine for elephants is a creeper called *Tinaspora noriflora,* or *sin done ma nwe,*" Dr. Ko Ko Lalt, one of 150 elephant veterinarians employed by MTE, told me. "It is antiparasitic and a tonic for colic and constipation. All elephants know this creeper. They know it is best and find it by themselves."

If wild elephants are about, males must be kept in camp so they won't fight. Females may be lured back to the wild by a seductive rogue. Come morning, the oozie may wander several miles, calling softly and listening for his elephant's distinctive bell, to find her and go to work. Thus is the traditional working elephant's life like the human clock-puncher's: slave by day, free at night. At age fifty-five, sixty if especially vigorous, timber elephants earn a retirement that does not include a trip to the proverbial glue factory. They continue to hang out with old friends in the field, sometimes carrying light baggage but no longer dragging logs.

Against what Lair calls the "disastrous declines" in mahoutship in Thailand and Sri Lanka, Burmese standards still seem high. But Khin Zaw says the profession's status and traditions are fading here as well: "When we were young, rural people — including me — loved to ride elephants, *wanted* to be mahouts, were very proud to be mahouts. Now it's not so." Blame the pay, and the inflation that has gutted the kyat's value. Even in Burma the private sector offers better opportunities.

Mahoutship isn't the only underpinning of the Burmese system that is eroding. Burmese keepers let baby elephants stay with their mothers for five years, far longer than their counterparts in other countries do. But they do not encourage births. Rather than taking mothers out of commission, then letting the babies stay with their mothers for five years (far longer than breeders elsewhere allow) and waiting twenty years for them to reach full working capacity, they found it was far cheaper to catch and break wild elephants. The government banned elephant captures in 1994, but unofficial reports filter out that they still continue, undermining wild populations. Births among timber elephants lag far behind deaths, and any captures are not enough to fill the gap. In 1948 the British turned about 5,000 elephants over to the new MTE, which in 1993 still owned 2,925. By 2000, that number had fallen below 2,500. "We could use five thousand," says Khin Zaw.

To fill the gap, the MTE contracts 2,000 private elephants. But outsourcing can be rough on logging elephants, as on software and sweatshop workers. The standard hauling quota for MTE elephants is 140 tons of teak a year, but their private counterparts may drag 250 or more. Some owners crisscross the porous, though strife-torn and mine-strewn, Thai-Burmese border, working where the working's good — at official logging in Burma and illegal logging in Thailand. Thai conservationists even claim that elephants bearing the MTE brand have shown up in Thailand. Khin Zaw concedes that the firm loses some elephants to poaching, but insists none have been stolen or exported alive.

Poaching is a growing peril. To learn more about it, I visited Saw Tun Khaing and Than Myint, local representatives of the New York–based Wildlife Conservation Society, one of the very few Western conservation groups operating in the pariah state of Myanmar. Their modern office sat on an upper floor of a ghostly high-rise that appeared nearly empty, like so many of Yangon's spanking-new hotels and office towers. "Formerly people took the tusk of the elephant," says Khaing. "Now they take everything — hides, meat. Most of it is exported to China and Thailand." Hides go into jackets labeled "buffalo" in Chiang Mai shops, he says. The shopkeepers discreetly tell customers they're really made of elephant skin. On the Chinese side, nearly any wild product anyone could want is openly sold: ivory and hides, pangolins and bear gall, "aphrodisiac" orchids.

Some of the highland minorities who don't keep elephants have no qualms about eating them. But the elephant-keeping Burmans, Karens, and Shans shun elephant meat — if they recognize it. "Hunters cheat the villagers," says park warden Y Htut Daw, just in from the anti-poaching frontlines. "They sell the meat as *sambar* [deer] or other game."

The MTE itself occasionally enters the local ivory market, auctioning tusks from captive bulls that die naturally. One official laments that such sales give cover to traffickers, who use legal certificates to launder contraband ivory. Nevertheless, a conservation ethic, or at least intent, has penetrated both the MTE and Forest Department. The latter's planning director, U Uga, begs me to send him information about biodiversity and land use issues in other developing countries — information being notoriously scarce in a country that bars foreign publications and the Internet. MTE's Khin Zaw, who concedes that he "didn't know anything about the environment before," attended a two-week seminar with the United Nations Environmental Program in Bangkok and came back zealous to share what he'd learned. He proudly displays the "Resource Book on Environmental Management and Environmental Impact Assessment" he prepared for his co-workers. "Making the decision-makers aware of the environment is the most important thing," he says, then pauses reflectively: "We have many bridges to cross."

The Myanmar regime tolerates an incipient conservation movement, whose activists are very different from the West's young firebrands. They are mostly retired government foresters, whose background confers expertise and a degree of political immunity and lets them serve as lightning rods for those still in the agency. In 1995 these veterans formed the Forest Resource Environment Development and Conservation Association (FREDA), the country's first such nongovernmental organization. They speak with mixed pride and alarm of their country's natural legacy. "Compared to India and Thailand we're still in good shape" as far as forests and elephants are concerned, says U Ohn, FREDA's general secretary. Half of Burma is still forested, and its population density is less than two-thirds Thailand's and one-third that of Vietnam, where elephants have nearly vanished. Wild elephants range from its upland forests to coastal mangrove swamps and — uniquely in the world — are still central to its economy. But all this is fast eroding as population surges and the regime tries to squeeze out revenue by selling concessions to Thai timber companies and pushing its own timber managers to produce more. "At MTE they talk about conservation," says forester-turned-conservationist Saw Tun Khaing, "but they're under pressure to cut so much volume."

At the same time, here as everywhere in tropical Asia, agriculture takes ever more land. Burmese conservation advocates and land managers alike complain of losing habitat to both illegal encroachment and deliberate policy. "The Agriculture Department is increasing production in an effort for food security," says one. The remaining forest, while vast, is increasingly fragmented; development cuts heedlessly across migration corridors, isolating elephant populations and threatening their genetic viability. And however well MTE may try to manage its logging, Thai and Chinese timber companies secure direct concessions in border areas, use bulldozers rather than elephants, and sweep the forests in one-time grabs rather than trying to log sustainably.

"We will be the last stronghold of wildlife in this region!" FREDA founder U Ohn says fervently. The Wildlife Conservation Society's Indiana Jones–like Alan Rabinowitz and Smithsonian biologist Chris Wemmer, two rare Western researchers working in Burma, second the hope. Burma is one of tropical Asia's least spoiled but also least studied reservoirs of biodiversity, with thousands of plant and animal species that have scarcely been documented. But those working to catalog and conserve these natural treasures must deal with a regime that much of the world scorns for suppressing human rights, oppressing its minorities, tolerating drug trafficking, and using forced labor. Burmese conservationists plead to be heard by the outside world, even as they try to coexist with the regime without getting co-opted by it. FREDA research chief Myint Than insists that the group is free to cooperate with outside governments and groups, even those on bad terms with the regime.

This balancing act is further complicated by the fact that much of Burma's forest is controlled by ethnic minorities that have fought as long as half a century to break from Rangoon's grip. Foreign observers assume that this means open season on lands and wildlife in the rebel areas, and Thai timber companies do take advantage of chaos and corruption here, as in Cambodia and Laos, to loot the forests bordering Thailand.

But not in at least one case, says U Ohn. The Karens, master elephant handlers who've fought longer and suffered more under military rule than any other minority, have actually "done a pretty good job of conservation . . . better [than the regime] against poaching. They know the local land and people, and control an area much more effectively than the government troops. And they need the forest for their own protection — just like in Vietnam."

At least this regime doesn't bomb elephants, as U.S. forces did in Vietnam. The irony is that on balance, civil war, isolation, and poverty may have helped protect Burma's wild lands and wild and tame elephants. The question will be how they fare when peace and prosperity — as in go-go Thailand — finally arrive.

This animal stood symbolically for the whole business of gold seeking. When a San Franciscan told a friend that he'd about decided to "see the elephant," he did not mean that he was going on a toot, but that he intended to take a flier at the mines.

— Stewart Edward White, *After Old California, In Picture and Story*

IV. The Circus Comes to Town

14

Bailey and Barnum, Jumbo and Bet

If it succeeds, I ought to have the whole credit and the honor, too, of course, for it will be a great thing to carry the first elephant to America.

— Captain Jacob Crowninshield in a letter to his brothers, November 2, 1795

He eats 130 weight a day, and drinks all kinds of spiritous aquas; some days he has drunk 30 bottles of porter, drawing the corks with his trunk. He is so tame that he travels loose, and has never attempted to hurt anyone.

— advertisement for "The Elephant," 1797

We must have that elephant.

— *New York Herald*, 1882

WITH ITS WHITE CLAPBOARD town hall overlooking a tidy brick library and quiet shaded green, Alfred, Maine, is the sort of picture-perfect New England town that has served writers of eerie stories from Nathaniel Hawthorne to Stephen King so well. Alfred has two claims to fame, but some local boosters wish it could be remembered for just one: America's oldest continuous courthouse records. They are doomed to disappointment. The real source of Alfred's fame — and chagrin — can be discerned on a small bronze plaque mounted on a tombstone-size granite slab in a grassy patch beside a drab commercial building, just past the county jail compound on the Saco road south of town. It reads:

JULY 24, 1816
SITE OF SLAYING OF ELEPHANT
EXHIBITED BY
HACKALIAH BAILEY AND GEORGE BROWN COMPANY
OF SOMERS, NEW YORK

Just as Pompey is still known for his bloody elephant circus, Alfred will be remembered, as long as it is remembered at all, as the site of one of the strangest and, even today, most mysterious murders in American history, an episode worthy of King or Hawthorne: the shooting of "Old Bet," the second and, till Jumbo arrived seven decades later, the most revered elephant in America. Old Bet was an unwitting and unlucky pioneer in two ways. Upon her broad back that hallowed American institution the circus was built. And she was the first in a century-long sequence of elephants to be sacrificed to the rambunctious new nation's hunger for entertainment.

Like so many elephant tales from Ganesha on, the facts of Old Bet's life and death are mired in legend, supposition, and contradictory versions. Many authorities describe her as "the first elephant in America," conflating her story with that of another elephant who arrived eight years earlier and was so singular a figure that he (or she — accounts vary) was known for the next two decades simply as "The Elephant."

The Elephant arrived in New York (or, some report less plausibly, Salem, Massachusetts) on April 13, 1796, on the ship *America*. A brief notice in the *New York Journal*'s shipping news reported that the young skipper, Jacob Crowninshield, had purchased a two-year-old elephant in Bengal some five months earlier. On April 23, Crowninshield sold the prize, for which he'd paid a reported $450, for an astonishing $10,000 (about $220,000 today) — "the greatest price ever given for an animal in Europe or America," the *Journal and Patriotic Register* surmised. The buyer was not named, but the circus historian James W. Shettel discovered that an enterprising

"Welshman named Owen" afterward owned and showed The Elephant. Owen seems to have milked the purchase price for all the publicity it was worth. He promptly exhibited The Elephant in New York, then took it on a national tour. In Philadelphia he charged adults a hefty fifty cents to see this living spectacle, but later dropped the price to a quarter.

America's first elephant got good notices. The *Philadelphia Aurora* lauded it as having "the adroitness of the beaver, the intelligence of the ape, and the fidelity of the dog." The Elephant, "caparisoned as for war," drew overflow crowds to the previously failing play *Alexander, the Great, or the Rival Queens,* though the contemporary historian William Dunlap nevertheless groused at seeing "the stage dishonoured" and a leading tragedian upstaged.

Owen and his elephant wintered in Charleston, South Carolina, then sailed north to tour again. Rick Brown, an antique newspaper dealer who tracks early elephant history, says they apparently continued until 1818, when the last published report placed The Elephant in York, Pennsylvania.

Meanwhile, traveling circuses derived from British equestrian shows, with trick riders as their centerpieces, were also establishing themselves in the thrill-starved new republic. The seeds of change, and of a distinctly American circus tradition, were planted in 1804, when an American skipper with an eye for a deal bought another elephant — this time an African one — for a reported twenty dollars at a London auction and brought it to New York. Sometime between then and 1808, a farmer in the Westchester County town of Somers named Hachaliah (or Hackaliah) Bailey (sometimes spelled Baily) paid around one thousand dollars for her. Some accounts make him the brother of the captain who charged this whopping markup, and one has it that he bought Old Bet (or Betty, or Betsey) to work his farm, but got other ideas when he saw what a sensation she made. A likelier tale is that Bailey, who also worked as a livestock driver, spotted her at the Bull's Head Tavern beside the cattle yards on New York's Bowery, and visions of dollars danced in his head. He wasn't a man to miss a chance; in addition to farming

Somers's second-largest landholding, Bailey ran the New York and Danbury stage lines, kept the turnpike tollgate, served as postmaster, Inspector of Common Schools, Militia Adjutant, Overseer of the Highway, and Pound Master for stray cattle, built a hotel — and founded the circus as we know it today.

In 1808, Bailey leased out a two-thirds share in Old Bet's earnings for more than the thousand dollars he'd paid for her. The next year he exchanged a one-quarter share for a half-share in "Nero, the Royal Tiger." Such dealings spawned a tale that, admiringly recounted by P. T. Barnum, has entered into folklore. When a partner, Nathan Howes, took Bet touring but failed to remit Bailey's half-share of the profits, the farmer-impresario supposedly tracked Howes to a New Bedford barn, stormed in, and demanded his share. When Howes refused, Bailey held a shotgun to Bet's head. When Howes protested that Bet was half *his* elephant as well, Bailey replied, "I am going to shoot my half." Howes paid.

And thus, deal by cold-blooded deal, Hack Bailey assembled a stable of traveling menagerie shows, variously including pigs, horses, trained dogs, bears, a lion, and other animals. But Old Bet remained the star. For eight more years, Bailey and his partners, hirelings, sons, and relations took her and any attendant creatures barnstorming the back roads of New England, as far north as Belfast, Maine. They walked at night so the curious could not see the elephant without paying their twenty-five cents. Enterprising lads contrived to beat this blackout. One group lured her with a trail of potato peelings to a bonfire, which they speedily ignited. The hallowed tradition of sneaking under the tent began even before circuses had tents.

Then, on July 24, 1816, tragedy struck in the form of a bad-tempered marksman fired up with liquor, religion, or a gatecrasher's sense of grievance. Bet's summertime tour of the north country had gone well, according to the scraps of evidence collected by Bruce Tucker, an Alfred aerospace engineer turned historian who has made the closest study of the now hazy events. Handbills urged Mainers to see her "NOW OR NEVER! The Largest and Most Sagacious Animal in the World." To see the elephant, a youth named

Neal Dow later recalled, "people thronged into Portland from many miles around, on foot, on horseback and in every conceivable kind of conveyance." Dow, who later became a prominent prohibitionist, marveled at Bet's knack for uncorking (and emptying) bottles of ale.

But as Bet's handlers were walking her out of Alfred, a certain Daniel Davis of nearby Shapleigh waited in ambush and shot her dead. "There goes my thirty thousand dollars," Bailey supposedly muttered, either as Old Bet died or when she was laid to rest. Evidently his investment had appreciated handily. He swore out a complaint and Davis was jailed for trespass for two days, then released and never tried.

The republic's first elephanticide was briefly a *cause célèbre*. A letter from an unnamed Alfred correspondent, published in Portland's *Eastern Argus* and the *Boston Gazette* and reprinted in the *New York Post*, suggests the passions that both the elephant and her murder incited:

INFERNAL TRANSACTION — DEATH OF THE ELEPHANT

The day before yesterday, as the Elephant was passing through this town, he was waylaid by some diabolical miscreant, and shot dead with a brace of musket balls. It does not appear what could have induced this infuriated desperado to be guilty of so foul a deed. . . . On such an occasion a whole community is disgraced. The act would disparage a nation of savages. Ah! noble, generous, high minded, intelligent animal, justly classed among the wonderful works of God! — Thou hadst past from the banks of the Ganges, to the shores of the new world, to gratify the just and laudable curiosity of mankind; to display the wonders of creation, and lead men to adore the maker and former of all things. And here thou hast come to fall by the hand of a miserable unknown caitiff, who only lives to disgrace his species — to dishonour God, and to be a scoundrel to his country.

The outrage rose so high it drew a backlash. The pacifist *Friend of Peace* complained that one elephant got more sympathy than human multitudes: "In this very country, where so much feeling is excited by the murder of *one* ELEPHANT, and so much infamy attached to the deed, how many people are extolled for murdering MEN in war!"

Down in Somers, Hack Bailey built an extraordinary memorial to his slain meal ticket: the Elephant Hotel, three stories of Georgian Revival brick and dignity. Before it he erected a gold-painted wooden statue of his first pachyderm star, Old Bet, which still stands, restored, twenty feet high atop a granite pedestal and wrought iron base. Today the Elephant Hotel is Somers's town hall, with its top floor given over to the Somers Historical Society's splendid little circus museum and archive. Its prize trophies are the harness, hook, leg chain, and sequined headgear used to tour Old Bet. In 1922, Ringling Brothers sent its star elephant, Old John, on a fifty-three-mile pilgrimage from Madison Square Garden to lay a wreath at Old Bet's monument, while six hundred schoolchildren sang "The Star-Spangled Banner." Thirty-one years later, Hunt's Circus's Rose laid another wreath to Old Bet and, writes Somers historian Mabel H. Addis, "even went as far as to gain admission to the Elephant Hotel."

But while Somers burnished its memories, the tale of Old Bet's death faded away, save in the rumors and recollections passed down by Alfred's old-timers. In the 1930s a local journalist got hold of it and wrote various (and, Tucker notes, highly variable) versions of Old Bet's saga, first for local papers, then for national magazines. The hubbub she sparked culminated in 1963, when the Circus Fans of America donated Bet's plaque. Controversy and uncertainty attended the dedication, recalls Alfred town clerk Elmer Williams: "They think the shooting happened at the dump, but of course they didn't want to put the plaque there." According to Tucker, the donor of the site chosen instead "wanted to tweak the town fathers. He said he didn't think that elephant was under that stone any more than it was under his living room."

Alfred's biggest story is still viewed dubiously there. Its history museum contains no trace of Old Bet. When Tucker began his research, he found that "everyone knew the tale but no one wanted to be responsible for telling it." Some told him the elephant actually died naturally as the show passed through, or dragged herself all the way to Waldoboro to die after she was shot. Or, if she died in Alfred, they noted that the shooter was from elsewhere. Tucker found them discomfited by a 1936 newspaper report that Davis had hired an Alfred man, who finally confessed on his deathbed, to do the shooting.

Even more doubts and debates shroud the killer's motive. Tucker says one woman "heard from her grandfather he was naked and crazy"; others said he was drunk. A 1933 story in Portland's *Sunday Press Herald* said "John Davis" had quarreled with the show's proprietor and shot the man's elephant to get even. According to another account, he feared his cows would stop giving milk after seeing the elephant. Or he thought it sinful to charge poor farmers twenty-five cents to see an animal. Out of such accounts grew a tale with mythic resonance and an appealing anti-Puritan twist — one that the writer James Agee recapitulated in the last of his famous letters to his mentor, Father James Flye: "Religious people decided that she was the reincarnation of Behemoth, and shot her dead."

The truth was probably more prosaic, and closer to innumerable other unhappy encounters between people and elephants. According to Tucker, an otherwise accurate newspaper account reported that Davis, who'd been drinking, taunted Bet with his bottle of liquor. She roughed him up; he was rescued and ejected, and came back armed. This tale nearly matches an oral account collected by Tucker and a 1939 newspaper story reporting that Davis teased Bet with food or slipped her a plug of tobacco, and she tore his vest.

Even in death, neither Bet nor her legend would lie still. According to several accounts, Bailey promptly exhumed her (if she was ever buried) and removed her hide and bones. In 1817 the *New York Post* announced that her skeleton could be seen, for the familiar price of twenty-five cents, at the American Museum on Broadway.

Old Bet's murder was not enough to put Bailey off show business or elephants. Three months later he commissioned a Calcutta-bound ship to bring him another star, Columbus, probably the first bull elephant in America, who toured for decades. Just before that animal arrived, Bailey bought another that happened to become available and named her "Little Bett, the Learned Elephant." Little Bett seemed to inherit Old Bet's luck as well as her name. On May 25, 1826, at age twelve, she was gunned down as she crossed the bridge at Chepachet, Rhode Island.

Legend and some published accounts have it that several local lads felt moved to test Little Bett's publicity, which declared her skin impervious to bullets. But the records of the local Friendship Lodge, several of whose members were implicated in the shooting, show that one Canton Smith instigated the crime after quarreling with Little Bett's owners when she played North Scituate the day before. According to *Woonsocket Call* columnist Jim Doherty, Smith and the other ruffians vowed revenge after sneaking into the show and being ejected. After the shooting, they were caught, tried, and assessed the elephant's value, $22,000. Bailey and his partners collected only a small portion. One of the fearless elephant hunters, Ben Brown, declared that "he would give them fifty dollars or they could send him to Hell or Texas." The partners recouped some of the loss by sending Bett's hide to the Boston Museum and her bones to another site for display. Canton Smith later sued and recovered several hundred dollars from another shooter, who had signed a contract pledging not to disclose Smith's role in the affair and then squealed. That was considered a worse transgression than murdering an elephant.

The people of Chepachet put the atrocity out of their minds for 150 years. But in 1976, as Bicentennial nostalgia swept the country, they decided to flaunt the distinction rather than duck the notoriety. They persuaded the state legislature to declare May 25 "Elephant Day" and installed a bronze plaque on the bridge; locals still call it "the Elephant Bridge." Down the road, outside the Chepachet Public Library, stands a large cartoonish statue of "The Learned Elephant" holding a book — though Little Bett is hardly an encouraging example of where learning will get you.

Hachaliah Bailey erected his monument to Old Bet the year Little Bett was shot, and it became the axis around which a circus world turned. Menageries and traveling shows sprang up like casinos in Nevada around Somers, in northern Westchester and Dutchess counties and in Putnam County, Connecticut. Many were offshoots of Bailey's enterprises; his own son Lewis became a prominent clown and circus operator, and his nephew George F. Bailey managed the Aaron Turner Circus, which toured as far as South America.

Hack Bailey did not stick around for the full flowering of the circus boom he and Old Bet had launched. He sold his last elephant and his Somers holdings and in 1836 decamped to northern Virginia. There he bought a large tract — today's Baileys Crossroads — and built training and wintering quarters for the traveling shows that now swarmed along America's roads. But his legacy endured in Somers and from there swept the nation — in the person of one Phineas T. Barnum, a farmer's son who operated a dry goods store in nearby Bethel, Connecticut.

Bailey visited Barnum's store just as Barnum was casting about for a new calling. The restless young merchant evidently drew a large draft of inspiration from the tales Bailey told. He later called Bailey the man he admired most after his own grandfather and hailed his show-biz success and the "fine Elephant Hotel" he'd parlayed from it. Barnum particularly noted that Bailey's elephant was "the foundation of his fortune." Half a century later he would make a much larger fortune from another elephant, and build the foundation of popular culture as we know it today. He would lay a path for Walt Disney, Colonel Parker, and all the master packagers of mass-market taste to come, and ignite a transoceanic frenzy of hype and orchestrated hysteria such as the world would not see again until the Beatles led another "British Invasion" of America. And, from the elephant that made it possible, he would give the language a new word for all that is outsized, especially in packaged products, expressing a new spirit of unbounded consumption: "Jumbo."

Barnum broke into show business with an assortment of touring curiosities, then worked a leveraged buyout of the stuffy American

Museum, where Old Bet's bones were shown. He replaced its mounted specimens with live animals, lively shows, and exotic spectacles, creating the prototype of all the amusement parks and entertainment palaces to come. He even made its exit an attraction. When the capacity crowds lingered too long, he posted an enticing sign: "This Way to the Egress."

Having seen what kind of promotional hay could be made of an elephant, Barnum determined to break into the traveling menagerie business with many elephants — America's first large pachyderm troupe. In 1850 he dispatched emissaries to Ceylon to acquire it. Finding no elephants to buy, they set out to catch them. Barnum, a kindly man, nevertheless boasted blithely in his autobiography that his posse "killed large numbers of the huge beasts" before finally catching ten, which he paraded up Broadway.

After four profitable years, Barnum parted out his "Great Asiatic Caravan," keeping one elephant for what he called "agricultural purposes." This he stationed, with a plow and a costumed keeper, in a field beside the New York and New Haven Railroad. "The keeper was furnished with a time-table of the road, with instruction to be busily engaged in his work whenever passenger trains from either direction were passing through." Sure enough, Barnum crowed, the American and European papers obligingly reported that the "proprietor of the celebrated American Museum in New York" had elephants doing his plowing. Letters poured in requesting particulars on farming with elephants. Alarmed that some poor sod might actually acquire one, Barnum replied that they were profitable only for farmers who also had museums to advertise.

Barnum entered the traveling circus business full-bore in the 1870s, but in 1880 he met his match. A rival show had enjoyed a lucky break, the first baby elephant born in America. Barnum, as aware as today's zoo and circus owners of such a tyke's drawing power, telegraphed an offer to buy it. But one of its owners, James A. Bailey, out-Barnumed Barnum. He printed up posters of Barnum's telegram, labeled "What Barnum thinks of THE baby elephant." Barnum saluted these "foemen 'worthy of my steel'" and opted to merge rather than fight. Barnum and Bailey eventually wound up sole partners, an odd but effective couple.

History records that Bailey was an orphaned stablehand who came up through the circus ranks and took the name "Bailey" after Hachaliah. But the story passed down among some of his relatives is that he was actually Hachaliah's illegitimate son. He was as dour, anxious, and methodical as Barnum was effusive, brash, and lax. After Barnum's passing, Bailey would turn the anything-goes circus into respectable family entertainment — and ordain a harsher fate for its elephants.

In 1882 one of Barnum's own elephants produced a baby, and he boasted of getting "more than fifty columns of details of the birth" in the papers and "unprecedented" crowds for its debut at Madison Square Garden. At the same time, an even grander elephant gambit presented itself. Jumbo, the cherished bull elephant of the London Zoo, already had a glamorous international career, as captive elephant careers go. Kidnapped around 1861 in Central Africa — probably after his mother and herd-mates were shot for their tusks — he'd landed in Paris's Jardin des Plantes. Three years later his keepers traded young Jumbo, who showed no sign of his future stature, to the London Zoological Society for a rhinoceros.

Perhaps the French later felt the way the Red Sox did after trading Babe Ruth to the Yankees — though if they hadn't traded Jumbo, he would likely have wound up as dinner for starving Parisians, as did so many animals during the Prussian siege six years later. In London, the long-legged Jumbo shot up until, topping six tons and eleven feet, he was the tallest elephant in Europe, though certainly not "the largest elephant ever seen, either wild or in captivity," as Barnum later claimed.

For fifteen years Jumbo greeted his London fans, ate the buns they handed him, and gave rides to thousands of their children (supposedly including those of Queen Victoria, a confirmed fan). These yielded a hefty bonus in tips for Matthew Scott, the only keeper who could handle him. The laconic Scott, like many keepers, seemed to prefer his beast's company to that of other humans, and with secret signals jealously guarded his control over him.

But in 1880–81, Jumbo's famous docility eroded. He fell into rages when confined indoors, nearly demolished his house, and drove his tusks right through its iron plates, breaking them off.

Then, evidently glad to leave his dark stall, he resumed giving rides, and Scottie resumed taking each rider's tuppence.

One modern elephant specialist, Sylvia K. Sikes, pins Jumbo's fits on teething pains, since he was at the age when the fifth of his six successive molar sets would emerge. But the Zoological's director, A. D. Bartlett, blamed musth and approached the conclusion that so many zoos and circuses would reach in the decades to come, with dire results for so many elephants: with their musth cycles, strength, and free-ranging ways, adult bulls were just too troublesome and dangerous to keep.

Bartlett had special cause to fear what was to come. As a boy, he had witnessed England's gaudiest elephant tragedy, the gory, fumbling execution of the popular Chuny, who had likewise lately reached the age of musth. "I well knew that this restless and frantic condition could be subdued by reducing the quantity of his food, fastening his limbs by chains, and an occasional flogging," Bartlett recounts in his fascinating memoir *cum* animal-care manual, "but this treatment would have called forth a multitude of protests from kind-hearted and sensitive people, and, in all probability, would have led to those concerned appearing before the magistrates at the police court charged with cruelty." So he kept Jumbo fed and asked his trustees for an elephant gun.

Just then, Barnum's agent came calling. Barnum had been assiduously trying to buy up hallowed British icons that would wow America. He'd nearly landed Shakespeare's birth cottage at Stratford and Madame Tussaud's museum, and even made an offer (sternly rebuffed) to exhibit Cetewayo, the newly captured Zulu king. He expected a similar rebuff when he asked about Jumbo, but the Zoological Society's trustees named a price: two thousand pounds (ten thousand dollars). Contrary to Barnum's usual practice, the two parties did not broadcast the deal; a single paragraph in *The Times* merely noted that a "large male African elephant" would leave for America.

Three weeks later, Barnum's men brought a crate to haul Jumbo to the docks. Jumbo refused to enter, kneeling in steadfast, eloquent, and, if anyone thought about it, highly suspicious protest.

The sight of him chained for the trip set off a firestorm. For five weeks the letters and editorials flew, debating what *The Times* called "the issue that has lately been agitating the country far beyond all political issues whatever." A few defended the prudence of selling Jumbo; one recalled all the elephants that had killed their keepers and been shot and argued that circus travel might work off Jumbo's rambunctiousness. But most Brits — including John Ruskin and the Prince of Wales — deplored the decision, begged the authorities not to let the crass Americans take away "our" Jumbo, and offered to raise the money to buy him back. Some wrote to Jumbo himself, and many sent him gifts: mountains of buns, bouquets, cigars, whiskey, jewelry, even twelve dozen oysters to give him strength to fight.

Marketers milked the mania by offering "Jumbo" hats, collars, cigars, ties, fans, stationery, earrings, boots, overcoats, underwear, perfume, fritters, stews, ice cream, and even kisses. Wags and versifiers had their day. One implored Barnum to take Prime Minister Gladstone instead. The *London Fun* suggested replacing the British lion with an elephant and revising the national motto to *"Dieu et Mon Jumbo."*

While Barnum's men labored to budge Jumbo, the zoo scored an attendance bonanza, logging more than ten times as many daily visitors as it had a year earlier. A lawsuit claimed that the sale violated the Zoological's royal charter, called it "immoral" to sell rather than kill an animal that was too dangerous to keep, and threatened further action on grounds of cruelty. Chancery Court upheld the zoo's right to sell the elephant.

Barnum relished this publicity, which money could not buy and even he could not contrive, and fanned it as best he could. When the *Daily Telegraph* asked him to cable, collect, his price to release Jumbo, Barnum replied that with "fifty-one millions of Americans anxiously awaiting Jumbo's arrival," no price would suffice. He then went on at length, and at the *Telegraph*'s expense, about his circus's attractions, noting that his "invariable practice of exhibiting the best that money could procure makes Jumbo's presence here imperative." Barnum's agent provoked further outrage when he told

The Times that Americans handled raging elephants as the Indians did, by chaining them and cutting their rations, however that might offend delicate English sensibilities: "Your definition of cruelty is not quite the same as ours."

The issue spread to Parliament, where one member fretted that human passengers wouldn't be safe shipping with Jumbo. Barnum fretted over threats of poison or violence to ensure that Jumbo never left. One American in London reported that *l'affaire Jumbo* had exercised the public more than the last assassination attempt on Queen Victoria. Across the Atlantic, the *New York Herald* editorialized, "It seems a sad thought that a war between England and America may break out at any moment [over] the thoughtless sale of Jumbo . . . but we must have that elephant."

Just as it seemed a real crisis would erupt, Bartlett realized why the otherwise obedient Jumbo was refusing to go: his keeper, loath to lose his meal ticket, was secretly cueing him to stay put. Bartlett punctured Scott's scheme by announcing that he would send him away so Barnum's team could master Jumbo. "At the same time," Bartlett recounted, "I remarked to Scott that Mr. Barnum had made him a most liberal offer if he would accompany the animal to America." Scott begged for one more day to try to budge Jumbo. Wonder of wonders, Jumbo suddenly cooperated. He was rolled to the docks at midnight, seen off by a "rough crowd" singing "Rule Britannia," and borne peaceably to New York aboard the suitably exotic-sounding *Assyrian Monarch*.

A measure of national pride departed with him. Improbable as it seems, in the year that Thomas Edison gave New York electric power and Robert Koch uncovered the tuberculosis bacillus, the world's most advanced industrial powers were squabbling like old-time Thai and Burmese kings over an *elephant*. Contemporary observers could scarcely guess at the cultural and political subtext, but for the Brits who pleaded to keep Jumbo and the Yanks who craved to take him, the elephant may have evoked a gathering shift in national stature. Britain was at the peak of its might, the seat of the widest empire the world had known — and on the verge of a long decline. The United States was an emergent colossus, sprawling across a continent and looking across the oceans. Commercial energy surged through this rough-and-ready giant like testosterone through a musth bull; small wonder it wanted "the largest elephant ever seen."

Once landed in America, Jumbo seemed to grow even faster. He epitomized the expansive optimism of those fond years before the 1893 depression restored a measure of humility. No longer did immensity seem menacing. In place of Moby Dick and the rumored monsters of Jefferson's day, America welcomed a gentle giant who gave children rides and plucked sweets from their mothers' hands.

Jumbo was Barnum's last great hit, the star of an enormous four-ring circus, as adored by the stateside multitudes as he had been in London. After just two weeks at Madison Square Garden, Barnum claimed that Jumbo had more than repaid the thirty thousand dollars he'd spent to bring him to America. "Jumbomania" entered the language. As in England, "Jumbo" trinkets and fashions appeared almost instantly. Advertisers hitched their products to Jumbo's star, blazing a path for Tony the Tiger, Charlie the Tuna, and every other marketing mascot to come. "Jumbo" trading cards proliferated, sponsored by competing sewing-supply companies. "This is 'Jumbo,' but the biggest thing out this season is the 'Hartford' Sewing Machine," read one. "Jumbo must go, because drawn by Willimantic Thread," read another, with giant spools dragging the unhappy giant toward a soaring banner reading "America Ahead!" J. & P. Coats showed Jumbo bound like Gulliver with its thread. "What is Jumbo's mission to the United States?" one colorful card asked, and answered, "To introduce Kerr's Dollar brand of six cord." The best cards, from yet another threadmaker, showed a cartoon Jumbo arriving in English bowler; "Jumbo at the Bar" hoisting barrels of beer; "Jumbo Eating Candy"; Jumbo feeding "Castoria" to a constipated baby elephant; and "Jumbo Aesthetic," posing like Oscar Wilde and wearing a flower as big as the Ritz.

In three seasons, Jumbo earned a million dollars, and Barnum craved another elephant showstopper. He thought he'd found one at the fabled court of Siam: a "sacred" white elephant, the last novelty left for audiences used to cute calves and giant bulls. Barnum enlisted the new U.S. ambassador to Siam, promising ten thousand dollars if he secured the prize. Another agent, J. B. Gaylord, managed to secure a white elephant from a Thai nobleman and smuggle it to Burma, long a receiver of purloined Thai elephants. But it died while passing through Singapore, apparently poisoned by Siamese agents or Buddhist zealots determined to prevent its being profaned.

Gaylord next turned to Burma, whose King Thebaw readily sold him a white elephant named Toung Taloung. This prize was first shipped to Jumbo's old quarters at the London Zoo, where the trouble began. Bartlett refused to let the Burmese musicians and priests Barnum had brought along hold "ceremonies" at the zoo. And neither Barnum's retinue nor all his documents attesting to Toung Taloung's pedigree could assuage the public's disappointment at discovering that the ballyhooed "white elephant" was actually mottled gray, buff, and pink.

Once again the newspapers erupted in elephantine debate. Old Asia hands and native Asians, including Siam's ambassador and Bengal's former chief elephant catcher, insisted either that white elephants weren't really all that special, or that they were much too sacred to ever leave Burma and so this couldn't possibly be one. Toung Taloung himself showed a decidedly secular taste for rum; several distillers offered to satisfy it but were rebuffed.

In New York, the "white elephant" did not get a Jumbo's welcome. Barnum tried to stoke the publicity machine with a device he'd earlier used to promote Jenny Lind, "the Swedish Nightingale": a poetry contest, with a prize of five hundred dollars for the best ode to Toung Taloung. But none of the entries measured up, and Barnum's partners barred him from fattening the purse. The contest was, however, fertile field for parody, at which the *New York Times* took the prize. It offered the purported entries of the era's most celebrated poets — Swinburne, Tennyson, Whitman — including this scandalous suggestion attributed to John Greenleaf Whittier:

Not sacred thou because the Burmese priests
Bow down before thy tusks with solemn hush.
But sacred since thy dark and heathen hide
Was touched by our black brother's whitewash brush.

This jibe eerily forecast the biggest blow yet to Barnum's ele-
phant-hyping schemes, a bit of competitive humbuggery so brazen
it shocked even the master humbug. His arch-rival, the butcher
turned circus operator Adam Forepaugh, loaded an elephant in
Liverpool, named it "Light of Asia," and had it painted bright white
en route. A reporter soon uncovered the hoax with a wet sponge
and sold his scoop to Barnum. According to one circus veteran,
the secret also came out (and the whitewash came off) when Forepaugh's circus parade got rained on. Barnum fumed and fulmi-
nated in the papers and offered ten thousand dollars if "Old 4
Paws" and company would swear in court that their white elephant
was authentic. Finally, he even paraded his own whitewashed elephant, "Light of America," under a banner reading "The White
Fraud." But Forepaugh bluffed through, and crowds flocked just to
see what the fuss was about. Finally he ducked out by announcing
that his white elephant had died. "It was simply *un*-dyed!" Barnum
sniffed.

Toung Taloung himself lasted only a few more years. In 1887,
Barnum's winter quarters burned, killing four of his thirty-four elephants and nearly all the rest of his menagerie. America's first and
last official "white elephant" rushed back into the blazing barn
and, as Barnum coolly put it, "determinedly committed suicide."
Barnum took a practical view of such losses, even the chance of
losing his greatest star — which, given the hazards of travel and
Jumbo's doubtful health, could happen at any time.

Nevertheless, Jumbo's fits ceased; touring seemed to suit him.
The transatlantic ill will melted away. Letters poured in from Britain addressed to Jumbo, and Barnum began planning the triumphal return he had promised. As the British biographer W. P. Jolly
writes, "Jumbo became one of those living links which bind the

two countries quite independently of the best and worst efforts of politicians and diplomats."

But this link would never make it back to London alive. After the September 15, 1885, show, near the end of their third touring season, Scott was walking Jumbo and the "dwarf elephant" Tom Thumb back along the railroad tracks in St. Thomas, Ontario; they were the last to load. An unannounced freight train roared up behind. They were hemmed in. The train's cowcatcher hurled Tom Thumb down the bank, breaking his leg. Jumbo nearly got clear, but was hit from behind and thrown against the parked circus train. The collision derailed the freight train. Jumbo, with a fractured skull and massive internal injuries, lay down and died; Scott, who was thrown clear, collapsed in grief atop him.

Afterward, Barnum told the papers, "Long ago I learned that to those who mean right and try to do right . . . all apparent evils are blessings in disguise." Indeed, Barnum had thought out how to make the best of a disaster like this. The Natural Science Establishment in Rochester, New York, was waiting on call to preserve Jumbo's hide and bones should he die. Its director arrived before souvenir hunters could steal more than a few scraps of hair.

Jolly writes that one enterprising soul threw up a fence and charged five cents to see the corpse, while others sold "pots of Jumbo grease" as "a sovereign remedy for most common ailments." Barnum had bigger plans. Even as the world press gave Jumbo obituaries fit for major statesmen, Barnum inflated his legend further. Jumbo did not die in vain, Barnum claimed: he had turned back to save Tom Thumb and face the locomotive in a final charge. Barnum wisely omitted this spurious claim from his own autobiography, but others have passed it down as fact.

Barnum stretched facts in the most literal way. While Jumbo lived, Barnum's ads and flyers showed him standing sixteen to twenty feet tall. Now Smithsonian Institution secretary Spencer Baird, who craved to get Jumbo's remains, hinted that the skin could be stretched even larger than life, and Barnum passed the directive on to his taxidermists: "It will be a grand thing to take all

advantage possible in this direction! Let him show as a mountain."
When the job was done, Barnum threw a splashy press party featuring a special dish: an aspic containing some of Jumbo's ground-
up tusk. Distinguished guests got inscribed cross-sections of tusk.
Barnum sent skin and skeleton on a national "double Jumbo" tour,
accompanied by Alice, another elephant from London — whom the
press and Barnum dubbed "Jumbo's wife," though he'd shown no
interest in her — decked in widow's weeds.

In 1889, Barnum kept his promise and brought Jumbo back to
England, albeit posthumously, as the skin-and-bones centerpiece
of a three-circus spectacle. This last hurrah tour was a huge hit.
Gladstone, Queen Victoria, and the Prince of Wales paid their re-
spects.

Soon after returning to America, Barnum took ill. But before dying he sent Jumbo's skeleton to the world's greatest boneyard, the
Museum of Natural History in New York, and his mounted skin to
the Barnum Museum of Natural History at Tufts College. The
bones survive; the Tufts museum burned down in 1975. But Tufts's
athletic teams are still called the "Jumbos," and a peanut butter jar
filled with Jumbo's ashes, rescued from the embers, still stands as a
totem in the athletic director's office.

In 1954, sixty-nine years after Jumbo's death, his ghost rose again
in a bizarre story in Bridgeport, Connecticut's, *Sunday News*, "They
Shot Jumbo! World's Most Famous Elephant Was Murdered." It reported, at third hand, that Barnum had hired a gunman to dispatch
Jumbo at St. Thomas, then pinned the blame on the railroad.
Jumbo had to go because of elephantine digestive problems: he
"smelled up all the tents and exhibition halls in the U.S.," as he had
the London zoo before it fobbed him off. The story was preposterous, but Barnum might have appreciated this posthumous dose of
notoriety. It demonstrated the enduring fascination of this improbable idol, the long-legged, broken-tusked giant who was the toast of
two continents. Wait and see if John F. Kennedy's legend endures as
long, and if crackpots and hoaxers still propound new theories of
his death in 2036.

15

Topsy Was Framed

I wouldn't trust one of those damned hides. They're the trickiest beasts that live. They know more than all the rest of the animals put together. They'll fool you for a long time, by allowing you to think they love you, when they are just waiting for a chance to put you out of business. . . . I hate them, though I'm a trainer. I rule them by brutality and fear, not by kindness.

— "Mike" of Forepaugh's Circus to the *New York Times*,
    April 28, 1901

At 9:30 that morning Tusko left me, dead from a blood clot in his heart.

May we meet again some day, where the grass is tall and green, and there are no chains.

— George "Slim" Lewis, *Elephant Tramp*

As ELEPHANTS BEGAN touring Europe and America, and dispatches about them trickled in from India and Africa, newspapers marveled at their cleverness, till "sagacious" became a standard trope to describe them. In 1830, "Mademoiselle d'Jeck, the celebrated elephant" and "sagacious animal," busked around England "accompanied only by an attendant on a pony" and bowing graciously to astonished toll-keepers. In 1844 a member of Wombwell's Menagerie showed his "sagacity" when, teased by a man who proffered and then withheld an apple, he picked not only the apple but a silk handkerchief and some halfpence from the teaser's pocket and swallowed them. That same year, one "sagacious beast" forced the lock holding him at Chapel-field near Norfolk and took the country air; another escapee snuck into a Welsh hotel's wine cellar and was found dozing contentedly amid the emptied bottles; and a "sagacious animal" at Canterbury, tormented with spitballs by a musician, scooped up trumpeter and trumpet and dropped them to the ground. In 1839 in Paris and 1840 aboard the U.S.S. *President,* wise elephants picked up wayward toddlers and safely returned them to their parents.

But something changed in the 1840s — not overnight, nor universally, but unmistakably: elephants were less and less often deemed "sagacious" and more often dubbed "mad" or "vicious." Endearing pranks came to seem menacing. This shift reflected both growing familiarity with elephants and persistent ignorance of one of their natural traits. Owners came to realize that their male elephants might go "mad," but ignored or mistook the recurrent onset of musth. Asian mahouts might have set them straight, but it was easier to hire local fellows. And audiences that had "seen the elephant" grew jaded and demanding. No longer could a single modest-sized animal arouse their awe and extract their coins; the elephant had to do tricks never before seen, or troop out with a pack of its fellows, or be the biggest and "fiercest" on earth. The owners sought powerful, big-tusked males — and often regretted the choice.

One of the first warnings came out of Venice at the dawn of the nineteenth century, when a touring elephant acted up and paid with its life. Its mistress, not dissuaded, acquired another — a male — and toured the continent with him until 1820. Then, while departing Geneva in the middle of the night, "without any apparent cause, he fell into a paroxysm of anger," as a contemporary report put it, and chased off his keepers. He let his mistress lead him back into his enclosure, "but finding him still intractable, she desired that he might be killed as speedily as possible." Speedily didn't come easily. The elephant readily quaffed brandy laced with three ounces of prussic acid, the sovereign poison of the day, rested briefly, and rose unharmed. Arsenic oxide likewise failed. Finally a cannon was wheeled in and his huge head blown open.

The Venice and Geneva killings provoked the first complaints about the show operators' use of elephants, raising "doubts of the propriety of suffering these animals to be taken about the country without greater precaution," as America's *Saturday Magazine* observed. In India, the writer noted with unusual insight, an elephant "seized with a paroxysm" would be confined between two or three others till he calmed down. Menagerie operators might not have the herds to do that, but if they'd plumbed Asia's experience, they'd have realized that these "paroxysms" would pass.

A turning point came with the execution of Chuny (or Chunee, or Chuney), the Jumbo of his day, star of the popular menagerie at London's Exeter Change. In the winter of 1812, Chuny had a dubious career as the first elephant on the London stage, bearing a sultan in the pantomime "The Golden Fish." Some nights he panicked and charged offstage, terrified sultan and all, "rumping" the audience on the way. *The Times* wondered whether "a wooden elephant is not more consonant to the dignity of the stage."

But Chuny remained a London favorite, and the great tragedian Edmund Kean often visited him at the Change. He endured his cramped cell agreeably for seventeen years, save once when he attacked a keeper who had driven nails into the wall where he scratched his head and once when he was berthed in a side building overnight and tore out his chains, opened a double-locked door, and strode up the stairs to his own cell. Then, at twenty-two — the age of musth — Chuny began showing "strong symptoms of madness." Ordered to turn around, he fatally clipped his keeper, then stood trembling as though remorseful. In a reprise of medieval animal trials, an inquest ruled the death an accident and fined Chuny a token shilling.

The law might hold an elephant liable, but it would not protect him. Next spring, in 1826, Chuny's "madness" erupted again, and his owners condemned him to die. A volunteer squad assembled and, later joined by soldiers from a nearby barracks, fired off and on for two hours — at least 152 rounds by one account, 180 by another. With the first and second volleys Chuny charged, bending a cell bar and knocking the door off a hinge. The other animals screamed and roared in panic, and the menagerie's operators feared Chuny would collapse the floor, bringing them — lions, monkeys, and all — down onto the bazaar below. But he retreated and, *The Times* reported, "gave no other symptoms of passion or pain, than an occasional groan or kick against the side of the den." He was finally "despatched with a sword, which, after being secured upon the end of a rifle, was plunged into his neck."

In the immediate aftermath, the papers reported that various persons had taken steaks carved from Chuny's corpse; one published elephant meat recipes. The alleged steak eaters demanded retractions. But the mood soon turned somber. One correspondent called it "inhuman" to "place an elephant, or any beast, without a mate, and in a box bearing no greater proportion to his bulk than a coffin does to a corpse," and blamed Chuny's "madness" on this torment. An outpouring of sensational prints and sentimental literature followed, including a successful play, *Chunyklah; or, the Death of the Elephant at Exeter 'Change.* The popular versifier Thomas Hood, who'd written an ode to the living Chuny, now memorialized the dead "gentle giant." Ten years later, Charles Dickens recalled in the *Morning Chronicle:* "The death of the elephant was a great shock to us; we knew him well; and having enjoyed the honour of his intimate acquaintance for some years, felt grieved — deeply grieved — that in a paroxysm of insanity he should have so far forgotten all his estimable and companionable qualities as to exhibit a sanguinary desire to scrunch his faithful valet."

The shows, and the carnage, continued. In 1837, "Miss Djeck," apparently the same "sagacious animal" that amazed the toll-takers, was killed — in Geneva, like the 1820 victim, with a cannon — "because of her extreme violence." In 1848 the Liverpool zoo's Rajah, much admired for his "docility and intelligence," was shot by soldiers after showing evident symptoms of musth. In 1852, the "enormous" elephant that King Victor Emmanuel II kept at his Stupinigi summer home tossed a groom who'd ill-treated him and was slowly suffocated with carbonic acid.

Considering how often the early show elephants were mishandled, it's a wonder more brutish keepers and reckless fans weren't killed. *The Times* received the reports from local English papers: In 1860 a would-be wrestler grabbed the iron rod binding the tusks of one "monstrous elephant." It lifted him high and dropped him unhurt in the mud, "amidst the hearty laughter of the spectators." In 1861, Manchesterite Henry Crowther teased a menagerie elephant till it gored him in the hip. In 1864 a groom in a circus performing on Jersey struck a thirsty elephant that was reaching for water, then commanded "the docile animal" to perform tricks until it wearied, grabbed him around the waist, and squashed him "half dead" against the wall.

The cycle of human imposition, elephant reaction, and fatal retribution continued across the Atlantic, where the shows were bigger and drunks and bullies at least as common as in Europe. But American circuses and menageries still craved big tuskers, and a violent reputation could be a plus. "It was considered good advertising to play up any jungle beast as dangerous beyond words," writes the circus historian Marian Murray. And so Van Amburgh's early menagerie touted the "almost unparalleled reputation for viciousness" of its big tusker Hannibal, imported in 1824 and reputed to have killed seven people. When Hannibal got worked up and smashed the wagons, Van Amburgh's publicity boasted, the crew would pacify him by chaining him down and stabbing him with pitchforks.

In 1830, Hannibal and another bull, one of many named Columbus, fought a knockdown-dragout battle on a Louisiana road. After they were separated, Columbus ran amok, killing horses, cattle, and people till he was finally gunned down.

For most animal shows, punishment was a means of control; at Coney Island it became a form of showmanship. Not that the irrepressible creators of Coney's Luna Park, Frederick Thompson and Elmer Dundy, had anything against animals. Coney historians Oliver Pilat and Jo Ranson note that "Thompson became almost fool-

ishly fond of elephants." He decorated his office with elephant curios, including the feet and hide of one favorite that "had to be
killed." He claimed to have the world's largest elephant show; its
stars slid down a water chute and strode through an oriental pageant.

But the frenzy and foolery of America's first great theme park
held less appeal for its chute-shooting elephants than for the clerks
and seamstresses who flocked there to forget their workaday
drudgery. In the wee hours of June 3, 1904, one of Thompson's
shoot-the-chutes elephants, Fanny, wriggled loose and swam across
the Jersey Narrows, giving one rowboatful of fishermen the shock
of their lives. She stepped lightly ashore near New Dorp on Staten
Island, where, according to the *New York Times,* police charged
"the monster of the jungle" with vagrancy, locked her up, and let
gawkers in to see her.

That unplanned stunt got the sort of ink Luna Park's press
agents slavered after. Nevertheless, Pilat and Ranson note, the
bloom was off the elephants at Coney, where ever more lurid spectacles competed for attention. Even Mom the dancing elephant and
Charleston-dancing baby elephants drew only a nod. An elephant
could "swim in the surf one day without causing a ripple in the
metropolitan press." But Dundy and Thompson did manage to
score one last, particularly gruesome elephant publicity coup.

The victim and centerpiece of this stunt, Topsy, gets a bad rap
in both contemporary and later accounts, which call her "ill-
tempered," a "bad elephant," "a triple murderer," and "the vicious
Topsy." "It was clear," Ric Burns's documentary *Coney Island* darkly
intones. "Topsy had to go." What's clear is that, cranky though
Topsy was, the humans around her behaved much worse. In May
1902, when she was with the Forepaugh Circus in Brooklyn, a
hanger-on named Blount lurched up to her holding a glass of whiskey and a lit cigar. Elephants can enjoy a snort as well as the next
big-brained mammal, but circus elephants soon learned to fear
booze on a keeper's breath; it meant they were in for abuse. One
veteran circus handler claimed that they also like tobacco — but
not burning on their tongues.

Some say Blount fed Topsy a lit cigarette; the next day's *Times* reported he shook her trunk, threw sand in her face, and, when a keeper shouted a warning, replied, "Don't you worry about me, brother, I know what I'm doing." Moments later he was swinging in the air, then lying crushed in the sawdust. Topsy's handler told the *Times* that she was "more amiable than most elephants" and had never killed before, and blamed the misadventure on her being thirteenth in Forepaugh's lineup. Later, when she was condemned at Coney Island, Blount would be described as her keeper, and she would be credited with also having killed two hands in Texas — perhaps to justify what was done to her.

Forepaugh sold Topsy to Luna Park, where she worked at building the park and giving children rides. One October day her keeper, a bender-prone fellow called Whitey, took her on an impromptu stroll and wound up in the Coney Island jail; Topsy tried to break in and join him. At year's end, he took her strolling again, sicced her on an Italian construction crew, which scattered to the high timbers, and was only persuaded "by threats and partially by force" to call her off.

"From that time," the *Times* declared, "Topsy's life was doomed." But it was for Whitey's sins that she would die. Luna's owners fired him and then, realizing that Topsy would obey no one else, decided to hang her. They built a scaffold, but the SPCA intervened and forced them to undertake a more humane execution.

Enter the entrepreneurial inventor Thomas Edison, then promoting his direct current as the wave of the electric future. Edison sought to prove that his rivals' alternating current was excruciatingly dangerous by staging AC electrocutions of dogs and persuading New York State to adopt the AC electric chair. Modern accounts say that he made similar use of Topsy: How better to demonstrate alternating current's perils than by zapping a five-ton elephant? But the day after her death, the *Commercial Advertiser* reported that the wires that ran to her came from the park's Edison-built DC lighting system.

Whichever current she faced, Topsy balked on the way to the scaffold, which Edison's crew had turned into a jumbo electric chair. The managers frantically sent for Whitey, promising that all would be forgiven and he'd get twenty-five dollars if he'd come lead his former charge to her death. Whitey refused, so Edison's men lugged the apparatus over to Topsy. Among them was a cameraman, making hers the very rare elephant execution recorded on film. First Topsy was fed two carrots stuffed with 460 grains of potassium cyanide, but didn't topple. She remained calm as the electrodes were fitted to her feet.

The hand-cranked film's jerky, ritualistic movements make the event all the more eerie. A puff of smoke rises from Topsy's hide and her body seems to scrunch inward. After a second that seems an hour, she crumples and collapses.

Other spectacular executions followed, most notably the 1916 hanging of the Parks Circus's Big Mary from a railroad crane after she stomped an errant trainer. The haphazard elimination of dangerous elephants grew steadily more concerted. James A. Bailey, Barnum's hardheaded partner, who had consolidated the biggest shows — Barnum & Bailey, Sells and Floto, Forepaugh — played a central role in this change. Bailey, it was widely said, had ordered the quiet elimination of male elephants whenever they got out of hand. During Barnum & Bailey's 1903 European tour, five of its elephants were killed for, as the *New York Times* put it, "being 'ugly.'" Keepers aboard ship declared that their biggest elephant, Mandarin, who had reportedly killed three men, might become fish food if he continued to act up, since "Mr. Bailey would never allow such an ugly elephant to be led through the streets of New York." Mandarin never made it to port.

In 1929, just two weeks before Wall Street's Black Monday, what the veteran handler Slim Lewis calls "a turning point in the history of male elephants in America" arrived with the execution of the Al G. Barnes Circus's giant Black Diamond. In Corsicana, Texas, Diamond's handler, Jack Grady, consented to let a former "bull hand" who'd once worked Diamond take charge to impress his neighbors. That handler imprudently let a local woman pet the big guy. By one account she was no stranger: the last time the circus passed through, she had hired away Diamond's beloved longtime handler right in front of him. Suddenly he sent the handler flying, knocked her down, and impaled her with both tusks.

Ordinarily, Lewis recounts in his raucous memoir, when an elephant killed an itinerant bull hand, the circus could brush it off or hush it up. The killer might be sold to another show and renamed ("Jumbos," "Jennies," "Charlies," and even "Topsies" proliferated over the years) and the incident forgotten until it was repeated. But this was a local victim, a pillar of the community. A lynch mob tried to storm the bull car where Diamond huddled, now meek and mild; Grady socked one pistol-wielding vigilante. Orders came to eliminate this troublesome bull. Other workers suggested turning him loose, but Grady knew what carnage that could cause.

And so, at the next stop, Black Diamond was offered bags of poisoned peanuts and oranges. He sniffed and took only the untainted ones. Finally a firing squad of straight-shooting Texans formed. Lewis writes that it took them 170 rounds to bring down Black Diamond.

The news traveled the circus grapevine: The public would no longer tolerate elephant "incidents." Other owners began weeding out worrisome elephants, unloading them on zoos or, as Lewis puts it, "shooting them after the slightest misbehavior."

In 1872, Forepaugh's giant Romeo had died peacefully at a ripe age after killing five keepers, smashing untold numbers of gardens, buildings, and bridges in his various escapes, losing an eye, and getting pocked with scars from the bullets and hot irons used to "subdue" him. Still he was eulogized by the *Times:* "He had many friends in various parts of the country, and his death will no doubt be sincerely mourned, notwithstanding the recollection of his crimes."

But the world was now less awestruck and tolerant, and owners were less attached to their star tuskers. The Ben Wallace Circus poisoned Big Charley after he drowned his handler. Barnum & Bailey's Tip and Forepaugh's Tip II (whom Forepaugh had given to the Central Park Zoo) were dispatched after attacking handlers — and in Tip II's case reportedly killing five. In 1920, Sells-Floto's star Snyder, father of four babies, was deemed unmanageable when his trainer disappeared while he was in musth. Cyanide couldn't down him; bullets did.

Often the zoos and private citizens who received circus refugees did not keep them long. The Los Angeles zoo had its circus veteran Billy Sunday shot; the former circus mates Romano and Sammy met the same fate at the San Antonio and Detroit zoos. Lewis recounts that zoos would typically justify killing a big bull on grounds that "he eats too much." Thus the headline after Pittsburgh's zoo shot its ex-circus elephant: "Danny Eats Himself to Death; Zoo Forced to Kill Costly Elephant." The depression, which forced the closure or merger of nearly all the big road shows, gave circuses and zoos more incentive to eliminate their biggest eaters — and feed them to the big cats.

This wasn't "a sort of elephant genocide" conducted "mostly under cover of night and carefully hushed up afterward," as one writer recently declared. The killings were individual responses to particular "problems." Often they were public spectacles reported in newspapers and popular books such as Lewis's; some owners made a point of inviting the press. But the outcome was devastating. In 1952, *Billboard* took a census of U.S. elephants; of 264 total, 124 of them in circuses, only six were bulls. American elephants did not breed for forty-four years.

If bullets and poison didn't get the circus stars, flames often did. When Coney Island's Dreamland burned in 1911, one elephant, Little Hip, waited obediently in his open stall for his absent trainer to tell him to leave. And in 1944, 40 elephants and nearly 170 people perished when Ringling's Big Top went up like a match.

Nearly fifty years later, elephant handling would undergo another radical reassessment, following a widely bruited report that it was the most dangerous job in the country. No one asked how dangerous it was to be a working elephant.

16

Our Kind of Elephants

It was an elephant forty feet high, made of scaffolding covered with masonry, carrying on its back a tower resembling a house, originally painted green by some housepainter, now painted black by the sky, rain, and weather. In this deserted, open corner of the square, the broad front of the colossus, its trunk, its tusks, its tower, its enormous rump, its four legs like columns, created, at night, under a starry sky, a surprising and terrible silhouette. It was hard to know what it meant. It was a sort of symbol of the popular force.

— Victor Hugo, *Les Misérables*

It started when I was a prisoner of war in Germany. Every man needs something to dream about. That's where the elephants came in. They were the most different thing I could think about.

— Morel in Romain Gary, *The Roots of Heaven*

TAKING A CAB in Bangkok is usually a horror or, at best, a nuisance. The city sprawls, the traffic is hell, and the driver is likely a newcomer who can't read a map, doesn't know the city much better than you, and isn't any happier to be stuck in gridlock. Or he's a city sharpie determined to extract every last baht from gullible foreigners, a strategy that didn't end when Bangkok mandated meters; the drivers refuse to use them or take long, looping routes.

But there's one way to soften even the most jaded Bangkok cabbie: Tell him to take you to "Chang Tower." He'll puzzle over your pronunciation, then grin and nod: "Ahhh . . . *Chang* Tower!" He'll know exactly where this one of all Bangkok's endless new peripheral office buildings stands. And you'll both feel like you're out for a lark instead of slogging through another urban errand.

Chang means "elephant" in Thai, and the Elephant Tower affords rare relief in a skyline that's high on brash commercialism and low on grace and whimsy. It is in fact three ordinary gray towers — two legs and a trunk — capped by a horizontal section that forms the belly of the beast. Add giant portholes for eyes, protruding dark bays for ears, a notch distinguishing head and trunk, and yellow skybridge-like tusks and *voilà* — an elephant!

This beguilingly zoomorphic skyscraper is the brainchild of Arun Chaiseri, an engineering executive who decided to become a developer just when everyone else in Bangkok did, in the booming early '90s. Though he's also president of Friends of the Asian Elephant, the idea of Chang Tower came to Chaiseri by serendipity. He owned a long, skinny parcel, and setback rules severely limited what he could build on it. His architect suggested boosting square footage with a joined, M-shaped trio of towers. "I looked at the sketch," Chaiseri recalled as we chatted in his Chang Tower office. "And I thought of an elephant."

That inspiration was a natural outgrowth of a private passion he'd nurtured for a decade, ever since he got stranded in Hong Kong at the end of a business trip. "It was Easter Sunday, and the plane was fully booked. I was stuck for five days, with nothing to do. But I like animals, so I started buying figures of them — elephants, turtles, owls." The elephants especially delighted him, and everywhere he traveled he bought more. "Even Germany, Denmark, Belgium — I discovered that *everyone* makes elephants. Right now I have about two thousand in my home office, from peanut-size to life-size." (Dozens more line one wall at Chang Tower.) "I even bought a piece of land — about two hundred acres — near Phetchabun in northern Thailand because I saw a stone there that reminded me of an elephant. I will build a park there, planted with all the flowers and trees that grow in Thailand, and give it to the public."

Already he's given that public its favorite skyline punctuation. Making his tower an elephant may also have paid off; the overbuilt Bangkok market crashed just before he finished it, leaving many developers holding unfinished hulks. But Chang Tower still drew tenants, some of whom said they were attracted by the elephant form; his cousin was hoping to strike the same gold by building a beer hall "shaped like a real elephant." Nevertheless, Chaiseri insisted he didn't share the traditional belief that the animal brings good luck: "I just like the elephant."

This urbane, globe-trotting engineer had unwittingly reenacted two ancient and enduring impulses: the urge to possess elephants in miniature form, and to re-create them larger than life. The elephant-collecting bug seizes otherwise sensible people all around the world. On a random sampling, the eBay auction site offered 6,253 "elephant" items — carved in wood, blown in glass, hung on chains, contrived a thousand different ways. "Elephants for collectors," proclaimed one seller; "LOVE ELEPHANTS WOW WOW" another. Elephant figurines are considered lucky in Brazil, so long as their trunks point up and their backs point to the door, as though they are entering the house. In Colombia, Seattle transplant Marta Pinto-Llorca recalls, "everyone was collecting elephants for good luck. You were supposed to set them with the tail pointing out. And they were supposed to be given or stolen, not bought."

Stealing aside, elephants were popular charms in depression-era America, when people were looking for luck. One writer traces the West's lucky elephants back to the Asian reverence for living elephants and to the auspicious Ganesha. I suspect that elephant images beckon especially to those who, like Chaiseri in Hong Kong or Romain Gary's guerrilla elephant protector Morel in prison, feel trapped by mundane circumstances and crave a larger sense of life.

Collecting curios is one thing; what type of person feels compelled to build elephants? For thousands of years, wherever elephants were known, they have been replicated, often large as life and sometimes much larger, in stone, wood, metal, paint, and cement. Among the oldest and most impressive representations are the stone elephants that run by the score and hundred, hypnotic in their repetition, along and around Asia's great temples and palaces, from the ancient Sri Lankan capital of Anuradhapura to Cambodia's Angkor Wat. The motive behind these "elephant walks" and elephant walls was devotional, invoking the elephant's spiritual power to protect and support the edifices above them. But emperors, real estate developers, and their ilk also build elephants for their own glory, appropriating the animal's stature and grandeur to themselves. Life-size elephants stand sentinel at Delhi Gate, over the Ming imperial tombs, and along a Copenhagen boulevard. One stone giant rules Bombay's Elephanta Island; another, in Calcutta, honors Prince Albert. One baroque elephant obelisk, designed by Bernini, caps Rome's Piazza della Minerva; another parts the traffic in Catania, Sicily.

Uncounted elephant finials, door knockers, capstones, and murals grace every sort of Indian shelter, from huts to palaces. No elephants now roam the northwestern state of Rajasthan, but it is the heartland of elephant decoration. Peasants paint simple elephants on their mud walls to ingratiate the wealth-giving goddess Lakshmi. Huge carved elephants guard the Elephant Gate at the Great Palace at Bundi and, facing the four directions as in the Hindu myth, cap the ornate pillars of the palace's Courtyard of Learning.

Charles François Robart tried to go one better when he designed "L'Éléphant Triomphale," an elephant-shaped palace honoring Louis XV, to stand at the center of Paris. But it remained unbuilt when the Revolution erupted, and Paris got Napoleon's Arc de Triomphe instead.

Elephant monumentalism reached its populist apotheosis in America's Gilded Age, under the promotional hand of a Philadelphia inventor, engineer, and land speculator named James V. Lafferty, Jr. In the early 1880s, Lafferty set out to turn a stretch of marshy beachfront into "South Atlantic City," but it was cut off from the real Atlantic City by a tidal creek. Lafferty, the *Hartford Courant* and *New York Times* noted, had "an elephant [as in white] on his hands."

Rather than despairing, Lafferty took the hint and built one of the first and most audacious of America's totemic roadside attractions. As local historian William McMahon notes, Lafferty even obtained a patent for "a building in the form of an animal, the body of which is floored and divided into rooms." Dubbed Lucy despite its male form, it stood sixty-five feet high at the howdah, with a painted tin skin over an elaborately carpentered frame. The *Courant* reported that Lucy cost a lavish twenty-five thousand dollars, "not because the material was expensive, but because the workmen had not built elephants" before. Lafferty claimed he spent thirty-eight thousand. Inside, she held a real estate office and a restaurant.

Lucy evidently boosted South Atlantic City enough to encourage Lafferty to build two more beachside tin elephants in 1884: the forty-foot "Light of Asia" at South Cape May, New Jersey, and the 122-foot giant promoted as "The Colossus of Architecture," but simply called "the Elephant," at Coney Island, New York — the perfect home for such a grand folly. Lafferty's timing was also perfect: two years after Barnum ignited "Jumbomania" across America, and two years before the Statue of Liberty became America's designated colossal greeter (though New York–bound passengers would still see Lafferty's Elephant first). Boardwalkers could view a diorama in one of its front legs or shop at a cigar store in the other. They could tramp up the circular staircase in one hind leg and down the other, pausing to view New York and New Jersey through the telescopes in the crowning howdah. Or they could engage one of the Colossus's thirty-one hotel rooms.

Standing smack in the middle of Coney's booming streetwalker trade, the Elephant was not a hotel for family custom or visiting royalty. Here, in what was probably the world's largest monument of simulated flesh, streetwalkers and their johns could consummate deals in chambers named after their sites in the animal's anatomy: the Throat Room, Shoulder Room, Thigh Room. "Seeing the elephant" was already a ubiquitous and versatile catchphrase in nineteenth-century America, usually meaning to see the world (and pay the price). Now it took on new meaning, as vaudeville comics snickered and boardwalk sirens cooed, "Hey, big fella, have you *seen the Elephant* yet?"

But novelty faded fast at Coney Island, and new amusement palaces soon overtook Lafferty's "Elephantine Colossus." After just two years it burned down — a frequent fate for Coney's attractions, as for circuses with living elephants. At Cape May, Lafferty's more modest Light of Asia lingered a few years longer. The receipts from the concession stand in its trunk never recouped its costs, and in 1900, two years after James Lafferty died, it was torn down.

But the tusker named Lucy hung on against all odds as a tourist attraction in South Atlantic City. One of the notables who paid the ten-cent charge to climb to her howdah was a young lawyer named Woodrow Wilson, who was so delighted, McMahon notes in *The Story of Lucy the Elephant,* that he tipped the guide a dollar — and repeated the climb years later as president of the United States.

A mini–Coney Island sprouted around Lucy. Her second owners acquired the onion-domed Turkish Pavilion from Philadelphia's Centennial Exposition, moved it next door, renamed a neighboring inn the Elephant Hotel, and made Lucy a summer home. But the great storm of 1903 nearly wrecked her, and she was moved upland and converted to a tavern; rowdy patrons set off a fire that nearly burned her down. Restored again, she lost her howdah in another storm. In 1969, Lucy's owners donated her, battered but standing, to the City of Margate (as South Atlantic City is now named), which had a vacant block available near the beach; Lucy might again become the beachfront attraction she was built to be. Volunteers raised money, schoolchildren held bake sales, architects pronounced Lucy sound, and she was jacked up and ready to roll. Then neighboring developers secured a last-minute injunction against the move, on grounds that an elephant next door would lower their property values. A judge tossed out the injunction in a dramatic weekend hearing, and Lucy paraded to her new home, mobbed by jubilant fans — an Americana version of India's elephant processions.

Today, restored to a shine, with historical displays inside and a new howdah on top, Lucy stands proud and anachronistic over the Jersey shore, supported entirely by donations, tours, and gift shop sales. As her publicity boasts, she's "the biggest elephant in the world" — unless you count the more abstract Chang Tower, and until a latter-day James Lafferty gets the bug and builds an even bigger one.

Parallel to elephant building runs another cultural current, from ancient religious art to modern popular culture: the use of elephants as vessels and standard-bearers for societies' most cherished ideas. Perhaps the animal's sheer size inspires people to project so many meanings and roles onto it. Like a roadside barn emblazoned with "Chew Mail Pouch," an elephant affords an irresistibly large canvas; indeed, the old touring circuses rented their elephants as walking billboards when they paraded into town. The meanings change, but the impulse endures.

To medieval Europeans, the elephant embodied all the spiritual virtues, but their more secular descendants had other notions to project. The raging, untameable tusker became a favorite trope of the industrial-colonial era and the centerpiece of the white hunter's Big Five trophy collection. Hemingway exalted this image; George Orwell turned it on its head in "Shooting an Elephant," his reminiscence of an unhappy career as a colonial policeman in Burma. There, to uphold his authority, Orwell had to slaughter an elephant that had already recovered from a musth-induced fit: "At that moment . . . I first grasped the hollowness, the futility of the white man's dominion in the East."

Hollywood magnified the rogue killer into the raging herd, a merciless natural juggernaut. In the 1927 quasi-documentary film *Chang*, Merian C. Cooper and Ernest Schoedsack honed the formula they would employ in *King Kong* and set the model for *Godzilla, Jurassic Park,* and all the other rampaging-creature features to come. In *Chang*, the stampeding elephants, the nemeses of the hard-working Thai farmers, fill the place of the human savages attacking European heroes in the usual exotic adventure. The farmers get justice and vindicate their species's supremacy by corralling the elephants, whom they will tame and transform into useful partners.

As the twentieth century progressed and elephants were decimated in the wild, their image in the movies and the wider culture was likewise transformed. They became sentimentalized pets — as in *Billy Rose's Jumbo* and Walt Disney's *Dumbo* — or selfless benefactors, like the cavalry that rescues Tarzan, the noble white savage, from native hordes and wicked white hunters. Conservation consciousness penetrated the formula. The Ceylonese elephants in the 1954 *Elephant Walk* are merely reclaiming their ancient migration route when they smash Peter Finch's tea estate and rescue him and Elizabeth Taylor from its morbid thrall. By 1958, when Gary's *Roots of Heaven* was filmed, the animals' image had come full circle: the heroes now risked their lives to rescue Africa's beleaguered elephants from their greedy fellow humans.

This evolution mirrors the outside world's changing views of the lands that elephants come from. In colonialism's heyday, elephants were the living image of savage, perilous lands begging to be conquered. Once the European powers consolidated their conquests, they viewed their colonies and elephants as prize possessions, wards to be schooled and civilized. And as they relinquished their colonies, they came to see elephants as likewise meriting freedom to live their own lives. And so you get the heartwarming spectacle of a shiftless fellow inheriting an elephant and walking it across America to return it to Thailand in the 1996 *Larger Than Life*.

These evolving attitudes are tellingly, if unwittingly, charted in some of the most widely cherished of all children's books, the thirty Babar tales written and drawn by Jean de Brunhoff and his son Laurent. Several latter-day critics have noted how closely Babar's saga reprises the colonial experience, as viewed through the rosy lens of the French *mission civilatrice*. What they don't note is how it also illuminates the attitudes of its time toward animals generally and elephants especially.

Certainly the Brunhoffs viewed the elephants sympathetically. *Père* Jean's first book, the 1931 *Story of Babar the Little Elephant,* begins with the baby Babar frolicking with his adoring mother in a tropical Eden. The elephants are still naked and quadrupedal, though humanoid touches have crept in: Mom swings Babar in a hammock strung between palm trees. Man first appears as a "wicked hunter" who kills Babar's mother. After the initial tears, this proves a blessing for the hero. He flees, and three days later (in one of the matter-of-fact marvels that give the books their charm) comes upon a perfect French city. Envying the city dwellers' "fine clothes," he promptly meets "a very rich Old Lady who has always been fond of little elephants" (Kenya's Samburu call elephants "old women"), who "understands right away that he is longing for a fine suit" and gives him her purse.

No more wicked hunters; Europeans henceforth appear as teachers, shopkeepers, and other benign, or at least well-intentioned, figures — even the ship's captain who rescues the stranded Babar and Céleste in *Travels of Babar* and gives them to a circus. The citizens of Célesteville, the city Babar founds after becoming king, face natural perils but never the ivory hunters who supplied the rich countries that also consumed Babar books.

Babar reverses Burroughs's Tarzan, the English lord who becomes an African ape: The African elephant becomes a French bourgeois and a storybook king. The land he returns to is unpopulated until he teaches his fellow elephants to cease being elephants and become people. When black Africans finally appear in the later *Travels of Babar* and *Babar's Picnic,* they are stereotypical "cannibals" in feather skirts and clownish blackface who dance, wave spears, fear the rain, and either try to eat the elephants or worship them as gods.

Watchdogs of political, racial, gender, and, if you will, species bias can find a feast of horrors in the *Babar* books. One librarian refused to read them at story hour because "Babar is a gigolo" — a teenager kept by a rich old lady. Ariel Dorfman argues that the tales present "the fulfillment of the dominant countries' colonial dream"; civilization transforms the benighted lands and animals "without interrupting their postcard existence." France finds the native proxy it always longed for, who happens to be an elephant.

The folklorist Donald J. Cosentino argues that the joke is really on colonialism and its champion, Babar, who mirrors "the farcical elephant king from the African trickster tradition." That figure, an effigy for human chiefs, is "big, dumb, and arrogant," a ready dupe for the hare, cock, and tortoise — commoners who make up for weakness with wits. Trouble is, Babar's the one who always wins by his wits. But whichever way the satire cuts, there is something irresistible and unspoilable about the dignified, earnest elephant dad in his proper green suit, puffing his pipe and making good citizens out of all creatures save a few rebellious rhinos.

Only an elephant could pull this off; a chimpanzee Babar would seem clownish or grotesque. As Jean de Brunhoff amplified the Babar mystique, he tapped into or chanced to evoke much older elephant myths. King Babar is visited by dark dreams of all the ills — Fear, Despair, Laziness, and so on — that threaten his City in the Forest. But a winged and trunked host of elephant angels — Work, Joy, Goodness, Love — chases the demons away, uncannily recalling both the early Christian view of elephants embodying all virtues and the mighty winged elephants of Hindu lore.

After Babar, humanized elephants proliferated in children's tales. The hero of the British *Olifant* books is a cheery, gregarious bumbler. Horton (who Hears a Who and Hatches the Egg) has the usual goofy Dr. Seuss look, but is steadfast, loyal, and nurturing — maternal, in short, though male. Disney's flap-eared flying Dumbo looks like the ultimate anti-elephant and penultimate example of Disney kitsch, but he too recalls India's winged elephants, and *Dumbo*'s depiction of circus cruelties is surprisingly sharp.

In 1942, one year after *Dumbo* soared and two years after Disney's *Fantasia* lent a certain respectability to large animals in tutus, Ringling Brothers boss John Ringling North realized a dream he'd long cherished: an elephant ballet. To create it, North recruited the great choreographer George Balanchine, who was then on the outs with New York's cultural powers and taking work where he found it. Why not? Balanchine asked a reporter. "Elephants are no harder to work with than ballerinas." He asked Igor Stravinsky, who also needed the money, to write the music. Stravinsky later recalled asking Balanchine how old the elephants would be. "Very young," replied Balanchine. "All right," said Stravinsky. "If they are very young elephants, I will do it."

Circus Polka debuted April 9, 1942, in Madison Square Garden, featuring Ringling's star elephant, Modoc, as "première ballerina," plus "Fifty Elephants and Fifty Beautiful Girls." Vera Zorina, Balanchine's own prima ballerina and wife, rode in terror atop Modoc, but didn't get the same billing. As might have been expected, Stravinsky's dissonant score, with scarcely a hint of polka meter, drove the elephants and circus band to near panic. Critic George Brinton Beal wrote that the elephants, who stepped readily to straightforward waltzes and marches, "flapped their ears in pain at the Stravinsky music. . . . Aside from the dancing of old Modoc, [it] was not a pretty sight." The starlets riding the elephants were bruised and frazzled from repeated falls. Trainers feared a stampede, and cheered when *Circus Polka* was retired after one season. Still the piece ended grandly, with Modoc and Zorina kneeling in the sawdust and touching foreheads. Stravinsky recounted that he later shook the foot of Bessie, the "young elephant" to whom he dedicated the score.

Not all the hoopla spun from elephants has been as elevated as a Balanchine ballet. But some has proven more enduring — and none more so than the Republican Party's elephant mascot. Its origin is, however, less exalted than some partisans might like to think. In 1874, the cartoonist Thomas Nast, playing off a hoax report of menagerie escapees roaming Central Park, portrayed the Republican vote as a panicked elephant fleeing a Democratic jackass wrapped in a lion's skin.

Other cartoonists reprised Nast's graphic jab, and the Grand Old Party proudly appropriated the emblem. Today the Republican elephant appears much more often than the Democratic donkey — more often, perhaps, than any other American mascot save Mickey Mouse and the national eagle. The political scholar Clinton Rossiter noted the aptness of "the majestic but ponderous Elephant —

the symbol of respectable Republicans." Adlai Stevenson offered further reasons why the elephant is a Republican: it "has a thick skin, a head full of ivory, and as everyone who has seen a circus parade knows, proceeds best by grasping the tail of its predecessor."

In the early 1900s, baseball's Philadelphia Athletics followed the Republicans in defiantly appropriating an elephant jab as an emblem after a rival manager sneered that new teams like the Athletics were costly "white elephants." But in the 1960s a brash new owner, Charlie Finley, substituted a jackass-like mule.

No longer did elephants exemplify all virtues; now they represented failings ranging from Republican hubris and hysteria to "white elephant" superfluity and the inebriation of seeing pink (or, in Britain, green) elephants. Still, for twentieth-century promoters as for triumphant Romans, nothing snagged the public's attention like elephants, especially in unexpected settings. Elephants were central to one of the greatest triumphs of hype: turning a remote, marshy sandbar into today's Miami Beach. In 1917, car-tycoon-turned-developer Carl Fisher's dream of an American Riviera was collapsing when a circus friend offered him a pet elephant. "I am going to get a lot of publicity out of him too," Fisher replied. "I am going to get a million dollars worth of advertising out of this elephant." Stealing a page from Barnum, Fisher had his elephant (named Carl II) haul rocks and mow the golf course whenever cameras were near. He acquired another and posed both with curvy models wearing the skimpiest bathing suits. The world finally noticed Miami Beach.

And the floodgates were open. The most diligent student of elephants in advertising is Sarasota businessman Wayne Hepburn, who has collected more than two hundred examples hawking everything from cornflakes, peanut butter, and toilet paper to credit cards and gasoline additives. According to Hepburn, elephants appear much more often in ads than any other wild animal, and on more greeting cards than any critters save the three sentimental standbys — cats, dogs, and teddy bears.

Even high-tech companies exploit elephant motifs: Adobe Image

Club showed an elephant in a little red wagon, and Hewlett Packard one on a bicycle, to demonstrate their products' reproduction quality. Their reputation for outsized appetite and indulgence makes elephants natural mascots for more sybaritic enterprises. Kenya's Tusker Lager, Thailand's Chang Beer, and America's Big Time Brewery all use elephant icons. Kathmandu's Eden Hashish Centre shows a roly-poly baby Ganesha. Street dealers have called heroin "elephant," angel dust "elephant tranquilizer," and crack cocaine "jumbo." Australians reportedly call breakfast cereal "elephant's dandruff." Elephants majestic and whimsical have graced Japanese, Indian, and Soviet matchboxes and French and British cigarette packs. A looming pink neon elephant with a heart spurting from his trunk marks Theatre Casa Rosso, Amsterdam's biggest sex club. The Wham-O executives who gave the world Frisbees and Hula Hoops gave their clients live elephants as practical jokes.

How does all this commercial use affect our views of the actual animals? In much the same way, I suspect, as humanized elephants in children's books and other popular art forms. They elicit delight and may keep elephants in view, after a fashion. But they tend to distract us from the animals' natural splendor and unnatural peril. And they may encourage a pernicious, unspoken complacency: Why should we fret about torment and extermination when we see so many happy elephants on the screens and billboards around us?

The animal is ripped from its living context, from life itself. Real elephants are complicated, troublesome creatures who demand space and freedom and refuse to abide by our fond stereotypes. Like martyred saints, dead rock stars, and vanished dinosaurs, they might be loved even more if they vanished from the earth, becoming safe figures of computer-generated spectacle and cozy emblems of nature's power and terror.

SEEING PINK ELEPHANTS: Drunk.

— Richard A. Spears, *The Slang and Jargon of Drugs and Drink*

V. Endings

17

The Elephant Island

Elephants are so numerous here that it is impossible to travel without people and drums. Also there are many cases when they, on meeting this or that person, have done great harm and killed them.

— François Valentijn, *Oud en Nieuw Oost-Indiën* (1674)

It is absolutely necessary for the comfort of the inhabitants and the prosperity of agriculture that the extirpation of these animals should be continued.

—The Reverend James Cordiner, *A Description of Ceylon* (1807)

ELEPHANT KITSCH is not confined to rich northern countries that see the living animals only in zoos and circuses. Nowhere save Thailand are elephants so widely splashed — across ads, signs, temples, and ballots — as in Sri Lanka. Stroll through sweltering Colombo and you'll see billboards for "Elephant Asbestos Cement" and the ubiquitous "Elephant House" ice cream and soda — just the thing to wash down one of the chocolate bars with the trumpeting tusker on the wrapper. You'll see dignified elephant heads guarding the main park's central Buddha and not-so-dignified pink and blue elephant cabs whirring in a nearby amusement park. Voters can mark the green elephant on their ballots, the symbol of the United Nationalist Party, which could advise its Republican counterparts on how to make the most of a mascot: "*The Elephant*

. . . is strong enough even to haul a nation out of a rut," campaign ads read. *"Place your trust in the Elephant. He will never let you down."*

You could mail a letter with the stamp honoring one illustrious elephant, Raja the Maligawa Tusker, for fifty-one years chief elephant of the great Temple of the Tooth in the old royal capital of Kandy and ceremonial bearer of Sinhalese Buddhism's holiest relic, a tooth of the Buddha narrowly rescued from Portuguese despoilers. In life, Raja was declared a national treasure, like Kenya's Ahmed and Nepal's Tula Hatti. In death he received a state funeral and his own museum beside the temple. Unlike every other museum I visited in five countries, the Tusker Raja Museum was packed, almost entirely with Sri Lankans.

Its centerpiece is Raja himself, standing proud and stuffed amidst his glittering robes and regalia — and dyed a mottled black that does not match his photos. Those photos hang by the score, neatly captioned and chronologically ordered: Raja leading peraheras, gracing ceremonies, greeting fans and dignitaries, surrounded by mourners who still throng to touch him. The gallery is bracketed by oversized photos of Sri Lankan presidents with Raja; they touch his trunk reverently, like pilgrims kissing the pope's ring.

The verdant, West Virginia–sized island of Lanka is to elephants what Venice's Piazza San Marco is to pigeons: their legendary heartland. Authorities as far away as Rome celebrated Lankan elephants as, in Aelian's words, "more powerful and bigger than those of the mainland" and "in every way" more clever. Distant potentates sought them for their courts and armies, and they became a valuable export.

Two centuries ago, when the British wrested Ceylon, as they called it, from Holland and the Kandy kings, it had an estimated 1.75 million human inhabitants and 20,000-plus elephants. Determined to turn lush upland habitat into plantations, the colonizers saw the elephants as obstructions with incidental export value. They designated them vermin and paid five- and ten-shilling bounties on 5,500 in the 1840s and '50s alone. The supreme exterminator, Major Thomas Rogers, killed 1,400 before being struck by lightning, a fate some Lankans saw as divine retribution. Thousands more were exported, to log in Burma and pirouette in American and European circuses.

When Ceylon gained independence in 1948, it had just 6 million people — plus high literacy, nature-venerating religious traditions, extensive forests, a two-thousand-year-old tradition of wildlife and forest protection, and a vigorous homegrown conservation movement. It was proclaimed a tropical Eden, the jewel in the crown of Third World conservation.

"This country had the perfect start," muses elderly Swiss-born Thilo Hoffmann, the dean of Sri Lankan environmentalism, who twenty-five years later led the fight to save the island's last intact rain forest. Now Hoffmann is deeply disillusioned. Population growth, cash crop globalization, and civil war have fractured and fragmented that wild base. The island now has nearly 20 million people and by most estimates three to four thousand elephants. Ivory poaching is the one modern bane that doesn't threaten Lankan elephants because, thanks to either centuries of hunting or a genetic fluke, few have tusks. Instead they get caught in the minefields and crossfire of a war centered on the strategic isthmus named Elephant Pass. Government forces and the Liberation Tigers of Tamil Elam have both given orders to spare elephants, and once joined in a cease-fire so the Red Cross could rescue an orphaned baby animal. But in Lanka's arid northeast, soldiers and Tigers alike fight the elephants for scarce water; one Tiger troop that repeatedly tried to drive off the thirsty rivals finally gave up and shot them. "There's been a lot of poaching by government troops and LTTE," says environmental attorney Lalanath de Silva. "Troops bulldoze right through national parks to create buffer zones and clear views between them. There's no management at all in those areas. Elephants fall into abandoned trenches and die, and also into irrigation canals."

But war is not the animals' worst enemy. More are displaced, harassed, and shot by farmers determined to grow crops where they are determined to forage. Elephants have the misfortune of favoring the same habitat as humans: "Rice paddy is perfect elephant feed," laments the biologist Sareth Kotagama, ex-director of the nation's Department of Wildlife Conservation. "You can't expect them not to go in a candy store." And you can't expect people to yield so elephants can wander freely. "A charismatic species is charismatic for us who are trying to raise the flag, not to the man who is being attacked by it. I blame conservationists for the current state of things. They didn't see the world as it is now."

It isn't so much elephant actions as human perceptions that have changed, explains Kotagama, who grew up amidst elephants on the island's wilder east side. Before, elephant attacks were another thing to endure, like droughts and typhoons. Each took its share of the crop, and peasants didn't fret as long as they had enough left to eat — as they almost always did in such a fertile land. But the usual global influences — trade, television, consumerism — have bred new expectations and resentments. "Today, it's cash," sighs Kotagama. "If an elephant knocks over your coconut tree, you're not seeing the coconut, you're thinking about all the rupees you lost.

"The older people are more complacent, more willing to compromise. The younger people are very angry at the elephants." Social change also saps cohesion and cooperation. Before, farmers joined in guarding their crops. "Now you're looking at a different kind of community," says Kotagama. When the government opened the massive Mahaweli reclamation project in east-central Sri Lanka, he recounts, each settler had to stand guard one or two nights each month. "It worked the first month," he says. "Then they didn't show up. The farmers in the back, who were buffered by the ones in front, didn't care about the elephants."

When their own crops are threatened, farmers fight back with a cruel and motley arsenal. They shoot elephants with ancient shotguns and homemade trap guns, throw acid in their faces, and set out sharpened stakes, poisoned nails, and live electric wires. They inject pumpkins with poison and stuff coconuts with ash and kerosene to make napalm-like bombs. In 2000 they killed 145 elephants and maimed or blinded many more. As a result, most of the 200-

plus "problem" elephants the Wildlife Conservation Department has relocated were already peppered with buckshot. This usually induces only painful sores and vengeful determination, unless it hits the eyes; the grandest-looking tusker at the national Pinnawela Elephant Orphanage hunches alone in his corral, shying from other bulls' attacks, entirely blind.

Nandana Atapattu, the veterinarian who for many years spearheaded these relocations, recalls removing a record nine pounds of shot from one almost entirely blinded rogue in 1996. Terrified locals called him Molekanna — "Brain Eater" — and claimed that he feasted on human flesh. "I never believed it. Elephants are not carnivores!" Atapattu exclaims. Then he found Brain Eater's seventeenth victim, a schoolteacher, headless — and "bundles of human hair" in his dung. "My explanation," says Atapattu, "is Molekanna was so harassed and angry, he didn't just kill, he took the head in his mouth and accidentally swallowed hair. After that, he may have done it purposefully." The rangers treated Brain Eater's wounds, restored his vision, and released him in a national park. Atapattu says he's been accepted into a herd and become a model elephant citizen and breeder, keeping his trunk clean and doing his bit for the shrinking gene pool.

It's an old script, reenacted in occupied lands from Oklahoma to Palestine. First, the invaders take the good land; then, when the bad lands prove useful, they take those too. In Ceylon, the British took the lush uplands for coffee, rubber, and tea plantations, pushing the elephants into the dry lowlands. Then independent Sri Lanka, backed by the usual international lenders, moved on those lowlands. A web of national parks and reserves was supposed to assure the elephants ample range and, equally important, migration corridors. But this network was never completed, and everyone from tobacco farmers to brick makers squatted in the corridors.

Push came to shove in the early 1980s, when the government joined with Britain's Booker Agriculture International to convert twenty thousand acres of prime corridor and habitat to sugar cane. The prospectus for their Pelwatte Sugar Company acknowledged "wandering elephants" as a business risk. Sure enough, the evicted elephants braved watchmen and electric fences to come back, eat cane, and haunt surrounding villages. In 1996, with yells and taunts and jumbo-sized firecrackers, rangers drove the 150 Pelwatte elephants to nearby Yala National Park, where tourists would flock to see them. With no deaths, the operation seemed a stunning success. But the elephants soon returned again and, finding their corridors blocked by illegal encroachers, drifted up into the tea country. Somewhere between eight and fourteen — all male, like most crop raiders; females are more cautious and easily discouraged — had worked the remote Koslanda district for six years. They did not eat the tea plants, nor the eucalyptus and Caribbean pine that unthinking foresters had planted in stately, sterile, fire- and erosion-prone groves along the slopes. But they raided the gardens that the tea pickers planted around their homes and the rice and toddy-palm wine they stored inside. I saw one newly patched tin roof and adobe wall that a pantry raider had smashed in.

The Koslanda Eight had killed five people, three of whom had stumbled, drunk, into elephants on the road at night. The lone female victim was a rubber tapper trudging to the groves at dawn.

And so the national elephant cops were heading out again. I stopped by the Wildlife Conservation Department offices to see if I might tag along. All right, Atapattu said briskly, if I could find his team out in the hills (he didn't know where they'd be staying), provide my own lodging and transportation, and get a release from the U.S. Embassy absolving him and his department of any liability should a charging elephant or some other disaster overtake me. But the American consul could only notarize a release I wrote myself. He warned me to be careful out there.

On the way to Koslanda, I stopped off to visit another famous giant named Rajah (Sri Lanka's biggest elephants are all Rajas and Rajahs) who had become a national *cause célèbre* and a legal trailblazer. Rajah had been a star of the daily circus-style elephant show at the national Dehiwala Zoo. Then one day he stepped out of line on the way to the stage, swatted his mahout, and queued back up as though nothing had happened. He seemed to be settling an old score, not rebelling, and his defenders claimed that the mahout drank and abused him. But he was sacked from the show and chained for a year and a half, until he snagged and killed another handler.

Dehiwala's director, Senarath Gunasena, already struggling to modernize the tattered zoo, had no time for a vengeful elephant. "There was pressure from the mahouts to get rid of him," he recalls. "Without their confidence I can't do anything. Psychologically, it was necessary." And so he put the zoo's fatal attraction up for auction — swapping a problem for a sure windfall. Elephants, which can no longer be taken from the wild, are prime status symbols for Sri Lanka's gem dealers and other nouveaux riches, just as they'd been for the old kings. As the acid-penned Colombo columnist Lucien Rajakarunanayake told me over whiskey and soda at his rugby club, "Once you've got the Rolls-Royce and the fancy house, what's left? The elephant!"

But Gunasena didn't count on Lucien's wife, Sagarica — zoo trustee, master writer of letters to the editor, and Sri Lanka's vanguard animal rights activist. She sued to stop the rush to sell Rajah without considering his welfare or a purchaser's ability to care for him. The zoo insisted it had no responsibility for animals after it handed them on, but finally settled. She agreed to drop her suit after she and a veterinarian verified that the gem dealer who'd paid twelve thousand dollars for Rajah was giving him good care.

Gunasena shrugs it all off as a teapot tempest, but attorney Lalanath de Silva, who pled Rajah's case, insists "it's a very big leap for Sri Lankan jurisprudence": the first time an animal's legal rights had been upheld. For Sagarica Rajakarunanayake, it reinforces the island's status as the seat of Buddhism, since "the Buddha preached the rights of animals over two thousand years ago." And, she argues, if the authorities can't blithely sell off troublesome elephants, they'll be under more pressure to preserve habitat for them.

My bus passed through Rajah's new home, the gem-mining mecca of Ratnapura. I got off, hired a trishaw driver who assumed I must be English to undertake anything so dotty, and spent the morning searching for Rajah. Our quarry was out on a logging job; the new rich are status-conscious enough to buy elephants but practical enough to rent them out when they aren't showing them off at peraheras.

Finally, after winding for two hours along back roads and jungle tracks, we found Rajah and his half-dozen attendants at work in the woods. He was huge, healthy, and slinging trees with a vigor that seemed downright eager. His new mahout called him "a good elephant, no problem," and had him rear up on his hind legs to prove it. Except for the lack of elephant companions, this life seemed to beat doing headstands at the zoo. Rajah, the double killer turned model logger, strained at his fetters and reached out his trunk. I'm sure he just wanted to give me a sniff.

COP THE ELEPHANT: To be tipsy.

— Partridge, *A Dictionary of Slang*

18

Catching an Elephant

This beast, tho' he be so big and wise, yet is easily catched.
— Robert Knox, *An Historical Relation of Ceylon* (1681)

THE BUS ROLLED on past a mountain called Adam's Peak —
where, the stories say, Buddha left his giant footprint, Adam landed
after being cast out of heaven, and the island's elephants went to die
— and a two-thousand-foot cliff called World's End, where Sri
Lanka's central highlands drop to steamy coastal plains. Then it de-
toured; the road to Koslanda had washed out. I jumped off at the
next hamlet and asked around for a car to rent. Over sweet milk tea
the district director named a price for his van. But then he asked
where I was going, and the deal was off. "It's too dangerous," he
said. "The elephants are there. They pursue the cars."

So I wound around on buses, overnighting at the last town
and catching the first morning bus, worrying that Dr. Nandana
Atapattu and his squad of wildlife rangers had already caught their
beast. The plantation country that unfolded out the bus window
seemed the last place to look for jungle creatures. This landscape
painted with tea was tidy to the point of surreality. The shiny,
viridian, uniformly sized and spaced tea bushes, hand-picked by
brightly garbed Tamil women, seemed coiffed with scissors, a bon-
sai world broken by the occasional blazing orange flame tree and
stone walls and umbrella-shaped pines straight out of Umbria.

Atapattu had told me to look for his elephant-catching posse around a plantation called Punnawela Estate. Its puzzled foreman took me to a gracious colonial bungalow, where the even more gracious plantation manager, Senarath Pahathkumbura, offered me the usual cup of milk tea, which was not usual at all. This was the proprietor's special stock — first-cut flowers, the Lafitte-Rothschild '64 of tea — and all cups I had drunk before suddenly seemed like stable sweepings. As I shook off the rapture, Pahathkumbura pointed across his postcard-perfect grounds. "Two weeks ago the elephants were here," he said mildly. "They wrecked some trees, but fortunately no one was injured."

As we left to find the elephant hunters, Pahathkumbura grabbed his Nikon, in case we should come across any elephants. He showed me prints from a camera safari he'd taken in Udawalawe National Park, where Sri Lanka's largest herds — about five hundred elephants — live. "That was a very good experience," he rhapsodized. "A herd of ten came over and surrounded our vehicles" five feet away. Those whom elephants afflict still delight in them; this man struggling to protect his plantation from elephants spends his free time photographing . . . elephants.

I needn't have fretted about arriving late; this capture wouldn't come easily. Dropping an elephant is easy, if you can get a clear shot with a tranquilizer dart. Getting him out is also easy in the flat African savanna, where nature shows and photo essays are customarily shot: you drive or, easier yet, fly where he drops and haul him out. Shooting an elephant is much harder in Asia's tangled undergrowth. And getting him out is *very* hard — and, for the elephant, perilous — in the vertical terrain out past World's End. Once darted, he'll bolt till he collapses or falls off a cliff. If he drops where you can't reach him in time to administer the tranquilizer's antidote, he'll fall over a metabolic precipice. And if he corners you, the life you lose may be your own.

Catching an elephant bears other risks, if he gets away. He may be even more elusive and more dangerous afterward, and may share what he's learned — elephant groups develop diverse "cultures" — with his fellows. In 1676, Jean Baptiste Tavernier, traveling in Golconda, India, reported hearing "an astonishing thing, which is wonderful if one could only believe it. It is that elephants which have once been caught and have escaped, if driven into the woods are always on their guard, and tear off a large branch of a tree with their trunks, with which they go along sounding everywhere before putting down their feet, to see if there are any holes, so as not to be caught a second time." Three elephants Tavernier's hosts had caught but lost had since eluded recapture, and killed "ten or twelve of the poor peasants who assisted in capturing them."

These too were streetwise elephants, schooled in evading vengeful villagers. And Atapattu was determined not to reprise his first capture hereabouts, in 1998. He'd darted that elephant a mile from the road and called in a *koonkie* — a "monitor elephant" used, like a prison trustee, to catch its fellows by body-slamming and pacifying them. It took three days to drag the captive to the truck, redoping him all the while. Never again, Atapattu swore. Henceforth he would get each elephant out in a day. And he renounced the "elephant slavery" of using koonkies; he couldn't find any well-trained ones in Sri Lanka anyway. Instead, he pled with his government and the U.S. Army for a helicopter to transport elephants South Africa– style. No dice. So he started calling in bulldozers — the very machines that are busting open wild elephants' habitat and making working ones obsolete.

Atapattu and his twenty rangers were parked in a rundown empty bungalow — relative luxury, he said; usually they camped in tents. He had selected his crew from parks and reserves around the country and convened them whenever elephants needed catching. Their specialties were finely tuned, from rodeo-style clowning and roping to scoping out thickets so dense an elephant could hide, silent and invisible, a few yards away. Even loading the gun required life-and-death precision. In the old days, massive doses of strychnine and cyanide failed to bring down condemned elephants; etorphine (Immobilon), the synthetic opiate used to dope them now, is considered ten thousand times stronger than morphine, and a

spilled drop can kill. The proper way to handle it, Atapattu explained with a chuckle, is with gloves, mask, and protective clothing. He wore none as he drew the yellow liquid and assembled
the cotton-wadded dart that would deliver it, barking orders all
the while. Anjit Kulasinha, Atapattu's gun bearer, did likewise, but
warily. The American-made darts were supposed to be used once,
Atapattu said, "but we retrieve them, straighten them, and use
them again. We have to. They cost fifty dollars each."

One name was missing from the roster: the man Atapattu called
"my best tracker, Manzoor," the scion of a traditional Pannikan
clan, hereditary Muslim elephant hunters supposedly descended
from Arab sailors who washed up centuries ago. "He'd been with
me for fifteen years," Atapattu recounted. Two years earlier, a darted
elephant had turned and charged, and Atapattu and Manzoor fled
up a narrow elephant path. "I always say *separate*, but in panic you
run the easiest way. He shouted at me, 'Jump, sir!' . . . I turned
ninety degrees into the brush." Atapattu looked back and saw Manzoor casting a Pannikan charm to stop the elephant. "Many times
I've seen it work. This time it didn't." Later they found Manzoor
trampled.

I bit my tongue and recalled what friends in Colombo had said:
"You're going into the bush with Atapattu? Be careful. People get
killed with him." That wasn't the only discouraging word I'd heard.
Conservationists in Colombo fumed at what they saw as the Wildlife Conservation Department's single-minded focus on elephants
and elephant-dependent tourism, its skittering from one hapless
strategy to another, and Atapattu's own haughty recklessness. One
of his most vehement critics was an urbane business executive
named Jayantha Jayewardene, author of the detailed study *The Elephant in Sri Lanka,* founder and managing trustee of a group called
the Biodiversity and Elephant Conservation Trust, and liaison to
many overseas wildlife organizations.

Jayewardene came to activism by an unusual route. He encountered elephants in adverse roles, first as a tea planter, then as general
manager of the Aswan-sized Mahaweli irrigation project, which
wound up displacing many of them. The problem, he says, was the

authorities' failure to stop farmers and businesses from moving into lands that were supposed to be reserved: "They could have limited intrusion and settlement if they'd wanted to, but the government was not interested." He was not reassured by the translocation program — "You're not solving the problem by moving the elephant around" — nor what he called the "cowboy way" Atapattu went about it.

Atapattu sneered at "so-called experts" like Jayewardene. What mattered, he insisted, was not what they said but what he did. Land use and environmental enforcement might be hopelessly tangled and compromised, but saving Sri Lanka's "flagship species" could still make a difference: "Preserve elephants and you preserve habitat for *all* the flora and fauna."

But even as he proclaimed this mission, Atapattu grumbled about penny-pinching by his government. He'd designed a truck with a hydraulic lift so recalcitrant elephants could be loaded at ground level; Malaysia had built one according to his design, but his government wouldn't put up enough money. It wouldn't supply a cell phone, or a powerful rifle for emergencies. "We carry two or three of these" — he lifted a shotgun, which might scare but wouldn't kill an elephant. "It gives the men confidence. But some may say it's foolish to get close to a wild elephant without a rifle" — though untold numbers of researchers do just that.

As for salary, Atapattu claimed he could earn more at a veterinary clinic he owned in Colombo "in a few days than in a month of this." His "boys," as he called them (they called him "the master"), received no bonus for dangerous overtime duty. So why do it? He smiled and said, as though the thought had just occurred, "I love adventure."

Atapattu plainly felt more at home here with his elephant scouts than in the bureaucratic corridors, where he'd shown a rogue elephant's gift for provoking the powers above him. About ten years ago, he was dismissed by one department director, then reinstated by a new one. Peredinya University zoologist Charles Santiapillai sums him up pithily: "A capable vet who took a lot of risks in tranquilizing and translocating elephants, but had a huge chip on his shoulder [and] that uncanny ability to annoy someone without any provocation."

It's easy to get a chip on your shoulder in this game. Everyone seemed to have an idea for solving the elephant problem. Atapattu urged a sort of habitat triage, vacating inhabitants — "less than one thousand families, and 75 percent are encroachers" — from essential corridors to dispensable areas. But the chance never came to attempt it. "Nandana is doing the short-term solution which the people who are being battered by elephants are asking for," said former Wildlife Conservation director Sareth Kotagama. "He understands what the problems are. But he can't sit down to make any long- or medium-term plans. There's always some emergency to deal with. Of course we're failing at long-term viability. No one is addressing the long range." Like police, the elephant cops kept chasing troublemakers and pushing problems over to the next jurisdiction. And, like drug peddlers and streetwalkers, the crop raiders popped up elsewhere.

Every strategy to confine wild elephants in shrinking habitat, employed everywhere from Sumatra to South Africa, can seem an exercise in tail-chasing and crisis management. Deep ditches work (elephants can't jump) but must be maintained, and aren't. Electric fences work till the elephants learn to knock them down with tusks or branches. "Elephants serve to demonstrate the complexity of effective conservation planning," the Sri Lankan biologist Rohan Pethiyagoda writes. "Almost anything (drives, corridors, electric fences, habitat enrichment) works in the short term, and almost nothing works in the long term."

Jayantha Jayewardene urges another solution. Since, he predicts, Sri Lanka will eventually support only about half as many wild elephants as today, problem animals should be removed permanently, though not lethally: "Capture them, tame them, and auction them off [or] give them to pre-selected owners who are financially qualified and expert at managing elephants. Better a live captive elephant than a dead wild elephant."

In 1993, the government proposed auctioning a fifth of its wild elephants and began enlisting bidders, but desisted when conservationists howled. Today its main haven for orphaned and refugee elephants is nearly bursting. The Pinnawela Elephant Orphanage opened in 1976 with twenty-three acres, five orphaned calves, and a planned capacity of ten. Today its population approaches seventy; it is a marvel that Pinnawela has functioned as safely as it has (with no human fatalities, just a few hushed-up injuries) for twenty-five years. Only five or six of its elephants are fully trained and ridden; the rest are kept in what Pinnewala veterinarian Chandana Rajapaksa calls a "half-tamed" state, like livestock. They are taught to follow a lead, are kept chained at night, and are walked to the nearby river to bathe, but otherwise wander the open grounds and function as a herd with minimal human contact.

That's how it's supposed to work. But the tourist imperative — natural curiosity plus the almighty dollar or euro — says otherwise. Pinnawela is a victim of its success, and a unique and profitable tourist attraction. Foreigners and Lankans crowd its grounds, where nothing separates them from four-ton beasts save their own discretion and a skeleton crew of handlers. Mahouts are supposed to keep visitors and pachyderms apart, but that's like banning gambling at a cockfight. Tips are inevitably exchanged, and tourists squeeze close to pat trunks and get their pictures taken. I offered no bribes, but one mahout offered me his coconut husk (the standard elephant scrub brush), and I waded into the muddy river and scraped his big girl's dander. For tourists seeking easy contact with mega-herbivores, Pinnawela is indeed an idyll. But it's a precarious one — the elephant equivalent of a 1960s free school, either a miraculous peaceable kingdom or a disaster waiting to happen.

The national zoo's director, Senarath Gunasena, who also oversees the orphanage, was trying to hire more mahouts and acquire more land at Pinnawela, but he was racing the population curve. More wild orphans keep appearing, and the orphanage had already had seven births of its own.

The Rajah ruckus left officials even warier of trying to sell off surplus elephants. Atapattu decried such sales as more "elephant slavery," and claimed success with the opposite approach: releasing five orphaned calves, raised on artificial milk, in the forest — contrary to the usual view that hand-raised elephants can't survive in the wild. The trick, he claimed, is to raise and release them together — "like schoolmates, like a herd" — while minimizing human contact. Captured adults had to be relocated so far away they couldn't wend their way back; as a bonus, that even disperses their genes.

But first Atapattu had to catch a Koslanda raider or two, which he hoped would make the rest decamp. And neither elephants, terrain, nor bystanders were cooperating. For five days the crew rose before dawn and, fueled only by jiggers of sweet tea, chased over hill, dale, and cliff seeking signs of elephants. Farmers and tea workers would report sightings that didn't pan out. "Out of one hundred times [they give tips], ninety-nine it's bogus," explained Atapattu. "It's not that they want to mislead us. They're so enthusiastic, they want to encourage us. They'll tell us what they saw three days ago as though it just happened."

We stood on a spectacular overlook. The land fell away in tree-fringed bands to the steamy green blur of the lowlands and, fifty miles off, a watery shimmer: the "tank," as artificial lakes are called here, at Udawalawe, where elephant herds were now taking their evening bath. Finally I discerned what experienced eyes spotted instantly: a kilometer off, two boulders moved — elephants, calmly grazing. Atapattu scanned the swooping terrain and muttered aloud, "No, we can't get one out from here."

Scant time remained before nightfall; darting and losing an elephant in the dark would kill him. But opportunity beckoned. One elephant strayed nearer a road. The rangers dashed off to surround him, trying to steer him with "crackers" — dynamite-sized noise bombs, the essential elephant-driving tool. But their target turned uncannily toward the only open escape route, over a steep ridge.

One morning, another elephant appeared in a perfect level spot near a paved road. But gawking villagers thronged to watch the catch. Most of them wore white, a color that incites elephants — a fact Darwin also noted. The trackers would tell me to hang back when elephants appeared because I was too pale. The elephant saw the villagers and bolted; Atapattu exploded and chased them off. The next morning we returned to the same spot, but the largest creatures we saw were a handful of plantation children playing stickball cricket while they waited for a ride to school — which started late so they would not be out in early morning, the elephants' favorite hour.

Low-tech elephant catching is like war and police work: dull hours of tramping and waiting, punctuated by moments of frenzy. At night, if anyone had enough rupees for a bottle of *arak* liquor, the rangers unwound with "get-together" singing parties. One played MC, cooing into a pantomime mike. Each ranger sang a couple of songs, from plaintive ballads to rollicking foot-stompers. Others grabbed tubs and buckets and pounded out a beat. The rest clapped and sang and danced along with the exuberance of a gospel congregation.

Atapattu and I watched and sipped beer, a rich man's drink in Sri Lanka. "The master" was exempt from singing, but the MC's finger inevitably pointed my way. Feeling like a cultural ambassador, I launched into "This Land Is Your Land" but, spooked by blank stares, stumbled somewhere between "sparkling sands" and "Gulf Stream waters." This audience wanted more beat; good thing I hadn't tried "Kumbaya."

The next night, a hand-clapping "Rock-a My Soul" went over better, though I felt a twinge at tricking good Buddhists and Hindus into singing along. On the next turn I decided to kick out the stops with "Satisfaction" — not Mick Jagger's preening original but Otis Redding's sweating, shouting, double-time live version. The elephant hunters joined in, delighted. We pranced and shook and howled at the Lankan moon: "I can't *get* no — dum-*dummm*-dadum-dum — I can't *get no* — dum-*dummmm*. . . ." The next morning the trackers' earlier wariness had vanished. I was in the fraternity — and got a bag of crackers to carry.

One morning we hit paydirt: fresh footprints, broken boughs, steaming droppings. Several elephants had strayed across the Koslanda road. One retreated into an opaque thicket of thorn bushes and lantana, a mint-like Mexican plant that has overrun tropical landscapes from Kauai to Kerala. The siege began. As the breakfast-free morning stretched into a scorching lunchless afternoon, I nibbled the tiny lantana blossoms when the stoic rangers weren't looking.

Atapattu feared that thunder flashes would panic the elephant and drive him into a sinkhole or landslide or over the steep ravine that lay below. And so for five hours, trackers and target played a blind game of cat-and-mouse. A few intrepid trackers climbed the ridge behind and started small rockslides to discourage their target from climbing. "That is a natural sound, so he does not panic," Atapattu explained, chain-smoking to stay calm himself; oddly dapper in a tweed fedora, he looked like a gambler waiting for his horse to come in. A grinning, gnarled old man walked up and showed us the dried root hanging from his neck — a charm to ward off elephants.

Finally the fugitive broke to flee. Crackers and shotgun blasts sounded to nudge him back, and Atapattu stepped into the thicket, rifle ready. Two shots rang, and he and his rangers hurtled out, chased by an angry elephant, who shook his huge head and started toward us, then cut across the road and down the slope toward the ravine. The rangers had already seen the danger and raced by foot and truck to head him off with crackers and shouts. Suddenly, silence fell.

By the time I reached the elephant, he was on his knees, wearing an oddly serene expression. He was going under too far, too fast. Atapattu quickly injected the antidote in his ear, then shouted at me to flap it for circulation. Tranquilizing is unpredictable, he explained later; you could only guess a hidden elephant's weight and the right dosage, and you might target a big specimen and hit a smaller one, or vice versa. Some elephants fall three minutes after they're darted, he told me, and some last thirty. This one took twelve minutes to fall.

Atapattu claimed that only three elephants had died in the 107 translocations he'd performed, while neighboring nations wound up killing as many as half the animals they tried to catch. But in 1999, Sri Lanka's Elephant Conservation Forum charged that through poor planning and over-long chaining, 70 to 80 percent of the elephants tranquilized and translocated in the preceding two years had perished. Such allegations would come back to haunt Atapattu.

This time the antidote took almost instantly. "Back!" shouted Atapattu, and we scattered like fleas shaken off a dog. The elephant rose and lurched toward us, then stopped, still groggy, and tossed a trunkful of dirt on his back. He was a tuskless male of middling size, in his early twenties. The crew had looped heavy ropes around his front feet, but these were unsecured, and his hind feet were entirely free. The master roper, Ranjit Viditha, sneaked up and, with a crook lashed from coconut fronds, managed to fish a twine leader attached to a three-inch rope around a rear leg, jumping back like a cat from a kick that could pulverize a wall. And again, so gently this time the elephant did not start, and he was roped.

Finally, at three-thirty, breakfast and lunch arrived. Revived, we began a tug-of-war. With thirty gawking villagers press-ganged into helping, we began to drag the big guy toward the road a quarter-mile away. But this was the Gandhi of elephants, a master of passive resistance. If only he'd charged, the rangers could have guided him under his own steam. But even when one named Abesekara, who had a specialty like a rodeo clown's, taunted him with palm fronds and a white flag, he just dug in his heels and his enormous rump. I knew an elephant could pull hard, having seen one dragging a company of soldiers at Thailand's Elephant Round-up. But you don't know how hard hard is until you're holding the rope.

Atapattu called a truce. If the living mountain would not come to Muhammad, Muhammad would cut a road to the mountain. He arranged for the local planters to provide a bulldozer the next day. We dragged Gandhi to the nearest palms (and to the limits of our strength) and tied him for the night.

Before dawn, a ranger who'd stayed to watch the prisoner burst into the bungalow shouting. Everyone dashed into the trucks and to the site, which was a wreck. Shattered wood and fronds were scattered everywhere. Gandhi's companions had returned and uprooted three of the four trees he was tied to; the fourth held by a splinter, and when it broke, he would be gone.

Atapattu waved everyone back, stared at the restive elephant, and called firmly. Gandhi stood still and stared back quizzically, like a chastened dog. Man and giant seemed to have reached an understanding. "That elephant is not a rogue," Atapattu murmured. "He never killed anyone."

The torturous process of snagging Gandhi's feet, fixing ropes, finding sturdy trees, and dragging him into position began again. Atapattu fumed at his planter hosts; neither the bulldozer nor a water bouser he'd requested had arrived. Without wetting, heatstroke overtakes elephants tied in the sun. Again the gawking crowd was recruited for a bucket brigade, and a ranger named Upali, the designated douser, warily splashed Gandhi with water.

It was afternoon before the 'dozer arrived and cut a road toward the prisoner. The rangers backed up the lorry and, lacking a hydraulic lift, build a dirt ramp to its elevated bed, which they concealed with more dirt and palm fronds. Again the mob hauled on the ropes while the rangers urged Gandhi on with white flags and thunder flashes. Once in range they hitched his ropes to the 'dozer, which towed him, like a slow-motion water-skier, onto the lorry. With his feet roped to its bed, he looked resigned and munched on a frond while one nimble ranger — our MC — gave first aid to his crop-raiding wounds. He'd been shot twenty-three times.

The truck would ride through the night, taking Gandhi to a park Atapattu would only say was "at least 250 kilometers away"; he never disclosed such destinations beforehand for fear that the locals, reacting as Americans do to sex offenders moving in next door, would block the "killer elephant's" arrival. But every villager and tea worker in the area lined the road to see off the giant who days before had terrified them. Children waved sadly, and crowds ran along behind the truck. Farther along, entire towns turned out to await the elephant, and several people, seeing my camera, asked for pictures of him. The mood was nostalgic and oddly festive, like a perahera procession. I recalled what Sareth Kotagama had said: "If a wild elephant becomes a problem, people will curse the animal and do whatever they can to kill it. But once it is captured, they do a 360-degree turnaround. They say, 'Oh, don't hurt the animal, it's suffering!' They come from all around, sympathize with the animal, bring it water. That is the attachment we have for the elephant in the village."

Six months later Atapattu wrote me that Gandhi was "faring very well" at Maduru Oya National Park. Atapattu himself hadn't fared so well. The Koslanda crop raiders proved persistent, and he returned to capture another. This one revived and charged, and Atapattu, barely escaping and seriously injured, was airlifted to Malaysia for treatment. By late August he had recovered and returned to Koslanda for another capture.

After that, I did not hear from Atapattu and could not reach him. By early 2001, both his home and office phones had been disconnected. After many tries I reached the Wildlife Department director, A. T. A. Gunasekara. He confirmed what I'd already heard, that Atapattu had been suspended again, but declined to name the grounds: "We can't give details on disciplinary matters. There are some serious issues under investigation here." Upon learning I'd attended an elephant capture, Gunasekara exploded: "He has no authority to take a foreigner out on an operation. He should have asked me about it. He has done another wrong thing!"

When pressed, Gunasekara acknowledged that one matter being investigated was the number of elephants that had died after capture. He said that this number seemed to be "much higher" than previously reported — as the Elephant Conservation Forum had earlier claimed.

The real problem may lie less in those results than in the unreasonable expectations nurtured by Atapattu's boasts and by media that, in Sri Lanka as elsewhere, crave animal stories with human heroes and happy endings. "The number of elephants killed accidentally by the veterinarians of the DWC [Department of Wildlife Conservation] pales into insignificance when compared with the number killed by angry farmers and poachers," zoologists Charles Santiapillai and Mangala de Silva recently wrote. They criticize the conservation groups for failing "to appreciate the problems and the inherent risks involved in the management of wild elephants" and for clamoring to sack the wildlife director "every time an elephant gets killed." Such pressure may prod shakeups but doesn't make peace between farmers and elephants. While the bureaucratic wheels turn and the rumors fly, the crop-raiding, trap-gunning, acid-hurling, and pumpkin-bombing continue.

Sure enough, Gunasekara himself was soon replaced as director. But the national government might finally be taking the elephant problem seriously. In the fall of 2001, President Chandrika Kumaratunga pulled Wildlife Conservation out of the ministry in which it had been buried and ordered it to report directly to her. She also ordered the drafting of a conservation master plan and appointed Jayantha Jayewardene and another well-connected figure, a former department director, as special advisers. "She is taking a personal interest in wildlife conservation," reported Jayewardene, "and it is doing much better than it has for a long time."

Still, Santiapillai muses, "truth comes in various shades in Sri Lanka. The impossible happens, and the probable never does. 'Today a fighting cock, tomorrow a feather duster' is the norm here. Nobody knows the truth of what's happening here." Nandana Atapattu, who might well dismiss all the latest moves as more armchair nattering, had disappeared from sight like an elephant in a lantana thicket.

DRAW THE ELEPHANT: To succeed in a most difficult undertaking.

— Mathews, *A Dictionary of Americanisms*

19

No Room in the Nilgiris

> There is undoubted cruelty in breaking the spirit and training wild
> elephants, after they have been captured by kheddaring. . . .
>   The wounds [they receive] are almost impossible to treat and
> they naturally become flyblown and ulcerated.
>   — J. H. Williams, *Elephant Bill*

I FOLLOWED the captive Gandhi up the road and kept on to Colombo, where I caught a plane to Trivandrum. While I wound
along India's elephant trail, through the states of Kerala, Karnataka,
and Tamil Nadu, two banner events occurred: lame duck Bill Clinton became the first U.S. president since Jimmy Carter to visit India, and India's population passed the 1 billion mark. The former
news was hailed as confirmation of the country's ascension to
global economic stature, and the latter seemed to inspire more
pride than alarm. The signs of new prosperity and familiar but
ever-worsening crowding were everywhere. The stately garden city
of Bangalore was now a booming high-tech mecca and sprawling
traffic jam. Just a few years earlier, the residents of a college dorm
on the outskirts of town had awakened to see a band of wild elephants foraging outside their windows.

With one-third the United States' area, India will likely overtake
China as the world's most populous nation. And yet it is home to
most of Asia's thirty-five to forty thousand surviving wild ele-

phants. You can explain this in terms of geography — the rugged mountains at its northeast and southwest edges, which hold the largest populations — or land use: its large forest reserves and national parks. But Raman Sukumar, director of the Asian Elephant Conservation Centre at Bangalore's prestigious Indian Institute of Science, suggests another explanation: "I'm convinced it's only because the elephant is sacred that it has survived in India."

Many of these survivors are hemmed into isolated pockets of doubtful viability, as in Sri Lanka and Southeast Asia. But a few large stretches of habitat still sustain thousands of elephants, and one of the most important is the fabled Nilgiri Biosphere Reserve at the junction of the two main southern mountain ranges, the Western and Eastern Ghats, where the states of Kerala, Karnataka, and Tamil Nadu also meet. Six national parks and sanctuaries, covering more than two thousand square miles, form a rare web of corridors and diverse habitats, from lush evergreen and deciduous forest to thorny scrub, and support more than four thousand elephants, one of Asia's densest populations. Compared to constricted Sri Lanka, this is vast elephant territory. It is paradise next to Sumatra, which has no elephant logging or mahout traditions, where timber companies and plantations are furiously bulldozing the forests and wild elephants are shot, poisoned, garroted at the legs with torturous wire snares, or captured and tethered in open-field concentration camps next to huge piles of their own manure.

I got a taste of the Nilgiris' wildness on my first improbable night there. I'd arranged to meet researchers from the Indian Institute of Science at the Bandipur Tiger Reserve, one of the biosphere's parks, that evening. But I'd caught the wrong bus at Sultan's Battery, looped far around, and finally had to hitch a ride in a long-haul truck with a sign that read "Love Is a Sweet Poison" afixed above its cab. Arriving around midnight, I found a reasonable sleeping spot behind the reserve's headquarters and then thought: perhaps a tiger reserve wasn't the best place to sleep on the ground. I spotted a ladder tenuously lashed together and crawled up to the rooftop. I slept, then woke under a clear black sky to a pattering that sounded like rain, but heavier and more distant. It came nearer, and the ground seemed to shake. I looked over the parapet and gasped: hundreds of spotted deer were milling around the illuminated clearing surrounding the building. At sunrise the deer were gone. My hosts explained that the leopards shunned the lights, so each night the deer gathered under them.

But despite such frissons, the Nilgiris are hardly pristine. Indian parks lack the tour-bus convoys and souvenir shops of their American counterparts, but the whole spectrum of Indian rural life coexists, often uneasily, with conservation. Sixty thousand villagers live in the Mudumalai Wildlife Sanctuary, near the Nilgiri Hills' center, along with twenty thousand cattle and sundry sheep, goats, and burros. The cows' horns are painted and gilded in Hindu observance, but they are not coddled. These are scrawny, light-footed "scrub cattle," able to withstand fierce heat and flee fiercer tigers. They live on what they can root out in the village alleys and surrounding countryside — and compete with elephants and deer for scanty dry-season forage. They provide at best a liter of milk a day, and are valued more for their dung. Women follow them about, collecting this fertilizer in wide flat baskets and selling it to the big plantations. "It's a major income for the poor people, with zero investment," N. Baskaran, a wildlife researcher from the Bombay Natural History Society working in Mudumalai, told me. But it's also a heavy burden on scarce plant resources. "Fortunately," says Baskaran, "they don't collect elephant dung, or no nutrients at all would go back to the system."

Fifteen hundred miles to the northeast, in Corbett National Park, elephant researcher Amirtharaj ("Christy") Williams sees the same vicious cycle. With declining forage, Corbett's nomadic tribespeople must keep twice as many buffalo as before to get the same amount of milk — which, along with erosion and water-fouling, compounds the decline in a feedback loop.

A different sort of incursion has lately overtaken many picturesque Mudumalai sites: the vacation homes of wealthy urbanites. Even Raman Sukumar, one of the world's best-known elephant authorities and advocates, has a country house in prime elephant habitat here. Others build illegal guest lodges disguised as private homes. Many care less about wildlife than Sukumar does. They plug their electric fences into main current rather than low-voltage solar generators and electrocute deer, gaur, elephants, and anything else that strays near their crops and gardens. If wildlife rangers come to investigate, the landowners may bribe them — and have them dispose of the corpses.

Corruption, from the lowest levels on up, is a recurrent drag on wildlife protection in the land that gave the world the term *baksheesh*. When I visited Ravindra Pal Sinh Katwal, Tamil Nadu's chief wildlife warden, at his headquarters in a Madras high-rise, he insisted that most of the poachers in his state came from neighboring Kerala, where people were "less respectful of the law" than Tamils. But he conceded that some of his staffers had assisted poachers — several were caught in a jeep with a hunting party — and covered up kills. "An elephant is very hard to hide," he noted. "But I have a case where an elephant carcass got burned." Such cover-ups don't necessarily signal collusion, he added — just rangers' fear of getting blamed for killings on their watch. His solution was to announce that they would not be blamed, though that wouldn't seem to promote accountability.

Katwal added that elephant poaching runs in waves: "All of a sudden it will happen, when orders for ivory come from Japan and the Arab states. I have lost four elephants in the last fifteen days." Kerala's close ties to the wealthy, ivory-craving Persian Gulf, where many Keralans work, provide a ready conduit for smuggling.

The dead elephants aren't the only victims; poaching affects survivors as well, disrupting elephant society and threatening the herds' breeding viability even when it does not obliterate their numbers. Poaching skims off the older, seasoned bulls who dominate mating and male social life. Without them, life's an elephant version of spring break at Fort Lauderdale. The young bucks — as impulsive and aggressive as their human counterparts — run rampant, mating incompetently and fighting incessantly. In Africa, they've challenged and killed many rhinos, and sometimes tried to mount them.

Because in Asia only the bulls have tusks, poachers don't target the cows as they do in Africa. But winnowing out males has badly skewed sex ratios in much of India. Periyar Wildlife Sanctuary, a tourist favorite in southern Kerala, has about one hundred cows for each bull — a recipe for inbreeding or a population crash. Five to one makes for healthy breeding, says Sukumar; in the Nilgiris, the ratio is twenty-five to one.

Sometimes poaching's signs are plain to see — like this one posted on a tree on the road to the Mudumalai village of Mahanvalla:

CAUTION
VEERAPPAN'S MOVEMENTS
SUSPECTED WARNED
AGAINST ENTRY INTO FORESTS
NILGIRIS FOREST DEPARTMENT

Koose Veerappan, always called just "Veerappan," was the most famous and destructive poacher of all, a dashing, mustachioed Robin Hood to some and a butcher to others. He was alleged, and himself claimed, to have killed 130 men and two thousand elephants, not to mention taking untold tons of wild sandalwood and kidnapping one movie star and many less famous people. This tally may, however, include others' crimes, conveniently pinned on Veerappan. Regardless, his specter stalks the mountains like a rogue bull. A small army of troops and police failed for a decade to catch him. Like the threat of forest fires, his presence could make authorities close an area. To guard against poaching, the trained tuskers at the famous Thepakkadu elephant camp in Mudumalai were tethered at night and denied forest foraging.

Despite the signage, locals say Mahanvalla is one area Veerappan hasn't infiltrated. Other poachers have. They commonly recruit the "tribals," indigenous hunting and gathering peoples who know the forest as nobody else does, as guides; often they ply them with booze, to which they're famously susceptible. Maneka, a member of the Honey Kumara tribe, told me through an interpreter that poachers will pay good money, up to ninety dollars, but it's a risky deal: "Once you're in that circle, you're trapped. If you try to stop, they'll think you must be betraying them. They may kill you, or threaten your family."

Squealing bears other risks, Maneka added. "People don't report poaching to the Forest Department because they'll pick *you* up. They're convinced you must be involved." The department also "tries to keep us out of the forest, our traditional place," Maneka complained, for fear his people would nab some game themselves. "We're meat eaters. How can you expect us to stop eating meat? We used to hunt, but now we just take carcasses."

That's true, wildlife researcher Rathinasam Aruguman told me; the tribals only scavenge now. Conservationists urge them to let the leopards and tigers eat their fill before taking their kills, and blink at this "illegal" appropriation.

Elephants, however, are inviolable: "We worship the elephant as a god," Maneka continued. He recalled an old man in his tribe who came upon an immense tusker, which charged. He jumped in a thicket and prayed to the tusker to forgive his transgressions and spare his life. The elephant came close, stared at him, and walked away. Maneka and others went to the thicket and, sure enough, found fresh dung and huge footprints.

The Kochi-based public interest attorney Daisy Tambi battles another sort of theft, carried out with official tolerance, that may do more harm than poaching: stealing the animals' forest habitat. Long ago the government granted growers cheap hundred-year leases on vast swaths of forest throughout the Western Ghats, specifically to grow cardamom and coffee. Because these grow in shade, they preserve much of the forest habitat. But the growers converted to tea, which doesn't need shade; good-bye, forests. Most continued to occupy the land without renewing the leases, and the government didn't bother collecting rents that inflation had reduced to pennies. And there's the loophole, Tambi explains: "Under the law, if land is occupied by private persons for thirty years, it reverts to them. So the government is losing the right to recover the land. Nobody does anything about it" — until the elephants get displaced, and tasty crops lure them into collisions with their proliferating human neighbors.

Human-elephant conflicts are more pronounced west of Mudumalai in Wayanad Sanctuary. "Wayanad" means "Land of Swamps," and it has more rain and fodder, with elephants feasting in its tree-high bamboo groves — and a hundred human settlements. Humans and elephants are packed so close, I spotted one wild group, grazing near the roadside, from a crowded public bus; a larger herd stopped traffic to cross another road. Madhusudan Annadaana, "Dr. Madhu," a Wayanad-based researcher with the Indian Institute of Science, blames much of the conflict on the government, which in its drive to boost food production in the 1950s and '60s leased tracts to farmers for pennies on the acre. Now most of Wayanad's namesake swamps are rice paddies, and cardamom and peppercorn plantations dot the slopes above. The settlements threaten elephant migration corridors that once stretched all along the Western Ghats: "Wayanad, in conjunction with [the neighboring reserves of] Nagarole and Bandipur, has a future" as habitat, says Madhu. "Wayanad by itself does not."

After years of tallying crop-raiding incidents and elephant movements, Madhu is deeply sympathetic to farmers and elephants alike. He scorns the term "rogue elephant" as unfair to the besieged animals. But he tells bloodcurdling tales of farmers' watchtowers toppled and smashed by raiders and the villager collecting firewood who bumped into an elephant in a bamboo thicket and did not live to light another fire. In one idyllic village, perched along a lush canyon, he takes me to meet the schoolteacher (one of a network of observers he maintains in some twenty villages). The teacher and his wife continue somberly recording each incidence of "human-elephant conflict" — even after losing a child to one. They've begged the government to move them elsewhere.

Such conflicts claim up to 250 human lives each year in India — far fewer than malaria, AIDS, auto accidents, or even snakebites.

But death by elephant is not a quiet fade-out. The casualties may be faceless peasants, but the elephants involved become notorious killers or celebrated victims — or both.

"One death is a tragedy," said Joseph Stalin, who knew more about such things than was good for the rest of the world. "A million deaths is a statistic." That's as true with charismatic megaspecies as with human victims. Killer whales can be starved and poisoned by the dozen and scarcely ruffle the world's attention. But millions of people got exercised and millions of dollars spent over one sad captive orca named Keiko who happened to play a sad captive orca in a movie.

Today, as when Jumbo was a superstar, people's views and sympathies are shaped not by statistics but by the individual animals they have known, at least vicariously. Thus did an unlucky "rogue" that wandered outside the Nilgiris become a *cause célèbre* like the Colombo zoo's Rajah, an incipient international incident like Jumbo, a cross-cultural flashpoint, and a case study in how elephant capture, taming, treatment, and politics can go awry.

The scene was Mudumalai's Thepakkadu Elephant Camp, commonly hailed as the best elephant camp in India, where journalists and television crews come to report the marvels of traditional elephant handling and the challenges of modern elephant conservation. Till 1989 it was a full-time logging camp; with fewer trees to cut, it now gives rides to tourists and a berth to uprooted elephants from around Tamil Nadu. Much of its glamour derives from Dr. Vaidyanathan Krishnamurthy, now retired from its helm but still a frequent consultant and bottomless fount of elephant lore.

The secret to training and treating elephants, Krishnamurthy expounds, is "to understand each one as an individual. . . . Accidents happen because someone did not follow that, tried to push the elephant around." Even when elephants kill, "nine times out of ten the animal is innocent, forced into the situation. It acts in pure self-defense." These axioms were forgotten in 1998, when a Thepakkadu posse was dispatched to catch a "rogue" that was terrorizing the surrounding countryside.

I did not know this elephant's reputation when I met him at Thepakkadu's feeding station, which resembles the sort of place where health food aficionados go for wheat grass and spirulina shakes. An intricate hand-painted chart like a railroad timetable spells out to the last gram the rations for each of twenty-seven elephants. On a wide concrete slab the mahouts — short, wiry, dark-skinned tribal men, distinct beside their taller, plumper, lighter-skinned supervisors and visitors from the cities — set out the ingredients: bricks of light millet and dark *raghi* mash, mounds of salt and special supplements. They knead these into melon-sized balls and hand-feed their waiting tuskers, a regime that instills loyalty and dependence but does not provide the roughage that is a mainstay of wild diets. It is an odd and unsettling sight, these giants of the jungle clamoring like baby birds to be fed by puny men.

One bull — a tuskless makhna, tall but a bit gaunt and stiff-legged — stood separate and received special attention. Babu Foster, Thepakkadu's bluff, cheery chief forester, insisted I plop coconuts into his mouth. "See?" he said, patting the makhna's trunk. "No problem now. Very good elephant — very gentle now, very happy." Forester Babu and the coconut-chomping bull seemed to grin and bob their heads in time.

Officials assumed "the Makhna" was the reason a Western writer would come to Thepakkadu now. He'd cut a wide crop-raiding swath across Mudumalai and Wayanad, and then his reputation, like Jesse James's, grew with the telling. According to Professor Sukumar and chief warden Katwal, he'd killed "about one dozen" people; Forester Babu told me he'd killed twenty-two; press reports ranged as high as thirty-three. But local residents and researchers who were closer to the ground said he'd killed just two men, both drunk, who blocked his way on the road.

The Thepakkadu crew darted the Makhna in July 1998 and, with four koonkie elephants, spent three days dragging him ten miles to the camp, by official accounts — eight days and twenty-six miles by an unofficial one. The catchers were ill prepared; their traditional bark rope, used to tether and drag animals because it does not cut as jute does, had rotted with disuse. So they hastily procured metal chains, which cut even worse. Foot-long sections of the chastened "rogue's" legs got flayed and infected. A dozen punctures on his upper body abscessed; officials ascribed these to earlier gunshots, but a videotape of the capture shows the koonkies jabbing him with their tusks.

At Thepakkadu, the Makhna was locked in a dilapidated sixteen-foot-square kraal built of heavy timbers, which he soon wrecked, and was chained again while a new one was thrown up. The mahouts set about breaking him in traditional fashion: with confinement and starvation, to be followed by beating, then food and soothing talk, in a bad cop–good cop sequence intended to leave him grateful and submissive. As his wounds worsened, members of the American-sponsored India Project for Animals and Nature (IPAN), which operates a shelter and mobile veterinary service for the area's neglected domestic animals, offered to help treat and feed the Makhna. IPAN's founder, Deanna Krantz, said she felt a spiritual bond with the resilient and surprisingly gentle giant and named him after the Norse messenger god Loki, as "the messenger to the world about the plight of the world's elephants." But Loki was also the god of mischief, a lethal sower of discord — foretelling, perhaps, what relations between the Indian authorities and outside volunteers would soon descend to.

The mahouts proceeded to the training's corporal stage; a forty-five minute tape of their striking "Loki" with switches and his screaming and moaning is painful listening. Krantz protested and urged that he be released into a sanctuary-style facility, which she offered to build, rather than trained to join the camp. As these criticisms escalated, so did official sensitivities. Forest managers barred her and her staff from visiting or further treating the elephant, whom they named "Murthy," after Dr. Krishnamurthy (though they still called him "Makhna"). They got the impression (abetted perhaps by some of Krantz's overeager supporters) that she sought to take Loki/Murthy away to her shelter, or even to California.

Krantz and her supporters publicized other incidents of mistreatment and instigated a barrage of faxes and letters — including one from U.S. Representative Sam Farr, the elephants' advocate in Congress — to Indian officials and India's and America's ambassadors. Prominent veterinarians and animal welfare activists from America and Africa inspected the Makhna and likewise criticized his care. In Washington, D.C., game show host and longtime animal rights advocate Bob Barker showed a tape of Loki's travails at a congressional press conference. *Salon* reported that "the frat party of House staffers crammed outside" wasn't much interested in the plight of the "elephant currently being tortured by a bunch of Indian thugs." Instead they wanted Barker's autograph. Celebrity fever also infected the expansive Indian coverage; a fair-haired, outspoken American woman challenging the conservation and political establishments was an editor's dream.

Those establishments only rallied and resisted. Sukumar and Krishnamurthy, who when asked concede that the capture went awry, publicly defended Thepakkadu and condemned outside meddling. India's crusading environment minister, Maneka Gandhi, scorned "the basic dishonesty" of foreign reports on India's animals. "No one asked Krantz about how Americans eliminated the bison and mail pigeon," Katwal complained. "America makes so much noise about conservation, but it should practice what it preaches."

Finally Krantz realized that she, rather than the elephant, had become the issue, and stepped back. By mid-2001, both the humans' rifts and the elephants' had further healed. IPAN's able Indian manager, Nigel Otter, was once again helping out at Thepakkadu. Poachers had nearly wiped out the wild tuskers in the area. Murthy/Loki, the messenger elephant, was still chained, limping, and docile. But he was spared further training. He won't have to carry tourists, but he'll never wander the Nilgiris again.

CRY UP THE ELEPHANT: To "talk up" something.
— Mathews, *A Dictionary of Americanisms*

20

Must This Show Go On?

For elephants forest dwelling only is ordained [by nature]; from not getting this, and from eating and drinking unwholesome and unpleasant things, from food that is unsuitable, indigestible . . . from sleeping in improper places on account of journeys . . . disturbances of the wind and other bodily humors are provoked, and quickly cause diseases to arise in the body and mind.

— Nilakantha, *Matangalila*

A circus is not a circus unless it has elephants.

— Earl Chapin May, elephant handler, in *The Circus from Rome to Ringling*

ON A SIDE TRACK at the Union Pacific rail yard, across the Willamette River from downtown Portland, Oregon, a hallowed American tradition is about to unfold. The half-dozen silver-painted train cars, lined with odd glassless windows and even odder signage, inch to a safe stop. A half-dozen motorcycle cops roar up and park across from one open freight door, waiting for someone or something to emerge. A small cluster of burly, hard-hatted yard workers also stand around expectantly. Farther back sits a line of sedans and pickups, like a slow night at a drive-in movie. Parents and young children — the families of railroad workers, alerted to this low-key arrival — crane out the windows and lean on hoods, waiting for the train to unload. They sit nearly three hours, until a city veterinarian arrives to check the passengers. But no one leaves; one mother nuzzles her daughter and says, "We'll just wait and see the elephant."

Finally a few small, dainty animals step lightly down the steel ramps leaning against one of the cars — angora goats, glowing white in the dark rail yard. Tiny white ponies follow, then white and black llamas, two white dromedaries, and horses of every size and color. At last the showstoppers loom, like upright shadows: ten elephants padding after their trainer, each holding the next one's tail, leading the menagerie on the last mile to the arena that a Microsoft co-founder built to house his basketball team. The elephant walk has begun. For four days the Rose Garden will be the stage for "The Greatest Show on Earth," the Ringling Brothers and Barnum & Bailey Circus.

Welcome to the great American circus parade, twenty-first-century style. Once it was a proud display, storming Main Street at midday with horns blaring and drums pounding, elephants transformed into walking billboards for local banks and car dealers, and entire towns turned out to watch. Now the circus arrives under cover of darkness, with police escort and a wary eye out. It is a quietly outlandish and incongruous spectacle, these exotic giants padding through the concrete night like ghosts of the mammoths that once trod here. None of the patient gawkers seems to mind the elephants' being late; they're still thrilled to see them. One seems a connoisseur of elephant walks: "You should see when they go back *in* the cars," he exclaims. "They have to kneel to get through the doorway!" Just seeing an elephant can have that effect, even in a digitally transmitted, simulated, and manipulated age; it enlarges our sense of the world's possibilities. Of course a moth or a spider can also enlarge that sense, but we must look closely and know what we're looking at. An elephant forces us to look.

Not that the circus wants to be seen tonight. Handlers still find walking the cheapest, safest way to transport their animals from rail yard to arena, and good exercise besides. But they walk at night, when the traffic is lighter, the weather is cooler, they can set up early the next day — and, if they're lucky, they can pass unnoticed.

Or they arrive as Ringling Brothers did in Seattle the week before, when protesters waited, despite the late hour and secret schedule, signs and slogans ready, to excoriate the circus for abusing animals generally and elephants especially. Ringling workers took a superior satisfaction at hearing one protester shout, "Send them back to Africa!" as the Asian elephants ambled past.

Ringling people rate cities according to the vehemence of their protests. "Seattle was the worst anywhere," says clown turned publicist Peggy Williams. "Norfolk came closest, but it's the headquarters of PETA [People for the Ethical Treatment of Animals]. They were well behaved in New York." The protesters are the first tier of an ardent campaign by animal rights and welfare groups, from the militant PETA to mainstream Humane Society, against using elephants and other "exotic" animals as captive performers. It's a battle fought on editorial pages nationwide and in legislation at every level from town councils to the U.S. Congress. Qualms about circuses' and zoos' treatment of animals have simmered since Chuny wowed 'em at Exeter Change, but they crescendoed as the millennium approached.

Sometimes the protesters wear elephant costumes as they hand out blood-curdling leaflets and checklists for patrons to record any abuses they see. Sometimes they lapse into misstatement and overstatement, which the circus defenders, led by Ringling's topnotch publicity cadre, leap on: If you can't tell Asian from African elephants, don't tell us how to care for them. The defense counters with its own slams at what Ringling P.R. chief Catherine Ort-Mabry calls "the animal rights industry" and its "integrated political campaign not just to remove animals from circuses, but to separate *all* people and animals in all ways."

That too is overkill, but a cultural dividing line does underlie the circus war. Seattle became a key battleground in early 2000 after its mayor and several City Council members proposed banning exotic animals from city-owned facilities. That would effectively drive out Ringling, which rents the civic arena each fall. The bill's two sponsors — young, single, and childless — hadn't seen a three-ring circus in many years. One, Heidi Wills, deplored undignified, unnatural spectacles like "elephants in tutus, bears on bicycles, and tigers jumping through burning hoops" (none of which Ringling shows) and the misleading "messages" these send. She compared the circus to the "violent video games" in a nearby amusement park (also on city property). And she suggested that fans see an animal-free circus like the more artistically refined Cirque du Soleil. "We live in a more enlightened age," she told me. "Seattle is a sophisticated city, with more discerning tastes about what we consider important."

Let the record show that I don't share this bias; I'm one of those kids who never quite outgrew the circus, who loves both the tinsel splendor of a traditional three-ringer and Cirque du Soleil's rarefied pantomimes. And I marvel that, in the virtual age, when video games are replacing books as universal texts and everything from "live-action" dinosaurs to ancient Rome is re-created on-screen by microprocessors, a hundred circuses still wend their flesh-and-blood, sawdust-and-greasepaint way across America. Let others sneer, as one activist did, that "if all we're going to do is say this is tradition, then I guess we should go back to slavery and sexual discrimination." I'd love to preserve this tradition, lions and tigers and elephants and all, if only it could be done conscionably.

A Seattle ban would have been a turning point; such laws had passed only in smaller jurisdictions, many of which didn't actually host circuses. To stop it, the Ringling show's owner, Feld Entertainment, pulled out the political stops. It hired top lobbyists, threatened to jerk its ice shows from Seattle, and brandished a poll showing three-quarters of Seattleites agreeing that "the circus is a wholesome and safe place to take children" and "animals are an essential part" of it. One Seattle council member with young children withdrew his support for the ban, saying he didn't "want to legislate morality," and the bill failed.

Since then, the anti-circus campaign has ebbed, at least in the corridors of power. A few smaller cities and counties banned exotic performing animals in 2001; Rhode Island and Maryland rejected bans; and Maine's split legislative houses compromised by requiring veterinary checkups and forbidding "public contact" with elephants — thus banning rides, a tidy moneymaker for many smaller circuses. (Ringling dropped elephant rides long ago, and the American Zoo and Aquarium Association recently forced its members to.)

The activists' biggest hope was the U.S. Captive Elephant Accident Prevention Act, instigated by an ex-animal trainer named Pat Derby and introduced by California Congressman Sam Farr. It would forbid elephant rides and the transport of elephants across state lines for entertainment purposes. Again Feld/Ringling fought back, spending a reported $30,000 on lobbying — including $2,400 in free circus tickets for members of Congress. The bill stalled in committee.

At a hearing on Farr's bill, Marine World elephant manager David Blasko, a former president of the Elephant Managers' Association, argued that rides give elephants much-needed exercise — an argument echoed by keepers at the Indianapolis Zoo, which was loath to give up rides. Circus operators also justify performing as exercise. By contrast, obesity is a frequent hazard for sedentary zoo elephants; Dennis Schmitt, a leading elephant veterinarian, suggested that the different obesity rates explained why only 60 percent of zoo elephant births are live compared to 90 percent of circus births. (Another reason may be that circus breeding is dominated by Ringling's highly specialized and experienced Elephant Conservation Center, while many zoos are just starting breeding.)

Schmitt's view gets support from a 2001 study, by animal scientist Ted Friend of Texas Agriculture and Mining University, of elephants' health and travel conditions in five big circus operations. The two sides view Friend differently: activists question his expertise (his prior experience was with agricultural livestock) and neutrality, but the circuses trumpeted his findings even before he submitted them to the U.S. Department of Agriculture.

"We've seen really no problems at all" at any of the five circuses, Friend told me. "Their elephants are generally in much better condition than zoo elephants, and their longevity is much better." He doesn't mention it, but that may reflect selection: healthier elephants keep touring while ailing ones go to zoos, sanctuaries, or

Ringling's retirement farm in Florida. Still, the circuses insist that performing doesn't just tone elephants' bodies — it nourishes their souls with stimulating travel, challenging work, and, most important, bonding in "partnership" with their trainers. "These animals see different things each day," argues Ringling animal superintendent Brian Cristiani. "They see different people, they're exercised continuously. Look at zoos. They get no interaction whatsoever" (a claim many zookeepers would fiercely dispute). Friend concurs, noting that some circuses "bring real old elephants along with them, just hanging out. If they leave them at home, they'll pine away and die."

Friend even puts a positive cast on the "stereotypic behavior" — weaving, swaying, pacing, and other repetitive motions — often displayed by captive animals. In circus elephants, he says, such behavior "increases a lot before feeding, watering, shows. When crowds show up for performances they start weaving like crazy in anticipation. We did a couple trials, kept a batch of elephants out for the performance. No question: if they could have broken loose they would have run right in the tent and joined in. They started doing their act outside as best they could, based on just the sound stimuli, the music. They're so accustomed to it, it's not as though you have to force them each time. It's probably a reinforcing habit, but I think it's stimulation — it gets them out of the boring pen or off the chains."

Parse that idea, however, and it seems a pretty bleak notion of "stimulation": compared to being penned up or chained, performing's not so bad. That suggests a rather narrow range of opportunities for circus elephants; even the stimulating travel Cristiani speaks of consists largely of close confinement in dark trucks or train cars piled with waste. But elephants, like other animals, are creatures of habit — "consistency, consistency, consistency" is the keeper's mantra — and become used to their performing routines ("reinforcing habits") as to anything else. These elephants have also been taught, at the point of a hook, to perform on their cues. If Friend's elephants were straining to get back and perform, they may have feared being punished for not showing up.

The circus lobby takes Friend's findings as proof that performing is enjoyable and "natural" for elephants — just as Ringling representatives point out that doing headstands is a "natural behavior" elephants use in play and to crack gourds. But animal behaviorists tend to view stereotypic behavior very differently, as adaptive behavior for coping with boredom, frustration, fear, distress, and/or helplessness. The British animal behaviorist David Shepherdson describes it as a response to "lack of control over external stimuli." Caged animals often pace at feeding time, but is this a sign of eager anticipation or vexation at waiting to be given what they would take for themselves in the wild?

Such questions soon enough lead to broader ones, such as "What is happiness?" — a question as fraught when asked of other animals as of humans. Oh, brave new circus that hath such creatures in it! The Seattle animal behaviorist and zookeeper Ellen Leach thinks that Friend's eager performers "at the best have a well-established routine and at the worst may have a very diminished behavioral repertoire, from being taught not to do anything unless told to. The elephants I am more familiar with would take the opportunities in an unstructured situation and explore whatever they could."

Carol Buckley, an ex–circus trainer, tries to give ex–circus elephants those opportunities. She acquired her first elephant in college, when she volunteered to care for a solitary six-month-old orphan used in tire-store promotions. Eventually Buckley trained her and took her on the road as a circus act. "Tara's a very patient animal," Buckley explains. "She waited a long time for me to get it. When she got to be a pre-teen I realized her life sucked. I thought she needed to be bred, to raise her own children to be happy. I've since learned better. I took her to a facility in Canada to be bred. That was my first exposure to full free contact" — the hands-on, often coercive management practiced by mahouts, circuses, and other traditional trainers — "in all its brutality and domination. That forced me to make a decision: Will you support this situation or support elephants?" And so she and her partner, Scott Blais, founded the Elephant Sanctuary in Hohenwald, Tennessee, where ailing, aged, abused, and surplus elephants could just "be ele-phants" in spacious open grounds.

Buckley's story parallels that of Pat Derby, who trained animals for Hollywood until she too had a change of heart and co-founded the Progressive Animal Welfare Society (PAWS), in California's griddle-flat Central Valley. Most PAWS residents, from parrots to lions, are caged, but the elephants have expansive paddocks. They come trotting eagerly — the Africans, true to form, are friskier — to greet and nuzzle when Derby and her partner, Ed Stewart, ap-proach. After proper introductions, I step forward to stroke their rippling inch-thick sandpaper skin, to be sniffed and poked by trunks that seem ubiquitous and imbued with wills of their own, embracing and lightly brushing at once. I get a warm misting of trunk spray and touch a rough cheek that vibrates like a drumhead and purrs like a cat or a Harley — a sound of contentment in ele-phants as well, so deep it seems to travel through the ground and up your bones. At such moments you understand the people, in-cluding those in circuses, who want nothing more or less in life than to care for, learn about, *be with* elephants. As a Seattle zoo-keeper said, "Once you've worked with elephants, you never want to go back to any other animals."

This elephilia crosses ideological lines; whatever brutes and incom-petents may still work circuses, other handlers show as much devo-tion as their opponents. Brian Cristiani, a seventh-generation cir-cus man and fourth-generation elephant handler, speaks softly and earnestly about how "these guys [Ringling's elephants] are really happy in this environment. . . . I love doing what I'm doing. I feel very proud of it." One of his colleagues, a white-haired veteran named Sonny, says hardly anything to anyone — at least any hu-man. After thirty years tending elephants, he moves like one him-self, with a measured economy and deliberation, guiding his charges with the slightest gestures, standing just as impassive and patient and with the same wry expression.

Dave Whaley, a former Ringling handler now with the Clyde Beatty–Cole Brothers Circus, is as voluble as an AM radio host.

Whaley speaks with evangelic fervor of "operant conditioning" and teaching tricks by "reward and repetition" rather than coercion. He describes the "enrichment" toys he's made — a twenty-foot tetherball, an abacus on metal rods, beer kegs drilled with various-sized holes and packed with food (which the elephants speedily smashed).

Friend sees the sort of trend in circuses he'd already observed in agriculture, "a new generation of elephant trainers coming along who are changing the style and methods, who are a little more in tune with the animals. It's more acceptable now to empathize and show concern for their welfare." But concern is still expressed by dominance: the trainer commands elephants and must be ready to enforce his or her commands with stick and chain. "I've known people in this business for thirty years," says Buckley. "I know they love elephants. What I had to learn to understand was, you can love someone in a very dysfunctional way."

Even Ringling Brothers' owner, Kenneth Feld, talks like an elephant lover. Slight, bespectacled, and intense, he looks more like a CPA than an elephant man, much less a circus boss. His rock-promoter father bought the struggling "Greatest Show on Earth" for $8 million in 1967, sold it to the toy company Mattel in 1971 for $50 million, and bought it back for $23 million after Mattel realized running a circus wasn't like selling Barbie dolls. From these beginnings, Feld has built what *Forbes* estimated to be a $675 million annual business and a $775 million personal fortune.

I watched Feld as he watched a near-final dress rehearsal of his Blue Show (Ringling's Red and Blue shows tour simultaneously and are redesigned in alternate years), noting miscues and other faults. He smiled for the first time and tapped his feet when the elephants paraded on. "I love it," he said during a break. "My whole house is filled with crystal elephants, elephant sculptures — only elephants. I've always collected them." Business and obsession coincide, he added: "We've done research. The primary reason people come is the animals." And the primary animal they come to see is the elephant — the circus's "number-one attraction," according to various surveys cited by Heidi Herriott, circus unit manager of the Outdoor Amusement Business Association. She complains that the pesky activists fixate on them for the same reason — "because elephants are high-profile, charismatic, endearing. When legislation is proposed, the conversation always turns to them."

Feld and Herriott insist they have a mission: to bring these charismatic "ambassadors for their species" to America's byways. "It's more important now than ever, with the shrinking natural environment, for people to see animals in the flesh," says Feld. Never mind that that flesh is standing on tubs and parading scantily clad glitter-babes around the ring. And so the circus tries to recast or repackage itself as a conservation and educational enterprise. Ringling's pre-show "Circus Experience" includes zoo-style displays on the parlous state of wild elephants and their habitat, which makes them seem even more precious: See 'em while we got 'em!

Ringling now packages the big girls as figures of story, not just spectacle. One young elephant steals the show and a bellyful of bread in a proboscidean variation on the classic Clown Café skit. Later, a platoon of clown suitors — from tycoon to Elvis — piles out of the clown car and woos the clown bride. She spurns them all, till one offers her the supreme gift: an elephant! Trumpets flourish, and in strides the caparisoned hundred-ton troop for the grand finale. "Here come the swing elephants," the Vegas-style ringmaster sings, "the ring-a-dinging elephants, party pachyderms. . . ." Demean elephants? the show seems to ask. We worship them!

Feld has put his money where his chorus line is, with a $5 million gated facility in central Florida he calls "the Center for Elephant Conservation" and activists call an "elephant puppy mill." In just six years the CEC has become the leading elephant-breeder in the Americas, with twenty-seven residents and eleven births as of mid-2001. After visiting, India's celebrated Dr. Krishnamurthy called it "a wonderful facility — that is how elephants should be kept!" It is indeed an impressive structure, ingeniously designed and scrupulously clean, a network of sturdy metal corrals interlinked so mating matches can be easily arranged and a single manager can do

much of the tending. Its barns are finished in baked-enamel alumi-
num, to shed whatever the residents may toss at walls and ceilings.

The CEC is also a stark, sterile-looking place, with no frills, little
evident enrichment or diversion, and an austere view of how animals should behave. The only visible toys for the younger elephants
the day I visited were truck tires stacked outside the pens. Jim Williams, then the CEC's manager, said he'd impounded them because
the young rowdies kept "rolling them out and bouncing them off
the fence. I'll keep them there for a while and then put them back.
They'll appreciate them more. It's just like when your mother took
away toys you didn't use." The difference is, these elephants lose
their toys because they do use them, and they have no others to
play with.

A one-tusked bull named Raja follows us along his pen's heavy
double fence, snorting and scuffing the ground like a cartoon bull.
"He's displaying his manhood," says Williams. "His focus is one
thing: to produce semen and properly deposit it. That's his one goal
in life." Raja and the other breeding bulls are left as wild and solitary as possible, trained just enough to receive medical and foot
care. "We want him that way. We want him to be aggressive — to
feel he has complete authority over all that domain."

Ringling people talk up their center's conservation mission and all
it's doing to enrich the gene pool. But it doesn't belong to the
Species Survival Plan that governs accredited breeding of Asian elephants. Feld says that joining the plan "will probably make sense
some day." But as he concedes, the Conservation Center's essential
purpose is to ensure the *circus's* survival, by assuring that it will
have elephants. Endangered species protection has made it all but
impossible to import Asian elephants since the 1970s and Africans
since the 1980s. According to one much-bruited analysis, North
America's Asian elephant population is not sustainable and, at current breeding rates and without imports, will number about ten
in fifty years. A companion study found that because its African
elephant population is younger, and so includes more breeding-

age females, it could be self-sustaining "if reproduction increases soon."

Baby elephants are a big draw for circuses, as for Thai resorts and American zoos. That gives incentive not only to breed them but also to wean them early and get them on tour. Ringling doesn't drag its toddlers away from their moms at six months, as some Thai promoters do, but neither does it let them nurse for four or five years, as they would in the wild or even in a Burmese logging camp. In early 1999, it tarnished its well-polished image of scrupulous elephant care when it took Doc and Angelica, two tykes less than two years old, from their mothers. U.S. Department of Agriculture inspectors, who regularly visit circuses unannounced, found "large visible lesions," evidently "rope burns, resulting from the separation process," on Doc's and Angelica's legs. USDA Undersecretary Mike Dunn declared this evidence sufficient to confirm that the tykes' handling violated the U.S. Animal Welfare Act and caused "unnecessary trauma, behavioral stress, and physical harm and discomfort."

Nevertheless, Ringling's publicity boasts that in the past thirty years it "has *never* been found in violation of the Animal Welfare Act." That's literally true — in part because the company avoids adjudication and formal findings through negotiated consent decrees. Ringling also struck such an agreement in an even more controversial 1998 case, when an ailing three-year-old elephant named Kenny collapsed and died, evidently of a gastrointestinal bug, after the third performance in a day. Ringling maintains that Kenny joined "voluntarily" (a puzzling term in this context) in the first two performances; when his illness became evident, he was placed near his stallmates at the third performance to "avoid the stress that could result from separation." It "neither admitted nor denied any violations" but agreed to donate $10,000 each to elephant medical research and Thailand's Elephant Hospital. And it secured a letter attesting that the USDA never alleged that Ringling was "responsible" for Kenny's death.

Other cases don't make it that far. In 1999, San Jose's police and

Humane Society accused Ringling of wounding seven elephants around the left ear, where handlers commonly tug with ankuses to guide animals. Ringling replied that any bleeding resulted from its vet's recently having drawn blood from the ears, and tried to discredit the investigating police sergeant with a photo showing her at an animal rights rally. Prosecutors declined the case for lack of evidence. In 2000 a former elephant groom, Tom Rider, testified to Congress that he had complained about Ringling's elephants, "including the baby Benjamin," being "beaten all the time when they do not perform properly" and was told "that's discipline." By then four-year-old Benjamin had drowned while bathing in a pond. Ringling's own necropsy concluded that Benjamin had an undiagnosed heart problem.

Other circuses' elephants have suffered travails worse than those recorded for Ringling's. In one ghastly 1997 incident, Albuquerque police found three elephants and eight llamas belonging to the King Royal Circus in a sweltering, filth-filled trailer in a motel parking lot. One elephant was dead, another malnourished; both were infected with salmonella. The circus's explanation: its owner's son had set out for home — San Antonio — from Nevada when one elephant got sick. Now that she'd died, he was awaiting a replacement driver to take her back to be properly buried. The USDA fined King Royal's owner a record $200,000 and permanently revoked his performing-animal license.

In 1997 the USDA also fined and suspended Manuel Ramos's Oscarian Brothers Circus for unsafe and unhealthy practices, including failure to provide sturdy elephant restraints. Three years later Kenya, an elephant Ramos had owned for fifteen years, broke from the tree she was chained to and killed a Ramos family performer. Ten days later she was found dead in her pen; an autopsy was inconclusive. This time the agency shut Ramos down. Again, the system worked — but too late to save one woman and one elephant.

In 1998 USDA inspectors reported finding "wounds caused by abusive use of an ankus" on two Clyde Beatty–Cole Brothers elephants, and on four elephants a few days later. The circus claimed that the fresh wounds were ingrown hairs and old scars on their legs were "calluses." It signed a no-fault consent decree with the government and received a suspended $10,000 fine. In the 1990s inspectors also repeatedly cited foot problems on Clyde Beatty elephants — no small matter: such problems are the prime cause of early death in captive elephants. By one theory, the pressure of standing in captivity (as opposed to walking all day and much of the night in the wild) clogs the sweat glands above the toenails, causing nail cracks under the cuticle which become infected. Without the natural scouring of walking, footpads also get overgrown and infected. Cold cement floors and accumulated urine and feces exacerbate these problems. Infections travel up the leg and eventually become systemic.

Clyde Beatty vice president Renée Storey concedes such problems plagued the circus "in the past." But she says that new staffers "more receptive to new ideas" are now correcting them: "We really have made a rapid entry into the present, after being rooted in the old ways." Indeed, the Beatty show has hired new, younger handlers (including Dave Whaley from Ringling) and finally instituted regular foot care. At a Long Island tour stop, its elephants were kept in outdoor hot-wire pens, as are Ringling's. "The only time I chain them is in transport," says their manager, Adam Hill, at his trailer beside their pen before a performance on Long Island. "I'm with the elephants twenty-four hours." A local volunteer drops by a large bundle of maple boughs for the Beatty three to munch. Unchained legs, a patch of ground, and fresh browse: small things, perhaps, but more than generations of captive elephants enjoyed.

No degree of elephant suffering is likely to make legislators ban elephants from performing or traveling, or stop circuses from finding an audience. But the violence inflicted in the name of elephant control has a flip side: the scores of circus workers and smaller number of circus patrons killed and injured by out-of-control elephants.

Circuses downplay or dismiss the risk. "At no time in its 130-

year history has Ringling Bros. had an animal-related incident that placed a member of the public at risk," that circus's publicity claims. That suggests an unusual idea of risk. In a widely reported 1950 incident at Ringling's Sarasota winter quarters, Dolly, a circus veteran previously considered gentle, grabbed a five-year-old boy who'd been feeding her peanuts and crushed his skull underfoot. The circus manager told a reporter the lad had reached under the guardrail to retrieve dropped peanuts and Dolly reacted "like a dog when someone takes a bone away."

Such killings of spectators are rare; only two have been reported in this country since 1980, both by the same elephant, Clyde Beatty's Frieda, in 1983 and 1992. One victim had climbed into Frieda's pen drunk after trying to ride other animals. The other case was problematic, with indications that the victim, a woman, had been murdered elsewhere and dumped in the pen. Frieda was still working in 1995 when she broke loose twice, the second time causing a panic in which twelve spectators were injured.

Patron injuries and worker fatalities are not so rare. A compilation of news and government reports by Ringling's nemesis, the Performing Animal Welfare Society, reports eleven U.S. circus worker deaths, nineteen worker injuries, and more than fifty patron injuries (several of them children thrown from riding elephants) in two decades, plus more in other countries. Ringling's own star trainer, Axel Gautier, was killed at its breeding farm. One attack occurred backstage at the *Live with Regis and Kathy Lee* show when a young elephant from the Great Moscow Circus severely injured a Russian translator.

Two of the most sensational incidents — and worst elephant rides of all time — involved the same unhappy animal. In 1989, Kelly, who'd already injured one trainer, broke from a petting zoo at the Southwest Florida Fair, charged through the midway, and plunged into a lake with three riders aboard. Three years later, renamed Janet and working in the Great American Circus, she stormed from the Big Top, again with three young riders. Hundreds of spectators dashed from the tent, then back in, as Janet raged outside. A brave worker on another elephant lifted the children off her back. Janet chased her trainer behind his car, smashed it and a couple of trailers, and trapped and very nearly killed a policeman, Blayne Doyle, who was there on traffic duty. Eight years later the encounter remains fresh in Doyle's mind: "Janet held me down with her foot and started to do a headstand on me. A circus worker ran up and poked her with a pitchfork, and she turned on him." The circus had no tranquilizer gun, and the rest of the crew fled like everyone else.

"Her owner told me, 'You're going to have to shoot her. She's a bad one,'" Doyle recalls. He refused, saying, "'All I've got is a nine-millimeter. It'll only make her mad.' But when she took off toward the tent, I emptied fifteen rounds in her." Janet got mad. More officers arrived and chased her around the tent, emptying their guns. "She fell down, trying to dig a hole, screaming," Doyle continues. Someone pulled a hunting rifle from his pickup, which likewise only pricked her. Finally a tactical officer finished her off with an armor-piercing bullet in the head.

"I've been shot, stabbed three times, taken forty-four stitches just in my head, been hit with bottles, sticks, you name it, crashed three police cars, a motorcycle, and an airplane," Doyle says with classic cop bravado. "None of this ever scared me. Trying to stop an eight thousand–pound elephant that was trying to do a headstand on me — *that* scared me!"

The next year another rampaging elephant met a death as gruesome as Janet's. Tyke, an African female that the Illinois-based Hawthorn Corporation rented out to traveling shows, had already torn loose and charged through an Altoona arena and a North Dakota fairground, where she nearly killed a groom. A year later, as a Honolulu circus audience watched, Tyke killed her trainer and mauled a groom, then stormed the downtown streets until eighty-six bullets brought her down.

Statistically, such events are rare. In the 1990s, according to Debbie Olson, the Indianapolis Zoo's science director, only four serious "incidents" were reported in 3.4 million rides at accredited zoos. Meanwhile, Heidi Herriott says, elephants safely bore 10 million riders at circuses and fairs. Ringling claims that all the spectators and bystanders injured in recent rampages were not trampled but rather stumbled while fleeing; most surely did. Panicked elephants may pursue their keepers, but they seem almost to avoid hurting bystanders — a testament to the animal's passive nature. The "rampaging rogue" of stereotype is a frightened animal trying to run away.

The circus trade has a long tradition of dubious practices: passing elephants from show to show; disguising dangerous ones like Kelly/Janet by changing their names; smuggling them across the border to Canada or Mexico; hiring unqualified casual help; stonewalling when things go wrong. The USDA has cracked down harder in recent years: witness the King Royal and Ramos closures. But Officer Blayne Doyle was not impressed with its efforts after Janet's wild ride: "If we investigated crimes against persons the way the USDA investigated this incident, no one would ever go to jail. In my opinion, USDA's main responsibility afterward was to ensure they had *their* ass covered." Animal welfare activists make similar complaints, and also claim that, however able and dedicated the agency's inspectors may be, they're too few for the job. The USDA has about eighty-two inspectors nationwide to cover circuses, zoos, slaughterhouses, animal dealers, laboratories, and all other enforcement of the Animal Welfare Act. Even its legal powers may not be sufficient to the task; a 1995 official audit concluded that the agency "does not have authority under existing legislation to effectively enforce the requirements of the [Animal Welfare] Act."

Circus operators nevertheless complain about undergoing ever more inspections, often prompted by activists' complaints. But former Ringling and Clyde Beatty handler Tom Rider told a congressional hearing that circus managers "always knew in advance" when inspectors would come, and told handlers "to clean up, don't hit the elephants. . . . Any attempt by the USDA to regulate circus[es] or to enforce the law is a joke."

One common response to anti-circus campaigns is the "you've got to be kidding" defense. Let people vote with their tickets, the defenders contend. Government has more important things to worry about than a couple of hundred elephants. Even some who wince at elephant performances fear the consequences of banning them. "They don't belong in the circus," says Thailand's "Professor Elephant," Richard Lair, "but where else are you going to send [Ringling's] seventy-nine elephants?" — not to mention the 130 or so in other circuses. "There is no zoo in the United States that wants or has room for any elephant except a very young female calf — which many of them want."

No, but sanctuaries have sprung up to receive show biz's castoffs. These include Pat Derby's PAWS, Carol Buckley's Elephant Sanctuary, and Riddle's Elephant Sanctuary in Arkansas — which animal welfare advocates scorn because of founder Scott Riddle's use of dominance training and involvement in two sensational zoo elephant incidents — and a number of smaller elephant havens. Ringling itself maintains a retirement facility in Williston, Florida, for some of its pachyderm veterans. PAWS has begun a large expansion, apparently funded (terms weren't disclosed) by the settlement of a lawsuit it filed accusing Ringling of infiltrating its organization and stealing records. After years of designing elephant management programs for zoos, California-based Active Environments plans to build its own residence for surplus bulls. Buckley's sanctuary, which recently doubled its original hundred acres, plans to add 1,840 more and, she says, "eventually accommodate about one hundred elephants."

Taking elephants off the roads, as the Farr bill would have done "doesn't mean Ringling Brothers would have to get rid of them," says PAWS founder Pat Derby. "Ringling would have a lot of options." She suggests that the company prove it's trying "to save the species" by opening "an elephant park." And if Ringling couldn't or wouldn't, "we'd just take care of the elephants."

Perhaps the Greatest Show on Earth would become a stationary show, or even a chain of circus theme parks. Feld tried that in the 1970s, with Circus World in Florida; it closed in the '80s. But audiences are ever more mobile — much more so than in the circus's heyday, when the only way for the circus to reach them was to go to them. Feld has already tried to move beyond its three-ring big show with a lavish Cirque du Soleil–scale tent show, "Barnum's Kaleidoscope." He claims the intent was "not at all" to do away with the exotic animals, but the Kaleidoscape used only domestic horses, ducks, and geese. It got rave reviews but cost a bundle and went into "hiatus" in mid-2001.

Feld insists the circus is here to stay, elephants and all: "I think the circus of yesterday *is* the circus of tomorrow. The reason it has survived and succeeded for centuries is that it's the most adaptable form of all." Perhaps; but adaptability means something else when all the world's an entertainment console and media forms change faster than the season's television lineup. The number of circuses has steadily shrunk for decades, and most that remain are struggling. "This is a declining industry," murmurs Feld's own senior elephant trainer, Gary Jacobson, as he waits to assemble the performers for the show. "It's been declining since 1910."

An autumnal foreboding colors the circus's merriment — even when the circus is as large and slick as Ringling's. That foreboding deepens to despair in India, where elephant training and acrobatic shows go back four thousand years and Western-style circuses were once hugely popular. Now, scorned as lowbrow, squeezed by movies and television, and harried by capricious regulation, India's remaining circuses claw for life, mainly in northern Kerala. I stopped there to see the Rajkamal Circus, "A Stupendous Entertainment of Regal Splendour." The splendour had faded; the tent was less than half full, and the clowns, acrobats, and motorcycle daredevils, though capable, seemed strangely listless. The audience sat silent until the elephants came out, and then finally applauded. India bans bears, tigers, and other wild animals from the circus, but still allows elephants. Without them, the whole business might blow away. And tradition is tradition.

21

Breaking Contact

The schoolchildren who witnessed the scene in the Zoo soon started neglecting their studies and turned into hooligans. It is reported that they drink liquor and break windows. And they no longer believe in elephants.

— Slawomir Mrozek, *The Elephant*

Prince, a precept I'd leave for you,
Coined in Eden, existing yet:
Skirt the parlor, and shun the zoo —
Women and elephants never forget.

— Dorothy Parker, "Ballade of Unfortunate Mammals"

WHATEVER SHORTCOMINGS circuses may have, surely zoos are another story. After all, they're nonprofit, often civic institutions, accredited by the American Zoo and Aquarium Association (AZA) and dedicated to protecting rather than exploiting animals. They provide animals homes rather than making them yo-yo around the country. They don't strap gaudy wraps on them and force them to march, prance, and stand on one another. And no one calls zoos "a declining industry"; their attendance climbed robustly in the 1990s.

But some in the elephant-keeping world aren't so sure of the difference. "A zoo is so sterile," says Elephant Sanctuary founder Carol Buckley. "It's as limited as any circus I was in. Neither is acceptable." Even some zookeepers echo the sentiment. "There's really no difference between what they're doing [at Seattle's Woodland Park Zoo] and what Ringling's doing," sighs Sally Joseph, the ex–circus handler who manages the elephants at Tacoma's Point Defiance Zoo. "They're both using free contact" — traditional direct, dominance-based, face-to-face control. The debate between partisans of free contact and advocates, like Joseph, of the newer, noncoercive "protected contact" approach has riven the elephant-keeping world, and reflects broader uncertainty in zoos at large. As that peculiar institution the zoological garden enters its third century, those who serve it are beginning to confront fundamental questions of mission and morality: Are zoos essentially conservation, education, or entertainment enterprises? Can they be all three? Should they measure success in the crowds they draw or the ways they serve their animals? Should they exist at all? Nothing brings these questions to the fore like the largest, most challenging, and (especially as babies) most popular zoo inmates, the elephants.

Such misgivings didn't arise yesterday. In 1912, the Bronx Zoo's sixteen-year-old male elephant, Gunda, attacked his keeper. Though Gunda remained calm after that, the zoo kept him tightly chained for two years because he had "murder in his eye," which meant testosterone in his veins. "There are only two things you can do with him," the zoo's director, Dr. William Hornaday, declared: "Kill him or keep him chained," and surely Gunda "preferred the latter. [He was] no worse off than any life prisoner."

This provoked an angry editorial in the *New York Times:*

> Dr. Hornaday thinks that Gunda prefers being chained to being shot, but that is mere anthropomorphism, since Gunda cannot comprehend the two fates — he can only resist each when it confronts him, and the decision must be made for him if at all. Dr. Hornaday believes in the maintenance of public menageries. He should therefore ponder well whether the chaining of Gunda may not strengthen the grave doubts which many of us already have on that subject and bring so many more to our point of view as to lead to the abolition of these prisons for animals.

Nearly a century later, no American zoo would get away with keeping an elephant chained for years, though some did so into the 1960s. And no daily newspaper would likely call for the abolition of that wholesome civic institution, the zoo. In 1997, according to the AZA, America's 184 accredited zoos and aquariums (grown by 2001 to 196) constituted a $1.3 billion business — with increasing emphasis on "business." They drew 134 million visitors, more than major league baseball, pro football, and pro basketball together. That's not counting some 1,800 USDA-licensed roadside zoos, menageries, and other exhibitors not accredited by the AZA.

In the past two decades, the hot zoo trend has been "landscape immersion," as pioneered at Seattle's Woodland Park under director David Hancocks in the 1970s. Rather than displaying animals like stamps in an album, zoos now propose to re-create their natural habitats, both for the critters' sake and to let visitors feel as if they're there in the rain forest or savanna themselves. Simulating habitat is relatively easy with, say, naked mole rats, which inhabit a larger version of a child's ant farm. But elephants, which forage over twenty or thirty miles a day, are a challenge of a whole other magnitude. I've seen only one zoo provide anything like the space elephants need to spend a day, let alone a year, as they would in the wild: the new Aringar Anna Zoological Park outside Chennai (Madras), India, at 510 acres the largest zoo in southern Asia. Its three elephants inhabit thirty acres, whose greenery grows faster than they can pluck it and tall enough to conceal them. Viewing them feels like viewing wild elephants — except that even they are isolated prisoners, cut off from the herd society, with all its familial connections, that envelops wild elephants.

"The elephant capital of the United States," in the words of the daily *Oregonian,* is Portland's Oregon Zoo. It is a media darling and a writer's dream; Sally Tisdale in *The New Yorker* and Shana Alexander in *The Astonishing Elephant* have extolled its breeding triumphs and keepers' wisdom. "Portland is the model, the inspiration," I once overheard a Calgary elephant keeper tell his Oregon counterparts. "Whatever you do, the whole world will be watching!" It was here in the 1970s that the veterinarian Michael Schmidt unraveled the mystery of the female elephant's sixteen-week estrous cycle, by far the longest among land animals, and here in the 1980s that Katy Payne proved elephants communicate by infrasound. Portland's is the only American zoo with its own museum — larger than the Royal Thai Elephant Museum — dedicated entirely to elephants.

The Oregon Zoo is famous above all for babies. In 1962 a young cow lent to Portland by the Seattle animal dealer Morgan Berry dropped the first elephant born in the United States in forty-four years. By 2001, twenty-six more calves had arrived, twenty-one of which survived. Seven were sired by that first calf, Packy, now grown into the largest Asian elephant in America — ten-and-a-half feet tall and up to seven tons at his pre-musth peaks (an elephant can drop a ton during musth). Packy is arguably the Rose City's most enduring celebrity; thousands turn out each April for his birthday party, even though he gets to eat all the cake.

Successful breeding indicates a modicum of well-being, and when you watch the barn's youngest resident, the irrepressible Rose-Tu, splash in its pool like a kid at the beach, you might think this is how the animals were meant to live. Oregon's elephants are not chained at night, as some zoo and most circus elephants are, and are allowed outdoors at all hours on rotation, weather permitting. Vienna zoo curator Harald Schwammer measured the causes of stereotypic behavior and found that "chaining was the main factor" and indoor confinement next.

But the dark side of elephant captivity shows even at Oregon's renowned zoo. Grand and famous though they are, Packy and Portland's other bulls brood away much of their time in dreary cells. Ray Hopper, in early 2000 the head elephant keeper, couldn't help wondering, as he guided a delegation of visiting elephant managers through those closed-off back rooms, "What are we doing, [keeping] our three bulls inside twenty-by-twenty-four-foot rooms?" Even that meager space is 20 percent more than the AZA requires in its new and stricter elephant care standards, which some zoos consider excessive.

Hopper pointed out a forbidding two-ton cement and steel door that a smaller bull, Hugo, had knocked off track, bending the half-inch steel I-beam holding it. Hugo and the other solitary captives are always teased by the scents and sounds of nearby females and rival males. Some years back, Packy and Hugo managed to connect by snaking their trunks through their cells' hay-feeding chutes. Then, for reasons that can only be guessed, Packy bit off the tip of poor Hugo's trunk. The keepers hand-fed Hugo till the stump healed. They later tried to reintroduce the two erstwhile chums, with a safe barrier between. At the sight of Packy, Hugo dropped into submissive posture and fled.

Confinement and jumbled social signals may be taking a psychological toll: the Oregon bulls' sperm production has plummeted in recent years, when they should be in their prime, putting the famous breeding program in remission. Rose-Tu, the last elephant born here, arrived in 1994. Six years later she was the victim of one of the most notorious cases of animal abuse in recent zookeeping.

Six-year-old elephants are often rambunctious, and Rose-Tu's spirits may have been further piqued by the arrival of another young elephant, Chendra, in November 2000. When they were later introduced, Rose-Tu reacted in the usual way of jealous stepsisters: she bit Chendra's tail.

Zoo managers had already decided that Rose-Tu, though not aggressive, suffered from "inconsistent handling" and, like many children of dysfunctional households, was slow to obey commands. They directed that only two senior keepers — Hopper and Fred Marion, a veteran with twenty-five years' experience, ten in Portland — handle her. On April 17, 2000, two months before they hosted their peers at the International Elephant Research Symposium, that decision went badly awry.

The subsequent police report records that Marion, who was supposed to be in charge, arrived late, smelling of alcohol. Without apparent provocation, the two junior keepers on duty avowed, he grabbed Rose-Tu by the tail, poked her with his ankus, gave contradictory commands, then chased her repeatedly around the yard mumbling commands, shouting obscenities, and hitting her. She screamed and threw dirt at him. The junior keepers saw Marion push the ankus's hook into Rose-Tu's anus and, according to one, "jerk down twice." Her knees buckled.

The other keepers were meanwhile occupied restraining the three other cows, who heard Rose-Tu's calls and tried to rush to her aid. They called on Marion to desist, finally got him to leave the yard, and then called in their supervisor, Hopper, and two top managers, who were all at home. Hopper counted 176 puncture wounds on Rose-Tu. He cleaned them but decided she didn't need immediate medical attention; a veterinarian looked at her the next day and examined her the day after.

As preceding events came to light, the biggest surprise was that Marion was still working with elephants at all. Four months earlier, in December 1999, a visitor, Karen Haberle, had complained that he suddenly hit Rose-Tu twice, swinging his ankus like a bat. "The hardest part was I had to answer to my child," recalls Haberle. "How do you answer a three-year-old asking, 'Why is the man hitting the baby elephant?' When I confronted [Marion] at the barn afterward, he laughed and said, 'You don't want to know what goes on around here.'" The zoo did not discipline Marion; its managers said Rose-Tu had tried to turn on him and had recently pulled a keeper against a wall. The USDA investigated but, unable to find wounds, pressed no charges.

Hopper told police that Marion had often come in drunk, sometimes stumbling, and been sent home for it. He'd brought in sharpened ankuses, which zoo rules forbade. Hopper had "had to counsel Marion at least a dozen times in the past eighteen months for inflicting hook injuries on various elephants," a police detective reported.

"It's just like with child abuse," says the Oregon representative of the Animal Protection Institute and a member of an official task force convened to review the incident. "The warning signs were there, but they weren't heeded." Silence prevailed up and down the line. Keepers and managers didn't talk enough, new keepers seemed reluctant to challenge their senior, and the zoo did not report the incident to police for a month — at which point prosecutors said the trail was too cold to file charges. (They later revived the case under public pressure; Marion pled no contest to second-degree animal abuse and was sentenced to community service and probation.) Marion's union protected him, and the zoo wound up paying him $18,000 in lost wages to avoid taking him back. It also paid a $10,000 federal fine. The Department of Agriculture declined to suspend the zoo's license, as activists urged, but did order more annual training for its elephant keepers. The Oregon legislature passed a "Rose-Tu Bill" assigning tougher penalties for animal abuse and closing a gaping loophole in defining it.

The kernel of the problem seems to have been that "the elephant capital of the United States" couldn't find anyone better to take care of its elephants. Marion evidently didn't want to anymore; in July 1999, after being accused of intoxication (and denying it), he had asked to be transferred. Another keeper was hired, but then yet another one left, and Marion stayed on with the elephants. The zoo's animal manager, Mike Keele, later told the task force that the only positions the zoo had difficulty filling were for elephant keepers, "and that's true around the country."

Many zoos face the same quandary. Elephant handling is a labor of love, since zookeeping, like circus work, doesn't tend to pay well. For some it's a dream job, but many who try soon quit. Some don't have the patience or nerve to work at close quarters with animals that can swat them like flies. Some just can't get along with elephants. And some don't like the odds.

Since the early 1990s, innumerable keepers, journalists, and even the occasional congressman have repeated the apocryphal claim that the U.S. Department of Labor rates elephant handling "the most dangerous occupation in the United States." In fact, the Labor Department doesn't rate handling because handlers are too few to constitute a statistically valid field. But in 1991 a National Zoo manager named John Lehnhardt, now animal operations director at Disney's Wild Kingdom, presented a paper arguing that, with a fifteen-year average of one fatality a year among some six hundred

handlers, elephant handling was three times as likely to kill its practitioners as coal mining, the most deadly occupation the feds listed.
And it was high time the profession managed its risks.

Lehnhardt's paper hit like a bombshell. One proof of its impact
is that ten years later, amid very different conditions, its findings
were still hotly debated. On top of that, fatalities climbed to two or
three a year in the early 1990s. Some keepers felt nearly as endangered as the animals they kept.

Thanks in good part to this alarum, fatalities have since dropped
to virtually nil at AZA-accredited zoos. Better training, including
annual AZA-sponsored classes in elephant management, is one
likely reason. Another is the weeding out of violent keepers, as in
Portland. And many zoos have installed elephant restraint chutes —
the term "crushes" is now frowned on and "huggers" never caught
on — powerful automated hydraulic cages something like the moving walls that used to threaten James Bond. These confine elephants so keepers can treat them from outside the bars. Often zoos
install chutes to convert to a protected-contact regimen, under
which keepers work with elephants only through protective bars.
But many zoos — including Oregon's, which devised the first crush
— have resisted the switch.

"Free contact" is a modern term for a very old approach: elephant handling as practiced since ancient days, with nothing standing between little man and mighty beast but their relationship and
all the fear and affection bound up in it. At its best, in traditional
logging camps and some zoos and circuses, it is a wonderfully close,
gentle, even loving relationship. But when gentleness and affection
fail, or when handlers lack the patience, skill, or character to exercise them, coercion enters in — ankuses, chains, electric prods,
and all.

"Operant conditioning" and "positive reinforcement" are the
names of the game in protected contact, "PC," which owes more to
Pavlov and Skinner than to ancient mahout traditions. It is new
only as a regimen for elephants; it's the unacknowledged way rhinos, hippos, dolphins, killer whales, and other large, dangerous, or
otherwise inaccessible animals have been managed for decades. In-

deed, elephants are the great anomaly — as Active Environments partner Gail Laule, one of the designers of protected contact, says, "the only animal in the zoo we even *consider* punishing when it does something we don't want."

Protected contact is not the "hands-off" system it is often painted as; keepers still pat and stroke their charges, but always safely behind bars, neither giving nor receiving hugs or blows. The only leverage they exert is the bestowing and withholding of rewards — apples, carrots, and attention, which matters even to solitary bulls. *Target training* is the trick. Once the elephants at Tacoma's Point Defiance Zoo understood that they should step up and position themselves — lifting their feet for pedicures, for example — when the "target," a styrofoam float on a pole, was presented, the new regime was a piece of cake, or apple. "It was just a matter of their realizing they get lots of goodies if they do what we want, instead of getting poked if they don't," says Tacoma's elephant manager, Sally Joseph. And if they still don't? "We can't make them. They just walk away." And the keepers wait for a better time.

Point Defiance's three middle-aged Asian females were poster children for protected contact. Each was a peculiar character — the terms "screwed-up" and "crazy" also come to mind — the product of traumatic birth or captivity. Cindy (since deceased) was the first of "the bad girls," as their keepers affectionately call them. For most of her childhood and adolescence she was Tacoma's only elephant, shuffling away her days in an apartment-sized barn, one of a generation of unsocialized solitary animals in small circuses and zoos. Besides the usual stereotypic swaying, she developed the tic of tugging one nipple, which now dangles a foot below her chest. When inexperienced keepers couldn't handle her, a consultant administered beatings and electric prods. In 1982, Cindy left for a crash course in socialization — a breeding loan to San Diego's Wild Animal Park. But in creatures as complex as elephants, sexuality is something learned, not just inherited. Cindy, who'd never learned, repelled every suitor and tried to kill keepers who came within range. They responded by beating her harder than ever. "A big chunk of her flesh was hanging down off her head, exposing part of the skull beneath," Ray Ryan, then a keeper at the Wild Animal Park, recounts in *Keepers of the Ark,* a chilling tell-all memoir fiercely critical of both the San Diego management and elephant-keeping practices generally. "Her legs had been hit so hard that it was weeks before she was able to walk without limping."

When Cindy's breeding contract passed unconsummated, she was barned in Portland for a couple of years, then returned to Tacoma. Cindy had become a one-man elephant, attaching herself to a single regular keeper and the rest of the world be damned. Zoo managers cringe at such dependency, which leaves them no control when that keeper isn't around. Tacoma raised funds, built a modern barn with hydraulic restraint chute and automated entries, and converted to protected contact.

The plucky little zoo set itself a mission as a home for wayward elephants. It next acquired Suki, a stocky circus veteran with brains, guile, and malice to spare. Suki, who came to dominate Tacoma's little herd, would probably command any environs she found herself in, or die trying. She took her lumps in the circus; she could not lift her trunk high, a result of taking too many beatings on its tender base. But she gave as good as she got, killing two grooms by doing headstands on them.

Suki bounced between facilities until she wound up at Dickerson Park Zoo in Springfield, Missouri, an important breeding center, where Sally Joseph happened to be working. With Joseph, Suki was a sweetheart; she had a soft spot for women and an abiding loathing of males, elephant and human. Some cows are that way: "They can smell the testosterone," said Joseph. One day Joseph spotted Suki standing over another worker, about to do her patented headstand: "She didn't want to kill *me* that day, so I was able to pull him out." Dickerson Park gladly sent Suki to Tacoma, where Joseph later joined her.

Hanako, the third "bad girl," was the tallest of the three — half-sister to Portland's mighty Packy — but the opposite sort of oddball. Hanako didn't pursue her keepers or, it seemed, any other goal. She was obsessively nervous and distracted, backing out of the barn in the morning as though she feared losing the way back. She shuffled along, quivering in her own private reverie. "She is the old lady that you see in the streets talking to herself," said Joseph. "The guys at Dickerson Park were convinced she'd spent too much time in the birth canal and suffered brain damage. If we had a lot of money and time, we could probably get her drug therapy and she'd be a wonderful elephant."

Wonderful is a lot to ask, but these three were doing about as well as could be expected — much better, certainly, than they and the people around them fared in trunk-to-face free contact. "We're letting them be elephants," Joseph crowed, and under Suki's doting tutelage, Cindy finally seemed to have learned how. Watching space-case Hanako tag along while man-hating Suki twined her trunk over Cindy, expressing dominance as well as affection, I remembered how diffident and aloof zoo elephants so often seem around one another, as though looking elsewhere for their cues. These girls were a society unto themselves. "You wouldn't want them this bonded with each other in free contact," explained Joseph. "You'd want to establish yourself as dominant. You wouldn't want to get in the middle here. Threaten one and they'd all be on you."

Safety and tranquility come at a price. Protected contact demands reservoirs of skill and patience; the San Diego Zoo's chief of behavior management, Gary Priest, writes that its elephants adjusted to the new system more readily than their keepers. In 2000, after Zoo Atlanta announced that it would move to protected contact, a soft-spoken and distinctly unswaggering young Atlanta keeper named Kim Leclerc told me she feared losing what she cherished most about her job: "You can get a much closer relationship with elephants in free contact." Even apostate ex-keeper Ray Ryan pines for the days when he would swim with the big Africans he managed at San Diego and be cradled in their trunks.

Sally Joseph knows how they feel. "I miss being hugged by elephants when they like you," she admits. "I miss taking them on walks. I miss being able to lean over and listen to them rumble. But

I don't miss what I had to do to get dominance over them — the physical coercion, the attitude I had to take. I don't miss seeing people get killed."

Dominance is the classic model in elephant handling. The logic is that elephants are hierarchical creatures; the only way puny humans can be safe around them is to establish themselves at the top of the pecking order — to become super-matriarchs. Sanctuary operator Carol Buckley disputes that view of elephant nature: "It's *not* a vertical hierarchy — it's a horizontal culture. You need to know the individual relationships *and* the collective relationship. The matriarch takes control in crises, but others may lead at other times. All these male keepers want to be *boss*. They don't even want to be matriarchs and meet the psychological needs of their elephants twenty-four hours a day." Ryan claims that some of the swaggering, club-swinging keepers he worked with resented elephants "because they're matriarchal" and longed to beat their souls right out of them.

There's a striking gender cast to the split in elephant-keeping philosophies. At one point at an elephant care conference, I noticed the two factions gathered at their tables like boys and girls in a middle school cafeteria. The old-school keepers, especially those most outspoken in defense of free contact, were almost all men. Protected-contact and anti-circus partisans tend to be women: Buckley, Joseph, Active Environments' Gail Laule and Margaret Whittaker, Oakland Zoo curator Colleen Kinzley, Seattle animal behaviorist and ex-keeper Ellen Leach, and, in the activist vanguard, PAWS founder Pat Derby and PETA campaigner Jane Garrison.

This division reflects a general shift in zookeeping, as women flock to what was an overwhelmingly male domain. India's Dr. Krishnamurthy marveled at the trend when he visited the States: "I found the women better handlers — their maternal instinct comes in play. They're more cautious. They can use love and affection on the animal, where men tend to use force."

Already, however, the divisions between the free- and protected-contact schools are starting to blur. Buckley practices a hybrid approach at her sanctuary, varying it according to each elephant's needs and temperament. Free-contact practitioners talk about moving beyond dominance and emphasizing "positive reinforcement" rather than intimidation. "I can't *make* an elephant do anything," says Chuck Doyle, chief curator at Syracuse's zoo, president of the Elephant Managers' Association, and a free-contact stalwart. "They choose to listen to me because they know I'm not going to put them in jeopardy, and they'll get something if they do." The notion of the keeper assuming top spot in the herd order is a fond illusion anyway, he adds. "We kid ourselves. The elephant knows you're not an elephant."

Seattle zoo innovator David Hancocks, later director of the Open Range Zoo at Werribee, Australia, also sees the issue as a red herring. "If zoos had traditionally treated elephants with respect and care, we would not now have the debate," he muses. "Protected contact would not now be on the agenda. [It] is a bureaucratic and legalistic cop-out to avoid the bigger problems of elephant care."

Some keepers still decry PC as abdicating responsibility — compromising their elephants' care to reduce their own exposure and their employers' insurance premiums. In one notorious incident, keepers had to stand by helplessly as a calf newly born in protected contact and neglected by its inexperienced mother was killed by its own grandmother. "Much of what elephants need to know about raising young is learned, not instinctive," says David Blasko, elephant manager at Six Flags Marine World and one of PC's most ardent critics. Zoo herds just starting to breed lack the multigenerational wisdom, the learning by example, that makes good mothers. Ergo, keepers must help as midwives.

But Houston and Oakland have had successful births in protected contact, and Disney's Animal Kingdom is undertaking artificial insemination under it. San Diego's big bull Chico received foot care for the first time in ten years after entering protected contact; before, keepers feared approaching him. The Oakland Zoo adopted protected contact after its bull, Smokey, killed a keeper.

Once freed from keeper dominance, Smokey received many medical procedures and, by all accounts, became a purring sweetheart.

And in Tacoma, Suki the Bad Girl, Sally Joseph's pal from the bad old days, sometimes rumbles softly to her through the bars that will always stand between them — out of reach but not out of touch.

SEE THE ELEPHANT: To see what there is to see; to experience something to the end; to become jaded or disappointed.

— Frederic G. Cassidy & Joan Houston Hall, *Dictionary of American Regional English*

22

Seeing the Elephant

An elephant by most accounts is wiser and is a better animal for its involvement with mankind.

— Jim Williams, Ringling Brothers' Center for Elephant Conservation

I know there are some really clever fellows who say my elephants are symbolic, allegoric, or whatever they call it. But that's not true at all. My elephants are a living thing — they breathe, they suffer, and they die, like you and me.

— Romain Gary, *The Roots of Heaven*

JUST UP THE INTERSTATE from Tacoma, Seattle's Woodland Park Zoo was in the throes of elephant mania. In early 1999 it achieved the holy grail of zoos, a pregnant elephant. Better yet, a pregnant Asian: Chai, the Seattle elephant barn's best-natured inmate — formerly trotted out on sunny weekends for the kids to pat — had been suitably serviced by the star stud bull Onyx on a breeding loan to Springfield's Dickerson Park. Best of all, as it later turned out, she bore a female calf, meaning the zoo wouldn't have to accommodate or dispose of a troublesome bull down the line, and that it could look forward to another generation of babies from that baby.

Woodland Park cranked up its publicity; even the breedings of Madonna and Demi Moore did not receive such intimate attention.

The *Seattle Times* ran regular "Chai's Baby Diary" updates, and Seattle's KING-5 positioned itself as the Baby Elephant Channel with continual "Pachyderm Project" reports. The hype hit overdrive on November 3, 2000, when Chai delivered a 235-pound bundle of fuzzy adorability. Despite a cold snap, fans waited three hours to ogle the tyke for five minutes. Attendants hustled them through. Zoo attendance rose 171 percent that month over the previous year and doubled projections through the winter and spring.

The mania peaked again in March with the zoo's "Name the Baby Elephant" contest, modeled on the contests the Indianapolis Zoo staged after its two births. A Thai theme was specified. Thai restaurateurs grumbled about all the patrons asking them how to say "Hope" in Thai. An appraiser who saw Asian art hanging in my house asked if I had a Thai dictionary. Sixteen thousand entries poured in; the winner, submitted by a first-grader, was *Hansa* — "Supreme Happiness." After two years of trauma, from riots to earthquakes to corporate upheavals, Seattle was ready for even a little cheer: "People needed something warm and fuzzy," says zoo marketing director Mary Lee Hanley. The Thais believed that white elephants could safeguard their peace and prosperity. Seattle turned to a baby elephant to lift its spirits and, maybe, its luck.

Hanley and other zoo marketers, in Seattle and Indianapolis, nevertheless bristle at headlines like "How Much Is Cute Worth? Baby Elephant Brings Long Lines, Big Bucks," in the *Seattle Times*. "Sure, it's a marketing dream," concedes Hanley. "But that's not why she was bred. We were 100 percent concerned about the viability of that birth." Judy Gagen, Hanley's counterpart at the Indianapolis Zoo, insists that its two African elephant calves, conceived through artificial insemination, "cost us more than we'll ever make." Perhaps. But what Indianapolis made is substantial: a half-million-dollar rise in ticket sales in the year its babies arrived and, more important, $10 million in donations largely credited to them. As Pat Maluy, the lead elephant keeper who accompanied Chai to Missouri, told me with a wry smile, "It's all show business."

Zoo director Mike Waller says that what with travel, stud fees, veterinarians, staffing, food, baby-proofing, and so on, Woodland Park spent about $165,000 to obtain Supreme Happiness. That sum sounds enormous against the funds available to protect wild elephants in impoverished countries like Burma, where a thousand dollars can keep fifty anti-poaching rangers in the field for a month. But it seemed a good investment. Seattle got a bigger attendance boost than Indianapolis. After Hansa's birth, voters eagerly approved a new zoo and parks levy.

"If you want to make a lot of money, get a baby elephant," one Indianapolis veteran was heard to say at a professional conference. Nothing else draws such crowds, except perhaps giant pandas, and it costs millions to rent them from China, if you can. Seattle tried, and failed.

Zoo officials in Seattle and elsewhere don't say that's why they go to such lengths to breed elephants. "Conservation" is the mission invoked, and SSPs — Species Survival Plans, a system established by the American Zoo and Aquarium Association in 1981 to ensure genetically dispersed "sustainable" breeding — the mission manual. The original rationale for SSPs, what AZA science director Michael Hutchins calls "the Noah's Ark concept," became a popular rallying cry. With habitat fast disappearing, zoos would become modern "arks," sustaining imperiled animals until they can be reintroduced at home. Zoos talked — often — about the handful of species that have been saved in captivity: the Arabian oryx, Bali mynah, Guam rail, European bison, Przewalski's horse, and Père David's deer.

Elephants are charismatic but difficult candidates for the modern ark, just as they doubtless were for Noah, and the troubling questions about captive breeding coalesce around them. Everything about them is enormous: their appetites, space needs, care demands (which protected contact doesn't diminish), gestation periods, and life cycles. Breeding exchanges can spread three sometimes deadly diseases now rampant among captive elephants: salmonella, tuberculosis (a strain that infects humans, and has crossed over in both directions), and a herpes virus borne asymptomatically by African elephants, that kills young Asians. Each day little Hansa nuzzled up against her African "auntie," Watoto, and her keepers watched anxiously for the purple mouth that indicates herpes.

Even if breeding exchanges don't spread infections, they can do psychological damage. Chai's began violently. She arrived tired and underweight after three days on the road and entered estrus early. With Maluy in attendance, the keepers at Dickerson Park set out to establish control by putting her through her commands. But they prodded her with their hooks on different, more sensitive "cueing points" than Woodland Park used. Stressed and confused, the docile Chai did something out of character: she swung her head at the lead keeper, knocking him down. The keepers retreated, conferred with zoo managers, and according to an internal report decided to counteract this "aggressive behavior." The lead keeper repeated the cues as before, and when she swung as before, he and two others administered "punishment" with wooden ax handles. Thereafter Chai submitted without incident.

The Elephant Sanctuary's Carol Buckley says one attendee at the beating told her, confidentially, that it lasted an hour or more. Dickerson Park spokesperson Melanie Mancuso says the actual beating took just "five minutes" out of an hour-long training session; Pat Maluy recalled "probably thirty seconds of striking." (He later left Seattle to work in the protected-contact elephant program at Disney's Animal Kingdom.) Buckley's disclosures prompted federal authorities to investigate, and in August 2001 they charged Dickerson Park with physically abusing Chai and moved to suspend its animal-keeping license. In November 2001, they settled, in the usual way of such animal-welfare cases. Without admitting guilt, the zoo agreed to pay a $5,000 civil penalty, $3,000 of it on an outside consultant to review its elephant-management practices. Dickerson Park director Mike Crocker told me the consultant would help the zoo convert from free- to protected-contact management, a change it had long wanted to make but had not been able to afford.

Although Chai never rebelled again, she showed new signs of stress, even after returning to Seattle and after giving birth. She began swaying and shuffling in a classic stereotypic pattern — behavior curator Bruce Bohmke says she had never displayed before. Zoo attendants and docents gave the public various improbable explanations: "The swaying motion on the drive to Missouri got her started. She still thinks she's on the truck." Or, "She learned it from an elephant in Dickerson Park." Or the familiar "It's anticipation, when she's waiting to get fed or go outside." Visitors to the zoo would often smile and say, "Oh, look, she's dancing." I never heard the attendants contradict that, or tell the public that the repetitive motions might be a response to stress or boredom.

"Calves unify elephant groups," biologist Bruce A. Schulte writes in *Zoo Biology*. Zoos commonly promote breeding as a social boon even for the nonbreeding elephants, enabling them to interact in more herd-like fashion and gain a fuller experience of elephant life. In the long run, that will likely be the case for Seattle's elephants. But for most of Baby Hansa's first year, her arrival spelled increased isolation, confinement, and stress for Seattle's other two Asian cows, nervous young Sri and testy older Bamboo. They were unfamiliar with baby elephants and did not take readily to Hansa. So keepers kept them separate — confined, each by herself, in smaller side chambers — while they focused on the new baby. According to the keepers' daily log, Bamboo and Sri were not allowed outside for seventeen days after the birth, and then went out only occasionally for an hour or two. Indoors, they showed pronounced stereotypic movements. Confinement seemed especially burdensome for Bamboo, an unusually clever and inquisitive elephant. The year before, keepers had observed her in the yard using a stalk of bamboo as a pole to fish distant boughs of scotch broom down into foraging reach — a type of tool use I've not seen noted in any of the elephant literature. Now she circled fiercely around the shower room in which she was confined, resuming a childhood stereotypic pattern she evidently acquired when she was kept in a round pit in a children's zoo. One animal behaviorist feared that this lockdown might actually hinder the older elephants' acceptance of the new calf; like a jealous housecat resenting a new roommate, they might associate the "deprivation" with Hansa's arrival.

Bohmke still hoped that all the Seattle elephants could be re-united in "a free-roaming herd situation," and by October 2001 they seemed well on their way. Bamboo now went outside with mom, baby, and Watoto, the zoo's sole African elephant, who took most readily to the role of auntie for the Asian baby. Sri and Hansa would nuzzle across a protective electric wire. But the prospect of confrontations among the elephants, occasioned by the calf's rambunctious presence, would soon make it too dangerous for keepers to go in among them. And so the zoo announced that because the new calf had "dramatically changed the social dynamics of the herd," it would move from free to protected contact (just as Dickerson Park would). Woodland Park director Mike Waller told me the underlying motive for the change was a moral one: "We don't have the right to do what we have to do to dominate these animals" in free contact.

Seattle's breeding travails pale against the tragedy of Phoenix's star Ruby, the most famous and apparently most accomplished of scores of "painting pachyderms" in zoos. Ruby, the bearer of a rare genetic line, was bred, but her fetus died in utero and, with no hope of removing it, she was euthanized.

Such risks and disruptions would surely be worth the cost if the ark concept worked — if elephant species really could be saved in captivity. But more and more zoo and conservation professionals, and the American Zoo and Aquarium Association itself, concede that Noah's Ark is a pipe dream. Captive breeding will not make appropriated habitat return; Mount Ararat is not going to rise up and receive whatever species the zoo arks have saved. And accelerating extinctions and habitat loss will overwhelm any conceivable resources zoos can field to save biodiversity. "There simply is not enough space in existing zoos and aquariums to maintain genetically and demographically viable populations for vast numbers of species," writes the AZA's Michael Hutchins, arguing "The Case against the Noah's Ark Concept." Hutchins and his collaborators calculate that the zoos could maintain just 16 of earth's 2,700 or so snake species and 141 of 9,672 birds. AZA institutions currently breed about 120 species under 80 survival plans — droplets in extinction's barrel. And most of these plans govern mammals, most of them large and exotic; just one covers a fish species and one an invertebrate. This is neither accidental nor surprising. As the AZA's own "Species Survival Plan Mission Statement" notes, "SSP species are often 'flagship species,' well-known animals which arouse strong feelings in the public." Zoos breed the animals that draw people to zoos.

But they still defend their breeding as "conservation," though they no longer proclaim themselves arks and vessels of biodiversity as often as they used to. The watchword now is "sustainable captive population": zoos and even circuses present themselves as habitats of last resort, virtual wildernesses where chosen species can endure while their wild ranges wither. Don't despair over dying rain forests and coral reefs; your neighborhood zoo will save the last tigers from the gathering darkness. This mission justifies the pleasure we get from viewing captive animals and the enrichment zoos derive from exhibiting them. Exploitation becomes salvation.

An elitist, cliquish appeal underlies this romance. A sea of extinction may wash over the world, but zoos will be safe islands — if only for the merest sliver of the bioverse. Let the snail darters vanish. Like Boccaccio's and Poe's fugitive courtiers escaping (or so they think) the Black Death, we will save our elephants and pandas.

This mission also seems to reconcile two warring modern impulses: a nostalgia for nature and craving for technological solutions. It appeals to both the inner earth child and, with the advent of artificial insemination and cryogenic gamete and embryo banks, the inner techno-geek. Already cloning's promoters invoke endangered species preservation to justify their technology; never mind that it would limit genetic diversity, producing a vulnerable race of identical Jumbos.

The fond notion of zoos as havens rests on a ground of despair that may prove self-fulfilling. Oregon keeper Ray Hopper speaks for many zoo people when he says, "I honestly believe the only place my grandchildren are going to see elephants will be in zoos and captivity." Hopper had been to Malaysia, and was understandably discouraged at the pell-mell exploitation of its forests. But such statements often come, loaded with sweeping presumption, from people who've never even been to the elephant's homelands and have no inkling of the brave efforts at conservation in India, Burma, and Sri Lanka — countries where elephants can survive.

I watched one Indian elephant researcher, Christy Williams, fume as he watched the proceedings at the 2000 International Elephant Research Symposium in Portland. Williams was one of just two speakers from the elephants' range countries at this international conference, and one of two speaking about wild elephants; the other, on both counts, was the Kenyan Wildlife Service's science adviser, Paula Kahumbu, who shared Williams's concern. Williams listened with mounting exasperation as one American or European expert after another described progress in foot care, nutrition, behavioral management, and, especially, artificial insemination — for captive elephants. Finally he erupted in a hallway conversation with American keepers. He noted the millions spent on captive breeding, and how much a tiny fraction of that could accomplish in the reserve where he worked: "Wouldn't it be better to take that money and preserve habitat?" He recalled the endangered Sumatran rhinoceroses that an AZA offshoot set out to save through captive breeding in the 1980s. Twelve of thirty-five rhinos taken from the wild for breeding soon died; the rest were scattered across Malaysia, Britain, and the United States; none bred; $2.5 million and thirty-five rare rhinos went down the hole. "If that money had been invested in buying up oil-palm plantations," asked Williams, "wouldn't it have done more for the rhinos?"

"Very possibly," an American keeper replied, and noted that the rhinos' failure to breed recalled "what we have now in this country with declining fertility in elephants." And that, he said, demonstrated the need for artificial insemination. The implication: they should have just used AI to breed those uncooperative rhinos. The American couldn't imagine habitat as a priority.

"Scientific research" and "technology development and transfer" are two of the justifications the AZA invokes for captive breeding, and zoos do provide scientists easy access for many kinds of research. Katy Payne monitored elephants' infrasound in Portland, and it's a lot easier to examine their reproductive systems in a cage than in the field. But "technology development" means mostly artificial insemination, notes Richard Farinato, director of captive wildlife protection for the Humane Society of the United States, and only captive elephants have any problem breeding. "Wild elephants don't need any help. They reproduce very well. In fact, they reproduce too well," overrunning parks where they're confined and protected from poachers.

AI's boosters argue that it could be used to prevent inbreeding by spreading genes among small, isolated populations. But that leads back to the same devilish bargain: having such tools makes it easier to throw in the towel on habitat and relinquish large reserves and migratory corridors. Confined on ever smaller parcels, wild elephants at some point become captive ones.

Even with AI and sperm imports from Asia's finest bulls, there's no assurance that the captive Asian population will be sustainable. The Fort Worth Zoo's Robert Wiese analyzed current and projected demographics and found that by 2012, accredited North American zoos will hold only thirty-four fertile cows. Assuming the best imaginable infant survival, each would have to bear a calf every four years to sustain the population. This is pushing the biological envelope; in practical terms, it is inconceivable.

Wiese does, however, offer a ghoulish-sounding alternative: intensively managed "extractive zoo reserves" that would "sustain an extractive harvest for use by zoos." Instead of keeping and showing elephants in order to save them, we will save them — or at least save breeding stocks on tropical elephant ranches — in order to show them.

Even without such reserves, American zoos do provide valuable technical and financial assistance to conservation projects in range countries. The New York Zoological Society, parent of both the

Bronx Zoo and the trailblazing Wildlife Conservation Society, is a stellar example. If all North American zoos — the best-heeled in the world, with budgets totaling about $1.3 billion — did their commensurate bit, the conservation results would far surpass anything they could achieve in their nurseries at home. Kenya's Paula Kahumbu suggests they commit to regular, ongoing support: "I'd like to see a 'one-percent for conservation' provision in all zoo construction, not just a one-off payment."

But important as such work is, zoos with their multiple missions may not be the most efficient mechanisms for it. "In the final analysis, the only justification for zoos is education," writes David Hancocks, who spearheaded the development of natural habitat enclosures in Seattle. "They have the potential to reach a huge audience, thereby mobilizing support for the far-reaching goals of conservation." People can't love what they don't see, goes the thinking; lure them with cute babies, then inform and impassion them. They'll learn to care first about elephants, then about all critters, and finally about saving the natural world that nurtures them.

How are zoos doing at that? Seattle's certainly tries, but it's an uphill battle. On a sunny Saturday I observed the hundreds of visitors clamoring to get a glimpse of Baby Hansa. Parents shared their ignorance with their children: "That's the baby elephant, that's the mommy elephant, and that [pointing to the African female] is the daddy elephant." At first the zoo handed out a leaflet, "Chai's Story," which included a paragraph on conservation issues, but it's long gone. The paths around the elephant compound are dotted with informative illustrated boards and kiosks, but the few who were curious were hampered; the zoo had roped off the displays opposite the viewing window to funnel the crowds through. In one hour I saw precisely seven people, all adults unaccompanied by children, look at any of the displays — not counting the young rowdy who pantomimed punching the elephant on one board describing human-elephant conflicts. At a random moment, ten were shopping in the compound's all-elephant gift shop.

That's entertainment — the financial imperative with which the zoos strike an uneasy balance. For all their best intentions, the spectacle of a baby elephant and the hoopla over her Thai name convey nothing about the circumstances of elephants in Thailand. They may even send a message of complacency: A baby elephant is frolicking here, all's right with the world.

The Humane Society argues that zoos simply shouldn't keep elephants, since they can't provide anything like the space they need. Hancocks, a heretic in the zoo world, has come to concur: Elephants "are actually very poor candidates for life in captivity," he told me. "I doubt if a dozen elephants worldwide are in truly good psychological, behavioral, and social conditions. Their requirements are so substantial . . . it is probably beyond the capabilities of most zoos to even begin to resolve them."

And yet, despite all these reservations and criticisms, I remember the little elephant who delighted us at the Saigon zoo more than forty years ago. Would I take as much notice of elephants now if that zoo had not had an elephant? Perhaps captive elephants can be "ambassadors for their species" in the full sense of the word — but only if they're allowed to show themselves as *elephants* rather than as pets or inmates. The new sanctuaries for zoo and circus refugees suggest a model. Give them space — hundreds of acres at least, dozens of acres per elephant, not the thousand or two square feet the AZA requires — to form something like their wild herds. If we let them breed (a big *if*), female elephants should stay with their families for life, generation after generation, and males should stay through adolescence, as they do in the wild. Zoos allow smaller social animals — mole rats, meerkats, and monkeys — their societies; they should do the same for the giants they profess to exalt so.

Carol Buckley admits no visitors to her sanctuary, letting them view it instead on a Webcam. But there is a way to accommodate visitors without intruding on the elephants: elevated viewpoints. Install telescopes, as at Niagara Falls, and let people watch them foraging, socializing, living their own lives — as in Africa. The thrill of seeing elephants in their world, even from a distance, far surpasses the thrill of seeing them close-up in ours. Certainly not every zoo could accommodate them in that way. But why should every zoo have elephants if it cannot provide them the space to live as a herd rather than a cellblock?

The honest answer would be that zoos, and the cities that host them, want elephants as icons and mascots — as living trophies. We come to see the elephant and see our own wishful projections, like the colored patterns painted on its skin for Indian festivals. Viewing the animal through what the anthropologist Peter Cuasay calls "the palimpset of wonder," we smudge troubling questions and urgent exigencies into comforting blurs. Each inquiry into the elephant-human tangle leads to paradox, even after thousands of years of undomesticated domestic partnership. While we prop our civilizations, literatures, and faiths upon its broad back, the animal remains untamed, and in many ways unknown.

Now, as in past years, our ignorance is gaping. For more than a century, Western circuses and zoos failed to profit from Asian experience, and banished and executed musth-prone bulls. Having only lately recognized infrasound communication, researchers now hypothesize that elephants send and receive *seismic* messages via unusual "reptilian" features in their ears, which would help them pinpoint one another's locations when other sounds don't. We are beginning to understand the "gentle great thing's" intelligence, capabilities, and sensibilities just as we are imperiling its survival.

So many myths and so much literature — from Ganesha to *Babar* — have used the elephant as a vessel for divine and human attributes. But not until 1998 did an accomplished writer, Barbara Gowdy, use a novelist's empathetic powers to imagine an elephant's life, from deepest dreams to the most mundane sensations, from the elephant's point of view. Befitting the times, the result, *The White Bone*, is also a tragic and terrifying elegy, recounting the slow destruction of an African elephant clan by drought and bullets.

"Elephant painting" has become a popular zoo entertainment and fundraiser. One fashion producer even made garments from elephant-painted fabric, hoping to launch a clothing line. The process is usually mechanical; the keeper chooses the colors, dips the brushes, and tells the elephant when to start and stop. Joan Embery, who started it all in San Diego, even rotated the paper to vary the stroke directions. But in 1979, before the fad spread, a Syracuse zoo attendant named David Gucwa got the idea from a different source — an elephant named Siri. He noticed her scratching distinctive patterns in her stall's floor with a pebble, gave her pencil and paper, pondered the results, and published them in a curious book, *To Whom It May Concern: An Investigation of the Art of Elephants.* Gucwa's superiors doubted and disowned his project and told him to stick with rides and circus-style tricks. Later writers on elephant art ignore it, except when they borrow the painter Willem de Kooning's response to Siri's drawing: "That's a damned talented elephant."

Laid off during a zoo closure, Gucwa now works as a carpenter and hasn't seen Siri in years. But the two of them made something of a breakthrough. Untold handlers and mahouts had doubtless seen their elephants scratching patterns in the dirt and thought nothing of it. Gucwa, as his collaborator, James Ehmann, writes, "was on virgin ground in the field of animal cognition." Even Desmond Morris's chimpanzees and other primates, celebrated for making pictures long before elephants were, did so only after humans showed them how. "*Elephas maximus,* on the other hand — like no species other than *Homo sapiens* — had discovered drawing on its own."

And drawings they were. Gucwa did not interject colors, and Siri's forms are graceful, distinctive (with characteristic winglike shapes), expressive of her moods, if Gucwa is to be believed, and beautiful.

Phoenix zoo publicist Dick George, who knew and wrote about Ruby, Phoenix's famous painting elephant, gave me a similar account of her painting. At first she swirled sand with her trunk; once she was shown how to paint, she "never got tired of it." She chose her colors and seemed to match hues she saw — red when a fire truck passed, the cranberry of a visitor's blouse. George even came to think that she was painting representationally. Art, he realized, was a "subtle and infinitely shaded" question. "I believe Ruby was painting as expressively as a human being."

Again, however, we've more to learn. We know elephants have retinal rods and cones that should enable them to see colors. We do not know whether they see the same colors we see.

Music is an even older elephant stunt than painting. An 1850s circus elephant named Romeo cranked a hand organ while "Juliet" danced, and the Forepaugh and Barnum & Bailey circuses deployed "elephant bands" wailing on simple horns. A century later, the elephantologist Richard Lair met a New York experimental composer named Dave Soldier. Over a bottle of whiskey, Lair and Soldier hatched the idea of getting elephants to make music. They built elephant-sized versions of traditional Thai xylophones, drums, gong, and bass, and occasionally added harmonicas, thunder sheet, and a synthesizer with an elephant-joystick keyboard. The elephants played as they wished but started and stopped on Lair's cues. Some showed no interest or aptitude and others threw themselves into the music — just like people. Soldier tried to determine whether one prodigy could recognize dissonance: "I put one bad note in the middle of her xylophone. She avoided playing that note — until one day she started playing it all the time. Had she discovered dissonance, and discovered that she liked it? She'd outsmarted the researchers."

The resulting recording by the Thai Elephant Orchestra is weird, trancelike, and, to the right ears, hypnotic. But is it music? I asked after playing the disk for five unsuspecting listeners, the equivalent of the Turing test for artificial intelligence. All answered yes ("in the broadest sense," one hedged, finding it "kind of random"). "They're really close to the earth," one opined. "Yes, there's intention there." "These guys are musical explorers." "It's like a Thai Residents." "CD seems to be so respectful of the conscious mind, avoids intruding with either Western or Asian themes. I might call it New Age meditative music, on the border of music and philosophical percussion. Not music to get a massage to, but music to free up the mind." All marveled when I told them that the musicians were elephants, then smiled as if to say, "But of course."

*   *   *

I believe it is necessary and right to unravel the webs of worship and myth, ritual and war, exploitation and art that we have wrapped the elephant in. But these strands say more about ourselves, in our noblest and basest aspects, than about the living animals. We still have much to learn about ourselves from our relationship with them, but we have so much more to learn about them and, perhaps, from them. If through greed and negligence we drive them from the earth, our story as well as theirs will be unfinished. When their lives are done, ours will be diminished too. The world will be a small and meager place when it has room only for us.

SEE THE ELEPHANT: To see or experience all that one can endure.

— *Random House Historical Dictionary of American Slang*

Notes

1. Human Nature and Elephant Nature

page
12   Van Couvering, "Proboscideans," 77 (notes).

     "If a woman dreams": Damiri, *Hayat al-Hayawan*, 587.

     Merrick's "Autobiography": from the pamphlet *The Great Freak of Nature!*
Half a Man and Half an Elephant, reprinted by Montagu, *Elephant Man*,
109–110.

13   *Boozing Jumbo:* Jolly, *Jumbo*, 133–135.

14   *Plugging bells:* Williams, *Elephant Bill*, 78.

16   *Sanderson on longevity: Thirteen Years*, 56.

     Pliny, *Natural History* 8.1–5, 3:3–13. His report of moon worship accords
eerily with Sinhalese astrology, which assigns an animal to each celestial
body — the elephant to the moon, which rules water and mind (Cannon
and Davis, *Aliya*, 16).

     Pious elephants: Pliny, *Natural History* 8.1, 3:3; Scullard, *Elephant in the
Greek and Roman World*, 208–209, 218.

     "That nobody may think it was a vulgar choice," Pliny adds that the ele-
phant's beloved flower girl was also "a remarkable favorite of the very celebrated scholar Aristophanes" (*Natural History* 8.5, 3:11–13).

     Elephants' breath, from Kim Eichlin's novel Elephant Winter *(187):* "Ele-
phant breath is a tonic. If you have a headache, the best thing in the world
is to stand quietly with an elephant, its trunk in your mouth." In his *Adventures of Leucippe and Cleitophon* (cited by Scullard, *Elephant in the
Greek and Roman World*, 233), Achilles Tatius adds that "the elephant
knows that it has this power of healing and will not open its mouth for
nothing, but like a rascally doctor insists on its fee first." No doubt its handler had taught it to get its drachma before sharing its sweet breath.

17   *Death by dung:* Elephant Research Foundation, *Elephant* 2.4 (January
2000), 105.

17   *"Sensations" and Giuliani:* Caleb Mason, "Remembrance of Things
      Trashed," *In These Times,* May 15, 2000, 30; artist Tufani Mayfield on *The
      Holy Virgin Mary,* www.tufani.com/commentary_sacredsacrilege.
      Writers often quote Donne's thirty-first stanza (*Complete Poetry,* 122) but
      omit the next, in which a mouse crawls up the "sinewy Proboscis" to the
      trusting elephant's brain, to "gnaw the life cords there" and perish with its
      host.
18   *"Two hearts":* Aelian, *On Animals* 14.6.

2. Mammoth Riches

20   Rosny (*Quest for Fire,* 23, 83, 86), writing in 1911, imagined a mammoth
      "fully thirty feet" tall.
21   *"Little Effie's head":* Cummings, *Poems,* 112.
      Dima: Lister and Bahn, *Mammoths,* 49.
22   *Giant, ghoulish rodents:* Strong, "North American Indian Traditions," 82;
      Lister and Bahn, *Mammoths,* 42, 151. The 1712 Chinese chronicler (Scott,
      "American Elephant," 471) recorded that the uncovered flesh "is of a very
      cooling sort, and is also used as a remedy for fever." Ides (*Travels,* 25–27)
      mentions a Chinese companion who hunted the mammoths' "teeth," and
      notes these were used throughout Muscovy "to make combs and all other
      such like things instead of Ivory."
      Darwin, *Voyage of the Beagle,* 139–140.
23   *Abel's Cyclops:* Mayor, *Fossil Hunters,* 35–36.
24   *Dragon's teeth:* Palaephatus, *Unbelievable Tales,* 33–34.
      Orontes, Pausanias, and Geryon: Mayor, *Fossil Hunters,* 73–75.
      Plutarch and other proto-paleontologists: Ibid., 55, and Lister and Bahn,
      Mammoths, 41. Mayor writes that the myth of Dionysus and elephants
      "must have arisen sometime after the fourth century B.C., after the Greeks
      first learned about elephants from Alexander's campaigns in India." But
      the Greeks had already learned of elephants from Herodotus and, almost
      surely, other travelers. The Persians, who invaded Greece in the early fifth
      century, kept elephants. See Chapter 9.
      Stiles on giants, in a 1784 letter to Jefferson: Papers of Thomas Jefferson,
      6:312–315.
25   *"Pinnacle of elephant evolution":* Eltringham, *Elephants,* 222–223, 230–231,
      237. The woolly mammoth evolved the most deeply ridged molars for ef-
      ficient grinding — a life-and-death matter in large herbivores — and its
      tusks' upward sweep afforded better leverage for chewing.
27   *"Evolutionary nursemaid":* Van Couvering, "Proboscideans," 70–71.
      Newly discovered remains: Haile-Selassie, "Late Miocene Hominids";

Wolde-Gabriel et al., "Geology and Palaeontology"; Gee, "Return to the Planet of the Apes."

29   *"Ape with a fastball"*: Van Couvering, "Proboscideans," 71; Isaac, "Throwing and Human Evolution," 3–17; Knüsel, "Throwing Hypothesis," 1–5.

Hand axes: O'Brien, "Projectile Capabilities," 76–79, and "What Was the Acheulian Hand Ax?" 20–24; Calvin, *Ascent of Mind,* 176–194; Ambrose, "Paleolithic Technology."

The savanna's origin: Vrba, "Ecological and Adaptive Changes"; Behrensmeyer et al., "Late Pliocene Faunal Turnover," 1589; Kerr, "New Mammal Data."

30   Dobson (*Conservation,* 40) cites beavers and leaf-cutter ants, but not elephants, as changing "ecosystem structure and function."

"Super-keystone species": Shoshani, "African Elephant," 57–58. The label is apt, though it carries some unfortunate elephantocentric baggage.

31   Payne (*Silent Thunder,* 251) concedes that she didn't observe any evidence of this "sonar" while watching elephants dig wells.

Kitum Caves: Redmond, "With Elephants Underground."

32   *Sinclair on the Serengeti:* Cited in Morell, "Return of the Forest."

Kigale Forest; Rhodesia: Wing and Buss, "Elephants and Forests," 62–67.

3. Overchill, Overkill, Over-ill, and Over the Hill

35   *Fayyum fossils:* Van Couvering, "Proboscideans," 66.

Hyraxes, manatees, and dugongs bear the closest anatomical resemblance to elephants, but researchers (S. Perkins, "Genes Seem to Link Unlikely Relatives," *Science News,* January 6, 2001, 4) now propose designating a new superorder, "Afrotheria," to include them with aardvarks, elephant shrews, and golden moles, all of which appear to have evolved in Africa and diverged from other mammals about 100 million ago.

36   *Bones and ovens:* William K. Stevens, "Suspects in Blitzkrieg Extinctions: Primitive Hunters," *New York Times,* March 28, 2000, F5; Miller et al., "Pleistocene Extinction"; "Tusk Tales," *Discover* 18.2 (February 1997), 22.

37   *Bog mastodon:* Thomas H. Maugh III, "Remains of Mastodon Reveal Diet," *Los Angeles Times,* May 4, 1991, A26; Shoshani and Fisher, "Extinction of the Elephant's 'Ancestors,'" 65.

Tooth residues: Gobetz and Bozarth, "Implications for Late Pleistocene Mastodon Diet," 115, 122.

Malaysian diet: Eltringham, *Elephants,* 97–99.

African diet: Anthony J. Hall-Martin, "The Question of Culling," 197.

Mastodon kills: Fisher, "Mastodon Butchery." For a fuller discussion of

Pleistocene extinctions and dental evidence, see Fisher, "Extinction of Proboscideans."

37 *"Proboscidean resilience"*: Haynes, *Mammoths, Mastodonts*, 316–317. Haynes notes that Africa's elephants withstood decades of "range loss, terrible droughts, and compression into overused habitat," but one decade's illegal poaching wiped out half of them.

Tudge, *The Time Before History*, 312. Tudge also notes (288–289) that the North American species such as bison that survived the Pleistocene blitzkrieg tended, like many African savanna herbivores, "to be unpredictable migrators."

38 *Keystone megaherbivores:* Owen-Smith, "Pleistocene Extinctions"; Zimov et al., "Steppe-Tundra Transition"; Stone, "Bold Plan."

"Hyperdisease": MacPhee and Marx, "The 40,000-Year Plague," and "Mammoths & Microbes."

39 *"Extinction spasm":* Wilson, *Diversity*, 280.

Deloria, *Red Earth*, 10.

40 Ben-Aaron, "Retrobreeding the Woolly Mammoth," 85.

41 *Goto's retrobreeding:* Stone, "Cloning the Woolly Mammoth"; Kakuya Ishida, "A Mammoth Undertaking," *Yomiuri Shimbun*, March 28, 2000, 10; Sutsuko Kamiya, "A Dream to Revive the Woolly Mammoth," *Japan Times*, October 19, 1999; "Mammoth Resurrection Eyed," *Japan Times*, December 21, 1999; Nigel Hawkes, "Mammoth Task in Siberia," *The Times*, August 18, 1999. This and the Buigues/Mammuthus effort are most fully described in Stone's *Mammoth*, published after the writing of this book.

43 *Mammuthus project:* Jeff Hecht, "Dead and Gone," *New Scientist*, November 13, 1999, 11.

44 *"Beast of Bardia":* Lister and Blashford-Snell, "Exceptional Size and Form"; Erlend Clouston, "Monster in the Mist," *The Guardian*, June 5, 1999, 12; Nancy Banks-Smith, "Bungle in the Jungle," *The Guardian*, July 22, 1996, T13 (on an earlier documentary by the same producers).

"Thai mammoth": Kamolthop Bai-Ngern, "Teams Tracking Hairy Tuskers," *The Nation* (Bangkok), December 7, 2000.

45 Adam Goodheart, "Bringing Back Woolly Mammoth Could Rewrite a Bit of Our History," *USA Today*, November 16, 1999, 19A.

4. Elephants in America

47 *Jefferson on mammoths: Notes on Virginia*, 43–54. Letters to George Rogers Clark, December 4, 1783, *Papers*, 6:371; Ezra Stiles, June 10, 1784, *Papers*, 7:8; July 17, 1785, *Papers*, 8:300; Robert Livingston, *Works*, 9:151. See also John Rutledge, Jr., September 9, 1788, *Papers*, 13:593.

48 *"Doctrine of Monsters":* Jefferson, *Papers,* 6:312–315. Stiles cites Scripture, Norse sagas, and an Elizabethan travelogue — sources not likely to have convinced the rationalist Jefferson.

49 *Annan on Washington:* cited by Scott, "American Elephant Myths," 471. *Jefferson's mockers:* Ellis, *American Sphinx,* 215.

50 Jefferson, icon of American populism, also suggested (*Works,* 9:373) that Peale offer three showings at different prices. The wealthy "would be glad to see a thing often, and would not regard paying every time, but that they revolt at being next with pickpockets, chimney sweeps &c."
   Giant "moose": Pierre F. X. de Charlevoix, *Journal of a Voyage to North America,* quoted in Strong, "Mammoth Traditions," 83; translation by the author.
   Naskapi, Djákabish: Strong, "Mammoth Traditions," 83–84.
   Like Saint Augustine, Mather ("Philosophical Transactions," cited by Scott, "American Elephant Myths," 471) took ancient elephantid bones as evidence of biblical giants.

51 Johnson ("Men and Elephants," 218–219) claims that Caesar's report of Germans hunting "elk," the largest animals then known, in the same fashion also reflected passed-down knowledge of mammoths.
   Daubenton, Hunter, Turner, and Ashe: Scott, "American Elephant Myths," 471–473.
   Scott (ibid., 472–473) describes Turner's, Ashe's, and Koch's imaginative flights. Montagu and Peterson ("Earliest Account," 407–419), however, argue that the "charlatan" Koch actually uncovered the first evidence that early Americans hunted megafauna, and found a fluted Folsom projectile point eighty years before the first "recognized" discovery: "It is the tragedy of such men as Koch that even when they speak the truth they are not believed."

52 *New Orleans "giant":* Scott ("American Elephant Myths," 473) notes that "the exhibitor was perfectly honest in his belief."
   Eiseley on "desire to please": "Myth and Mammoth," 86, on myths, "Mastodon and Early Man" and "Men, Mastodons, and Myth," and, on hunters' unimportance, "Archeological Observations."

53 Lister and Bahn (*Mammoths,* 138) also recount claims of actual mammoth sightings in Siberia in the sixteenth and early twentieth centuries.
   Mayan "elephants": Stephens, *Incidents,* 122; Smith, *Elephants and Ethnologists,* 62, 87, and passim; Smith, "Pre-Columbian Representations." Travelers still see elephants in Mayan ruins: Molly Maguire, "The Mayans Left Clues," *San Diego Union-Tribune,* February 28, 1985, C1; Robin Lloyd, "A Child's-Eye View of Chichen Itza," *Washington Post,* September 25, 1994; Jim Hutchison, "Romancing the Stones," *Los Angeles Times,* January 12, 1987.

54   *Elephant and tapir terms:* Clark, "Note," 247–260.

55   Gourlay, in "Elephant in South America," *Man,* 40 (June 1940), 86–88,
      conceded that his discovery was unconvincing "as an elephant portrait"
      but presented "a problem demanding solution."
      Petroglyphs: Farley, "Elephant Petroglyph" and *In Plain Sight,* 66–67, 403–
      407; Davis and Keeler, "Georgia Elephant Disk"; Fell, "Elephant Petro-
      glyph." See Chapter 6, regarding elephants and rain in Hindu myth.

56   *"Ingenious accomplishments":* Engle, "Mayan Genius," C7.
      Rewilding: Martin and Burney, "Bring Back the Elephants," and Davis,
      "Pros and Cons," 70–74; Zimov et al., "Steppe-Tundra Transition," 782–
      783; Stone, "Bold Plan," 33.

5. Dances with Elephants

62   Although February is the prime season for processions in southern India
      and Colombo, Sri Lanka's biggest festival season comes in July and Au-
      gust, capped by the Kandy Esala Perahera.

64   *Queen Sirikit's gift:* "Majesty and Religious Rite," *Bangkok Post,* January 30,
      2001.

65   *Sinhalese nationalism:* Tambiah, *Buddhism Betrayed?* esp. 123–128; de Silva,
      History of Sri Lanka, esp. 350–363; Daniel, *Charred Lullabies.* For a Tamil
      nationalist view, see www.tamilnation.org, esp. "Sinhala Buddhist Funda-
      mentalism — the Record Speaks."

66   Lair's informative, often saddening, surprisingly entertaining *Gone Astray:
      The Care and Management of the Asian Elephant in Domesticity* is available
      from the United Nations Food and Agriculture Organization in Bangkok,
      fao-frap@fao.org.

67   Seneviratne (*Work of Kings,* 229) writes that Galboda "crossed over to the
      nationalist protest" when President J. R. Jayewardene agreed to let an In-
      dian force keep the peace in the breakaway Tamil region. Galboda's rheto-
      ric hasn't been as inflammatory as that of some senior monks. But his pa-
      tron, the late President Premadasa, helped reignite the civil war when he
      expelled the Indian Peace Keeping Force and used death squads to sup-
      press a Marxist uprising.
      Galboda and Kandy: Ibid., 227.

69   *"Great Elephant March":* "Visit Kerala (God's Country — and Yours!)"
      Web site, www.keralatourism.com.

70   *Chenda melam:* "Discover India" Web site on Trichur, www.meadev.gov
      .in/tourism/states/ker/trichur.

6. The Elephant Treasure

76 Airavata's origin presages the recent theory that elephants' mammal ancestors were probably aquatic. In 1999, A. P. Gaeth and other biologists in Melbourne announced in the *Proceedings of the National Academy of Sciences* that embryonic and fetal African elephants have vestigial kidney ducts, called nephrostomes, which occur in fish and frogs but rapidly disappear from other embryonic mammals. Furthermore, elephants' testes lie deep in the abdomen, as do marine mammals', to protect against cold waters. The trunk, present even in early fetuses, may have evolved as a snorkel. Elephants are famously good swimmers, able to cover long distances largely submerged, breathing through their trunks.

   Origin of elephants: Nilakantha, *Matangalila*, 41–54.

   Musth fluid: Bedi, *Elephant: Lord of the Jungle*, 95.

77 *"Tree of life":* Ibid., 7.

   "Heavenly beings": Abu L-Fazl, *A'ini Akbari*, 128.

78 *Marks of character:* Nilakantha, *Matangalila*, 74–79.

   "Charlatan science": Peris, "Abusing the Elephant," 53–55.

79 *Gajalakshmi:* Naravane, *Elephant and the Lotus*, 59.

   Kama: Gröning and Saller, *Elephants*, 125.

80 *Krishna and the milkmaids:* Andrews, "Elephant in Industry and Art."

81 *Buddha's birth:* Naravane, *Elephant and the Lotus*, 60.

   Jataka tales: Francis and Thomas, *Jataka Tales*, "The Crab and the Elephant," 211–213; "The Quail's Friends," 247–250; "The Pet Elephant," 140–141; "The White Six-Tusked Elephant," 395–409.

82 *Demon Mara:* Chutiwongs et al., *Paintings of Sri Lanka*, 54, 116; M. M. J. Marasinghe, "Theravada Buddhism," 37.

83 *Al-Fil: The Koran*, 432; Damiri, *Hayat al-Hayawan*, 575–580. Ad-Damiri also recounts Abu's rescue.

   Cures and curses: Ibid., 584–585.

84 *Elephant dreams:* Ibid., 586–587.

   On biblical ivories, see Chapter 12. The Old Testament also contains one cryptic reference, noted by Kurian (*Dictionary*, 138), to Solomon's receiving from India *shen-habbim*, "teeth of *habbim*," which may correspond to the Sanskrit *ibha* (elephant).

85 *Ganesha as scribe:* Rajagopalachari, *Mahabharata*, pp. 17–19. See also Courtwright, *Gaṇeśa*, 151–153.

   Aryan poet: Pal, *Elephants and Ivories*, p. 26.

   Bhartrihari's poems: translated by Barbara Stoler Miller in *The Hermit and the Love Thief: Sanskrit Poems of Bhartrihari and Bilhana*, cited by Courtright in *Gaṇeśa*, 29–30.

86 *Polymorphous sexual symbolism:* Courtright, *Gaṇeśa*, 30–31.

86   *"Low union":* Vatsayana, *Kama Sutra* 2.1, 23–24.
      "Old women": Cosentino, "Elephant as Metaphor," 85.
      Yoruba: Ibid., 86.
      Mende spirits: Ibid., 81, 83.
      Pygmies: Turnbull, "Legends of the Bambuti," 54.

7. The Elephant-Headed God

89   *Atmavilas Ganesha shrine:* Rao, *Mysore Palace,* 29.
90   *"Oh, Elephant-faced One":* Saint Nambiandiyadigal's prayer in Subramu-
      niyaswami, *Loving Gaṇeśa,* 295.
      "Milk miracle": Vinitra Srivastava, "Milking a Miracle," *Village Voice,* Oc-
      tober 17, 1995, 12; Lavina Melwani, "Question of Faith," *Little India,* Octo-
      ber 31, 1995, 49; "Of Milk and Media," *Hinduism Today,* January 31, 1996, 1;
      K. S. Jayaraman, "India's Milk Miracle Is Hard to Swallow," *Nature* 377
      (September 1995), 280; Joe Nickell, "Milk-Drinking Idols," *Skeptical In-
      quirer* 20.2 (March 1996), 7; and Subramuniyaswami, *Loving Gaṇeśa,* xii–
      xxv. Tim McGirk in *The Independent* ("Not Another Drop, Says Ganesh
      the Elephant God," September 24, 1995, 3) and Stuart Wavell in *The
      Sunday Times* ("In the Lap of the Gods," September 24, 1995) explore the
      miracle and the Chandra Swami connection.
92   *Shiva's and Parvati's restraint:* Courtright, *Gaṇeśa,* 42.
      "One thousand goblins": Millner, "Indian Mythology," 69.
      The version in which Airavata's head is sacrificed for Ganesha is cited (as
      "the" origin tale) by O'Flaherty in "Hinduism," 31.
93   The absence of Ganesha's origin in art, which puzzled me as I traveled
      in India, is confirmed by Robert Brown in his introduction to *Ganesh:
      Studies,* 5. The conferring of Ganesha's elephant head, Brown writes, has
      never "to my knowledge been depicted in art."
94   Lakshmi Lal recounts the origin myths involving Sani and Ganga in
      Ganesha: Beyond the Form.
      Aum: Courtright, *Gaṇeśa,* 31–32.
95   *Elephant aspect:* Narain, "Idea and Icon," 34–35.
      "Greek artists": Dhavalikar, "Myth and Reality," 55.
      "Demon of the Jungle": Foucher, introduction to Getty's *Gaṇeśa,* xxii–xxiii.
      In Foucher's exquisitely French interpretation, this "divine Opportunist"
      grew cozy and corpulent as he worked his way into the Hindu pantheon,
      assuming "the aspect of a *bon bourgeois.*"
      Transformation: Narain, "Idea and Icon," 35.
96   *"Scattering of the sweetmeat":* Werner, *Popular Dictionary,* 67–68.
97   *"Sun-worshipping Dravidians":* Getty, *Gaṇeśa,* 1. See Scullard, *Elephant in*

the Greek and Roman World, 254–255, on sarcophagi showing Dionysus returning in triumph from India riding or being drawn by elephants: "Since Dionysiac processions symbolically reflected the joy of victory over death, the presence of elephants which were believed to be favourites of the Sun-god gave further point to the triumph of light over darkness."

Garuda Purāna: Summarized by Redig in *Gaṇeśa: Images*, 29, along with a gentler version in the *Skanda Purāna*, in which a mouse nibbles Ganesha's *modaka* and becomes immortal. So much for elephants' fabled fear of mice.

Crashing and sneaking: Zimmer, *Myths and Symbols*, 13.

8. The Land of the White Elephant

98   *Oldest Thai depiction:* Ringis, *Elephants of Thailand*, 60.
      Oldest Thai inscription: Lair, *Gone Astray*, 211.
100   *The regent trapped:* Ringis, *Elephants of Thailand*, 67–68.
      Mahachakrapat and Naresuan: Ibid., 68–74; Warren and Amranand, *Elephant in Thai Life*, 60, 114–116.
      The Burmese demonstrated their own devotion to white elephants when an orphan calf was left at Mandalay Palace. "It was suckled daily by twenty young Burmese women" (Williams, *Elephant Bill*, 62).
101   *Flag:* Another explanation (from Richard Lair, personal communication) is that Rama VI resented the fact that some flags were so poorly made that "the elephants looked like pigs." The Royal Thai Navy still uses the white elephant ensign.
      Western bedazzlement over white elephants and the mystic East are most poignantly expressed in a March 8, 1878, *New York Times* article ("Funeral of a Siamese God," 2). It calls the Thais "Indians" and reports that "mandarins" attend each elephant. The royal elephants might have been gifts of the gods, but they certainly weren't gods themselves. Suthilak Ambhanwong summarizes the 1921 Thai law describing these noble elephants in his *Chang Thai*, translated and excerpted in Warren and Amranand, *Elephant in Thai Life*, 120–121. Whoever concealed or released such an elephant could be fined or imprisoned.
104   *"Divine madness":* Chadwick, *Fate of the Elephant*, 352.
      Elephant numbers: Lair (*Gone Astray*, 167) considers 100,000 "not impossible." Contemporary estimates are from the Forest Industry Organization of Thailand's *Elephant Status* report, posted in December 2000 at www.thaielephant.com/e_trial. Lair (165) in 1997 gave ranges of 1,300 to 2,000 wild and 3,800 to 4,000 domesticated elephants. Alongkorn Mahannop of the Dusit Zoo believes that only 2,000 to 2,200 domesticated animals re-

main. To resolve uncertainties and track populations and health data, Lair (242) recommends an "International Registry of Domesticated Elephants."

105   *Amphetamine addiction:* Lair, *Gone Astray,* 201.

106   *Captive babies:* Sitthidej Mahasawangkul, "Trading of Baby Elephants/The Tragedy of Thai Elephants," in the FIO report "Elephant Status." Thai hotels were not alone in this practice; as of 1972, according to Royal (*Speaking of Elephants,* 9), the Six Flags over Texas amusement park got a new baby elephant mascot each year. Each was named "Sis Flagg" and was sold at season's end.

107   *The Sui:* Cuasay, "Marginal Animals," 6–7.
       Bangkok buskers: Mick Elmore, "A Day in the Life of Jumbo in the Concrete Jungle," *T&I Traveller* (August–September 1999), 78; Artit Khwankhom, "Elephants in Bangkok to Be Seized," *The Nation* (Bangkok), March 15, 2000, A2; Anjira Assavanonda, "Back on the Road to Nowhere," *Bangkok Post,* March 8, 2000, 2.

108   *Nong Nooch goring:* "Girl Killed by Rogue Elephant," *Daily Mail,* April 26, 2000, 2; "Animal Show Clampdown," *The Nation,* April 27, 2000, 1; "Elephant Shows Go on After Killing of Tourist," *Daily Telegraph,* April 27, 2000, 15; "Big Steps Toward Safety," *Travel Trade Gazette* (U.K. and Ireland), May 15, 2000, 48; "Killer Elephant to Work Again," *Daily Mail,* July 29, 2000, 44.

110   *Elephant Village:* "More Elephant Stories," *Thai News* 23 (August–September 2000).

112   *Elephant meat:* Lair, *Gone Astray,* 212; for the hype, Busaba Sivasomboon, "Taste for Elephant Meat Spreads Among Northern Thais," AP Worldstream, May 31, 2000; "Activists Say Elephants Being Killed for Meat," *Bangkok Post,* June 4, 2000; Anusak Konglang, "Slaughter of Thai Elephants for Meat on the Rise," Agence France Presse, June 7, 2000.
       Trunk tips: Pliny, *Natural History* 8.10.31, 2:25; Gale, *Burmese Timber Elephant,* 13, a captivating record of teak culture and elephant care, rich in firsthand science and lore.

9. Warriors and Giants

117   Lair (*Gone Astray,* 12–13) cites Lahiri-Choudhury's 1995 article "History of Elephants in Captivity in India and Their Use: An Overview." The question, he adds, is "how many elephants must be kept over what period of time before qualifying as true domestication."

119   *Egypt's menageries:* Murray, *Circus!* 29–31.
       Elephant-head coin: Kunz, *Ivory,* 170, 172.
       Hanno's voyage: Scullard, *Elephant in the Greek and Roman World,* 33.

It seems that Herodotus (*Persian Wars* 4.91, 367) never saw an elephant, or the other, even stranger creatures he described.

120 *Ctesias' tales:* Scullard, *Elephant in the Greek and Roman World*, 33–34.

Trung sisters: Nguyen, *Vietnam*, 27; "Vietnam Stamps" Web site, www.best-signs.com/vinhtran/1959/1959b.htm; "Women in World History" Web site, www.womeninworldhistory.com/heroine10.html.

121 *Alexander versus Darius:* Tarn, *Alexander*, 1:47.

Alexander versus Porus: Arrian, *Anabasis*, 2:43–67; Tarn, *Alexander*, 93–99; Fox, *Alexander*, 358–361; Kunz, *Ivory*, 146.

122 *Quintus Curtius:* Scullard (*Elephant in the Greek and Roman World*, 72–73) dismisses this "nonsense" about the uselessness of elephants that "Curtius puts into [Alexander's] mouth," insisting that "the men who fought against Porus knew better."

Alexander in Babylon: Ibid., 74–76.

Funeral carriage: Diodorus 18.27, 91.

123 *The elephant Ajax:* Philostratus, "Apollonius" 2.12, 43. The bones found outside Troy and believed to be those of the original warrior Ajax probably belonged to a prehistoric elephant. Philostratus also recounts that Apollonius, prompted by the sight of a boy "grievously goading" his elephant, asked his companion Damis, in the Socratic manner, "What constitutes a good rider?" Apollonius concluded that credit should go to the ridden elephant, not the rider: "This is by far the most docile of all animals, and when once it has been tamed by a man it lets him do anything to it and always shows him the same obedience. It delights to take food from his hand like a puppy; it caresses him with its trunk when he comes near; it lets him put his head into its jaws, holding them open as long as he likes, as we saw done among the nomads. Yet it is said to lament over its bondage at night, not with its usual trumpeting but with a mournful and piteous moaning; yet if the man comes to it while mourning so, the elephant stops its complaining as if ashamed. Thus it is its own master, Damis, and its tractable disposition manages and rules more than its rider does."

Ptolemy at the parapet: Diodorus 18.34, 107–109.

Perdiccas' breakwater: Ibid. 18.35, 109–111.

124 *Seleucus' victory:* Scullard, *Elephant in the Greek and Roman World*, 97–99. Diodorus (19.14–15, 269–273) notes that Eudamus acquired these beasts "by treacherously slaying King Porus," then traded them to Seleucus.

Pyrrhus' voyage to Tarentum: Scullard, *Elephant in the Greek and Roman World*, 101–103.

Pyrrhus at Rome: Plutarch, *Lives*, 481. Defeat at Beneventum, ibid., 486.

Fear of pigs: Aelian, *On Animals* 7.38(i), 57. Scullard (*Elephant in the Greek and Roman World*, 114–115) notes that the same story was later told when Antigonus Gonatas attacked Megara.

125   *Pyrrhus in Macedonia and Sparta:* Plutarch, *Lives,* 486–490. Death at Argos, ibid., 490–403. See also Scullard, *Elephant in the Greek and Roman World,* 105–119.
       Carthage's elephants: John Noble Wilford. "The Mystery of Hannibal's Elephants," *New York Times,* September 18, 1984, C2.
       Romans routed: Polybius, *Histories* 1.33–35, 39, 1:38–41, 45.
126   *Caecilius' victory:* Ibid. 1.40, 1:46–47.
       Hannibal at the Pyrenees and Rhône: Ibid. 3.41–43, 46, 1:202–203, 206–207; Livy, *History* 21.26–28, 4:24–27.
       Reenactments: De Beer, *Hannibal,* 172–173; John Hoyte, "Trunk Road for Hannibal," *Daily Telegraph,* September 13 and 17, 1979, 1; "Two Rented Elephants to Trace Alpine Trek," *New York Times,* September 13, 1979, 4; David Plummer, "Botham Ignores Sacking Questions as First Alps Elephant Goes Lame," *The Guardian,* March 31, 1988; Tony Rocca, "Even the Legion Retreats as Botham Advances," *The Sunday Times,* April 3, 1988.
127   *Trebia battle:* Polybius, *Histories* 3.72–74, 1:232–234; Livy, *History* 21.55–56, 3:52–53.
       Carthage's fall: Wernick, "Carthage"; *Columbia Encyclopedia,* s.v. "Punic Wars."

10. Blood and Circuses

128   *Domitius' Provence procession:* Suetonius, "Nero," from *Lives,* cited by Scullard, *Elephant in the Greek and Roman World,* 192.
       Caesar's coin: Hayes, *Ancient Coins,* 17. Cederlind is an ancient-coin dealer in Portland, Oregon.
129   *Caesar versus Pompey:* Caesar, "The African War," in *Civil War,* 253–255.
       Caesar's triumph and funeral: Suetonius, "The Deified Julius," in *Lives* 1.37, 84, 1:51, 113.
       Ptolemy II's parade: Murray, *Circus!* 31–32.
130   I never saw arak (distilled palm juice) slipped to elephants in India or Sri Lanka, but I did hear of elephants who had broken into storerooms to steal arak and toddy wine. Arak is a notorious vice among mahouts; with a cup-size pouch of it costing about twenty U.S. cents in India, it's often the only booze they can afford. Considering their job risks, it's not surprising they drink, although this may make them more likely to abuse their elephants and to be injured or killed in turn.
       India's elephant bouts: Varadarajaiyer, *Elephant in the Tamil Land,* 73; Bernier, *Travels,* 314–316; Carrington, *Elephants,* 199. Bernier, who barely escaped trampling at one bout, notes that the mahouts received a hefty bonus if they survived, and their families still received their salaries if they didn't.

131   *Caracalla and elephants:* Scullard, *Elephants in the Greek and Roman World,* 258. Scullard also cites Dio Cassius' observation that the emperor "took about with him many elephants in imitation of Alexander, or rather of Dionysus."

      Pompey's Circus: Cicero, *Letters to His Friends,* 2:7; Pliny, *Natural History* 8.7.20–22, 2:15–17; Seneca, "On the Shortness of Life," 74–75; Dio Cassius, *Roman History* 34.38.2–6, 3:361–363; Toynbee, *Animals in Roman Life,* 22–23.

132   *Augustus', Trajan's, and Commodus' Circus slaughters:* Toynbee, *Animals in Roman Life,* 21–22.

133   *Elephant executions:* Deraniyagala, *Some Extinct Elephants,* 68; Balaban, notes to *Spring Essence,* 121. Edwardes, *Ralph Fitch,* 99. Such executions weren't confined to the East. Diodorus Seculus (*Diodorus* 25.2.3, 11:47) recounts that Hamilcar, Hannibal's father, suspended his usual leniency and had rebel mercenaries who had mutilated captured Carthaginians trampled by elephants. It seems likely that the method was employed elsewhere around the Mediterranean.

134   "Stomping Out Software Piracy," *Seattle Times,* April 28, 1999, A3.

      Babur and Akbar: Hendley, "Elephant in State Ceremonies," 18.

      "What strange practice": Digby, *War-Horse and Elephant,* 50–51.

135   *Aurangzeb:* Tavernier (*Travels,* 179–180) adds that Aurangzeb attacked on Sunday, believing that the Christian Portuguese, "like Jews, would not defend themselves on their Sabbath." Disabused of that notion, "this Prince has wished to have nothing more to do with Christians."

136   *"Seeing the elephant":* soldier's letter dated 1847, collected by James M. McCaffrey in *Manifest Destiny,* and J. M. G. Brown, *Rice Paddy Grunt,* both cited in the *Random House Dictionary of American Slang,* 702. Bartlett (*Dictionary of Americanisms*) credits a "Mr. Kendall" in his "Narrative of the Texan Santa Fé Expedition" with first publication of the expression. It became versatile and ubiquitous in the later nineteenth century, variously meaning to see combat, see the sights, experience the world, get cheated, be seduced, and lose one's innocence. Partridge (*Dictionary of Slang*) notes an English variation, "to see the king." Mathews (*Dictionary of Americanisms*) notes "*to draw up the elephant* [means] to succeed in a most difficult undertaking," and "*to cry up the elephant* [means] to 'talk up' something."

      Marshal Blücher's false pregnancy: Longford, *Wellington,* 406.

      Kunz (*Ivory,* 153) mentions Hagenbeck's drafted draft elephant. Gröning and Saller describe her, and the British, Burmese, and Cambodian elephant corps, in *Elephants,* 232–235.

      Japanese elephants and British bombing: Williams, *Elephant Bill,* 228–230, 244–247. Williams also notes that though the Japanese did not mistreat their elephants outright, they effectively starved them by tying them up at night rather than letting them range for fodder in the usual fashion. They also "had a passion for ivory, and practically every tusker elephant which had been in Japanese hands had his tusks sawn off as near to the nerve as possible" (246).

11. Ambassadors from the East

138 *Enmity with snakes:* White, *Book of Beasts,* 26–27.
  Timotheus' fragmentary *On Animals* (31–32) also notes, "They are law-abiding and moderate, and have a leader and pass by rivers carrying their young."
  "Modest and shamefast": Topsell, *Historie,* 197.

139 *Crusades:* Sanderson (*Dynasty of Abu,* 146) and Carrington (*Elephants,* 200) mention Charlemagne's and Henry's elephants but omit Frederick's. Popham ("Elephantographia," 180–181) includes it and gives a fuller account of Louis's gift to Henry. He opines that a realistic elephant carved among the chimeras on Notre Dame Cathedral was based on Louis's elephant and was "the first authentic likeness . . . drawn or carved since Roman times, different indeed from the extraordinary creatures purporting to be elephants, which decorate the pages of thirteenth-century romances." Sanderson (147) mentions accurate carvings of elephants in several obscure French churches, including one of an African at Souvigny, but gives no dates.

140 *Punctured myths:* Albert the Great (Albertus Magnus), *Man and the Beasts,* 100–101.

141 *Manuel I:* Bedini, *The Pope's Elephant,* 30.
  Elephant versus rhino: Ibid., 112–121.
  Leo X and Hanno: Kunz, *Ivory,* 154; Carrington, *Elephants,* 201; Popham, "Elephantographia," 183–185; and, most thoroughly, Bedini, *The Pope's Elephant.* Bedini was evidently unaware of these and other previous references (including one by Jacob Burckhardt in 1878) when he set out to confirm the tantalizing rumor of an elephant or rhinoceros that appeared at the Vatican long ago. The famous Vatican archives contained no mention of the Vatican's own elephant, and one after another Vatican official knew nothing of it. Finally, Bedini chased down the tale and discovered parts of it had often been told before.
  Hanno reaches Italy: Popham, "Elephantographia," 183; Bedini, *The Pope's Elephant,* 39–44.
  "Genuflected three times": Popham, "Elephantographia," 183; Gröning and Saller, *Elephants,* 249.
  "King of the poets": Bedini, *The Pope's Elephant,* 90–100; woodcut (ibid., 93). Popham ("Elephantographia," 184) notes that Hanno not only ejected

Baraballo but also, when fitted with a towering howdah to march at Giuliano de Medici's wedding, panicked at a cannon salute and threw himself, turret and all, into the Tiber. This prompted the false belief (Gröning and Saller, *Elephants*, 249) that he had drowned.

142 *Fra Bonaventura:* Bedini, *The Pope's Elephant*, 138–141.

Rome's finest physicians: Ibid., 142–143.

Hanno suffocated: Gröning and Saller, *Elephants*, 249.

Hanno's epitaph: Ibid., 145; Popham, "Elephantographia," 185.

143 *Maximilian's elephant:* Popham, "Elephantographia," 186–187.

Bohemia, Guicciardini, and Lipsius: Ibid., 186–188. Translations by the author.

144 *Gift from Calcutta:* "The Queen and the Teetotallers," *The Times*, August 29, 1840.

Mongkut's letter: Ringis, *Elephants of Thailand*, 90.

145 Bowring described the "Royal Elephant of Siam" in the *Fortnightly Review*, reprinted in *The Times*, October 2, 1865. Despite their fascination with white elephants, British colonial authorities refused "for sanitary reasons" to let King Thebaw of Burma's deceased royal elephant lie in state for three days (*The Times*, December 12, 1885).

146 *Order of the Elephant:* Royal Danish Embassy, www.denmarkemb.org/orders.

12. White Gold

147 The revered missionary-explorer David Livingstone had argued passionately for missionaries' "undoubted right" to the ivory wealth their exertions opened up, at the same time denying that they actually profited from it: "Though poor, we make others rich" (*South African Papers*, 116, 120).

148 *Japanese import volumes:* Barbier et al., *Elephants, Economics, and Ivory,* 9–10, 60.

149 *Japanese ivory industry:* Takeshi Nakanishi, "Ivory Ban"; Jonathan Watts, "Lifting of Ivory Ban Gets Seal of Approval in Japan," *The Guardian,* July 4, 1997, 12; Kakuchi, "Ivory Imports"; "Lifting of Ivory Import Ban Fuels Fear of New Poaching," *Yomiuri Shimbun*, March 17, 1999, 2; M. V. Balaji, "India Lobbies Against the Ivory Hunters in Bid to Save Jumbo," Deutsche Presse-Agentur, April 7, 2000.

151 Mungo Park, *Travels,* 235–236. Park surmised that local elephants frequently broke their tusks prying up edible roots because "such a large proportion of broken ivory is daily offered for sale."

152 *"Devil's work balls":* Oriental Ceramics Society, *Chinese Ivories*, 187.

153 *Czech mammoth carving:* Lister and Baum, *Mammoths*, 98.

Egyptian ivories: Scullard, *Elephant in the Greek and Roman World,* 27–28.

153   *Influences:* Beihoff, *Ivory Sculpture,* 9.
       "Chinese" carving from Italy: Ibid., 28–29.
       Chinese adaptation of Western figures: The Oriental Ceramics Society
       (*Chinese Ivories,* 41–43) notes that these figurines, euphemistically de-
       scribed as "medicine ladies" to "prudish westerners," were in fact erotic
       toys, not medical models.

154   *Biblical ivories:* 1 Kings 10:18, 10:22, 22:39; 2 Chronicles 9:17, 9:21; Psalms
       45:8; Song of Songs 5:14, 7:4; Amos 3:15, 6:4.
       Trunk meat: Pliny, *Natural History* 8.10, 25.
       Christianized Roman ivories: Joice, Knight, and McClusky, *Ivories,* 17.

155   *Value of slaves and tusks:* Ross, "Imagining Elephants," 39.
       Opponents of slavery such as Livingstone made much of the connection
       between the ivory and slave trades, using the horrors of one to pique hor-
       ror at the other. But Alpers ("Ivory Trade," 356) contends that the nexus
       "was not so pronounced historically as is often portrayed." He concedes
       that the Yao in Mozambique and Arab-Swahili traders in East Central Af-
       rica used slaves they transported as ivory porters. But elsewhere, "ivory
       porterage was a prestigious undertaking, and came to represent for many
       young men something of a rite of passage . . . that can be compared to la-
       bor migration in the present century." However it uprooted them, the
       trade certainly sapped labor from farming and disrupted village life.
       Hybrid ivories: Fagg and Forman, *Afro-Portuguese Ivories.*

156   *Crocodile "chalice":* Ibid., 10.
       Portuguese ivory buying: Vogel, *Africa and the Renaissance,* 13–18. Pamela
       McClusky, the Seattle Art Museum curator who introduced me to the
       Afro-Portuguese ivories, notes one lingering mystery: "No one knows if
       African carvers were taken to Europe, or if they just carved in Africa from
       European pictures."
       Ivory at Manyuema: Stanley, *How I Found Livingstone,* 460–461.

157   Livingstone, *Missionary Correspondence,* 184, notes "ivory rotting in the
       sun."
       Leopold's advance man: Hochschild, *Leopold's Ghost,* 30–31, 64–65.

158   *Annual ivory harvest:* Eltringham, *Elephants,* 207–208; McLynn, *Hearts of
       Darkness,* 183; Alpers, "Ivory Trade."
       "Elephant Marsh": Livingstone, *Narrative of an Expedition to the Zambesi,*
       cited by Alpers, *Ivory and Slaves,* 27; Joseph Thomson cited by McLynn,
       Hearts of Darkness, 184.

159   *Billiard balls per tusk:* Ludwig, *The Nile,* 183–184.
       Building a better ball: "Industrial Symbols: Moulding History," *The Econo-
       mist,* October 19, 1996, R13; Alpers, "Ivory Trade," 356; Elizabeth Holmes,
       "Billiards and Ivory," *Buzzworm* (May 1992), 24. Billiards specialist Holmes
       notes the abiding "passion for ivory" of the cue stick elite who declare,
       "Only ivory balls hold English after the third bank."

160   *Piano keys:* Wier, *The Piano,* 71–72.
161   *Taming Africans:* Bartlett, *Wild Animals in Captivity,* 62.
      Gordon in Sudan: Frank Buckland, "Working Elephants," *New York Times,*
      March 24, 1879, 2. Buckland relied on a report in the "influential" newspa-
      per *Colonies,* which seconded Gordon's idea.
      Congo project: Smith, "Domestication Centre," 152–154; Melland, *Elephants
      in Africa,* 133–144; Watson, "King Leopold's Elephants"; "Taming African
      Elephants: School Work in the Congo," *New York Times,* April 9, 1927, 11.
      Cornacs and mahouts: Gavron, *King Leopold's Dream,* 272; Smith, "Do-
      mestication Centre," 152.
      Public relations bonus: "Trying to Save the African Elephants," *New York
      Times,* December 28, 1902, 4.
162   *WWF's pullout:* Fred Pearce, "Rumble in the Jungle," *New Scientist,* No-
      vember 7, 1998, 16; Watson, "King Leopold's Elephants."

13. Brown Ivory

164   *The oak crisis:* Marcus, *Age of Nelson,* 244–245. Knight, *Shipbuilding Tim-
      ber,* 10–18.
      Shipbuilding boom: Knight, *Shipbuilding Timber,* 12–13.
      "Fatal want": Ibid., 14.
      Teak's qualities: Tewari, *Monograph on Teak,* preface; Sanderson, *Dynasty
      of Abu,* 174–175.
165   *"Manifold uses" of elephants:* Symes (*Embassy to Ava,* 277) noted that "his
      Birman Majesty is said to possess 6,000."
      "Political necessity": ibid., 455–460.
      Indian shipyards: Knight, *Shipbuilding Timber,* 18. Clowes (*The Royal
      Navy,* 13) writes that the first naval order from the Bombay yard was
      launched in 1805, but ships previously built in India had been presented to
      the navy.
      "Sorry plight": Sanderson, *Dynasty of Abu,* 178.
166   *"Living museum":* Lair, *Gone Astray,* 101.
167   *MTE elephant husbandry:* Zaw, "Utilization of Elephants"; Chris Wem-
      mer, "The Elephant-Wallahs' Microcosm" (unpublished paper).
172   *Forest exploitation:* World Resources Institute, "Logging Burma's Frontier
      Forests," at www.wri.org/ffi/burma.

14. Bailey and Barnum, Jumbo and Bet

178   *America's first and second elephants:* Carrington, *Elephants,* 202; Whitt; *El-
      ephants and Quaker Guns,* 13–14; *Portland Sunday Telegram,* "First Ele-

phant Brought to U.S. Said to Be Buried at Alfred," July 2, 1933; "Elephant Burial Ground" Web site, www.roadsideamerica.com/pet/oldbet.

178   Shettel cites the log kept by Nathaniel Hawthorne's father, a member of Crowninshield's crew, and the *New York Journal* notice ("First Elephant," 6–7). He also notes (14) that Crowninshield was later elected to Congress and appointed secretary of the navy by President Jefferson.

179   *"Stage dishonoured"*: Shettel (ibid. 8–10) cites The Elephant's publicity and the pan in Dunlap's 1832 *History of the American Theatre* and notes, "It must be remembered that Dunlap had no love for the circus." With circuses presenting themselves as "wholesome" alternatives to the theater, which was often castigated and suppressed for immorality, it's no wonder that its defenders resented them. Shettel (6–7, 12) describes a John Davis, who reported meeting Owen and his elephant in South Carolina. Davis marveled at "the solemn majesty" with which the latter received gifts but noted that "an old negro man" remembered much larger elephants in Africa and called this one a mere "calf."

180   *Bailey and Howes:* Barnum, *Funny Stories,* 46–48; Addis, "Somers History," 121.
       Bet's handbill: Eastern Argus (Portland), May 22, 1816, 3.

181   Dow, *Reminiscences,* 46–47.
       "Death of the Elephant": Boston Gazette, July 29, 1816. A slightly different version in the *Portland Eastern Argus* (July 30, 1816, 3) gets Bet's gender right.

182   *Pilgrimages to Bet's monument:* Addis, "Somers History," 128–129. On Somers's growth as a circus center, see ibid., 119–137.
       Alternate accounts of Bet's murder: Tucker's unpublished "Old Bet Lives — Dammit," provided by the Alfred Historical Society, the most thorough examination of the facts and fancies attending on Old Bet's death.

183   This, Agee's final letter to Father Flye (*Letters,* 228–232), was sitting on his mantel when he died of a heart attack five days after writing it. In it, the author of *A Death in the Family* and the *African Queen* screenplay described "a movie idea I've recently had": to recount the bitter saga of circus elephants, beginning at the point when God consigns them to their fate and urges them to "be your own good selves, and through so being, you may convert those heathen, those barbarians, where all else has failed."

184   The Chepachet shooting is described in the statement taken by Friendship Lodge historian Frank H. Potter from Jedediah Sprague, who lived beside the bridge, and in Glocester historian Ena M. Kent's *Glocester.* Extracts from both are in the Somers Historical Society archives.
       "Impervious to bullets": Kelley, *Fun by the Ton,* 14.
       Doherty (*Woonsocket Call,* November 24, 1994) also cites an 1872 newspaper story about an elderly man who, crossing the bridge at night, "saw the

ghost of the elephant that was shot here 40 years ago. He declines to say how big the ghost was, but he is willing to swear that lightning is slow compared to his own gait homeward."

185 *Barnum's debt to Bailey:* Barnum, *Funny Stories,* 48, and *Life* (1855 version), cited by Saxon in *P. T. Barnum,* 358–359; Whitt, *Elephants and Quaker Guns,* 14.

"Jumbo" has also come to mean "a person of great skill or success" and a "trade-name for a shade of grey" *(Oxford English Dictionary);* crack cocaine; and, in Jacqueline Susann's *Valley of the Dolls,* a prominent Hollywood talent. Other applications: "jumboburger," "jumbo jet," "jumboesque," "jumboesqueness," "jumboism," and "jumbomania" *(O.E.D.),* and, in cinema, an abrupt "jumbo cut."

186 *Barnum's elephant hunt:* Barnum, *Struggles and Triumphs,* 355–356.

Barnum's "agricultural" elephant: Ibid., 357–359. A. H. Saxon, in his fine biography *P. T. Barnum* (286), notes that Barnum would entice famous friends such as Oliver Wendell Holmes to visit Bridgeport by promising to show them "Jumbo & 40 other elephants." He "was particularly intrigued by the elephants," and even tried to ride one, Albert, who "later killed his keeper and was shot in New Hampshire." Barnum's essay on mahoutship "ended ignominiously in a mud puddle."

Barnum, Bailey, and the baby elephants: Fenner, *The Circus;* Kelley, *It Was Better than Work,* 120. Barnum (*Life,* 330) glosses over his rivals' coup.

187 Barnum (*Life,* 330) recounted that his agents had scoured Europe for "novelties" and that he had "often looked wistfully at Jumbo."

Giving rides: Bartlett, *Wild Animals in Captivity,* 48.

Jumbo's outbursts: Ibid., 45–47; Jolly, *Jumbo,* 39–45; Saxon, *P. T. Barnum,* 292, 404–405; Sikes, *Natural History,* 293–294.

188 *Chuny and Jumbo:* Bartlett, *Wild Animals in Captivity,* 44.

Jumbo's sale: Ibid., 49–50; *The Times,* February 21, 1882 (10), 22 (12), 23 (12), 24 (10), and 28 (10), March 2 (11), 7 (12), 8 (7), 9 (9), and 10 (5).

189 *Other captive elephants killed: The Times,* February 25, 1882, 10.

"Jumbo" products and jokes: Haley, "Jumbo," 66; "Jumbo, King of Elephants," *Tufts College Bulletin,* May 15, 1927, 1.

Lawsuit: The Times, March 6, 1882, 7.

Chancery Court decision: March 9, 1882, 9.

Barnum's cable: Barnum, *Life,* 331; Root, *Unknown Barnum,* 340–341; Jolly, *Jumbo,* 65.

190 *Threats against Jumbo and attempt on Queen Victoria:* Saxon, *P. T. Barnum,* 293; Jolly, *Jumbo,* 82.

Scott's stalling: Bartlett, *Wild Animals in Captivity,* 50–51.

191 *Jumbo's earnings:* Barnum, *Life,* 333; Bondeson, *Feejee Mermaid,* 120.

Jumbo ads: Lanauer, "Jumbo's Influence," 43–49; ads and trinkets: Saxon, *P. T. Barnum,* 293.

192 Burma had a long tradition of using white elephants to extract money from foreigners. Ralph Fitch (Tragen, *Elizabethan Venture*, 110; Edwardes, *Ralph Fitch*, 106–107) and other visitors to Pegu had to view the king's four — and pay half a ducat.

193 *Forepaugh's whitewashed elephant:* Barnum, *Life*, 338; Saxon, *P. T. Barnum*, 304–307; Kelley, *It Was Better Than Work*, 120; Fenner, *The Circus*, 19. *"Living link":* Jolly, *Jumbo*, 145.

194 *Jumbo's death:* "The Death of Jumbo," *The Times*, September 17, 1885, 3c, and 18, 5a; Barnum, *Life*, 344–345; Saxon, *P. T. Barnum*, 297–299; Jolly, *Jumbo*, 147–152.
Myth: "Jumbo sacrificed his life for the love of a baby elephant. . . . Evidently angered at this huge demon that was about to attack the little elephant, Jumbo charged full force ahead to meet the locomotive." O'Brien, *Circus*, 61.

195 *Jumbo aspic:* Goodwin, "Whatever Became of Jumbo?" 21. *"Go Jumbos!":* Tufts University Web site, http://ase.tufts.edu/athletics. *Conspiracy:* John Chapman, "Wuxtry! They Shot Jumbo!" *Bridgeport Sunday News*, September 26, 1954.

15. Topsy Was Framed

197 *"Sagacious beasts":* *The Times*, October 6, 1830; "Not to Be 'Done,'" October 19, 1844; news item, July 30, 1839; "Van Amburgh's Elephant," September 26, 1844; "Escape of an Elephant," November 2, 1844; "A Roving Elephant," August 14, 1844.
Rescuing children: "A Sagacious Elephant," *New York Times*, August 30, 1839; *The Times*, December 7, 1840.
Elephant attacks reported in The Times: "A Boy Gored by an Elephant," March 12, 1861; "A Vicious Elephant," December 23, 1864; "An Elephant's Revenge," December 29, 1866.

198 *Geneva elephant killed: Gospel Advocate* 1 (1821), 259; *Saturday Magazine*, May 11, 1822, 415.
Chuny on stage: The Times, January 18, 1812, 3; *European Magazine* 61 (1812), 53. The latter notes that as early as 1707, a Dorset garden theater arranged to put an elephant on stage, but it was too large for the entry.

198–99 *Chuny's outbursts and death: The Times*, "Coroner's Inquests," November 2, 1825, 3; "Destruction of the Elephant at Exeter Change," March 2, 1826, 3; "Exeter Change Elephant," March 3, 1826, 4. Also *Annual Register* (1825), "November: Coroner's Inquest," 153–154; (1826), "March: Death of the Elephant at Exeter Exchange," 25. Jolly, *Jumbo*, 17. Altick (*Shows*, 310–315) summarizes the contemporary accounts.
Chuny steaks: "Dissection of the Elephant," *The Times*, March 8, 1826, 4;

Mirror of Literature, 7, quoted by Altick, *Shows,* 314. Two years later, Chuny's skeleton was mounted and shown to a public that still had not forgotten him (*The Times,* December 13, 1828).

"Inhuman" treatment: Letter from "Chuny," *The Times,* March 8, 1826.

Chuniana: Altick, *Shows,* 315; Thomas Hood, "Address to Mr. Cross, of Exeter 'Change, on the Death of the Elephant," *New Monthly Magazine* 16 (1826), 343–344.

Dickens omitted this passage (reprinted in Butt, *Dickens at Work,* 55) when he adapted the piece that included it, "Scotland Yard," in *Sketches by Boz.*

Miss Djeck killed: Journal des Débats, reprinted in *The Times,* July 4, 1837.

Liverpool execution: The Times, June 19, 1845.

Victor Emmanuel (*The Times,* November 15, 1852) had his elephant stuffed for the Turin Museum.

200 *Hannibal:* Murray, *Circus!* 260–262; "Death of Hannibal," *New York Times,* June 2, 1865, 8.

Luna Park: Oliver Pilat and Jo Ranson, *Sodom by the Sea,* 148–149.

201 Fanny's escape ("Elephant Lands in Jail for Swimming Narrows," *New York Times,* June 4, 1904) was surpassed by two others. The mighty Tusko rampaged through thirty miles of Washington towns, farms, woods, and logging camps, overturning cars, barns, and telephone poles before meekly submitting to recapture (*New York Times,* May 18, 1922, 12). In British Columbia in 1931, eleven Sells-Floto elephants stampeded upon unloading, and three lit out into the East Kootenay Mountains. The little trick elephant Charlie Ed eluded hundreds of pursuers, including Indian trackers, for six weeks, until the first snowfall (Eric D. Sisney, "Elephants Wandered Through East Kootenay," in the Thirty-seventh Annual Report of the Okanagan Historical Society, Vernon, British Columbia, November 1, 1973).

Topsy: "An Elephant Killed Him," *New York Times,* May 2, 1902; "Coney Elephant Killed," *New York Times,* January 5, 1903, 1; "Bad Elephant Killed," *Commercial Advertiser,* January 5, 1903 (reprinted at www.railwaybridge.co.uk/Topsy); Coney Island History Site (naid.sppsr.ucla.edu/coney island/articles/lunapark); "Topsy, Electrocuted by Edison" (www.roadside america.com); Ric Burns, *Coney Island* (film); *New York Clipper,* January 10, 1903, 1022, cited in the Charles W. Reynolds Papers (Reynolds, "Elephant Biographies").

203 *Mary's hanging:* Reynolds, "Elephant Biographies"; "Big Mary," www.roadsideamerica.com/pet/bigmary.

Mandarin: "Ugly Elephant May Have to Be Killed on Steamship," *New York Times,* November 9, 1903; Reynolds, "Elephant Biographies."

Lewis (*Elephant Tramp,* 76–88) had a ringside seat to the killing; he was handling another elephant behind Black Diamond. See also "Black Diamond," www.roadsideamerica.com/pet.

204   *Romeo:* "Elephant Romeo," *New York Times,* December 21, 1867, 1, and "An
       American Elephant," June 13, 1872; *The Times,* July 4, 1872; Murray, *Circus!*
       264; Reynolds, "Elephant Biographies."
       Executions: Royal, *Speaking of Elephants,* 1–11; "Elephant Forgets Not,"
       New York Times, April 28, 1901.
       Tip II: "Killer Elephant's Mummy Rides in State," *The Times,* May 16, 1956;
       Reynolds, "Elephant Biographies."
205   *Zoo killings:* Lewis, *Elephant Tramp,* 90–91.
       "Elephant genocide": Alexander, *Astonishing Elephant,* 125.
       Eliminating "problems": Lewis, *Elephant Tramp,* 89–91; Murray, *Circus!*
       264.
       Billboard *census:* Lewis, *Elephant Tramp,* 10–11.
       Dreamland fire: Pilat and Ranson, *Sodom by the Sea,* 169. Ringling fire: Ka-
       ren Goldberg, "The Hartford Circus Fire of 1944," *Concord Review* 3.2
       (Winter 1990). Many of P. T. Barnum's elephants also perished in fires. See
       his *Life,* 352–353.

16. Our Kind of Elephants

207   *Elephant Tower:* "A Passion for Pachyderms," *Bangkok Post,* December 14,
       1996.
209   *Rajasthan murals:* Gröning and Saller, *Elephants,* 156–157. Bundi palace:
       Maharaja of Baroda, *Palaces of India,* 60–69.
       Elephant monuments illustrated: Delort, *Life and Lore,* shows Ming tombs
       (42–43) and the Elephant of the Bastille (90–91). Gröning and Saller, *Ele-
       phants,* shows Bernini's obelisk (391), the Berlin Zoo (392), Horst Rel-
       lecke's *Glass Elephant* conversion of a coal mine plant (394), Ribart's plan
       (395), and Lucy and the Coney Island Colossus mistakenly conflated (395).
210   *Lucy:* William McMahon's amply illustrated booklet *The Story of Lucy the
       Elephant,* available from the Save Lucy Committee (P.O. Box 3336,
       Margate, N.J. 08402). Also "Atlantic City's Elephant," *New York Times,*
       August 20, 1882; "Lucy the Margate Elephant" page, www.childrens
       furniture.net, and the Save Lucy Committee's www.lucytheelephant
       .org.
       Coney Island Elephant: McCullough, *Good Old Coney Island,* 55–57;
       McMahon, *Story of Lucy the Elephant,* 13–14. Much of Kevin Baker's lavish
       novel *Dreamland* is set in and around the Elephant.
212   *"Shooting an Elephant":* Orwell, *Reader,* 6.
214   Babar and friends even adopt human diets. Penned up in *The Travels of
       Babar,* he fumes, "We are fed hay, as though we were donkeys!" In *Babar's
       Fair,* his children gorge on sausages at a fair to which all the beasts are in-
       vited; which ones become sausage is not noted.

"*The Sad Truth About Babar the 'Gigolo'*": Kristine Maitland, *Toronto Star*, July 29, 1997.

"*Colonial dream*": Dorfman, *The Empire's Old Clothes*, 25–26. See also Kohl, *Should We Burn Babar?* 3–19.

215   *Trickster tales*: Cosentino, "Elephant as Metaphor," 92–95.

216   *Circus Polka*: Buckle, *George Balanchine*, 139–140; Taper, *Balanchine: A Biography*. 177–178, 181–182; White, *Stravinsky*, 178–179, 372–375; New York City Ballet repertory notes; George Brinton Beal, "Entr'acte: Stravinsky and the Elephants," in the *Concert Bulletin of the Boston Symphony Orchestra*, cited by White, *Stravinsky*. Balanchine and Jerome Robbins would later present the renamed *Circus Polka for Wind Symphony* with human dancers, and the score became a concert standby.

    Republican elephant: Safire (*New Language of Politics*, 166–167, 186–187) describes Nast's cartoon and cites Rossiter and Stevenson.

217   *Philadelphia Athletics*: Gwathmey, *Enchantment*, 57.

    Seeing green elephants: Williams, *Elephant Bill*, 180. Other English terms for drunkenness include "cop the elephant" and "elephant's trunk" (Partridge, *Dictionary of Slang*) and "jumbo's trunk" (Spears, *Slang and Jargon*).

    Fisher's Miami elephants: Fisher, *Pacesetter*, 241–245; *The American Experience*, "Mr. Miami Beach" (transcript at www.pbs.org/wgbh/amex/miami). Hepburn plans a museum to show his 3,400-plus elephant objects and images, a selection of which, along with many useful links, are on his Web site, www.wildheart.com.

218   *Cigarette packs*: Gwathmey, *Enchantment*, 57.

    Wham-O gift elephants: "King Barbie," *Los Angeles Magazine*, October 8, 1994, 62.

17. The Elephant Island

222   Tula Hatti (Lister and Blashford-Snell, "Exceptional Size," 36) suffered a rather deflating fate for a national treasure: in 1995 he was killed by a land mine set for wild pigs.

    Elephant population and bounties: Jayewardene, *Elephant in Sri Lanka*, 59–61; de Silva, "Man versus Elephant in Ceylon," 252.

223   *Major Rogers*: Ibid., 254; Santiapillai and Jackson, *The Asian Elephant*, 62.

224   Atapattu claimed that male crop raiders "often become homosexual," something I've never seen in the literature. But homosexual activity has been reported among other highly intelligent mammals, including male baboons, bonobos, and dolphins.

225   Although elephants are herbivores, "Brain Eater" had some captive predecessors. In Thailand, W. A. R. Wood (*Consul*, 133) knew a grave-robber

elephant who covertly dug up and ate recently buried corpses: "In every other respect this elephant was a most tractable and lovable animal." Lewis (*Elephant Tramp*, 99–100) describes the grimmest elephant anthrophage of all, who grew up spoiled from infancy in the Zurich zoo and had the run of the grounds till he grew too large. An office worker pitied his confinement and slipped in to give him a loaf of bread. The next day keepers found blood on the floor and a human hand in the straw. Clothes and a handbag appeared later. These were hardly starving elephants; more likely they sought visceral vengeance after years of repression. Lewis (66) also describes a particularly ill-tempered circus trouper, "the only fish-eating elephant I ever knew," who would try to bite men but couldn't lash them because her trunk was "almost paralyzed," a sign of heavy beatings. Whenever she could slip her chains, she'd raid the sea lions' icebox.

18. Catching an Elephant

230   *Metabolic precipice:* Gale (*Burmese Timber Elephant*, 109) recounts rare cases of captives committing suicide by standing on their own trunks and suffocating, despite all efforts to budge them.

231   *Koonkies and helicopters:* Niresh Eliatamby, "Sri Lankans Trying to Save Elephants from Clashes with Man," Associated Press, April 13, 1998.
      In 1950, Williams (*Elephant Bill*, 179–180) noted that elephants loathed the bulldozer's roar above all other sounds, as though they sensed the doom it foretold.

234   *"Nothing works":* Pethiyagoda, *Ours to Protect*, 131.
      Auctions: "Wealthy Sri Lankans Flock to Elephant Sale," *London Observer*, March 1993.

236   *Darwin (*Descent of Man, *852):* "Sir S. Baker repeatedly observed that the African elephant and rhinoceros attacked white or grey horses with special fury."

238   *Lantana:* Shanika Sriyananda, "Uda Walawe National Park: Falling Prey to 'Lantana' Plants?" *Sunday Observer* (Colombo), October 10, 1999.

239   *Translocation deaths:* Dhaneshi Yatawara, "A Huge Problem," *Midweek Mirror* (Colombo), October 13, 1999; Udene R. Attygalle and Shane Sevneviratne, "Fresh Probe Sought on Elephant's Death," *Sunday Times* (Colombo), September 9, 1999.

241   *Atapattu injured:* "Sri Lanka Elephant Expert Hospitalized After Attack," Agence France Presse, July 11, 2000.

19. No Room in the Nilgiris

243   *Elephants at the dorm:* Sukumar, "Wildlife-Human Conflict," 303.
252   *Loki debate:* Statements of Krantz's India Project for Animals and Nature,

letters by Raman Sukumar, Maneka Gandhi, and others, posted at www.gcci.org/ipan/loki.

253 Jake Tapper's July 14, 1999, *Salon* piece was inevitably titled "A Media Circus." One could fill a volume with news stories on performing-elephant issues headlined "Media Circus" or "Political Circus." I wrote one myself.

20. Must This Show Go On?

256 *Circus bans:* Greg Avery, "Sorry, Flipper: Boulder Bans Exotic Pets," Scripps Howard News Service, July 4, 2001; "Wild About Animals," *Los Angeles Business Journal* (Pasadena), June 25, 2001; Performing Animal Welfare Society, "Circus & Animal Ride Incidents," in *Everything You Should Know about Elephants* (self-published report), 1999.

257 *Feld's lobbying outlays:* "Lobbyists Not Hurt by Reforms," *Baltimore Sun,* June 3, 2001, 1B.

258 David Blasko, Dr. Dennis Schmitt, Tom Rider, Debbie Olson, and Blayne Doyle testified before the Crime Subcommittee of the House Judiciary Committee in Washington, D.C., on June 13, 2000.

260 *"Lack of control":* Shepherdson, "Stereotypic Behaviour," 100.

262 *Feld Entertainment:* Davide Dukcevich, "Forbes Faces: Kenneth Feld," *Forbes,* January 9, 2001.

264 *Captive North American populations:* Wiese, "Asian Elephants Are Not Self-Sustaining"; Olson and Wiese, "African Elephant Population."

265 Doc and Angelica, Kenny, and other Animal Welfare Act cases: U.S. Department of Agriculture inspection reports, complaints, and consent decisions.
Sufficient evidence: Mike Dunn, letter to Pat Derby, December 23, 1999.
"Never been found in violation": Ringling Bros., "Proposed Seattle Circus Ban Fact Sheet," publicity release.
Training methods: "Ringling Bros. and Barnum & Bailey Animal Care Fact Sheet," publicity release.

266 *San Jose wounds:* Linda Goldston, "Investigators Found Signs of Elephant Mistreatment," *San Jose Mercury News,* May 9, 2000.
King Royal Circus: U.S. Department of Agriculture, "In re John D. Davenport"; "Circus Loses Appeal," *Houston Chronicle,* January 13, 1999, A18; Tania Soussan, "Elephants Fit into Family," *Albuquerque Journal,* August 7, 1999, E1.

268 *Ringling death: New York Times,* March 26, 1950, 1; March 30, 1950, 33.

270 *Cross-border elephant:* Mark Stevenson, "Benny, a Border & the Big Top," *Seattle Post-Intelligencer,* February 1, 2001, A4.
USDA audit: Inspector General Roger C. Viadero, testimony before House Appropriations Committee, Washington, D.C., February 16, 1995.

21. Breaking Contact

274   *Gunda's plight: New York Times,* "Bronx Zoo Elephant Chained for Two Years," June 23, 1914, 3; "Gunda's Plight Deserves Consideration," June 24, 1914, 10. Either Gunda was later rehabilitated, or Hornaday was shameless about exploiting his memory. In 1919 he published a brief article on elephants, "Citizens of the Jungle," in *The Mentor* 7.16 (serial 188) with a photo of the tusker bearing two keepers on his back, posing as though knocking on the zoo director's office door. The caption: "Gunda Complains — Gunda Was a Celebrated Giant Elephant of the New York Zoological Park."

275   *Zoo attendance:* American Zoo and Aquarium Association, "The Collective Impact of America's Zoos and Aquariums," report, January 1999; Tom Arrandale, "The Zoo Biz," *Governing Magazine* (July 1995), 38.

         "Elephant capital": Matt Palmquist, "Chendra Ambles into View for an Eager Crowd at the Zoo," *Oregonian,* February 13, 2000, D9.

276   *Schwammer on chaining:* "Reducing Stereotypical Behavior of African Elephants," presentation to the Fifth Annual International Elephant Research Symposium, Portland, Oregon, June 2, 2000.

277   Fred Marion could not be reached. His attorney, Kenneth Lerner, says that "he always denied he'd been drinking," no breath test was performed, and 176 did not seem an accurate count of the number of blows he struck. Lerner said he couldn't discuss the case further and didn't think Marion would want to.

279   *December 1999 incident:* Roger Anthony, "Zoo Cleared of Cruelty Charges," *Oregonian,* January 7, 2000.

280   *Occupational fatalities:* Toscano and Windau, "Changing Character," 17; Lehnhardt, "Elephant Handling"; Chapple and Ridgway, "Elephant Handling."

281   *Tacoma's "bad girls":* David O. Seal, "The Most Dangerous Elephant in the Country," and Eric Scigliano, "Seattle's Zoo: Clinging to Free Contact," *Seattle Weekly,* February 17, 1993, 15–16, 22; Nancy Roberts Trott, "Tacoma Zoo Looking for Another Nasty Elephant to Train," *Seattle Post-Intelligencer,* January 2, 1997, B1; Ruth Schubert, "Two African Elephants in Tacoma Will Be Packing Their Trunks for Florida," *Seattle Post-Intelligencer,* June 5, 1997, B1; Paula Bock, "Big-Time Attitude," *Seattle Times Pacific Northwest Magazine,* April 12, 1998, 13–22.

283   *San Diego changes:* Gary Priest, "Zoo Story," *Inc.,* October 1994, 27.

22. Seeing the Elephant

288   *Baby elephant mania:* Mark Ramirez, "How Much Is Cute Worth?" *Seattle Times,* November 12, 2000, B1, B6; "Pachyderm Pride," Woodland Park Zoo, @ *the Zoo* (Fall 1999), 14–17; "Small Miracle," @ *the Zoo* (Spring 2001), 9–13.

289   *SSPs:* "AZA Species Survival Plan ®Program," www.aza.org/ ConScienceSSPFact/; "Species Survival Plan©," www.centralflorida- zoo.org/ssp. *The World Zoo Conservation Strategy* can be viewed at www.wzo.org/conservation/wc2s.php.
      "Noah's Ark": Hutchins, Wiese, and Willis, "Why We Need Captive Breeding," 78.

290   *"Internal report":* Patrick Maluy to Lee Werle, "Breeding Loan Report for Asian Elephant Calf," Woodland Park Zoo, March 14, 2001.

292   *"Long-considered move":* Woodland Park Zoo, press release, February 7, 2001.

293   *SSPs' benefits:* Smith and Hutchins, "Value of Captive Breeding."

294   *Sumatran rhinos:* Rabinowitz, "Helping a Species Go Extinct."

296   *"The only justification":* David Hancocks, "Leaky Arks," *Seattle Weekly,* September 16, 1992, 17. See also Hancocks, *A Different Nature,* xviii–xix.

298   *Seismic communication:* O'Connell, Hart, and Amason, "Comments on 'Elephant Hearing'"; Langbauer, "Elephant Communication," 443.

300   *Thai Elephant Orchestra:* Eric Scigliano, "A Band with a Lot More to Offer than Talented Trumpeters," *New York Times,* December 16, 2000, A19; Mulatta Records website, www.mulatta.org.

Bibliography

Abu L-Fazl. *The A'ini Akbari [by] Abu'l-Fazl 'Allami*. Trans. H. Blochmann. Ed. S. L. Goomer. Delhi: Aadiesh Book Depot, 1965.

Addis, Mabel H. "Somers History Closely Intertwined with Circus Show World." In *Somers: Its People and Places*. Somers, N.Y.: Somers Historical Society, 1989.

Aelian, *On the Characteristics of Animals*. Trans. A. F. Scholfield. Cambridge, Mass.: Harvard University Press, 1948.

Agee, James. *Letters of James Agee to Father Flye*. New York: George Braziller, 1962.

Albertus Magnus, *Man and the Beasts: De Animalibus*. Trans. James J. Scanlan. Binghamton, N.Y.: Medieval and Renaissance Texts Studies, 1987.

Alexander, Shana. *The Astonishing Elephant*. New York: Random House, 2000.

Allan, Francis D. *Lone Star Ballads*. Galveston: J. D. Sawyer, 1874.

Alpers, Edward A. *Ivory and Slaves: Changing Patterns of International Trade in East Central Africa to the Later Nineteenth Century*. Berkeley: University of California Press, 1975.

———. "The Ivory Trade in Africa." In *Elephant: The Animal and Its Ivory in African Culture*. Ed. Doran H. Ross. Los Angeles: Fowler Museum of Cultural History/University of California, 1992.

Altick, Richard D. *The Shows of London*. Cambridge, Mass.: Harvard University Press, 1978.

Ambrose, Stanley H. "Paleolithic Technology and Human Evolution." *Science* (March 2, 2001), 1748–1753.

Andrews, F. H. "The Elephant in Industry and Art." *Journal of Indian Art and Industry* 10.88 (1904).

Aristotle. *History of Animals*. Books 7–10. Ed. and trans. D. M. Balme. Cambridge, Mass.: Harvard University Press, 1991.

Arrian. *Anabasis Alexandri (Books V–VII)* and *Indica (Book VIII)*. Cambridge, Mass.: Harvard University Press, 1964.

Baker, Kevin. *Dreamland*. New York: HarperCollins, 1999.

Baker, Sidney J. *The Australian Language*. Sydney: Currawong Publishing, 1966.

Balaban, John, trans. *Spring Essence: The Poetry of Hồ Xuân Hu'o'ng*. Port Townsend, Wash.: Copper Canyon Press, 2000.

Balter, Michael. "Anthropologists Duel over Modern Human Origins." *Science*, March 2, 2001, 1728–1729.

Barbier, Edward D., Joanne C. Burgess, Timothy M. Swanson, and David W. Pearce. *Elephants, Economics, and Ivory*. London: Earthscan Publications, 1990.

Barnum, Phineas Taylor. *Funny Stories*. London: George Routledge and Sons, 1890.

———. *Life of P. T. Barnum*. Buffalo: Courier Co., 1888.

———. *Struggles and Triumphs; or Forty Years' Recollections of P. T. Barnum*. Buffalo: Courier Co., 1875.

Baroda, Maharaja of. *The Palaces of India*. Paris: Vendome, 1980.

Bartlett, A. D. *Wild Animals in Captivity, Being an Account of the Habits, Food, Management, and Treatment of the Beasts and Birds at the "Zoo," with Reminiscences and Anecdotes*. London: Chapman and Hall, 1899.

Bartlett, John Russell. *Dictionary of Americanisms*. Boston: Little, Brown, 1860.

Bashan, A. L., ed. *A Cultural History of India*. Oxford: Clarendon Press, 1975.

Bassani, Ezio, and William B. Fagg. *Africa and the Renaissance: Art and Ivory*. New York: Center for African Art, 1988.

Bedi, Ramesh. *Elephant: Lord of the Jungle*. New Delhi: National Book Trust, 1969.

Bedini, Silvio A. *The Pope's Elephant: An Elephant's Journey from Deep in India to the Heart of Rome*. New York: Penguin Books, 1997.

Behrensmeyer, Anna K., Nancy E. Todd, Richard Potts, and Geraldine E. McBrinn. "Late Pliocene Faunal Turnover in the Turkana Basin, Kenya and Ethiopia." *Science*, November 28, 1997.

Beihoff, Norbert J. *Ivory Sculpture Through the Ages*. Milwaukee: Public Museum, 1961.

Ben-Aaron, Diana. "Retrobreeding the Woolly Mammoth." *Technology Review* 87 (April 1984).

Bernier, Francis. *Travels in the Mogul Empire*. Trans. Irving Brock. London: William Pickering, 1826.

Bondeson, Jan. *The Feejee Mermaid and Other Essays in Natural and Unnatural History*. Ithaca, N.Y.: Cornell University Press, 1999.

Brown, Robert L., ed. *Ganesh: Studies of an Asian God*. Albany: State University of New York Press, 1991.

Brunhoff, Jean de. *Babar the King*. Trans. Merle S. Haas. New York: Random House, 1935.

――. *The Story of Babar the Little Elephant.* Trans. Merle S. Haas. New York: Random House, 1933.

――. *The Travels of Babar.* Trans. Merle S. Haas. New York: Random House, 1934.

Brunhoff, Laurent de. *Babar's Fair.* Trans. Merle S. Haas. New York: Random House, 1954.

――. *Babar's Picnic.* Trans. Merle S. Haas. New York: Random House, 1949.

Buckle, Richard, with John Taras. *George Balanchine: Ballet Master.* New York: Random House, 1988.

Butt, John, and Kathleen Tillotson. *Dickens at Work.* London: Methuen, 1957.

Caesar, Julius. *The Civil War Together with The Alexandrian War, The African War, and the Spanish War by Other Hands.* Trans. Jane F. Gardner. London: Penguin Books, 1967.

Calvin, William H. *The Ascent of Mind.* New York: Bantam Books, 1990.

Camphausen, Rufus C. *The Encyclopedia of Erotic Wisdom.* Rochester, Vt.: Inner Traditions International, 1991.

Cannon, Teresa, and Peter Davis. *Aliya: Stories of the Elephants of Sri Lanka.* Melbourne, Australia: Airavata Press, 1995.

Carrington, Richard. *Elephants: A Short Account of Their Natural History, Evolution, and Influence on Mankind.* New York: Basic Books, 1959.

Chadwick, Douglas. *The Fate of the Elephant.* San Francisco: Sierra Club Books, 1992.

Chamberlin, Henry Harmon. *The Age of Ivory.* Boston: Richard G. Badger, 1904.

Chapple, Patrick, and Darcy Ridgway. "Elephant Handling and Analysis of the Risks." *Journal of the Elephant Managers Association* 11.3 (September–December 2000), 163–165.

Chutiwongs, Nandane, et al. *Paintings of Sri Lanka: Telvatta.* Colombo: Archaeological Survey of Sri Lanka/Centenary Publications, 1990.

Cicero, Marcus Tullius. "Letter to M. Marius." In *The Letters to His Friends.* Trans. W. Glynn Williams. London: William Heineman, 1928.

Clark, Hyde. "Note on Serpent and Siva Worship." *Journal of the Anthropological Institute of Great Britain and Ireland* 6 (1877).

Clowes, W. Laird. *The Royal Navy: A History from the Earliest Times to the Present.* Vol. 5. London: Sampson Low, Marston, 1900.

Collis, Maurice. *British Merchant Adventurers.* London: William Collins, 1942.

Conrad, Joseph. *Heart of Darkness and Other Tales.* Oxford: Oxford University Press, 1990.

Cordiner, Reverend James. *A Description of Ceylon, Containing an Account of the Country, Inhabitants, and Natural Productions.* New Delhi: Navrang Publishers, 1983.

Cosentino, Donald J. "Elephant as Metaphor in African Myth and Folklore." In *Elephant: The Animal and Its Ivory in African Culture.* Ed. Doran H. Ross.

Los Angeles: Fowler Museum of Cultural History/University of California, 1992.

Courtright, Paul B. *Gaṇeśa: Lord of Obstacles, Lord of Beginnings*. New York: Oxford University Press, 1985.

Cox, Warren E. *Chinese Ivory Sculpture*. New York: Bonanza Books, 1946.

Croft-Cooke, Rupert, and Peter Cotes. *Circus: A World History*. New York: Macmillan, 1977.

Cuasay, Peter. "Marginal Animals and a Magical Minority of South Isan." *Seaspan* 13.2 (Southeast Asian Studies Consortium, 2000), 6–7.

Cummings, E. E. "here is little Effie's head." In *Selected Poems*. New York: Liveright, 1994.

Curtius, Quintus. *History of Alexander*. Trans. J. C. Rolfe. 2 vols. Cambridge, Mass.: Harvard University Press, 1956.

Damiri, Muhammad Ibn Musa. *Ad-Damiri's Hayat al-Hayawan, a Zoological Lexicon*. Trans. A. S. G. Jayakar. London: Luzac, 1906.

Daniel, E. Valentine. *Charred Lullabies: Chapters in an Anthropography of Violence*. Princeton: Princeton University Press, 1996.

Darwin, Charles. *The Origin of Species* and *The Descent of Man*. New York: Modern Library, n.d.

———. *The Voyage of the Beagle*. Cambridge, Mass.: Harvard Classics, 1909.

Davis, Bubba, and Clyde Keeler. "The Georgia Elephant Disk." *The Epigraphic Society Occasional Publications* 8.199 (November 1979), 162–164.

Davis, John. "Pros and Cons of Bringing Asian and African Elephants to North America." *Whole Earth*, March 22, 2000.

De Beer, Sir Gavin. *Hannibal: Challenging Rome's Supremacy*. New York: Viking, 1969.

Deloria, Vine, Jr. *Red Earth, White Lies*. New York: Scribner, 1995.

Delort, Robert. *The Life and Lore of the Elephant*. New York: Harry N. Abrams, 1992.

Deraniyagala, P. E. P. *Some Extinct Elephants, Their Relatives, and the Two Living Species*. Colombo: Ceylon National Museums, 1955.

De Silva, K. M. *A History of Sri Lanka*. Delhi: Oxford University Press, 1981.

Dhavalikar, M. K. "Gaṇeśa: Myth and Reality." In *Ganesh: Studies of an Asian God*. Ed. Robert L. Brown. Albany: State University of New York Press, 1991.

Digby, Simon. *War-Horse and Elephant in the Delhi Sultanate: A Study of Military Supplies*. Oxford: Orient Monographs, 1971.

Dio Cassius. *Dio's Roman History*. Trans. Earnest Cary. Cambridge, Mass.: Harvard University Press, 1954.

Diodorus Siculus. *Diodorus of Sicily*. Trans. Russel M. Geer. Vols. 9–11. Books 18–22. Cambridge, Mass.: Harvard University Press, 1947.

Dobson, Andrew P. *Conservation and Biodiversity*. New York: Scientific American Library, 1996.

Donne, John. "The Progress of the Soul." In *The Complete Poetry and Prose of John Donne*. Ed. Charles M. Coffin. New York: Modern Library, 1952.

Dorfman, Ariel. *The Empire's Old Clothes: What the Lone Ranger, Babar, and Other Innocent Heroes Do to Our Minds*. New York: Pantheon, 1983.

Dow, Neal. *Civil War General, Temperance Crusader: Reminiscences of Neal Dow*. Portland, Maine: Evening Express Publishing, 1898.

Edwardes, Michael. *Ralph Fitch, Elizabethan in the Indies*. London: Faber and Faber, 1972.

Eichlin, Kim. *Elephant Winter*. New York: Carroll & Graf, 1997.

Eiseley, Loren C. "Archeological Observations on the Problem of Post-glacial Extinction." *American Antiquity* 8.3 (January 1943), 209–217.

———. "The Mastodon and Early Man in America." *Science*, August 3, 1945, 108–110.

———. "Men, Mastodons, and Myth." *Scientific Monthly* 62:515 (June 1946), 517–524.

———. "Myth and Mammoth in Archeology." *American Anthropologist* 47.1 (January–March 1945).

Ellis, Joseph. *American Sphinx: The Character of Thomas Jefferson*. New York: Alfred A. Knopf, 1998.

Eltringham, S. K. *Elephants*. Poole, England: Blandford Press, 1982.

Engle, Margarita Mondrus. "Mayan Genius No Mystery, but a Gift of Native Americans." *San Diego Union-Tribune*, October 14, 1984.

Fagg, W. P., and W. B. B. Forman. *Afro-Portuguese Ivories*. London: Batchworth Press, 1959.

Farley, Gloria. "An Elephant Petroglyph." *Epigraphic Society Occasional Publications* 17 (1988), 195–196.

———. *In Plain Sight: Old World Records in Ancient America*. Columbus, Ga.: Isac Press, 1994.

Farmer, J. S., and W. E. Henley. *Slang and Its Analogues* (1890–1904). New York: Arno Press, 1970.

Fell, Barry. "An Elephant Petroglyph in Glen Canyon, Colorado." *Epigraphic Society Occasional Publications* 14. 161 (1985), 22–27.

Fenner, Mildred Sandison and Wolcott. *The Circus: Lure and Legend*. New York: Prentice-Hall, 1970.

"Fetal Elephants Point to Wet Beginnings." *Science*, May 21, 1999.

Fisher, Daniel C. "Extinction of Proboscideans on North America." In *The Proboscidea*. Ed. Jeheskel Shoshani and Pascal Tassy. Oxford: Oxford University Press, 1996.

———. "Mastodon Butchery by North American Paleo-Indians." *Nature*, March 15, 1984, 271–272.

Fisher, Jerry M. *The Pacesetter: The Untold Story of Carl G. Fisher*. Fort Bragg, Calif.: Lost Coast Press, 1998.

Forest Industry Organization of Thailand. "Elephant Status" report. www.thai elephant.com/e_trial.

Foucher, Alfred. Introduction to Alice Getty, Gaṇeśa: A Monograph on the Elephant-Faced God. New Delhi: Munshiram Manoharlal, 1974.

Fox, Robin Lane. Alexander the Great. New York: Dial Press, 1974.

Francis, H. T., and E. J. Thomas, eds. Jataka Tales. Cambridge: Cambridge University Press, 1916.

The Friend of Peace ["Philo Pacificus"]. Boston: Massachusetts Peace Society, 1815.

Gaeth, A. P., R. V. Short, and M. B. Renfree. "The Developing Renal, Reproductive, and Respiratory Systems of the African Elephant Suggest an Aquatic Ancestry." Proceedings of the National Academy of Science 96 (May 1999), 5555–58.

Gale, U Toke. Burmese Timber Elephant. Rangoon: Trade Corporation, 1974.

Gary, Romain. The Roots of Heaven. Trans. Jonathan Griffin. New York: Simon and Schuster, 1958.

Gavron, Jeremy. King Leopold's Dream. New York: Pantheon, 1993.

Gee, Henry. "Return to the Planet of the Apes." Nature, July 12, 2001, 131–132.

Getty, Alice. Gaṇeśa: A Monograph on the Elephant-Faced God. New Delhi: Munshiram Manoharlal, 1974.

Gobetz, Katrina E., and Steven R. Bozarth. "Implications for Late Pleistocene Mastodon Diet from Opal Phytoliths in Tooth Calculus." Quarternary Research 55 (March 2001), 115–122.

Godagama, Wasatha Kumari. "An Ethno-Zoological Study of Domesticated Elephants in Sri Lanka." Master's thesis. University of Colombo, 1996.

Goodwin, George G. "Whatever Became of Jumbo?" Natural History, January 1952, 16–20, 45.

Gowdy, Barbara. The White Bone. New York: Picador USA, 1998.

Greenwood, Alex D., et al. "Nuclear DNA Sequences from Late Pleistocene Megafauna." Molecular Biology and Evolution 16.11 (November 1999), 1466–73.

Gröning, Karl, and Martin Saller. Elephants: A Cultural and Natural History. Cologne: Könemann Verlagsgesellschaft, 1999.

Gucwa, David, and James Ehmann. To Whom It May Concern: An Investigation of the Art of Elephants. New York: W. W. Norton, 1965.

Guilday, John E. "Differential Extinction During Late Pleistocene and Recent Times." In Pleistocene Extinctions: The Search for a Cause. Vol. 6 of Proceedings of the International Association for Quaternary Research. New Haven: Yale University Press, 1967.

Gwathmey, Emily. An Enchantment of Elephants. New York: Clarkson N. Potter, 1993.

Haile-Selassie, Yohannes. "Late Miocene Hominids from the Middle Awash, Ethiopia." Nature, July 12, 2001, 178–180.

Haley, James L. "Jumbo: The Colossus of His Kind." *American Heritage* 24 (1973), 62–68, 82–85.

Hall-Martin, Anthony J. "The Question of Culling." In *Elephants, Magnificent Creatures of the Wild.* Ed. Jeheskel Shoshani. Emmaus, Pa.: Rodale Press, by arrangement with Weldon Owen, 1992.

Hammarstrom, David Lewis. *Big Top Boss: John Ringling North and the Circus.* Urbana: University of Illinois Press, 1992.

Hancocks, David. *A Different Nature: The Paradoxical World of Zoos and Their Uncertain Future.* Berkeley: University of California Press, 2001.

Hare, E. M., trans. *The Book of the Gradual Sayings (Anguttara-Nikāya).* Vol. 3. London: Luzac & Co./Pali Text Society, 1961.

Harrington, John E. "The Stravinsky Page," www.geocities.com/Vienna/1807/strav.html.

Harris, Charles N. "American Circus Elephants." *Circus Scrap Book* 1.5 (1930).

Hawkins, Captaine Williame. "His Relations of Occurrents Which Happened in the Time of His Residence in India." In *Report for 1878.* London: Hakluyt Society, 1879.

Hayes, William. *Ancient Coins.* Cambridge, Mass.: Fogg Art Museum, 1956.

Haynes, Gary. *Mammoths, Mastodonts, and Elephants: Biology, Behavior, and the Fossil Record.* Cambridge: Cambridge University Press, 1991.

Hellen, Nicholas. "Rush on to Create Real Jurassic Park." *Sunday Times,* March 5, 2000.

Hendley, Colonel T. H. "The Elephant in State Ceremonies." *Journal of Indian Art and Industry* 16.122–128 (October 1914), 18–22.

Herodotus. *The Persian Wars.* Trans. George Rawlinson. New York: Modern Library, 1942.

Hochschild, Adam. *King Leopold's Ghost.* Boston: Houghton Mifflin, 1998.

Hugo, Victor. *Les Misérables.* Trans. Lascelles Wraxall. Boston: Little Brown, 1887.

Hutchins, Michael, Robert Wiese, and Kevin Willis. "Why We Need Captive Breeding." *AZA Regional Conference Proceedings* (1996), 77–85.

Ides, E. Ysbrants. *Three Years Travels from Moscow Over-land to China.* London: W. Freeman, 1706.

"Infernal Transaction — Death of the Elephant." *Boston Gazette,* July 29, 1816.

Isaac, Barbara. "Throwing and Human Evolution." *African Archaeological Review* 5 (1987), 3–17.

Jayaraman, K. S. "India's 'Milk Miracle' Is Hard to Swallow." *Nature,* September 28, 1995, 280.

Jayewardene, Jayantha. *The Elephant in Sri Lanka.* Colombo: Wildlife Heritage Trust of Sri Lanka, 1994.

Jefferson, Thomas. *The Jeffersonian Cyclopedia.* Ed. John P. Foley. New York, London: Funk & Wagnalls, 1900.

———. *Notes on the State of Virginia.* Ed. William Penn. Chapel Hill: University of North Carolina Press, 1955.

———. *The Papers of Thomas Jefferson.* Ed. Julian P. Boyd. Princeton: Princeton University Press, 1956.

———. *The Works of Thomas Jefferson.* Ed. Paul Leicester Ford. New York: G. P. Putnam's Sons, 1905.

Johnson, Ludwell H., III. "Men and Elephants in America." *Scientific Monthly* 75 (October 1952), 215–221.

Joice, Gail, Michael Knight, and Pamela McClusky. *Ivories in the Collection of the Seattle Art Museum.* Seattle: Seattle Art Museum, 1987.

Jolly, W. P. *Jumbo.* London: Constable, 1976.

Kakuchi, Suvendrini. "Ivory Imports May Seal Elephants' Fate." Inter Press Service (Tokyo), February 11, 1999.

Kelley, F. Beverly. *It Was Better than Work.* Gerald, Mo.: Patrice Press, 1982.

Kent, Ena M. *Glocester: The Way Up Country.* Providence: Glocester Bicentennial Commission/A. Mowbray Co., 1976.

Kerr, Richard A. "New Mammal Data Challenge Evolutionary Pulse Theory." *Science,* July 26, 1996, 431–432.

Kimes, Marion. *Namoratung'a.* Winston, Ore.: Nine Muses, 2000.

Knappert, Jan. *Myths and Legends of the Congo.* London: Heineman, 1971.

Knight, R. J. B. Introduction to *Shipbuilding Timber for the British Navy: Parliamentary Papers, 1729–1792.* Delmar, N.Y.: Scholars' Facsimiles & Reprints, 1993.

Knüsel, C. J. "The Throwing Hypothesis and Hominid Origins." *Human Evolution* 7.1 (1992), 1–7.

Kohl, Herbert. *Should We Burn Babar? Essays on Children's Literature and the Power of Stories.* New York: New Press, 1995.

The Koran. Trans. N. J. Dawood. London: Penguin Books, 1995.

Kotzwinkle, William. *Elephant Bangs Train.* New York: Equinox, 1974.

Kunz, George Frederick. *Ivory and the Elephant in Art, in Archaeology, and in Science.* Garden City, N.Y.: Doubleday, 1916.

Kurian, G. B. T., ed. *Dictionary of Indian English.* Madras: Indian Universities Press, 1966.

Lair, Richard C. *Gone Astray: The Care and Management of the Asian Elephant in Domesticity.* Bangkok: FAO Regional Office for Asia and the Pacific, 1997.

Lal, Lakshmi. *Ganesha: Beyond the Form.* Bombay: IBH Publishers, 1991.

Lanauer, Bella C. "Jumbo's Influence on Advertising." Photocopy.

Langbauer, W. R., Jr. "Elephant Communication." *Zoo Biology* 19 (2000), 425–445.

Lehnhardt, John. "Elephant Handling: A Problem of Risk Management and Resource Allocation" (1991). *Journal of the Elephant Managers Association* 11.3 (September–December 2000), 167–171.

Lewis, B., Charles Pellat, and J. Schacht. *Encyclopedia of Islam.* London: Luzac & Co., 1995.

Lewis, George "Slim," with Byron Fish. *Elephant Tramp*. Boston: Little, Brown, 1955.

Lister, Adrian, and Paul Bahn. *Mammoths*. New York: Macmillan, 1994.

Lister, Adrian M., and John Blashford-Snell. "Exceptional Size and Form of Asian Elephants in Western Nepal." Elephant Research Foundation. *Elephant* 2.4 (January 2000), 33–36.

Livingstone, David. *Livingstone's African Journal, 1853–1856*. Ed. I. Schapera. London: Chatto & Windus, 1963.

———. *Livingstone's Missionary Correspondence 1841–1856*. Edited by I. Schapera. Berkeley: University of California Press, 1961.

———. *Livingstone's Private Journals, 1851–1853*. Ed. I. Schapera. London: Chatto & Windus, 1960.

———. *South African Papers, 1849–1853*. Ed. I. Schapera. Cape Town: Van Riebeck Society, 1974.

Livy [Titus Livius]. *The History of Rome*. Vols. 2–3. London: J. M. Dent, 1914.

Longford, Elizabeth. *Wellington: The Years of the Sword*. London: Weidenfeld and Nicholson, 1969.

Lu Zoe [San Lwin]. *Myanmar Proverbs*. Bangkok: Ava Publishing House, 1996.

Ludolphus, the Learned Job. *History of Ethiopia*. London: Samuel Smith, 1684.

Ludwig, Emil. *The Nile: The Life-Story of a River*. Trans. Mary H. Lindsay. New York: Viking, 1937.

Macaulay, Elizabeth. "In Celebration of Somers Grand Old Elephant Hotel." In *Somers: Its People and Places*. Somers, N.Y.: Somers Historical Society, 1989.

MacPhee, Ross D. E., and Preston A. Marx. "The 40,000-Year Plague: Humans, Hyperdisease, and First-Contact Extinctions." In *Natural Change and Human Impact in Madagascar*. Ed. S. M. Goodman and B. D. Patterson. 169–217. Washington, D.C.: Smithsonian Institution Press, 1997.

———. "Mammoths and Microbes: Hyperdisease Attacked the New World." *Discovering Archaeology*, September–October 1999, 54–59.

Marasinghe, M. M. J. "Theravada Buddhism." In *Mythology: An Illustrated Encyclopedia*. Ed. Richard Cavendish. New York: Barnes & Noble/Little, Brown, 1993.

Marcus, G. J. *The Age of Nelson: The Royal Navy, 1793–1815*. New York: Viking Press, 1971.

Martin, Paul S. "Prehistoric Overkill." In *Pleistocene Extinctions: The Search for Cause*. Vol. 6 of *Proceedings of the International Association for Quaternary Research*. New Haven: Yale University Press, 1967.

Martin, Paul S., and David A. Burney. "Bring Back the Elephants." *Whole Earth*, March 22, 2000, 70–74.

Mathews, Mitford M., ed. *A Dictionary of Americanisms on Historical Principles*. Chicago: University of Chicago Press, 1951.

Mattocks, Charles. *Unspoiled Heart: The Journal of Charles Mattocks of the 17th Maine*. Ed. Philip N. Racine. Knoxville: University of Tennessee Press, 1994.

May, Earl Chapin. *The Circus from Rome to Ringling*. New York: Dover, 1932.

Mayor, Adrienne. *The First Fossil Hunters: Paleontology in Greek and Roman Times*. Princeton: Princeton University Press, 2000.

McCullough, Edo. *Good Old Coney Island: A Sentimental Journey*. New York: Scribner, 1957.

McLynn, Frank. *Hearts of Darkness: The European Exploration of Africa*. London: Hutchinson, 1992.

McMahon, William. *The Story of Lucy the Elephant*. Margate, N.J.: Save Lucy Committee, 1988.

Melland, Frank. *Elephants in Africa*. London: Country Life, 1938.

Melwani, Lavina. "Question of Faith: A Global Miracle." *Little India*, October 31, 1995, 49.

Miller, Gifford H., et al. "Pleistocene Extinction of *Genyornis newtoni*: Human Impact on Australian Megafauna." *Science*, January 8, 1999, 205–208.

Millner, Liz. "Indian Mythology." In *An Introduction to Oriental Mythology*. Ed. Clio Whittaker. London: Quintet, 1989.

Montagu, Ashley. *The Elephant Man: A Study in Human Dignity*. Lafayette, La.: Acadian House, 1971.

———. "An Indian Tradition Relating to the Mastodon." *American Anthropologist* 46 (1944), 568–571.

Montagu, Ashley, and C. Bernard Peterson. "The Earliest Account of the Association of Human Artifacts with Fossil Mammals in North America." *Proceedings of the American Philosophical Society*, May 5, 1944, 407–419.

Morell, Virginia. "Return of the Forest." *Science*, December 19, 1997, 2059.

Mrozek, Slawomir. *The Elephant*. Trans. Konrad Syrop. New York: Grove Press, 1962.

Murray, Marian. *Circus! From Rome to Ringling*. New York: Appleton-Century-Crofts, 1956.

Nakanishi, Takeshi. "Ivory Ban Hits Traditional Carving Industry in Japan." Associated Press (Tokyo), January 17, 1990.

Narain, A. K. "Gaṇeśa: A Protohistory of the Idea and the Icon." In *Ganesh: Studies of an Asian God*. Ed. Robert L. Brown. Albany: State University of New York Press, 1991.

Naravane, V. S. *The Elephant and the Lotus: Essays in Philosophy and Culture*. Bombay: Asia Publishing House, 1965.

Narayan, R. K. *The Man-Eater of Malgudi*. New York: Viking Press, 1961.

Neumann, Arthur H. *Elephant-Hunting in East Equatorial Africa*. New York: St. Martin's Press, 1994.

Nguyen Khac Vien, *Vietnam: A Long History*. Hanoi: Foreign Languages Publishing House, 1987.

Nickell, Joe. "Milk-Drinking Idols." *Skeptical Inquirer* 20.2 (March 1996).

Nilakantha. *The Elephant-Lore of the Hindus (Matangalila)*. Trans. Franklin Edgerton. Delhi: Motilal Banarsidass, 1985.

O'Brien, Eileen M. "The Projectile Capabilities of an Acheulian Handaxe from Olorgesailie." *Current Anthropology* 22.1 (February 1981), 76–79.

——. "What Was the Acheulian Hand Ax?" *Natural History,* July 1984, 20–24.

O'Brien, Esse Forrester. *Circus: Cinders to Sawdust.* San Antonio: Naylor, 1959.

O'Connell, Caitlin, Lynette A. Hart, and Byron T. Amason. "Comments on 'Elephant Hearing.'" *Journal of the Acoustic Society of America* 105.3 (March 1999), 2051–52.

O'Flaherty, Wendy. "Hinduism." In *Mythology: An Illustrated Encyclopedia.* Ed. Richard Cavendish. New York: Barnes & Noble/Little, Brown, 1993.

Olson, Deborah, and Robert J. Wiese. "State of the North American African Elephant Population and Projections for the Future." *Zoo Biology* 19 (2000), 311–320.

Oriental Ceramic Society. *Chinese Ivories from the Shang to the Qing.* London: British Museum Publications, 1984.

Orwell, George. "Shooting an Elephant." In *The Orwell Reader: Fiction, Essays, and Reportage.* New York: Harcourt, Brace, 1956.

Owen-Smith, Norman. "Pleistocene Extinctions: The Pivotal Role of Megaherbivores." *Paleobiology* 13.3 (1987), 351–362.

Pal, Pratapaditya. *Elephants and Ivories in South Asia.* Los Angeles: Los Angeles County Museum of Art, 1981.

Palaephatus. *On Unbelievable Tales.* Trans. Jacob Stern. Wauconda, Ill.: Bolchazy-Carducci, 1996.

Park, Mungo. *Travels in the Interior Districts of Africa.* New York: Arno Press, 1971.

Parker, Dorothy. *The Collected Poetry.* New York: Modern Library, n.d.

Partridge, Eric. *A Dictionary of Slang and Unconventional English.* Ed. Paul Beale. London: Routledge & Kegan Paul, 1984.

Payne, Katy. *Silent Thunder: In the Presence of Elephants.* New York: Simon & Schuster, 1998.

Peris, Merlin. "Abusing the Elephant: Pseudo-specification and Prognostication in Ancient Elephant Lore." *Gajah: Journal of the Elephant Specialist Group* 20 (January 2001), 51–59.

Pethiyagoda, Rohan. *Ours to Protect: Sri Lanka's Biodiversity Heritage.* Colombo: Wildlife Heritage Trust of Sri Lanka, 1998.

Philostratus the Elder. "Life and Times of Apollonius of Tyana." Stanford University Publications University Series. *Language and Literature* 2.1 (1923).

Pilat, Oliver, and Jo Ranson. *Sodom by the Sea: An Affectionate History of Coney Island.* Garden City, N.Y.: Garden City Publishing, 1943.

Pliny. *Natural History.* Trans. H. Rackham. Cambridge, Mass.: Harvard University Press, 1956.

Plutarch. "Pyrrhus." In *The Lives of the Noble Grecians and Romans*. Trans. John Dryden. New York: Modern Library, n.d.

Polybius. *The Histories*. Trans. Evelyn S. Shuckburgh. Bloomington: Indiana University Press, 1962.

Popham, A. E. "Elephantographia." *Life & Letters* 5 (July–December 1930). New York: Kraus Reprint Corporation, 1967.

Rabinowitz, Alan. "Helping a Species Go Extinct: The Sumatran Rhino in Borneo." *Conservation Biology* 9.3 (June 1995). 482–488.

Rajagopalachari, C. *Mahabharata*. Bombay: Bharatiya Vidya Bhavan, 1978.

Random House Historical Dictionary of American Slang. Ed. J. E. Lighter. New York: Random House, 1994.

Rao, M. S. Nagaraja. *The Mysore Palace*. Mysore: Directorate of Archaeology and Museums, 1989.

Rayner, Richard. *The Elephant*. New York: Turtle Bay, 1992.

Redig, I. Wayan. *Gaṇeśa: Images from India and Indonesia*. Delhi: Sundeep Prakahan, 1996.

Redmond, Ian. "With Elephants Underground." In *Elephants: The Deciding Decade*. Ed. Ronald Orenstein. San Francisco: Sierra Club Books, 1991.

Reynolds, Charles W. "Elephant Biographies." Charles W. Reynolds Papers. Robert L. Parkinson Library and Research Center, Circus World Museum, Baraboo, Wisc.

Ringis, Rita. *Elephants of Thailand in Myth, Art, and Reality*. Kuala Lumpur: Oxford University Press, 1996.

Ritvo, Harriet. *The Animal Estate: The English and Other Creatures in the Victorian Age*. Cambridge, Mass.: Harvard University Press, 1987.

Root, Harvey W. *The Unknown Barnum*. New York: Harper & Brothers, 1927.

Rosny, J. H. *The Quest for Fire: A Novel of Prehistoric Times*. Trans. Harold Talbott. New York: Pantheon, 1967.

Ross, Doran H. "Imagining Elephants." In *Elephant: The Animal and Its Ivory in African Culture*. Ed. Doran H. Ross. Los Angeles: Fowler Museum of Cultural History/University of California, 1992.

Royal, Bruce R. *Speaking of Elephants, and the Circus Under Canvas*. Waco: Texian Press, 1973.

Ryan, R. J. *Keepers of the Ark: An Elephants' View of Captivity*. Xlibris, 1999.

Ryley, J. Horton. *Ralph Fitch: England's Pioneer to India and Burma*. London: T. Fisher Unwin, 1899.

Safire, William. *The New Language of Politics*. New York: Collier, 1972.

Sanderson, G. P. *Thirteen Years Among the Wild Beasts of India*. London: Wm. H. Allen & Co., 1879.

Sanderson, Ivan. *The Dynasty of Abu: A History and Natural History of the Elephants and Their Relatives Past and Present*. New York: Alfred A. Knopf, 1962.

Santiapillai, Charles, and Peter Jackson. *The Asian Elephant: An Action Plan for*

Its Conservation. Gland: International Union for the Conservation of Nature, 1990.

Saxon, A. H. *P. T. Barnum: The Legend and the Man.* New York: Columbia University Press, 1989.

Schulte, Bruce A. "Social Structure and Helping Behavior in Captive Elephants." *Zoo Biology* 19 (2000).

Scott, W. B. "American Elephant Myths." *Scribner's Magazine* 1.4 (April 1887), 469–478.

Scullard, H. H. *The Elephant in the Greek and Roman World.* Ithaca, N.Y.: Cornell University Press, 1974.

Seneca, "On the Shortness of Life." In *Dialogues and Letters.* Ed. and trans. C. D. N. Costa. London: Penguin Books, 1997.

Seneviratne, H. L. *The Work of Kings: The New Buddhism in Sri Lanka.* London: Oxford University Press, 1999.

Seuss, Dr. [Theodor Seuss Geisel]. *Horton Hatches the Egg.* New York: Random House, 1940.

Shepherdson, David. "Stereotypic Behaviour: What Is It and How Can It Be Eliminated or Prevented?" *Ratel/Journal of the Association of British Wild Animal Keepers* 16.4 (August 1989), 100–105.

Shettel, James W. "The First Elephant in the United States." *Circus Scrap Book* 1.3 (July 1929), 5–14.

Shoshani, Jeheskel. "The African Elephant and Its Environment." *Elephant: The Animal and Its Ivory in African Culture.* Ed. Dorian H. Ross. Los Angeles: Fowler Museum of Cultural History/University of California, 1992.

Shoshani, Jeheskel, and Daniel C. Fisher. "Extinction of the Elephants' 'Ancestors.'" In *Elephants, Magnificent Creatures of the Wild.* Ed. Jeheskel Shoshani. Emmaus, Pa.: Rodale Press, by arrangement with Weldon Owen, 1992.

Sikes, Sylvia K. *The Natural History of the African Elephant.* New York: American Elsevier Publishing, 1971.

Silva, Ian de. "Man versus Elephant in Ceylon." *Loris* (Colombo) 11.6 (June 1969).

Smith, Brandie, and Michael Hutchins. "The Value of Captive Breeding Programmes to Field Conservation: Elephants as an Example." *Pachyderm* 28 (January–June 2000), 101–109.

Smith, G. Elliot. *Elephants and Ethnologists.* London: Kegan Paul, Trench, Trubner & Co., 1924.

——. "Pre-Columbian Representations of the Elephant in America" (letter), *Nature,* with responses by Alfred M. Tozzer and Herbert J. Spinden, November 25 and December 16, 1915, and January 27, 1916.

Smith, Kes Hillman. "The Elephant Domestication Centre of Central Africa." In *Elephants: Majestic Creatures of the Wild.* Ed. Jeheskel Shoshani. Emmaus, Pa.: Rodale Press, by arrangement with Weldon Owen, 1992.

Spears, Richard A. *The Slang and Jargon of Drugs and Drink.* Metuchen, N.J.: Scarecrow Press, 1986.

Spinden, Herbert J. "Pre-Columbian Representations of the Elephant in America" (letter). *Nature,* January 27, 1916.

Srivastava, Vinita. "Milking a Miracle: Why Lord Ganesh Got Thirsty — a Report from Queens." *Village Voice,* October 17, 1995.

Stanley, Henry M. *The Congo and the Founding of Its Free State: A Story of Work and Exploration.* New York: Harper & Brothers, 1885.

———. *H. M. Stanley's Wonderful Adventures in Africa.* Ed. J. T. Headley and Willis Fletcher Johnson. Philadelphia: Hubbard Brothers, 1890.

———. *How I Found Livingstone: Travels, Adventures, and Discoveries in Central Africa.* New York: Scribner, Armstrong & Co., 1872.

Stephens, John L. *Incidents of Travel in Central America, Chiapas, and Yucatan.* New Brunswick, N.J.: Rutgers University Press, 1949.

Stone, Richard. "A Bold Plan to Re-create a Long-Lost Siberian Ecosystem." *Science,* October 2, 1998, 31–34.

———. "Bringing Back the Beast." *Moscow Times,* July 3, 1999.

———. "Cloning the Woolly Mammoth." *Discover* 20.4 (April 1999).

———. "The Cold Zone." *Discover* 22.2 (February 2001), 59–65.

———. *Mammoth.* Cambridge, Mass.: Perseus Publishing, 2001.

Strong, W. D. "North American Indian Traditions Suggesting a Knowledge of the Mammoth." *American Anthropologist* 36 (1934), 81–88.

Subramuniyaswami, Satguru Sivaya. *Loving Gaṇeśa.* Kappa, Hawaii: Himalayan Academy, 1996.

Suetonius. *The Lives of the Caesars.* In *Suetonius.* Vol. 1. Trans. J. C. Rolfe. Cambridge, Mass.: Harvard University Press, 1974.

Sukumar, Raman "Wildlife-Human Conflict in India: An Ecological and Social Perspective." In *Social Ecology.* Ed. R. Guha. New Delhi: Oxford University Press, 1994.

Symes, Michael. *An Account of an Embassy to the Kingdom of Ava, sent by the Governor-General of India, in the Year 1795.* London: W. Bulmer, 1800.

Tambiah, Stanley Jeyaraja. *Buddhism Betrayed? Religion, Politics, and Violence in Sri Lanka.* Chicago: University of Chicago Press, 1992.

Taper, Bernard. *Balanchine: A Biography.* New York: Times Books, 1984.

Tarn, W. W. *Alexander the Great.* Cambridge: Cambridge University Press, 1951.

Tavernier, Jean Baptiste. *Travels in India.* Trans. V. Ball. London: Macmillan, 1889.

Tewari, D. N. *A Monograph on Teak.* Dehra Dun, India: International Book Distributors, 1992.

Timotheus of Gaza. *On Animals.* Trans. F. S. Bodenheimer and A. Rabinowitz. Paris: Académie Internationale d'Histoire des Sciences, n.d.

Topsell, Edward. *The Historie of Foure-Footed Beastes.* London: W. Iaggard, 1607.

Toscano, Guy, and Janice Windau. "The Changing Character of Fatal Work Injuries." *U.S. Department of Labor Monthly Labor Review* 117.10 (October 1994), 17.

Toynbee, J. M. C. *Animals in Roman Life and Art.* Ithaca, N.Y.: Cornell University Press, 1973.

Tozzer, Alfred M. "Pre-Columbian Representations of the Elephant in America" (letter). *Nature,* January 27, 1916.

Tragen, Cecil. *Elizabethan Venture.* London: H. F. & G. Witherby, 1953.

Tucker, Bruce. "Old Bet Lives — Dammit: The Elephant We'd Like to Forget, or, Pondering Maine's Only Successful Elephant Hunt." Unpublished paper, University of Southern Maine.

Tudge, Colin. *The Time Before History: Five Million Years of Human Impact.* New York: Scribner, 1996.

Turnbull, Colin M. "Legends of the Bambuti." *Journal of the Royal Anthropological Institute of Great Britain and Ireland* 89.1 (January–June 1959), 45–60.

U.S. Department of Agriculture. "In re John D. Davenport, d/b/a King Royal Circus." *Agriculture Reports* 57 (December 189[ ]), 189–194.

Valentijn, François. *François Valentijn's Description of Ceylon (Oud en Nieuw Oost-Indiën).* Trans. and ed. Sinnappah Arasaratnam. London: Hakluyt Society, 1978.

Van Couvering, John A. "Proboscideans, Hominids, and Prehistory." In *Elephant: The Animal and Its Ivory in African Culture.* Ed. Doran H. Ross. Los Angeles: Fowler Museum of Cultural History/University of California, 1992.

Varadarajaiyer, E. S. *The Elephant in the Tamil Land.* Annamalainagar, India: Annamalai University, 1945.

Vatsyayana. *Kama Sutra: The Hindu Ritual of Love.* New York: Castle Books, 1963.

Vogel, Susan. Introduction to *Africa and the Renaissance: Art in Ivory.* New York: Center for African Art, 1988.

Vrba, E. S. "Ecological and Adaptive Changes Associated with Early Hominid Evolution." *Ancestors: The Hard Evidence.* Proceedings of the Symposium held at the American Museum of Natural History April 6–10, 1984. Ed. Eric Delson. New York: Alan R. Liss, 1985.

Wallace, Irving. *The World's Greatest Showman.* London: Hutchinson, 1960.

Ward, Peter D. *The Call of Distant Mammoths: Why the Last Ice Age Mammals Disappeared.* New York: Springer-Verlag, 1997.

Warmington, E. H. *The Commerce Between the Roman Empire and India.* London: Curzon Press, 1974.

Warren, William, and Ping Amranand. *The Elephant in Thai Life and Legend.* Bangkok: Monsoon Editions, 1998.

Watson, Rupert. "King Leopold's Elephants: Legacy of Belgian King Leopold II of Taming Elephants in Zaire." *New Scientist,* December 22, 1990, 25.

Werner, Karel. *A Popular Dictionary of Hinduism.* Richmond, England: Curzon Press, 1994.

Wernick, Robert. "Carthage." *Smithsonian* 25.1 (April 1994), 124.

White, Eric Walter. *Stravinsky: The Composer and His Works.* Berkeley: University of California Press, 1966.

White, T. H. *A Book of Beasts: Being a Translation from a Latin Bestiary of the Twelfth Century.* New York: Putnam, 1954.

Whitt, Jane Chapman. *Elephants and Quaker Guns: A History of Civil War and Circus Days.* New York: Vantage Press, 1966.

Wier, Albert E. *The Piano: Its History, Makers, Players, and Music.* London: Longmans, Green, 1940.

Wiese, Robert J. "Asian Elephants Are Not Self-sustaining in North America." *Zoo Biology* 19 (2000), 299–309.

Williams, Heathcote. *Sacred Elephant.* New York: Harmony, 1989.

Williams, J. H. *Elephant Bill.* Garden City, N.Y.: Doubleday, 1950.

Wilson, Edward O. *The Diversity of Life.* Cambridge, Mass.: Harvard University Press, 1992.

Wing, Larry D., and Irven O. Buss. "Elephants and Forests." *Wildlife Monographs,* no. 19 (February 1970), 6–71.

Wolde-Gabriel, Giday, et al. "Geology and Palaeontology of the Late Miocene Middle Awash Valley, Afar Rift, Ethiopia." *Nature,* July 12, 2001, 175–178.

Wood, W. A. R. *Consul in Paradise: Sixty-nine Years in Siam.* Chiang Mai, Thailand: Trasvin Publications, 1991.

Zaw, U Khin. "Utilization of Elephants in Timber Harvesting." Presentation to 1995 Environmental Management Conference, Yangon.

Zimmer, Heinrich. *Myths and Symbols in Indian Art and Civilization.* New York: Pantheon, 1946.

Zimov, S. A., V. I. Chuprynin, A. P. Oreshko, F. S. Chapin III, J. F. Reynolds, and M. C. Chapin. "Steppe-Tundra Transition: A Herbivore-Driven Biome Shift at the End of the Pleistocene." *American Naturalist* 146.5 (November 1995), 764–783.

Index